S. J. Taylor is a writer living in North London. Her previous books are *Stalin's Apologist, Walter Duranty: the New York Times's Man in Moscow* and *Shock! Horror! The Tabloids in Action.*

THE GREAT OUTSIDERS

OUTSIDERS

Northcliffe, Rothermere and
the *Daily Mail*

S. J. Taylor

A PHOENIX GIANT PAPERBACK

First published in Great Britain
by Weidenfeld & Nicolson in 1996
This paperback edition published in 1998
by Phoenix, a division of Orion Books Ltd,
Orion House, 5 Upper St Martin's Lane,
London WC2H 9EA

A CIP catalogue record for this book
is available from the British Library.

ISBN: 0 75380 455 7

Printed and bound in Great Britain by
Butler & Tanner Ltd, Frome and London

This book is for Sherrie Good

CONTENTS

ILLUSTRATIONS

Sections of photographs appear between pages 82 and 83, 146 and 147, and 178 and 179

The Publishers wish to thank Associated Newspapers, the *Daily Mail* Library, and individual members of the Harmsworth family who have kindly made available photographs from their personal archives.

The Publishers also wish to acknowledge the Estate of Max Beerbohm (for the Max Beerbohm cartoon), Hulton Deutsch (for Louis Blériot with Lord Northcliffe, and Northcliffe and Churchill at the Hendon Aviation Meeting) and Popperfoto (for Lord Beaverbrook and Lord Rothermere).

NOTE TO THE READER

For clarity's sake, I have called Alfred, Harold, Esmond and Vere Harmsworth by their Christian names until, in the course of the narrative, each succeeds to his title. Otherwise, practically every character in this book, man and woman, with a few self-explanatory exceptions, is called by their surname – in keeping with modern style.

ACKNOWLEDGEMENTS

I want to thank authors Keith Kyle, Nicholas Faith and Dr Peter Beal for reading this book in manuscript. Dr Beal also helped with research by looking up queries at short notice, and I remain extremely grateful to him.

In a more official capacity, *Daily Mail* librarian Paul Rossiter was indefatigable in researching queries related to the early history of the newspaper, and I thank him. Of my research assistant Anna Webster, I can only say there is not a single aspect of the book she did not help with. She is intelligent, perceptive and funny, and I could not have done without her. Vyvyan Harmsworth, Director of Corporate Affairs at the Daily Mail & General Trust, plc, lent his support right through to the selection of the illustrations.

Similarly, Esmond Harmsworth in the United States gave me access to materials that completely changed my thinking, and Roger Pyke in Newfoundland was patient and informative. In Montreal, Robert Morrow, QC, showed exhaustive recall of corporate events.

My other research assistant Janet Cavallo was tireless and thoroughgoing, and Steve Allen was nothing less than brilliant in programming the research material into useful files. Enoch Ayree gave solid computing support, as did Andrew Pieri, Computer Systems Manager at Associated Newspapers. Mike Gray, David Greensmith and John Wheaton in Photo Services helped with the illustrations at short notice.

I am also grateful to the Publishing Director of Weidenfeld & Nicolson, Ion Trewin, who is my editor. He's given enormous help.

On a more personal level, these people were particularly kind to me: Linda Melvern, Genevieve Cooper, Kathy Campbell, David Feingold, Jim and Julie Boydston, Jonathan and Claudia Harmsworth, Gina Ellis-Johnson, Larry Ashmead, Peter McKay, Jane Gunther and Dr Colin Franey.

I am also grateful to the artists' colony YADDO who made me resident for several months.

Finally, I wish to thank Vere Rothermere who long ago imagined that a book like this should be written. It was my good fortune to be the one to write it.

ALFRED

1

'The Revenge of the Y.H.W.'

'If you can get good looks,' Geraldine Harmsworth, matriarch of the Harmsworth family and mother of Northcliffe, once said, 'then you have something.' It seemed a strange remark, coming from a woman who bore fourteen children in twenty years, buried three of them at birth, and frequently had to wrap the younger ones in newspapers on cold winter nights to keep them warm.

But it perhaps explains why the Harmsworth newspaper dynasty, Lord Northcliffe and three Rothermeres, all their brothers and sisters, and most of their progeny, were blessed by extraordinary good looks. Of Northcliffe himself it was said that he had the face 'of a young Apollo', and a schoolmate, recalling his arresting appearance as a youth, later said, 'He had golden hair and blue eyes and carried himself in a commanding way. People often turned to look at him in the street.'

One popular theory amongst the army of journalists and historians who have written about the founder of the *Mail* empire is that Northcliffe's mother had been badly spoiled, meaning primarily that she had been educated – and even permitted to travel abroad. As a young woman, she visited England, France and Germany, doing something of a continental tour, unusual for a young woman of the age. The daughter of a wealthy Dublin land agent, Geraldine was strong willed and accustomed to having her own way, so goes the thesis. Thus, enlisting her father's support against other members of her family, she defied their disapproval and married an insignificant English schoolmaster, Alfred Harmsworth, who had left his post in Truro in order to teach at the Hiberian Military School in Phoenix Park, Dublin.

Alfred had long, lanky legs, the languid air of a man of the world, a literary bent and the eyes of a visionary. He wore his dark hair swept romantically to the side and curled into a single lock, and, in the stern Victorian style of the day, his sideburns led into a heavy beard, giving him a harsh look at odds with his character. Geraldine Maffett married Alfred Harmsworth for looks and for love, and what she got for her trouble was a hungry brood. She would have done better to learn sewing and cooking, according to this version of events.

Another line has Geraldine meeting Alfred on a park bench, 'the whole affair being very low class', her father having begun his career delivering groceries and his father as a greengrocer and coal-merchant, honours therefore remaining 'more or less even'. The pair and their increasing family, forced to live off the charity of an ageing relative, would eventually achieve a makeshift life of their own, but Geraldine would always remain a slave in her affections to her husband, as evidenced by her willingness, at an advanced stage of pregnancy, to run up a flight of stairs to procure for him a forgotten handkerchief. Strangely, this particular chronicle of events belongs to Cecil King, himself a grandson of Geraldine and Alfred and the nephew of Northcliffe. Later, given his main chance by his uncle Rothermere, and eventually succeeding as far as the chairmanship of the International Publishing Corporation, King seemed to have spent his life resenting the help he received, and as a result remaining ever ready to denigrate the Harmsworth family name, even to the point of damaging his own.

The truth was that Geraldine Harmsworth was a young woman of the newly emerging Victorian middle classes, of good family and breeding, who was as pretty as her husband was handsome. At the time of her marriage, she had a round, plump face, strangely sad eyes and an air of intense vulnerability; by the time Alfred junior was born, her look would have changed to the more businesslike and commonsensical woman she was destined to become. She was ambitious, and she drove her husband to make something of himself.

Alfred Harmsworth also came from the middle class, hardworking yeoman stock who in two generations had worked their way up from being common farm labourers to merchants. Alfred dreamed of becoming a poet or novelist, like his hero Charles Dickens, and, whilst it remained uninspired, his fiction fell easily into the second tier, sufficiently competent to give him status amongst local literary types, but simply not good enough to make him a name of the day. He was a brilliant talker; a mediocre writer. What he lacked was not the talent, but the drive. He knew a good idea when he heard it though, and when his young wife proposed he read law, Alfred complied, and was called first to the Irish Bar, then to the English Bar at the Middle Temple. His career as a barrister, however, was doomed to remain as undistinguished as his literary endeavours.

He was well liked and convivial but lacking in backbone, this resulting from a fondness for the bottle – a fact that became generally known in the Temple. It prevented his advancement despite his undeniable ability. His own father, Charles Harmsworth, had been an alcoholic, dying at fifty-three of cirrhosis of the liver; now Alfred's drinking would become the central problem of his wife's life, and later the lives of his children.

Alfred Harmsworth junior, the future Northcliffe, was born in 1865 in Sunnybank, a cottage on the bank of the River Liffey at Chapelizod. The family, who, like all families, created their own mythology, believed his head too large for his body. Alfred himself would later joke, 'You see, I had a swelled head even as a baby.' He had a low tolerance for noise and was genuinely upset when his brothers and sisters became too loud at play. As he grew older, he came to dominate the nursery, forcing the other children to become quiet at his command. He was very efficient at imposing his will, even from an early age.

One oft-repeated anecdote that purports to give early insight into the young Alfred's character is an exchange with his mother, in which she tells him, 'Those who ask shan't have, and those who don't ask won't get.' Alfred worked his way round the conundrum by saying, 'Yes, Mother, but I take.' Maybe so, but whatever else his failings, Alfred Harmsworth was no taker; his business skills as a young entrepreneur were so dismal he stood in danger of losing his early advantage had he not been prevented by the advent of his younger brother Harold, whose keen business sense would turn out to save the day. Alfred was the leader, the visionary whose dreams were monitored by the more prosaic, less gifted, but infinitely more practical Harold. Harold had a bent for arithmetic; he was the type who went about doing mental calculations of rent and mortgages to occupy his mind. If anyone, it was Harold who would take, and the reasons weren't difficult to understand.

The Harmsworths lived on the edge, and they were all keenly aware of what happened to those who went over it. When Alfred and Harold were boys, the family in the house next to them went bankrupt, and all committed suicide. Alfred brushed it aside, redoubling his determination to succeed and to make money. But Harold was shaken to the core. During the last decade of his life, he would still remember his terror at the event, passing the story on to his grandchildren.* Another time, after he had become Viscount Rothermere, 'the third richest man in England', Harold would surprise one of his guests by bursting into tears when a particular fish dish was served as a second course. He told his shocked guest, 'We

* Interview with the 3rd Viscount Rothermere, London, 1 February 1993. In the version found in the Reginald Pound and Geoffrey Harmsworth biography of Northcliffe, the neighbour is a City stockbroker who commits suicide when he goes bankrupt. The fate that befell his family is unrecorded.

lived on that fish for days at a time. My mother couldn't afford to get us anything else.'

The indifference of Alfred senior to his family's plight was typical of the alcoholic. At times, he was the self-aggrandizing patriarch, calling to his sons after a night of heavy drinking to remove his boots because he was 'a descendant of kings'. He was referring to the persistent family legend that his mother was the illegitimate daughter of either the Duke of York or the Duke of Cumberland. The Harmsworth children half believed, half doubted his claims, later investing some credence in the possibility in an attempt to explain why the descendants of common labourers had achieved so much.* At other times, less enamoured of his own genealogy, and racked with guilt, Alfred senior would haul himself over the coals for making 'a fool of myself last evening. No more drink,' he would write in his diary; 'took too much wine'; 'very seedy, my own fault, too much drink again.'

In spite of his mood swings at home, Alfred senior kept his public sense of humour. After listening to one of his recitals of financial distress, a friend of his remarked, 'You don't appear to be worrying overmuch'; Harmsworth replied: 'I imagine my creditors are doing all the worrying that is necessary.' Underneath the joking was a strain of bitterness unsuspected by his cronies, but all too apparent to his family. One year, when ham and peas were all Geraldine could afford for his birthday dinner, her drunken husband delivered a particularly sarcastic soliloquy: 'Never in my life have I enjoyed anything more, and what food could a man desire better than bacon and green peas?' In fact, he had a rich friend who actually preferred bacon and green peas to any of the fine and expensive foods he could afford. After this condescending speech, Alfred retired to his study to continue with his drinking.

He whiled away his time at the King of Bohemia in Hampstead High Street, not far from the Vale of Health, where the family had moved in the early 1870s in search of cheap lodgings. When they first came to London from Dublin, they had set up in St John's Wood, but as their fortunes declined, they were forced to move further from town, the Heath being a distant and inexpensive suburb of London at the time.† Despite

---

* References to the presence of royal blood in the family can be found in Cecil King's book *Strictly Personal*, where he discounted the idea, p. 51; Paul Ferris was equally sceptical, pp. 10–11; Reginald Pound and Geoffrey Harmsworth remain uncommitted, pp. 4–5; and through family legend (see interview with Rothermere). The absence of any record of the birth of Hannah Wickens, née Carter, later Hannah Harmsworth and mother of Alfred snr, prevents evidentiary confirmation.

† The rose-covered house was renamed 'Hunt Cottage' by Ernest Rhys, editor of Everyman's Library after Leigh Hunt, the poet and essayist.

their poverty, the family benefited from living there, establishing a reputation for wit and charm, and making important contacts.

Alfred senior became one of Hampstead's founder members of the Sylvan
Debating Club, whose topics – 'Horseflesh as Food', 'The Morality of
Music-Halls', 'The Abolition of Capital Punishment' – sound suspiciously
like the kind of little snippets upon which his son Alfred would found his
publication empire. Northcliffe called such ideas 'talking points', and
nearly a hundred years later staff members at the *Daily Mail* would still be
discussing the most important 'talking point' in the day's issue. Significantly, George Jealous, founder of the respected local newspaper *The
Hampstead & Highgate Express*, gave little Alfred a toy printing set. Half a
century later, Northcliffe would tell a trade unionist that this was how he
became acquainted 'with printers and their ways'.

But, for now, Alfred junior's way of dealing with his father's increasing
estrangement from the family was by formulating great ideas. He determined at an early age to rid himself of the money problem once and for
all, but discovered it wasn't as easy as it looked. Noting the wealth of
patent medicine purveyors, he came up with the hare-brained scheme of
manufacturing and selling Tonk's Pills ('cure all ills'), putting the younger
children to work dispatching the wonder-drug, made mainly of soap,
across north London. This first attempt at becoming rich failed dismally,
and Alfred had to endure a great deal of ridicule from all who had helped
in the project.

He nevertheless remained buoyant, energetic, optimistic; much admired
by adult acquaintances of his family, obeyed without question by his
younger siblings. Like his father, however, he was subject to the peculiar
duality found in the character of so many of the Harmsworth family. It
would surface time and again in various generations and it would take a
variety of forms: rising optimism followed by periods of great pessimism,
confidence shaken by minor crises, lengthy disclosures followed by long
silences; and always a pensiveness that gave others the impression, at
best, they were being ignored, at worst, rejected. There would be this
preoccupation as if with another dimension, a kind of mental 'knitting'
that excluded present company.

In the case of the young Alfred Harmsworth, periods of great effort were
frequently followed by serious illness. He was subject to 'nervous attacks',
brought on by emotional fears. Real enough, though, were his bouts with
influenza, sore throats and, during his teenage years, pneumonia. He was
a constant worry to his mother, even as a baby, and no doubt the amount
of concern and attention he received both gratified and frightened him,
leading to his own tendencies towards hypochondria.

In the background to all this, he was aware constantly of the victimization of his mother by his father, her suffering from actual deprivation, and the fights between parents that he and the other children witnessed over Alfred senior's drinking. Alfred's mother was his mainstay when his father failed; a sense of loyalty and devotion to her would dominate his life, inspiring him to greater and greater achievement.

'She ruled them all,' Northcliffe's great nephew, the third Viscount Rothermere, would say, decades later. 'They were all very much under her influence all their lives. I think perhaps that, to release all their energy, they needed to have a firm emotional anchor; there's simply no firmer an emotional anchor than a strong mother.'

And just as future generations of Harmsworths would know Northcliffe's mother was strong, they would also know his father as 'the weak link'. But even for Alfred senior, whose every moment had been marred by the knowledge of his own failure, there would be compensation. Just before he died, at fifty-two, like his father of cirrhosis of the liver, he said to a friend: 'I have a marvellously clever boy. We shall see him come up right to the top of the tree!'

Young Alfred Harmsworth's passion was words, just as his father's had been. He loved Dickens, Defoe, Thackeray; he devoured the classics. But the 1860s had brought about a new kind of literature, one less lofty but more accessible, and with the new technology it was cheap and plentiful.

The British Government's policy of Votes for All, when Alfred was only a babe in arms, had prompted concern about the proper education of the working classes. This in turn had led to the passage of Forster's Education Act of 1870, which made child labour illegal and introduced elementary education for all children. Thus, at a single stroke, a new audience of tens of thousands of working-class readers, with leisure time on their hands, was created. Alfred and his entire generation were suddenly awash in magazines like *Youth*, *Young Folks' Tales*, *Scraps*, *Lots o' Fun* and, the outlet for a most suspicious and potentially corrupting new sport, *Bicycling News*. This was the up-market end of the new mass publications industry.

On the down-market side was the frightful 'penny-dreadful', devoured by the millions by horrified yet spellbound youngsters. These were tales of 'love, mystery and crime', featuring the exploits of fearful underworld figures and their molls. *Sweeney Todd: The Demon Barber of Fleet Street* terrified his young readers, who were likewise amazed and dismayed by Frank Read's *Electric Birds*. These featured bat wings and webbed feet, Victorian pterodactyls that haunted the dreams of small children. But the best selling of all was Edward Viles's *Black Bess*, the story of a famed highwayman, so popular it was published in weekly parts for five years, at a penny a go. At its conclusion, public demand was so high Viles wrote two sequels, *The Black Highwayman* and *Blueskin*.

Less wholesome were the torture, shipwreck, mutilations and executions that featured heavily in the plots of many of these cheap publications. In *The Wolves of Wake-up*, for example, the young hero is buried up to his neck by the villain: 'There you are!' Dark Dan announced, when the 'planting' was finished. 'You grow up to seed, unless the wolves get ye. Anyhow, it can't be said we murdered you!'

Alfred devoured all of it, the wholesome along with the frankly dreadful, gaining, subconsciously at least, a sense of what others wanted to read. He was a gifted writer; one of his early teachers used his essays to demonstrate her own teaching skills. And by the time he was in his early teens, George Jealous had enlisted him to write short articles for the *Ham & High* during the summer holiday. Alfred's interest was intense; before he reached his sixteenth birthday, he had talked his reluctant schoolmaster, J.V. Milne, into letting him publish a school magazine, the *Henley House School Magazine*.

The magazine was entertaining, wholesome and cheeky, Alfred showing an early flair for self-promotion. 'I have it on the best authority,' he wrote in the 'Entre Nous' section of the first issue, March 1881, 'that the H.H.S. Magazine is to be a marked success.' In the very next issue, he confirmed his own clairvoyance: 'I am glad to say that my prediction as to the success of this magazine proved correct.' The magazine was also noteworthy for a section entitled 'Answers to Correspondents', a question-and-answer column invented by Alfred. It would resurface a few years later, tailored into a flashy, readable fount of diverse and amazing information, to become the flagship of Alfred's publications empire.

Alfred was popular at Henley House School, noted for his dazzling good looks, and captain of both the cricket and the football teams. But his real enthusiasm was reserved for cycling. As a child, Alfred's father had taken him for a train ride, and the engine-driver had let the boy ride with him in the front. The young boy, his face blackened with ash, returned home vowing to become a railroad man. By his teens, however, Alfred had developed a positive mania for the bicycle. He joined a cycling club, each of its members wearing a handsome uniform and one carrying a bugle. He loved the open road, and would never forget the freedom the bicycle afforded him in his youth.

More significantly, he understood what the bicycle, and later the motor car, portended for the future. 'Road-minded people', he would say a few years on, 'don't think like rail-minded people. The rails steer you, but on the road you steer yourself. Believe me, that's tantamount to a change of character.'

It was a change many feared. The bicycle was viewed as a suspicious contraption threatening the livelihoods of coach drivers, hindering horse-and-carriage transport and encouraging the wanton movement of the lower classes. It was not uncommon for cyclists to suffer abuse from passing coachmen; in some cases they were actually attacked, or implements were thrown into the spokes of their moving wheels.

Even without the ill will of fellow travellers, bicycling was a precarious sport. Alfred had part-ownership in a penny farthing, a forty-eight-inch Coventry model which he rode wildly, at high speed, and sometimes foolishly. Once, after a return trip to St Albans, Hertfordshire, Alfred and his biking friend Max Pemberton accepted a challenge to ride on to Eastbourne, more than fifty miles away. Another time, they raced to Bournemouth, without once dismounting.

After one such exploit, in driving rain, Alfred came down with pneumonia. Amongst his family members, it was a commonly held belief that early biking feats like this one permanently damaged his health, accounting for the many bouts of ill-health he suffered in adulthood. But really, Alfred's tendency towards superhuman exertion, followed by a collapse – either in health or spirit – was becoming a discernible behavioural mode. His quick recoveries were followed by a dispiriting lethargy that came as a shock to those who had seen the bravura side of his character.

With his easy optimism, good looks and confident style, the young Alfred Harmsworth didn't seem a complex character; quite the opposite. Friends and colleagues who knew him for years rarely glimpsed what lay behind the facile surface of his observations and pronouncements. It was a legacy of suppressed inferiority, poverty and alienation. He was an outsider, underprivileged in a class-ridden society; he had not attended Cambridge or Oxford; he had no money, nor the artistic temperament to gain access even to the counter-culture of the age. If he was to go anywhere in life, Alfred Harmsworth junior had to bluff his way in. The only asset he could muster was his family, and he was his family's only asset.

When he was seventeen, he managed to talk his way into a position as a travelling companion on a continental tour with a young man ten years his senior. The Reverend and Honourable E.V.R. Powys, third son of the third Lord Lilford, discounted Alfred's age immediately, once he discovered how personable and pleasant his demeanour. Behind the scenes, however, a domestic tragedy was playing out. Only a short time before, Alfred, aged sixteen, had made the family's young maid-servant pregnant; she returned home in disgrace to bear their illegitimate child. Alfred's father was furious, but, more terrible still, his mother rejected him, an intolerable state for the young man who loved her to distraction and depended upon her for stability and strength. The unhappy state of affairs was swept under the carpet for the sake of the family – and the future.

Despite the emotional confusion, anger and recriminations, however, the family scrambled together, everyone contributing enough money for an inexpensive grey travelling suit so that Alfred had the chance to make his way in the world – if he could – with the advantage of acceptable attire. After his return from the tour, he still had to confront his mother's wrath: she would no longer have Alfred in the house, and he was forced to take lodgings. As to the suit, Alfred made it last for years. On the streets in London, he took comfort from the fact drivers of hansom cabs approached him for fares; 'It shows we look all right,' he said to a friend.

On his own for the first time, Alfred went straight to Fleet Street, taking whatever free-lance work he could get for whatever it paid. A chance meeting on the steps of the British Museum renewed his friendship with Max Pemberton. 'Give editors the kind of thing they want – less British Museum and more life,' he lectured Pemberton, and soon they had joined forces and lodgings, looking for their main chance. Ironically, Pemberton, who in later years would become a famous novelist, got his main chance from knowing Alfred; as Alfred rose, Max went with him.

One afternoon, fed up with a market-place indifferent to their ideas, the pair trudged up the steps to the offices of George Newnes, owner and editor of *Tit-Bits*, who, unlike most Fleet Street editors, was not only available to free-lancers, but sat amongst his staff, at a table, eating a sandwich as he worked. On his wife's whim, Newnes had prospered by converting his hobby into a magazine. For years, he had clipped stories, little snippets on a variety of subjects that interested him, often reading them aloud to his wife in the evening. She suggested he should compile them into a magazine for the enjoyment of others.

There was a long tradition in Britain of what Newnes was doing, but he knew nothing about it. Ever since the sixteenth century, scholars had formed the habit of collecting ideas – about law, theology, classics, and literature – in their own 'commonplace' books. And what began as a scholarly aid became more and more a thing compiled for entertainment, first by the aristocracy, then by the middle classes. Examples of humour, poems that pleased, ideas to remember, pictures, cartoons, all these were collected, degenerating as they grew more and more popular, into scrap-books. By the Victorian age, stationers sold mass-produced scraps and paper dolls for children to paste into ready-made books; the same was done for autographs of well-known personalities. What Newnes had accomplished was the application of the new printing technology to the scrap-book principle – a miscellany of little-known facts assembled for amusement.

Newnes had started small, in Manchester where he lived, but his business had grown rapidly, and he had only recently moved to London where it was thought by experienced hands in the publishing trade that he would fall flat on his face. After all, his detractors opined, what he produced was the worst sort of 'trash', interesting only to 'workers and maid-servants and office-boys'.

But Alfred knew instinctively the full import of what Newnes had stumbled upon. 'The Board Schools', he told Pemberton, 'are turning out hundreds of thousands of boys and girls annually who are anxious to read. They do not care for the ordinary newspaper. They have no interest in society, but they will read anything which is simple and is sufficiently interesting. The man who has produced this *Tit-Bits* has got hold of a bigger thing than he imagines. He is only at the very beginning of a development which is going to change the whole face of journalism. I shall try to get in with him. We could start one of these papers for a couple of thousand pounds, and we ought to be able to find the money. At any rate, I am going to make the attempt.'*

He didn't let the grass grow under his feet. By the time Alfred was nineteen, he had taken over as the editor of *Youth* for £2 a week; by the time he was twenty, *Youth* had folded and he had moved on to Coventry where he became editor of *Bicycling News*, owned by William Iliffe. By then, the circulation of the biking magazine had slumped to three hundred, and Alfred went to work at once, cutting paragraph lengths and enlivening the layout. He took the unprecedented step of hiring a woman correspondent, Lillias Campbell Davidson, with an eye to encouraging women to take up biking. Such an idea was thought ludicrous, and music-halls made hay from what they considered a figure of fun:

> My eye! Here's a lady bicyclist ...
> She's put her petticoats up the spout,
> And now she has to go without;
> She hopes her mother won't find out,
> And thinks they won't be missed.

* See Max Pemberton, *Lord Northcliffe: A Memoir*, p. 30; see also Reginald Pound and Geoffrey Harmsworth, *Northcliffe*, p. 54; also Paul Ferris, *The House of Northcliffe: The Harmsworths of Fleet Street*, p. 27; also Hamilton Fyfe, *Northcliffe: An Intimate Biography*, pp. 11–13.

But Alfred saw no reason why women and girls shouldn't bike alongside men and boys. Alfred liked women; he also recognized them as potential customers for his publications.

He also wrote extensively about a character named Ah Fong, a Chinese bicyclist who would soon visit Coventry to encourage biking amongst the populations of China and England. The whole affair turned out to be an elaborate hoax, hyped up to increase readership and advertisements. And it worked. Far from being angry when Ah Fong didn't appear, as had been promised, on Christmas Day, Alfred's readers found the whole thing tremendously amusing, and circulation rose as news of the hoax spread.

But not everything Alfred did met with approval. Throwing himself into his work like a maniac, he infuriated one of the leader writers with his slash-and-burn editing style; Lacey Hillier retaliated by calling Alfred 'the yellow-headed worm', a term taken up by the printers and abbreviated to 'the Y.H.W.'. Years later, when Alfred had occasion to write to Hillier, he would good-naturedly sign his letter, 'the Y.H.W.'. But despite Hillier's ill will and the irksome suspicion of the printers that, by using his charm, Alfred was getting far more work out of them than they were being paid for, Alfred was developing a winning manner that 'inclined people to do things for him'. In the end, Alfred succeeded in Coventry, beyond his proprietor's wildest dreams – or desires. William Iliffe had never intended *Bicycling News* to become his top sports magazine, preferring it to pick up the slack from his pace-setter publications. In the end, he let Alfred go, carefully preserving his friendship with the young man. His explanation for Alfred's leaving was simple: 'He was too hot for me.'

It was okay with Alfred, because he now had enough experience to put his master-plan into effect. He would publish a magazine to compete with George Newnes's *Tit-Bits*. More than that, he would found a magazine empire, this according to his Schemo Magnifico – a detailed plan of action and the source of Alfred's ambitions for years to come. He was known to carry it about with him, referring to it from time to time, although he kept it rolled up and took care that nobody besides himself saw the contents.

The first step in realizing his magnificent scheme was to secure capital. He approached William Iliffe, but was rebuffed. Never mind, Alfred talked him into printing his first magazine on credit. If you can't get what you want, get what you can, was Alfred's motto, and in fact Iliffe should have bought into Alfred's venture. As it turned out, Iliffe's delays in receiving payment in the early days were tantamount to a hefty capital investment. Had Iliffe formally underwritten the project, he would have become a rich man. Instead, Alfred turned to a friend of his family's, W.F. Dargaville Carr, who was willing to put up enough capital to establish Alfred as a publisher, but not enough to get his first magazine into publication.

The rest had to be found elsewhere, and eventually, with the aid of a barrister who also wrote for the *Daily Telegraph*, the deed was accomplished. Edward Marwick knew of one Captain Beaumont, a retired officer of the Royal Welch Fusiliers. According to anti-Northcliffe lore, Beaumont was a homosexual who, while married to a woman fourteen years his senior, rather fancied the attractive young publisher. Thus, when asked by Marwick for £1,000, Beaumont forthwith put up the amount, giving Alfred and Marwick 'Joy', as Marwick put it in the telegram to Alfred informing him of his success. If Beaumont actually was homosexual, Alfred, who was exclusively inclined towards women, was happily oblivious to his benefactor's proclivities, for both Beaumont and his wife became great friends; the three of them keeping up a lively correspondence, and eventually managing a few social visits back and forth to Italy where the Beaumonts kept a villa.

In the meantime, Alfred, with characteristic impetuosity, married his long-time sweetheart, Mary Milner, on 11 April 1888. The couple honeymooned in Folkestone, as close to Europe as they could afford, Alfred's mother, who was against the marriage, predicting, 'They will have so many children and no money.' It was destined to become a much quoted sentiment, since the couple were fated to have no children at all and so very much money.

In the early days, they were pathetically poor, though this state of affairs suited Alfred well enough. He and Mary, or Molly as she called herself, took cheap lodgings in West Hampstead, in a little house in Pandora Road, and side by side, Alfred barking out orders, his wife obeying, they put out Alfred's first magazine. Alfred called these years the happiest of his life: strewn about the flat were clippings, papers, paste and scissors, and proofs draped over chairs. Unable to afford the bus fare, he often walked the four miles to his office off Fleet Street in the morning and back again at night, presumably on air; Alfred never complained.

He began with the third issue of *Answers to Correspondents*, on 16 June 1888: 'A weekly storehouse of interesting knowledge; a weekly paper of surpassing interest; Praised by the Clergy, the Press and the Public.' It was a claim difficult to substantiate since there had been no previous issues. How could there have been if the publication answered the queries of its correspondents?*

* Sewell Stokes, 'Lord Rothermere Came to Lunch', *Listener*, 22 May 1958, p. 851; see also Reginald Pound and Geoffrey Harmsworth, *Northcliffe*, pp. 81–2.

'Horseflesh as Food' was an early topic, clearly borrowed from his father's debates at the Sylvan Debating Club; Dickens, too, popped up in a query of what the great writer himself liked to read. But the range of articles in *Answers* was as diverse as Alfred's imagination: 'How Madmen Write', 'How Divers Dress', 'An Electrical Flying Machine', 'A Year only Eighty-Seven Days Long'. In one article, the reader was taken into an opium den in Soho and allowed to experience vicariously the opulent Oriental fantasies produced by smoking the drug.

Alfred went stunt-crazy as well, sending his pal Pemberton for a ride in a locomotive engine, in a postal railway van, down in a diver's bell, up a steeple – all for *Answers*. Inside the office, at 26 Paternoster Square, anything could happen. In response to one article, doubting whether grass could grow in highly urbanized districts, enthusiastic readers proved it did by cutting their grass and sending it along to *Answers*. The office, Alfred complained, had turned into a haystack; one packet weighed forty-eight pounds, and, as it was nine pence short on postage, Alfred, ignorant of its contents, had actually paid the postage due in order to receive it.

As always, the family played its part. Alfred's brother Cecil, reading for his exams at the British Library, was asked to research material on the Bank of England. He noticed, somewhat cynically, his article appeared later with the preface, 'J.F. Smith writes from Birmingham as follows'. Alfred's sister Geraldine conducted similar research, learning typewriting as well in order to help in the firm. Alfred believed women should learn negotiable skills, and whatever Alfred believed, the family put into action. Earlier, during a brief period when Alfred had worked for an American sports magazine, *Outing*, he actually succeeded in talking his brothers into marching along the streets of London as '"superior sandwichmen" dressed as fishermen, huntsmen, and yachtsmen'. Aside from such frolics, however, the family existed as a survival unit, willing to act in unison whenever danger threatened any single member.

In the same year that saw the launch of *Answers*, some two hundred new publications appeared on the market. Newnes himself admitted *Answers* was his first real competition, and why shouldn't it have been? Alfred had helped himself to Newnes's front-page layout, taking the basic uptilted masthead, but ridding himself of the serif and shadowed type in a surround of ornate, curling flowers. Alfred gave his title-page typographical clarity by using startling black on white. '*Tit-Bits*', Newnes's masthead proclaimed, 'from all the most interesting books periodicals and newspapers in the world.' '*Answers to Correspondents*', Alfred heralded, 'on every subject under the sun'; '*Interesting*', '*Extraordinary*', '*Amusing*'. Symmetrical, silhouetted fingers appeared pointing inwards on either side of the important message. Another of Alfred's ploys was to give away virtual mountains of the first issues; it was the only advertising he could afford. His efforts paid off: of all Newnes's new competitors that year, *Answers* was the only one to survive.

It was a close thing. Within weeks, Alfred, whose profits were rapidly sinking, was in a near panic. 'I cannot make it pay,' he wailed. By autumn, with circulation actually falling off, he blamed the heavy fog that was blanketing London; this, plus the 'Jack the Ripper scare', then at its height. He could think of only one person who could save the business – his brother Harold.

Harold had gone to work for the Civil Service as a clerk in the Mercantile Marine Department of the Board of Trade. The whole family felt the good fortune of his having got the position – as he could expect, at the end of forty-five years' service, to receive a pension of £160 per year. For Harold, it would be a long forty-five years: since taking the post, his most exciting moment on the job had occurred when a rat ran up the leg of his trousers. Despite the decades of servitude he faced, however, Alfred's request plunged the family into deep crisis. Should Harold abandon his best and surest option to heed his brother's desperate cry, or should he stay the safe course?

In one version of events, Harold had to be persuaded by a relative to come to Alfred's aid. Alfred, so goes the story, gave a cousin three shillings to take Harold to the theatre, there to convince him to come into the business. The two young men didn't have the bus fare home, and it was during the long walk back that the cousin finally succeeded in winning Harold over to the scheme. But, given the loyalty of the family members to one another, the story doesn't add up. Even if he had entertained grave misgivings, Harold would have joined Alfred's firm – if for no other reason, out of family loyalty.

So important was Harold's contribution to the business that his brother Cecil would later write, 'Harold's letter of resignation from the Civil Service was "the most important single document in the history of the family".' So Harold quit his safe job and went to work with Alfred, where, it was said, the first evening he examined the firm's books, he actually wept from the mess they were in.

Now Harold was thrust into a strange and unenviable role: he had to convert Alfred's energy and genius into a paying proposition, and everything depended upon his succeeding at this task. This meant he had to exercise the most painstaking and minute control over outgoings, both financial and creative – the two almost inevitably going hand in hand. In the early days, Harold acted from necessity; later, he would respond almost without thinking. When the news was good, he would conjure up an entire range of potentially bad repercussions. When a project went off successfully, Harold would dwell on where it could go wrong. To Alfred's optimistic motto, 'You have to lose money to make it', he would stolidly reply, 'Stick to the money you have got and don't waste it on new ventures.'

He became known within the firm for his cutting of costs. In one famous memorandum sent to Alfred, Harold wrote, 'If I were you I should not extend that small type in Answers. To a person with weak eyes like myself it is almost unreadable. Our bad paper and cheap printing will not stand much in the way of small type. To railway travellers also the small type will of course be unreadable.'* Alfred's respect for Harold's opinion was practically unassailable. He deferred to him in most financial matters: 'Has Harold been into that?' he would ask before giving his own opinion, or he would dismiss a matter out of hand, saying, 'Harold says there is nothing in it.' If staffers complained of Harold's mean ways, Alfred would only reply, 'Harold has a knack of being right.'

For his part, Harold worried constantly and became easily depressed. In his personality, the Harmsworthian duality of character came into sharp relief. Exceedingly shy to the point of introversion, he discovered within himself the ability to perform a number of unpleasant tasks Alfred would never have been capable of.

It was Harold who squeezed out the Beaumonts, after it became apparent the company no longer needed their capital. 'In this kind of business skill and ability account for everything and capital for nothing,' he wrote to Alfred, blowing a minor disagreement into a full-blown rift. After many harsh words, most of them exempting Alfred, the Beaumonts eventually agreed to accept the life annuity of £2,400 per year Harold offered in place of partial ownership – but not without rancour. The trouble between Harold and the Beaumonts made Alfred physically ill, and he withdrew to his bed, where he suffered one of his worst bouts of nervous exhaustion.

Harold, himself undismayed, quickly formed the company Answers Ltd, offering special shares to newsagents. Thus he ensured the prominent display of the firm's publications.

Free now to concentrate on the editorial side of *Answers*, Alfred came up with the first of several zany promotional schemes. The most outlandish was a puzzle called Pigs in Clover, the object of which was to get little rolling balls in a glass box into the right holes in order to spell the word

* Paul Ferris, *The House of Northcliffe: The Harmsworths of Fleet Street*, p. 45. The date of the memorandum was 10 February 1892.

'Answers'. It was a terrific success, with *Answers* puzzle clubs springing up across the country and circulation rising as a result. The magazine claimed that two and a half million of these puzzles were sold on three continents.

But the most successful promotion, and the one that assured not only the survival of *Answers* but also its continuing success, was Alfred's £1-a-Week-for-Life scheme. 'On this sum,' Alfred told his readers, 'the young man who has been waiting to marry could probably be united to the object of his affections, and what an heiress would be the girl who secured the prize!'

The idea for the contest was said to have come from a tramp who, encountering Alfred and Harold on the Embankment, told them of his dream of having an income of a pound a week for the rest of his life. With this princely sum, he said, he could find happiness. Alfred seized upon the idea, and in October 1889 he announced 'The Most Gigantic and the Simplest Competition the World has ever seen'. The winner would have to guess correctly the amount in the National Treasury on a given day. It seemed that Alfred had hit upon a nerve, because *Answers* received 718,000 entries for the competition. Since each entry had to have the signatures of five others, Alfred boasted that for £1,100 – the amount needed to capitalize the prize money – he had advertised his magazine to some five million potential readers. And to top Alfred's good luck, it turned out that the winner was indeed a young man who used the money to marry his sweetheart.

This was the turning point for *Answers*, and indeed for Alfred and the firm. By the year after the stunt, the magazine's annual profit had soared to £30,000, and although a similar lottery was prohibited by the Government the following year, the £1-a-Week Competition enabled Alfred to put his Schemo Magnifico into full operation.

His first effort was a comic magazine, *Comic Cuts*, which quickly turned into a gold mine. Alfred's method of getting the magazine into production was simple: he took a staffer from *Answers* and ordered him to get the thing out in four days. By the night *Comic Cuts* went to press, the editor was vomiting into a wastepaper basket from anxiety. He needn't have worried: the first issue sold over 118,000 copies. Within only a few weeks, it was outselling *Answers*.

The slogan for the eight-page, halfpenny weekly was 'Amusing Without Being Vulgar'.* But *Comic Cuts* was vulgar, wonderfully vulgar, making full use of a suspicious innovation in the world of publications – the

* It is possible Oscar Wilde was referring to this slogan of *Comic Cuts* when he said a particular production of *Hamlet* was 'Amusing without being vulgar.'

speech balloon – along with inflated, colourful characters who spouted terrible jokes. 'The police magistrate may not enjoy himself even when he is having a *fine* time,' the magazine punned. 'It is never too late to mend. This is why the bootmaker never has your boots done at the time promised.' Condemned as 'office-boy humour', *Comic Cuts* succeeded because it targeted exactly that market. The magazine made so much money the Harmsworths themselves decided to bring out the first imitation – *Illustrated Chips* – which also sold exceedingly well.

Although Alfred would never have admitted it, these comic magazines had been inspired by a character named Ally Sloper, who was the star of a popular Victorian penny dreadful. In fact, Alfred had made the 'penny 'orribles', as he called them, the object of his continuing scorn. He dubbed their writers 'miserable beer-swilling wretches', urging his readers to take up 'our pure, healthy tales' instead. In every issue of *Answers*, Alfred slammed into the ''orribles', warning

> about errand boys who, after an overdose of sub-literary trash, chloroformed their bosses, pilfered the petty cash, and attempted to make their getaway to the States in rowing boats. In addition, every issue contained some testimonial, whether a statement by a metropolitan magistrate or a young railway clerk's letter, lauding the clean, pure fiction put out by Harmsworth.

This was Alfred's path to the next great market – that of the adolescent boy. Almost yearly, a new boys' magazine was added to the growing list of Harmsworth publications: *Boys' Home Journal, Pluck, Marvel, Boys' Friend* were a few of them. But just because they offered a 'purer' alternative to the penny dreadful didn't mean the Harmsworths weren't above a little derring-do. Harold had shown the pair's true colours when he suggested to Alfred they call *Marvel* the *Boys' Weekly Reader*; 'It sounds respectable,' he wrote, 'and would act as a cloak for one or two fiery stories.' Alfred stuck to his own title and found his drama in tales of 'deeds and bravery of those who laid the foundations of the Empire'.

In fact, the Imperialist theme was such a fecund source of revenue it quickly found its way into its own magazine – *Union Jack*. It became known for its stories of the Brits in exotic locales: 'More than forty natives sprang on Cyril,' one story recited, as it rose to a climax, 'and, although his resistance was desperate, he was quickly reminded how surely numbers tell, even though they be black ones.'

Now, Schemo Magnifico was no longer a fantasy; it was a steamroller flattening all competitors in its path. Alfred and Harold, turning to the women's market, developed *Home Sweet Home, Forget-Me-Not* and *Home Chat* ('The Daintiest Little Magazine in the World'), each following quickly after the other. *The Wonder* and *Sunday Companion* also appeared in turn. 'Knife it,' Harold would shout, if the publication didn't turn quickly to gold. But Alfred held out, and many that made poor starts quickly found their level.

Towards his flagship publication, Alfred maintained an attitude of reverence: he found a pun based on the hymn, 'I *knead* thee every hour', far too vulgar for inclusion in *Answers*, and rewarded the editor who questioned it. Indeed, after *Answers* was bound, he placed the copies among his collections of Socrates, Cicero, Homer and Virgil.

More and more, the distance between the Harmsworth brothers and their disadvantaged beginning lengthened, and Harold's letters to Alfred reflected their growing prosperity. 'I am paying off the mortgage of 94 Boundary Road,' he would write to Alfred, or 'I am advancing mother money,' or 'The figures are very good this week, and we can hope now permanently to remain over the three quarters million.' But for Harold, the threat of fresh competition, such as *Pearson's Weekly* or some other publication, was enough to set him back to his perennial state of worry.*

Certainly, the brothers had made their enemies – to Harold's concern and Alfred's delight. Alfred himself gleefully published an anonymous criticism of *Answers* that took him and his brother to task:

> Who is the editor of this excerpt publication and where will he and his brother conspirators ultimately go? The intellect of the few, their wit and humour, joys and sorrows, all are got into the machine, the handle turned, everything is bruised, crushed, and pulverised; then comes the mixing powder of adulteration, and this dreadful weekly *Answers to Correspondents* is ready for issue.

It was certainly the end of civilization as the Victorians knew it, and the beginning of a new age of mass consumption and magical cheapness. Alfred revelled in catering to the common man, just as he loved confounding his newly gained enemies.

He had brought his family out of poverty. He had increased his circulation from 20,000 to a combined weekly sales figure of 1,009,067 copies, the largest circulation of any magazine company in the world. This in just four years.

By 1892, with the steady assistance of his brother Harold and occasional aid of his younger siblings, Alfred had managed to establish a publications empire; eliminate his original investors and become the sole proprietor;

* Excerpts from letters written by Harold to Alfred are held in the Harmsworth Archives, owned by the Daily Mail & General Trust, plc. Generally, they are more cordial than biographies of Northcliffe have tended to report. There, Harold is generally characterized as writing only terse circulation reports, and very little else.

buy an estate in Broadstairs for himself and his wife; pay for a house for his mother; educate his younger brothers and sisters – *and* he paid contributors to his publications *on acceptance*.

By the time he had achieved all these things, Alfred was twenty-seven years old, and his brother Harold was twenty-four.

2

'This Paper Will Go'

No one could accuse Frank Harris, the roguish editor of the *Evening News* from 1883 to 1887, of a niggardly style of living. He lunched regularly at Kettner's, in private rooms, so that his guests were spared any appraisal by other diners. He supped at the Criterion and the Café Royal – whose cellar, he assured his friends, was the best in the world. He favoured Perrier-Jouet of 1874 and very pretty, vacant young women, of whom there were quite a few if Harris's sensational memoirs are to be believed. He was a man received in all the best houses in London – *once!*, as his friend Oscar Wilde put it.

Harris was acquainted with the American expatriate Henry James, who was redefining the modern novel, and the young French playwright Edmond Rostand, whose *Cyrano de Bergerac* had just been staged triumphantly with Sarah Bernhardt. He was personal friends with George Bernard Shaw, James McNeill Whistler, Max Beerbohm, Sir Henry Irving, Lillie Langtry, Bram Stoker, the list goes on. The only well-known figure of the age with whom Harris did not claim at least a limited intimacy was Jack the Ripper.

Yellow was the favourite colour of the age, and the most celebrated literary organ was called, appropriately enough, *The Yellow Book*. Begun in 1889, a year after Alfred Harmsworth's *Answers*, it embodied everything his publication did not – élitism, aestheticism, extremist views. Its art editor was the gifted illustrator Aubrey Beardsley – still another of Harris's friends – whose works celebrating male tumescence and female reluctance were perhaps less well known. It was *fin-de-siècle* London, a time of literary and social decadence, a time that was rapidly unravelling the conventions of its own making. Deeply enamoured of the witty, if cynical literati, Harris was fond of quoting a line of overripe verse about a century that was 'dying into a dance,/An agony of trance'. This from a man whose success as editor of the *Evening News*, by his own estimation, depended upon his decision to cover fully the divorce of Lady Colin Campbell, including 'the most scabrous details'.

'I gave up the whole of the right-hand centre page to it', he boasted, later defending himself successfully against a charge of obscene libel. From this incident and a few others like it, Harris came to the conclusion that his readers had a literary age of thirteen or fourteen, and, like all good thirteen- and fourteen-year-olds, 'kissing and fighting' were the only things they cared to read about.

Harris obliged them. After three years of sensational crime stories and court cases, the paper's circulation increased, and for the first time since it was founded in 1881 it had begun to make money. Thus Harris continued for several years, a foot in either camp; his friends, the aesthetes of the age, his readers the asses. By 1887, his proprietor, Kennard Coleridge, had had enough of Harris's self-important posturing and contemptibly low publication standards. He forced his editor out. Harris went immediately to the *Fortnightly Review*, joining in the chorus of disapproval against populist upstarts like the Harmsworth brothers. As for the *Evening News*, it began its inevitable circulation slide, gradual at first, then snowballing, until the paper's losses made it a liability no sane man would consider buying. It was said Coleridge personally squandered something in the region of £100,000 trying to make the *Evening News* pay. By 1894, and several editors later, the *News* had become such a loss-maker that Liberal wags on the stock market put up its shares for sale in bushel baskets.

Coleridge decided to take steps. He would sell the paper cheaply to some obvious rube – or he would fold it.

At the same time Frank Harris was sensationalizing the *Evening News*, W.T. Stead, editor of the *Pall Mall Gazette* and Harris's major competitor, was staking out new ground for journalism. For centuries journalism had been a profession of disrepute. Since 1799, public reading rooms had been considered for legal purposes the same as brothels: 'any house, room, or place for the purpose of reading books, pamphlets, newspapers or other publications without a licence', the law stated, 'shall be otherwise punished as ... disorderly houses.' The idea of wine-soaked hacks eking out a living in Grub Street with their truthless prose had never really left the public consciousness, even though the hacks had long since moved to Fleet Street and a steady influx of well-intentioned, well-educated newsgatherers had entered the profession. Nevertheless, the long tradition of killing the messenger persisted.

A puritanical man of deeply held convictions, Stead steadily pursued issues of major social concern in the pages of the *Pall Mall Gazette*, actually raising the paper's circulation by appealing to the moral sensibilities of his middle-class readers. His best-known campaign was against the enslavement of children and young girls into prostitution, and in place of the usual empty platitudes abjuring such practices, he particularized an active traffic in vice, including the procurement of virgins for deflowering in exchange for money, the selling of children for sexual violation, atrocities and unnatural acts, and other theretofore unspeakable practices. On Monday, 6 July 1885, he published the transcript of his interview with a sixteen-year-old girl who was prepared to sell him her virginity for £4, although she had no understanding of what that act entailed.

Condemned as a vicarious lecher in some camps, praised as a moral crusader in others, Stead actually went to prison for his campaign, along the way changing the face of journalism in Great Britain. In America, the *New York Sun* hailed him as 'England's version of Horace Greeley, a man who came nearer to governing Great Britain than any other man in the kingdom'. Stead was a journalist's journalist; in fact, T.P. O'Connor, editor of the *Star*, another forerunner in the field, welcomed Stead's approach as 'the new journalism'. In an important article published in October 1889 in the *New Review*, O'Connor delineated 'a new departure in English journalism...'.

'The main point of difference', he wrote, 'is the more personal tone of the more modern methods.' O'Connor condemned long and 'lifeless' reports not easily accessible to the new readership. Instead, he lauded journalism that emphasized the personality of the subject, 'the habits, the clothes, or the home and social life of any person'. This, said O'Connor, had now become subject to fair commentary by the press. To defend his views, O'Connor referred to the great historian Lord Macaulay, who, O'Connor emphasized,

> did not neglect ... the smallest detail in making up one of these portraits – the kind of wig his hero wore; the food he loved; the way he tied his shoe ... [the] picture is the more interesting from the infinitude of its petty details ... quite in the style of the New Journalism. But apart from the value of personal journalism as historical material, I hold that the desire for personal details with regard to public men is healthy, rational, and should be yielded to.

Despite this emphasis upon the personal, O'Connor nevertheless condemned out of hand any tendency of journalism to descend to the level of mere gossip.

The unexpected interest of the public in issues of social concern, the ferment of the argument as to whether personal conduct was a proper focus for journalism, the new technology that created the potential for a mass readership – all these things caused practitioners of the trade to re-evaluate their mission. George Newnes, the founder of *Tit-Bits*, writing to W.T. Stead, explained it this way:

There is one kind of journalism which directs the affairs of nations and makes and unmakes Cabinets; it upsets Governments, builds up navies, and does many other great things. That is your journalism. There is another kind which has no such great ambitions. It is content to plod on, year after year, giving wholesome and harmless entertainments to crowds of hard-working people craving for a little fun and amusement. It is quite humble and unpretentious. That is my journalism.

True enough. But little did Newnes suspect that his major competitor, Alfred Harmsworth – the man who had built an empire on queries and answers, comic books, boys' adventure stories and ladies' domestic concerns; the very man who was about to take the *Evening News* off the hands of Kennard Coleridge – would be able to do both.

At street level, the reporters on T.P. O'Connor's *Star* were busy. Bank robbing and homicide being at a low ebb for the moment, the hacks were deeply involved in a game of skill and chance – 'a kind of indoor quoits', one of them called it. The object of the game was to spin playing cards into a turned-up top hat, or 'topper' as it was called, at an agreed range for an agreed wager. Whoever succeeded in 'topping' the most cards won the wager. The *Star* men were therefore unanimous in their approval of a dress code that required a silk hat to lend respectability to the trade whilst at the same time providing a golden opportunity to improve their powers of observation and manual dexterity.

On that first day of publication in 1888, the *Star* had called itself 'an epoch in journalism', but the men who made it work were a bit less lofty. There were Lincoln Springfield, Tom Marlowe, Walter J. Evans and the ever-popular Charlie Hands.

Of Hands it was said an evening's enjoyment consisted of attending not a single music-hall, but a dozen, taking a turn at the bar of each, before returning home apparently none the worse for drink.

Hands once substituted the name of his colleague Lincoln Springfield for that of a notorious co-respondent in a well-known divorce case of the time. He then posted it on the wall of the reporters' office at the *Star* under the heading 'Serpent Springfield: How a Man May Have Curly Hair and Be a Villain' – just in time for a visit from Springfield's wife. After a few minutes of serious consternation, she commented drily, 'I see Satan still finds mischief for idle Hands to do.'

Even as his boss T.P. O'Connor rattled on about the noble cause of the new journalism, Hands was at work exposing a matrimonial newsletter that brought couples together for purposes that Hands believed showed 'the Dark Continent of Human Nature'.

> Broadly speaking, the men wanted the money and the women wanted the love; but in each case the desire was impersonal. The men didn't care the toss of a button who brought the money, and the women didn't care much who the man was.

Chorus girls of the age usually didn't involve themselves in the activities of the *Matrimonial News*. But in one case an under-aged beauty did so, and finding herself seduced, not by a client but by the publisher himself, sued on breach of promise, and, for her trouble, was awarded £10,000. The publisher fled to Paris, giving Hands the opportunity to publish in the *Star* letter after letter he had taken from the files of the marriage service. The serial was brought to an abrupt end when it was discovered a director of the *Star* was one of the most prolific of the letter-writers. It was this kind of high-minded exposé that made Charlie Hands the darling of the newsroom.

Another disciple of the darker side of human nature was the gifted sub-editor Walter J. Evans. A short man whose scholarly appearance belied a mischievous nature, Evans ceaselessly smoked shag tobacco as he tore through reams of copy. His greatest claim to fame, aside from his ability to take in prodigious amounts of drink without apparent effect, was to subsist on nothing more than a single hard-boiled egg a day.

Meanwhile, the Promenade Empire, closed for a time by the 'Prudes on the Prowl' Crusade, had just reopened 'with a flourish of strumpets', as one well-known clergyman put it, and it was there that the young Tom Marlowe found himself in a serious scrape. Known as something of a hothead, Marlowe, thinking himself insulted on an important point he later could not remember, attacked the boxer who had gone a hundred rounds with John L. Sullivan, and was only saved from extinction by Lincoln Springfield, who dragged him, struggling, from the bar-room floor and safely to his home.

Springfield himself was eventually lured away from the *Star* to the *Pall Mall Gazette* by Harry Cust, the paper's newly named editor. The *Gazette* had been purchased by American millionaire William Waldorf Astor who, it was said, was hoping for a peerage by becoming an English newspaper proprietor. Springfield was allowed to bring one colleague with him, so Evans and Hands drew lots, Hands winning, and away they went to the *Gazette*, there to meet up with a young leader writer by the name of George Warrington Steevens. Steevens wore pince-nez, was distinguished by dark good looks and, unexpectedly, had been a Balliol senior scholar who gained a first in 'Mods' and 'Greats' and a fellowship to Pembroke College. Unlike his colleagues, he was of a sensitive nature and preferred research and writing to bar-room brawls. Springfield immediately took Steevens under his wing in order to introduce him to a few of the finer things Fleet Street had to offer.

It was also down to Springfield for encouraging a young Birmingham reporter, Kennedy Jones, to leave his post and seek his fortune in the Street, for, as Springfield explained to the fledgling Jones, there was 'nothing sacrosanct or preternaturally capable about the London journalists as compared with the average copy-slogger in the provinces'.

Many years later, when Kennedy Jones, or 'K.J.', as he called himself, became the right-hand man of Alfred Harmsworth, first on the *Evening News* and then on the *Daily Mail* – earning the rubric 'the most hated man in Fleet Street' – Springfield found himself threatened with 'a burning at the stake or a boiling in oil' for bringing to Fleet Street the man 'who had caused so much misfortune'.

For all these reporters – Springfield, Evans, Hands, Steevens, Kennedy Jones, and a host of others – this was indeed the dawn of a new journalism. They were all about to be taken up by Alfred Harmsworth as he built a newspaper empire to rival and even exceed what he had achieved in the world of magazines.

In 1894, London had nine evening papers, four of them halfpenny papers, the others a penny. All of them were in trouble. Most notably, the *Evening News*, known for its affiliation with the Conservative Party, had been a notorious loss-maker despite a circulation of close to 100,000. On the eve of its closing and with three days to spare, a pair of ambitious young newsmen, Louis Tracy and Kennedy Jones, being informed that Alfred Harmsworth had 'more money than the Bank of England', made a visit to the young magazine magnate to try to convince him and his brother Harold to purchase the ailing *Evening News*. Alfred, golden haired and swathed in what Jones perceived as innocence, seemed vaguely interested in the proposition; his brother Harold was more difficult to read.

Jones, a tough cookie who had worked the mean streets of Glasgow and Manchester, later admitted he suffered several sleepless nights after the initial interview with the two brothers. What Jones didn't know was that they were fascinated by the prospect of owning the *News*, which fitted nicely into their own hidden agenda, but only under conditions laid down by Harold.

'My Dear Alfred,' Harold wrote in an undated letter to his brother,

Kay Robinson has not a very high opinion of Tracy and Jones. He says they have not got that reputation as journalists which they would like us to believe. He, however, fully believes that the E. News might be made to pay...

If we could pick the paper up for a song it would be worth our while to have it, but not otherwise.

Yours,
HAROLD

In fact, owning the *Evening News* was just the ticket for the Harmsworth brothers, because it gave them the opportunity to have a go, and fairly cheaply, at the newspaper market, which they intended to invade in much the same way that they had invaded the magazine field. The plan to launch a daily newspaper had always been at the back of Alfred's mind. Here was the chance for a test-drive, as it were, and for only £25,000 – a fraction of what it would cost to launch a paper from scratch. Thus it was that the brothers decided to buy the *News*, 'our gold brick', as Harold was wont to call it.

From that day on, Alfred later wrote,

After a hard day's work in editing, managing and writing for periodicals, my brother and I met Mr Jones night after night in the ramshackle building in Whitefriars Street in the endeavour to find out what was wrong with the *Evening News*, and why it was that a newspaper in which the Conservative Party had embarked between three and four hundred thousand pounds was such a failure ... Our combined efforts soon discovered the faults in the *Evening News*. They were mainly – lack of continuity of policy and lack of managerial control.

Fleet Street didn't very much care what steps the Harmsworths might take to save the *Evening News*. The brothers were viewed as hopeless naïves by old hands in the business, and generally held in contempt. The very night the brothers were digging the pits to install new rotary presses, 'a waggish enemy spy' decided to pay a visit. He allowed as how the pits were big enough to swallow up the Harmsworths' entire hard-earned fortune. 'Better be satisfied with what you have done,' he advised the brothers.

Alfred Harmsworth, never satisfied with what he had done, disregarded the ill wishes of his new-found enemies, and set about to enliven the paper, Harmsworth-style. For a start, he adopted a newer and more modern typeface, emphasizing important news with bold headlines. The leaders were cut to the bare bones, the political writing trimmed. Regular features were put in the same place day after day, so the reader could easily find what he wanted. Wherever possible, Alfred laid in maps beside the foreign news – and, in a stroke of pure genius, he introduced the football pools. Items like 'How Time-Tables Are Made', 'Two Delectable Drinks', 'About Smoking in Cemeteries' and 'Swell Criminals' ('Is Crime a Mental Disease? – A Prison Governor's Views') found their way into the paper. Alfred wrote about famous ventriloquists or the origin of the bicycle with the same seriousness of purpose his new partner K.J. reserved for murder and mayhem.

K.J. was horrified by the growing proliferation of Alfred's 'talking points'. 'God, man,' he complained, 'you're not going to turn the paper into an evening *Answers*, are you?' Worse still, from K.J.'s point of view, was Alfred's insistence on women's pages. To the macho K.J., such a move was destined to alienate male readers. It would be many months before Jones could bring himself to admit that Alfred was right about the women's market.

In the meantime, Harold set about to overhaul the distribution of the *News*. He examined the points throughout the city where the crowd was at its peak, and, using a well-synchronized system of delivery, put the paper at the right place at the right time. He also organized the net sales certificate, considered controversial at the time, which verified readership claims for advertisers. Shortly afterwards, he raised the *Evening News* advertising rates to £40 a half-page. His competitors thought he was mad, predicting the Harmsworths would come a cropper.

Investigating the ledgers of the paper, Harold discovered that much of the paper's losses, which amounted to some £170 per week, resulted from the uninformed purchase of newsprint. In the first week of the brothers' ownership of the *Evening News*, the paper's losses went down to £100. By the second, the paper was running a £7 profit, by the third, £50. Within six months of the Harmsworths' takeover, circulation had risen to 122,000, by far the largest sale of any evening paper in the city.

A celebration was clearly in order, and K.J. and the Harmsworths engaged for dinner at Kettner's, Frank Harris's old hangout. While Alfred and Harold were putting in eighteen-hour days, Harris had been flirting with his decadent literary crowd, enjoying the pleasures of his own notoriety. Now the Harmsworths had joined in the fray, and having made it up the first rung of the ladder in newspaper management, they felt that Kettner's was the ideal place to celebrate.

For his part, though, Harold was depressed, and did not enjoy his meal at all. 'It will take us years to wipe off those debentures,' he informed Alfred with characteristic pessimism. Alfred himself ate little. Unimpressed by the famous Soho establishment where so many journalists wined and dined, he never bothered to return. A pattern was thus emerging; these were men who enjoyed the labours of success more than its fruits. It was in this spirit of worry and workaholism that the Harmsworths made their first foray into Fleet Street.

Walter J. Evans, deserted by Lincoln Springfield and Charlie Hands when they went off to work on the *Pall Mall Gazette*, also quickly abandoned the *Star* in order to join Kennedy Jones on the Harmsworths' new acquisition. By early May 1896, K.J. having gone on to bigger and better things, Evans found himself editor-in-chief of the evening paper in one of those fast upward shifts of staff for which the Harmsworths were rapidly becoming known.

He now paid a visit to his old pal Springfield, who, he said, was to return with him to the offices of Alfred Harmsworth, where he would be made an offer he couldn't afford to refuse.

It happened that Springfield's opinion of Harmsworth reflected the popular assessment currently making the rounds of Fleet Street – that he was a one-day phenomenon destined in the not-too-distant future for the rubbish heap – and he refused to budge an inch from his comfortable office chair. But Evans persisted. He had given his word he would return with Springfield; now Springfield must go and hear what the man had to say. Reluctantly, Springfield agreed.

Thus did Lincoln Springfield find himself unexpectedly in the presence of an eager, energetic and handsome young man who would one day own more than half the titles in Fleet Street. Harmsworth stated his case without ado. He had just started a new morning newspaper, he explained, and it was doing well, but occasionally his staff missed big stories other papers managed to pick up. Would Lincoln Springfield undertake to become his news editor?

Unimpressed, Springfield decided to put an end to the matter once and for all. He wouldn't consider the job, he said flippantly, for less than ten guineas a week.

'Certainly,' Harmsworth replied, 'we'll give you that.'

Springfield, who prided himself on his composure, found himself flustered and, perhaps for the first time in his life, speechless. Harmsworth continued. That weekend, he said, Springfield would stay with him at Elmwood, his estate in Broadstairs. There, the two men would become acquainted with one another and assess how best their work could proceed.

This is how Springfield found himself amongst the increasing ranks of men who called Harmsworth 'Chief', men who suddenly found themselves not only well paid and respected for their work but also subject to the easy charm and charisma of Alfred Harmsworth. Just before Springfield caught his train back to London on Monday morning, the two men took a walk along the beach at Broadstairs. There, they came upon a coconut shy and, after a brief contest, Springfield came out ahead.

'Look here, Springfield,' the young entrepreneur said, 'since you have been down you have beaten me at lawn tennis, you have beaten me at billiards, and now you have whacked me at coconut shying. Do you think you are being quite tactful?' It was typical Harmsworthian sportsmanship, with a touch of wit thrown in for good measure, but Springfield would soon learn, as others before and after him, that Alfred was less charming when it came to his new morning newspaper, the *Daily Mail*.

Alfred had determined this paper would become the market leader, and characteristically he had left very little to chance. The brothers had been planning for a daily newspaper ('our next scheme') since 1894, just before they had bought the *Evening News*.

By the time the first issue of the *Daily Mail* finally appeared, on 4 May 1896, over sixty-five dummy runs had taken place, the first of them beginning six weeks earlier on 15 February. For each of the runs, reporters covered stories the public would never read, their copy was subbed and set up on linotype machines, stereo plates were cast, and the paper put to bed to a strict deadline, exactly as if the paper were being published and distributed. Before the public ever viewed a single copy, over £40,000 had been spent on newsprint, staff, salaries, wire services and telegrams. Such a thing had never before been done on Fleet Street.

The front page had been created by making composite photographs of all the daily newspapers on the market – the *Standard*, the *Daily Telegraph*, the *Daily News*, the *Chronicle*, the *Morning Post* and *The Times* – super-imposing these one upon the other, and taking the best features of each. At the top of the page, on either side of the title, were the *Daily Mail*'s twin mottos – 'A Penny Newspaper for One Halfpenny', and 'The Busy Man's Daily Journal'.

Harold believed the name for the *Mail* came from the *Glasgow Daily Mail & Record*, which he bought in 1895 when he and Alfred were considering setting up a chain of provincials. But Kennedy Jones also claimed credit for the name, saying it derived from the *Birmingham Daily Mail*, where he had first begun his reporting career. Even Leicester Harmsworth, Alfred and Harold's younger brother, laid claim to the newspaper's title, saying that Alfred had originally preferred the name 'Arrow', but came around to Leicester's suggestion because he thought *Mail* would sound better when yelled out by paperboys.

However the name actually did come about, the *Mail*, Alfred decided, was to be a national newspaper, with distribution in the provinces. Here Harold's experience with the *Evening News* was invaluable. Close studies 'proved to us to how large an extent sales were affected by the hour at which the paper was available', Kennedy Jones later reported. The team set about using the railways to get the papers to central distribution points at the right time.

Another of Alfred's ideas was that the *Daily Mail* would encapsulate the news of the entire world in a bulletin form, and he worked out a strategy by which a team of worldwide correspondents contributed to this feature – another first for Fleet Street. The concept was part and parcel of *Daily Mail* policy: 'All the news in the smallest space'; and in this case 'all' meant *all*.

Money seemed not to be an issue with Alfred, and later on it would be rumoured the entire cost of putting the *Mail* into operation eventually topped half a million, an immense sum in the last decade of the nineteenth century. In addition to the new linotype machines, which revolutionized typesetting, Alfred also installed a state-of-the-art printing room that not only printed the paper but folded and cut it as well. 'The process is so rapid', Alfred would later write of his most outstanding innovation,

> that the eye fails to follow it. The paper is literally flowing in like a rushing stream, and at the other end the papers are being tossed out in dozens; the one machine having printed, cut, folded, and counted them. The papers are thrown from the machine on to a kind of multiple lift, consisting of an endless chain continually raising a series of shelves to the publishing room above. You hear a sudden whirl as the machines start, and almost at the same moment great bundles of papers are thrown out to the carts in waiting and the race for the railway stations and the newspaper distributing agencies begins.

The gigantic rolls of paper sped through the machine at twenty miles per hour, printing between 48,000 and 96,000 copies in an hour. Even at that, it was not enough. The first issue of the *Daily Mail* sold 397,215 copies, so many more than Alfred originally estimated that on that first night it was necessary to hire the use of machinery from several other evening newspapers and two large printing companies.

Readers had been cajoled into buying the first issue with an intriguing advertisement: 'Four leading articles, a page of Parliament, and columns of speeches will NOT be found in the *Daily Mail* on 4 May, a halfpenny.' What the reader did find on that first Monday morning were leaders on the 'London Tramways Scheme', a brief warning about a growing 'Cycle of Crime', and an obvious favourite of Alfred, 'Motor Car Travel'.

There was also an article entitled 'The Explanation', which undertook to de-mystify the question of how the *Daily Mail* was able to deliver 'all the news of the penny morning Press for a halfpenny'. The answer was found in 'remarkable new inventions':

> Our type is set by machinery, and we can produce many thousands of papers per hour cut, folded and if necessary with the pages pasted together. It is the use of these new inventions on a scale unprecedented in any English newspaper office that enables the Daily Mail to effect a saving of from 30 to 50 per cent and be sold for half the price of its contemporaries. That is the whole explanation of what would otherwise appear a mystery.*

Finally, Alfred had installed and was putting to practical business use a wonderful, relatively new communication device – the telephone – in which two parties could speak to one another as if in each other's presence, by means of a wire. By June, he had even set up telephone connections between the *Mail* in London and *Le Journal* in Paris.

All these improvements, as well as emphasis upon concise and entertaining writing, distinguished the *Mail* from its competitors.

As if all this were not enough, the *Mail* made an unexpected claim, one that was bound to cause trouble in the family – that the paper would have less advertising space than other dailies. Advertisements, Alfred decided, 'spoilt the paper'; Harold, on the other hand, would have preferred to cut news content for ad space. By the same token, Harold wanted to use cheap tinted paper for the *Daily Mail*; Alfred wanted a high-quality white. It was a gentle rift between the pair at first, but in fact it represented a good deal more – a genuine difference in point of view, even in the temperament of the two brothers. Long term versus short term; coverage versus cash outlay; editorial versus management; courage versus fear – this was the classic declension that would cause discord between Alfred and Harold in later years. Later still, it would affect the *Daily Mail* itself.

As for Harold, whose distribution and business genius had informed the success of the magazine empire and of the *Evening News*, he now found himself shunted aside by Alfred, who had, in his obsession with his new newspaper, come to fear Harold's thrift, suspicious that he would cheapen the *Daily Mail* with false savings. The family seemed to go with Alfred. But for Alfred's resistance, Leicester said, Harold's management might have made the *Mail* into 'a farthing paper for a halfpenny'.

*

---

* Kennedy Jones writes that the press could produce 200,000 copies per hour on p. 138–9 of *Fleet Street and Downing Street*, in contradiction to Alfred Harmsworth at p. 17, n. 42 in *The Romance of the Daily Mail*, where he writes that the press could produce up to 96,000 copies per hour. I have taken Harmsworth as the accurate number and so indicated in quoting Jones.

This was probably the reason that Alfred, in building up the *Daily Mail*, turned to Kennedy Jones, the two of them making the unlikeliest pair of bedfellows in the history of journalism. K.J. had a brusque and dismissive manner that earned him the hatred of employee and competitor alike. Said one colleague, who actually liked him, K.J. had a particularly 'acidulated humour that meant he laughed at you rather than with you'. He smoked up to a hundred cigarettes a day, swore expressively and managed to offend almost everyone around him. He pushed for crime, mystery, football, racing and cricket, often neglecting other sections of the paper. And he viewed Alfred as a total innocent in the rough-and-tumble world of Fleet Street.

Kennedy Jones had taken an early lead over the man who had originally conspired with him to convince Alfred Harmsworth to buy the *Evening News*. In fact, soon after signing on, Louis Tracy had voluntarily bowed out, sold his shares at a decent profit and turned to his first love, novel-writing, at which he excelled. As a result, the early success of the *Daily Mail* depended almost exclusively upon the bizarre combination of Alfred's unique brand of 'new journalism' and K.J.'s dogmatic adherence to blood-and-guts formulas. In the early days on the *Evening News*, one early crime story, about the execution of the murderer James Canham Read, who had shot a pregnant woman, clearly shows the kind of collaboration the pair were perfecting. It was K.J.'s selection of event, Alfred's emphasis upon details.

'The man who is executed at Chelmsford', the story read, 'is pinioned in his cell, is walked quickly from there to a strange little room, with its gaudy, dark red paint and unpleasantly clean whitewash, and is sunk into eternity in less than sixty seconds.' K.J. understood the reader's morbid curiosity about the death of a murderer; Alfred focused on Read's red socks and excellent appetite at breakfast on the morning of his execution. On the first day of the series on Read, circulation of the *News* was 187,000; by the last, it had risen to 390,000.

By the time the pair turned to the *Daily Mail*, they had learned to work in perfect harmony. On that first day, Alfred was all over the place; nervous, fussy, frantic. Legend has it that he worked two days and nights straight, and then, as soon as he saw the paper was a success, went home to sleep for twenty-two hours. The actual entry in his diary reads, 'After a severe struggle got the paper to press with many misgivings at 1.20 a.m.' He autographed the first copy for his mother and went home, whether or not to sleep for twenty-two hours he neglected to record.

For his part, K.J. was serenely confident of the new product. It happened the paper was founded on his birthday, and he was so certain of success he said, 'It is my hope that when in 1996 its centenary is celebrated, then shall K.J. be freshly remembered, and it will be recalled that had he lived to see that day, he would have been 131 years old.' Later, when the pair were told of the first day's phenomenal sales, K.J.'s seeming arrogance was more than vindicated. 'We've struck a gold mine!' Alfred exclaimed to his colleague.

Maybe so. But not everybody approved of Alfred Harmsworth's latest incursion into the world of journalism. Although Lord Salisbury, then Prime Minister, sent a congratulatory telegram to Alfred on the outstanding success of his new paper, behind his back he made one of the best-remembered gibes: paraphrasing Thackeray's Pendennis, who started a newspaper 'by gentlemen for gentlemen', the *Daily Mail*, said Salisbury, was 'a newspaper produced by officeboys for officeboys'. The *Saturday Review* condemned the paper for its 'snippet' journalism, and the aesthetes and intellectuals of the day dismissed the paper as 'that rag'.

In his rooms at 5 Old Palace Yard, however, one shrewd customer was looking at the *Mail* in a different light. Henry Labouchere, editor of the respected journal *Truth*, slowly leafed through Alfred Harmsworth's brainchild with extreme interest. At last he threw it lightly on his desk and shrugged. 'This paper will go,' he said to one of his colleagues.

And it did.

For someone naïve about the Street and its workings, Alfred Harmsworth never seemed to lack for an idea. He pounded his staff daily with what he believed to be a winning strategy: 'Every day there is an event which ought to be the outstanding feature of the news column. The clever news editor puts his finger upon that; the other man misses it altogether.' He barked out his observations ceaselessly: 'It is hard news that catches readers,' he advised the staff, 'features that hold them. Always have a woman's story at the top of all the main news pages in your paper.' Again, it was Alfred Harmsworth who first said that when a dog bites a man, that's not news; when a man bites a dog, that is.

Under Alfred's tutelage, the *Daily Mail* would become 'a writer's paper'. 'Explain, simplify, clarify!' he constantly exclaimed. Foreign currencies had always to be explained in terms of pounds and pence; foreign phrases had to be defined in English. One staffer who used the phrase *fait accompli* found it asterisked in the newspaper as 'accomplished fact'.

For his women readers, Alfred laid in stories on cookery and clothes; he also instituted an entirely new idea in daily journalism, the first magazine page ever used in a daily newspaper. Its subtitle was 'a page for leisure moments'. He personally supervised the writing of serials, whose average length was 100,000 words. The opening episode had to be a spellbinder of 5,000 words, with exciting follow-ups of 1,500 to 2,000 words every day. If Alfred found a commissioned work lacking, he sat down with the writer and, together, they rewrote the story until it held the suspense Alfred wanted for his readers.

Underlying all this effort was Alfred's profound respect for the rising middle classes of the late Victorian age. 'The new century was close at hand and hundreds of thousands of people to whom the old papers had nothing to tell were ready and eager for the *Daily Mail* to rise up and interpret its meaning,' said one staffer, trying to explain the impact the *Mail* was making on the public at large. But if Alfred respected his readers, his partner Kennedy Jones took the opposite view.

'Don't forget you are writing for the meanest intelligence,' the crude Glaswegian would remind the staff. At his relentless insistence, crime and sensationalism became vital parts of the paper. Typical was a report about a man who infected victims intentionally with a deadly disease simply because he himself had become accidentally infected: 'Professor and Poisoner; kills fifteen victims by cholera bacilli; sensational suicide; MYSTERIOUS MURDER of an aged chemist at Nottingham; no clue.'

Aside from this strange capacity to co-operate, the two men had little in common. For one thing, Kennedy Jones had an inflexibility that prevented him from adopting the style and class his new-found success and wealth could have afforded him. When he purchased a lavish new home in Muswell Hill, North London, the decorations for which cost in excess of £20,000, his assistant had to convince him to buy new furnishings and get rid of the old stuff. It sold for £20. K.J. also had to be told to smoke a less offensive blend of tobacco. His response was typically K.J. 'Uh, OK,' he said, and switched the same day. It had never occurred to him he could afford something better. His favourite saying was, 'Nothing really matters,' and he meant it.

To Alfred, everything mattered. And yet, despite the differences between the two men, they would work together harmoniously for the next two decades, Alfred's opinion of K.J. remaining high: 'It is a great relief to me,' he would write eighteen years after they had launched the *Daily Mail*, 'always to have so reliable a colleague at the other end of the wire.'

K.J. *was* reliable; he was shrewd and competent. But his salient characteristic was cynicism. When, on 31 December 1895, the Scottish Dr Jameson, acting as an agent of the British-owned South African Company, led a raid of some five to six hundred troops into the Boer province of Transvaal, Jameson became a rallying point for British Imperialism, a symbol of Empire. At this time, K.J. was working with Alfred on the *Evening*

News, and the event hit the Glaswegian like a lightning bolt. He realized for the first time that:

> one of the greatest forces, almost untapped, at the disposal of the Press was the depth and volume of public interest in Imperial questions ... The instant we lifted the Jameson raid out of the miasmal fog of party politics and put it in the clear light of reason and honourable motive the heartiest support was accorded cordially to our paper by all classes.

Thus having discovered Queen and Country as a profit centre on the *Evening News*, it became clear to K.J. that the new newspaper, the *Daily Mail*, had to stand 'for the power, the supremacy and the greatness of the British Empire'. The paper became 'the embodiment and mouthpiece of the Imperial idea'.

'If Kipling be called the Voice of Empire in English Literature, we may fairly claim to [be] the Voice of Empire in London Journalism,' K.J. proclaimed. In this, both Alfred and K.J. agreed.

The only difference was that Alfred believed it.

3

'Dead! and ... Never
Called Me Mother!'

The dislike engendered by Alfred Harmsworth and his flagship publication, the *Daily Mail*, now reached wondrous proportions. By 1 September 1896, daily circulation of the *Mail* had reached 222,405. As to the *Evening News*, that newspaper was rapidly approaching the 800,000 mark, with annual profits a shameless £50,000.

This was not what Fleet Street had predicted, and Fleet Street was not pleased. Although the profession of journalism was then held in low esteem by the public – 'To be a journalist,' Alfred once said, 'is to be a leper' – seldom have so many in any single trade shown so much self-regard. Unlike themselves, Alfred had come up the wrong way, from magazines; worse even than that, from popular magazines. He was a jumped-up, ill-educated opportunist who had made his start on a *bicycling* magazine published in Coventry, of all places. This certainly wasn't the way things were done, although inexplicably Alfred seemed to have done it.

The Old Guard also found Alfred's success, well, somehow distasteful. His first visit to Printing House Square was met with disdain. Arthur Walter, the proprietor of *The Times*, explained in no uncertain terms that Alfred could not buy shares in his newspaper because these must be handed down from family member to family member. Never mind that the shareholders themselves were champing at the bit to sell to the newly emerging press baron. Said Walter, any rumours that Alfred Harmsworth might be involved in a possible takeover were 'so absurd in themselves, and so utterly baseless in point of fact, that it might seem unnecessary to pay any attention to them'. Meanwhile, in the *Saturday Review*, Frank Harris was summing up the reactions of the intellectual community. Alfred, he wrote, was 'brainless, formless, familiar and impudent'.

Alfred Harmsworth was a harbinger of the future, and as such he was a dangerous man. He symbolized the approaching twentieth century, its attitudes and inventions. He was enthralled by the telephone, the bicycle, electric lighting and photography. A gramophone recording of sneezing and snoring left Alfred laughing long after others had ceased. He had a boyish love of gadgets and gizmos, often spending hours playing with model trains. As for the motor car, it was 'like being massaged in high wind'.

The *Daily Mail* openly welcomed the 'Coming Street Revolution', and on the day before motor cars were made legal by an Act of Parliament the newspaper predicted that on the morrow they would fill the streets of London:

> The electric cabs may not be ready just yet, and the horseless hearse which has been built may not have an engagement for the first day; but motor vehicles of all sorts are being got ready for an early spin through the City and the West-end, and the Post-office parcels express motor-van, which has already been seen in the streets, preceded by a lad on foot carrying the red flag of permission, will prance about unfettered by any such danger signals ... Already prospectuses as to the insurance of motor-cars are freely flying about.

Four days later, on 17 November, an electrically powered carriage sponsored by the London Electric Cab Company made its appearance. So important an event was this that even stockbrokers left their desks in order to watch the vehicle travel 'easily through the crowded streets', the gentlemen inside the cab denying the existence of any vibration whatsoever.

So devoted was Alfred to the new motor car industry that he prohibited reports of automobile accidents in the *Daily Mail*. He also campaigned to repeal a law that prevented motor vehicles from travelling faster than three miles per hour, saying it 'made England lag far behind Continental countries'. Another *Mail* campaign called for an important new feature – safety mirrors that allowed the driver of the motor car to view what was behind him.

By 1899 the newspaper was lauding the motorcycle, which could travel an incredible thirty-six miles per hour. A race at the Crystal Palace showed that 'it came out of the test with flying colours', leaving far behind all records made by riders of the 'leg-propelled bicycle'. Watching the motorized cyclists whirl around corners, said the reporter, made 'one [shiver] at the thought of what would happen if there was a collision'.

Indeed, 'Automobilism' was becoming more and more an important part of life. Fashionable French ladies were making their morning social calls in the new motor car, and Parisians were planning their summer holidays in large automobiles arranged 'as conveniently as a houseboat'.

> The car is divided into compartments: the first is reserved for the owner, and can be transformed from sitting-room to dining-room and bed-room, the remainder

being arranged for servants, kitchen, and luggage. This house on wheels, which is propelled by an engine of thirty horse-power, can cover twenty-two miles an hour, and mount with ease the steepest hills. The above manner of seeing the country is said to be delightful.

Before one could even imagine such a thing, the *Mail* said, fire engines were likely to become motor driven.

Early one morning at four a.m., a young man of eighteen who was watching the news tapes on the *Mail* found himself suddenly in the presence of a man in a 'motor dust-coat . . . and wearing a tweed cap whose ear-flaps served the purpose of wind screens'. Who was in charge? the man demanded to know. The youth admitted he was. 'You!' the man exclaimed. 'But, my good fellow, what would you do if the Queen died?' The youth gave a step-by-step explanation of the procedure he would follow, adding that he wouldn't 'forget to turn the column rules'.

'Quite right, my lad . . . Good night to you, my lad!'

And Alfred was suddenly gone, driving, like Mr Toad, at improbably high speed back to Elmwood in his Mercedes, after checking out 'what those dashed fellows got up to in the night'.

Alfred Harmsworth, it was said by old hands who knew their way around, had jobs to give; easy enough to get but hard to keep. The watchword at street level was, 'The *Mail* will suck out your brains, then sack you.' To an extent it was true. Kennedy Jones, having suffered rebuff after rebuff in his early days on Fleet Street, had determined on a policy he deemed fair: anybody could try; few would succeed. Legend had it that a receptionist, asked whether a particular staff member was in, answered that he couldn't say as he hadn't yet seen a list of '*today*'s sub-editors'.

J.E. MacManus, poised between life and death as acting editor, was technically the first editor of the *Daily Mail*, although Alfred and K.J. were ever underfoot. MacManus was a solicitor who had never practised law but instead had given himself over to plays and verse, at one time writing the lyrics for patriotic songs sung by the well-known music-hall performer Leo Stormont. It was MacManus's casual manner and preference for pipe and whisky over work that finally did him in. When Alfred sacked him, he went over to the ill-fated *Morning Post*, which folded shortly thereafter.

While the Angel of Death was mercifully swift, those who did earn the approval of the 'Chief' could suddenly find themselves receiving unexpected perks. Lincoln Springfield, who worked twelve-hour days without giving much thought to it, found his remarkable ten guineas a week increased to fifteen without his even asking. Similarly, a young

Australian who wrote an amusing snippet about a contest of fisticuffs between a tram conductor and a passenger, and the resulting half-mile tailback on the line, received a cheque for £50 written out personally by Alfred to pay his fiancée's passage to England. 'If all millionaires were like Harmsworth,' said the astonished reporter, 'there wouldn't be the long-standing prejudice there is to the entrance of the rich man into the Kingdom of Heaven.'

Even fops, if they were sufficiently talented, were welcome to try their hand on the *Mail*. About the time he began publishing his fabulous cartoons, Max Beerbohm wormed his way on to the staff after sending a grovelling card to Alfred. Beerbohm's tie, gloves and socks, all in matching lavender, did little to instil confidence in his writing. His regular column, 'A Commentary Made by Max Beerbohm', was dismissed as 'literary cav-iare' by one disapproving staffer. And even Alfred found it expedient to attach a disclaimer: 'Readers will understand that we do not accept the very wide responsibility of identifying ourselves with Mr Beerbohm's opinions.' Just as well, since Beerbohm was as likely as not to write about the pleasures of pyromania. In one column, with the Turko-Greek War pending, and Jerome K. Jerome known to have sent a telegram of support to the Greeks, Beerbohm wrote, 'Yet Jerome never struck me as being a man of Attic temperament, although his humour, at least, has always been Greek to me.'

Other staffers dared defy Alfred and lived to tell the tale. Along with his beloved 'talking points', Alfred also invented the letter to the editor. The very first one was headed 'Should the Clergy Dance?' and signed 'Pained Parishioner'. Two weeks and thirty letters later, the subject of the 'dancing curates' had worn thin, if not on the *Mail*'s readers, at least on its staff. Subjects like the ethics of flogging schoolboys soon followed. This trend led the Bohemian journalist Hannen Swaffer to pose the journalistic query, 'Is Oatmeal a Poison?'

'What's all this nonsense about oatmeal?' yelled Alfred. 'You've cost us thousands of pounds. All the proprietors of patent foods are damning us. Get this contradicted by three o'clock or you're fired.' Not only did Swaffer survive, he prospered.

The talented Philip Gibbs (later knighted for his reportage of the First World War) put in a short apprenticeship on the *Mail* as its literary editor. By the time he joined Alfred, aged twenty-one, he had already published his successful book, *Founders of the Empire*, and headed up a literary syndicate. And, of course, the ever-popular Charlie Hands was soon on the staff, stolen from the *Pall Mall Gazette* by his pal Lincoln Springfield, against the advice and wishes of the hard-nosed Kennedy Jones. Hands's first assignment seemed to confirm K.J.'s reluctance to take him on board. 'You didn't send much from Dublin,' Jones said, confronting Hands on his return. No, Hands allowed, but Jones would no doubt be pleased by the 'several columns of expenses account' he would soon be submitting.

Hands wasn't the only reporter who managed to get away with murder. Duncombe Jewell, who fancied himself a literary type, was sent to Blackwall, at the Thames Ironworks, where HMS *Albion* was to be launched. He returned with a report that was 'the nearest thing to a Turner sunset that you could get in manuscript'; this just as the news reached the editor's desk that thirty had drowned at the launching. Confronted by his apoplectic editor, Jewell languidly replied, 'Well, I did see some people bobbing about in the water, as I came away, but...'

Kennedy Jones himself turned out not to be infallible. On 29 June 1897, news reached the *Mail* offices that the steamship *Aden* had gone down off the island of Socotra in the Arabian Sea, with the loss of nearly a hundred lives. A few survivors, adrift for seventeen days before they were picked up, were outside the reach of any reporters when someone on the *Mail* staff came up with the idea of contacting the local postmaster, and asking that he cable the newspaper with their story. It was a harrowing tale, of mighty waves that swept overboard one after another, of the miserable creatures who were clinging to the deck of the sinking ship. Food supplies sank to only fifteen nuts each day for each of those left and a tiny quantity of soda-water. With the bad weather continuing, the small band gave up hope until, on 22 June, somebody said, 'Why, it's Jubilee Day! Is there anything we could do?' And, despite the raging winds and misery of all, the rag-tag group stood and sang a hymn before making a toast to the Queen and drinking to her honour out of that day's allotment of soda-water.

Jones, reading the cable recounting this dramatic event, slashed the story with his blue pencil, complaining that such 'exalted slush' had to be fiction. The postmaster, he said, quoting Disraeli's famous comment on Gladstone, had become 'intoxicated with the exuberance of his own verbosity'. If such a report were published, K.J. continued, the *Mail* would become a laughing stock. Two weeks later, when the survivors reached Plymouth, they cabled their own version; every word K.J. had ordered expunged turned out to be true.

Many at the *Daily Mail* believed that the enlistment of the shy scholar George Warrington Steevens was the greatest coup of all for the newspaper. Steevens had quit the *Pall Mall Gazette* in protest at the firing of his editor Harry Cust by William Waldorf Astor. Alfred Harmsworth was quick to pick him up. Given leaders to write at first, Steevens failed to measure up to Alfred's standards. When Alfred, perplexed, asked Steevens what he believed he could do, he reckoned anything 'from tying parcels downward'. His modesty was rewarded by Alfred sending him to report the Richmond Horse Show, where he showed an 'extraordinary power of observation'. 'There were the usual number of unborn babies in the crowd,' wrote Steevens, thereby securing his position with Alfred.

Steevens was selected to go on an American tour, where he wrote a set of articles under the title 'The Land of the Dollar'. It was reckoned to be so good that it was reprinted as a slim volume which quickly became a bestseller. Typical of Steevens's style was his treatment of Chicago. It was, Steevens wrote, 'the queen and guttersnipe of cities, the cynosure and cesspool of the world, the most beautiful and the most squalid, where women rode straddle-ways, and millionaires dined at midday – the chosen seat of public spirit and successful boodle'.

Those signed up by the *Daily Mail* were interpreting an age in transition, and the ones who lasted on the staff were extraordinary in their own right. For these men, no ordinary proprietor would do. Their 'Chief' had to be smart, cunning, clever and witty; he had to be whimsical, larger than life and street-wise, with perhaps a touch of mystery about his person. Alfred encompassed all these characteristics, and more. And as with all great newspaper men, there was more than a little of the impresario in his nature.

The year before he founded the *Daily Mail*, Alfred had initiated an expedition to the North Pole. Such a project was underway in the United States, and Alfred's competitive spirit and pride in Empire required that he underwrite a British effort – at a cost of £30,000, more even than he had paid for the *Evening News*. He enlisted the British explorer Frederick George Jackson, and although Jackson and his companions didn't make it to the Pole, they did find and rescue the Norwegian explorer Fridtjof Nansen, who had been lost for nearly twelve months.

Alfred himself got little out of the deal – a 2,000-foot land mass named after his wife, and an island named after himself. In an age of trophies, he could display on his grounds at Elmwood the *Windward*, the lifeboat from the ship used on the journey, and in the front hall, a stuffed polar bear. 'And *that* cost me £30,000,' he was apt to say to visitors, indicating the bear, with the ironic twist that came more and more to characterize his humour.

The same year, he tested his popular appeal in the political arena – only to find he wasn't suited to the life of a politician. He had accepted an invitation to stand as Unionist candidate for Portsmouth, and with typical éclat Harold and Kennedy Jones bought a local newspaper, whilst Alfred, ever the showman, commissioned a serial he expected would bring about his victory. 'The Siege of Portsmouth' was a fictional account of an attack by foreign soldiers upon the town, with actual citizens of Portsmouth appearing as characters in the narrative. It was one of Alfred's more bizarre stunts, and it was mostly ignored by voters in Portsmouth. Imagination, it seemed, didn't make for a good politician; in most cases, quite the contrary.

So far as public speaking went, Alfred lacked personal magnetism. On the podium, he receded. Unable to perform on demand, he found neither debate nor bombast his strong suits. He had the endurance all right; he covered town meetings, local teas, classrooms, pensioners' meetings, whatever was going. One local reporter said afterwards, 'Harmsworth nearly wore us out.' But, in the end, the voters declined to elect him to Parliament.

In defeat, he was slightly pompous: 'At my age a defeat does one good,' he said, pontificating with all the sagacity of his thirty years. 'Too much success in life is bad for one.' Privately, he admitted he had found the experience degrading. 'It was like swimming in a sea of filth,' he told intimates. At any rate, politicians henceforth lost most of the allure they might otherwise have had for him. Certainly, in later life, he wasn't inclined to take them at face value, remaining sceptical about their motives.

It was a lesson more important than it seemed at the time. Queen and Country had carried important symbolic value until now, and they would continue to do so; but the idea that a country needed protecting from within as well as without hadn't previously occurred to Alfred, even less that he would be the man to do it. Newspapering was what he was good at, that was all, and if that was where his talents lay, then he knew how to proceed. It would be many years before he understood the full extent of the power this gave him, and years more before he grasped the responsibility that went with it. For now, he was content to beat the drum of Imperialism simply because of his own enthusiasm and because he did that best.

Britain ruled the waves. Fully one-fourth of the globe's surface fell under the dominion of the Union Jack, and the British provided the ideal of freedom and democracy throughout the world. London was the home of international finance; the country's industrial output was known for its inherent superiority. As arbiters of the world's squabbles and architects of one of the most advanced legal systems in the world, the British set the global standard for a sense of fair play. At home, most men believed in individual responsibility, and if a man's word was not his bond, then his place in the community was diminished. Abroad, Britain was 'the nearest thing to a world government that man had yet known'.

Inside his own country, Alfred Harmsworth, for better or worse, was himself becoming the symbol of the strength and power of the Empire. By 1897, as Queen Victoria celebrated her Diamond Jubilee and Alfred's enthusiasm was brought to bear upon the event, his fame would spread beyond the shores of the British Isles. With the full co-operation of the royal family, Harmsworth Brothers Ltd prepared a ten-volume history of the Queen's reign: *Sixty Years a Queen*. Hailed as 'the publishing triumph of the Jubilee', the 'lavishly illustrated' volumes were issued at fortnightly intervals at 6d. each, the last two parts written by Alfred himself.

As to the *Daily Mail*, for weeks before the actual day of celebration, the newspaper had been featuring special columns called 'Diamond Jubilettes', one-line briefs about various members of the royal family. On Jubilee Day itself, the newspaper reported, there would be twenty miles of fireworks along the Thames, and a sea of brightly coloured roses – 'the Jubilee is upon us indeed'. The *Mail* also lauded what it termed 'Jubilee Snapshooters' in this 'greatest day the science of photography has ever had'. Over eleven thousand feet of film had been sold to French photographers alone, and balcony space was being rented out along the route of the procession for as much as £100.

By the day before the spectacle, the *Mail* was publishing 'the Complete Procession Guide', with timetables of when the Queen would pass certain landmarks and 'Important Hints to Jubilers', reminding them to take along food ('Go early, but don't go hungry'). Thousands of pounds, the *Mail* continued, had gone into illumination, and on the night of 22 June London would be transformed into 'a city of light', the London and North-Western Railway Company's offices 'flanked on either side by beacons of fire, [surmounted by] a magnificent and imposing electric lighted picture of Britannia panoplied with helmet and trident'.

A leader published on 22 June proclaimed: 'The jubilonged-for day is upon us at last. Before these lines are read six million people will have started out to jubiline the streets by day and jubilluminate them by night ...' On the following day, 100,000 copies of the *Daily Mail* were printed in gold at a cost of 6d. each. The lead story was headlined: 'Queen and Empire: Pageant of unparalleled meaning and magnificence: Thanksgiving at St Paul's: In Queen's weather the great celebration passes without hitch or accident.' On page seven appeared a full-page line drawing of the view from St Paul's Cathedral, 'the largest news illustration ever printed by any daily paper in this country'.

The night before the great event, Alfred and his wife gave a party at their house in Berkeley Square, purchased specifically by Mary for entertaining London Society. Invitations to the affair were inscribed 'To Meet the Colonial Premiers' who had arrived in London to attend the Jubilee. The guest list demonstrated how far Alfred had come in the nine years since the founding of *Answers*. Well-known actors and actresses, princesses, ambassadors, Members of Parliament, Society figures – all thronged the house. The great Australian soprano Nellie Melba sang; Paderewski played. With fabulous floral arrangements at every turn and the chef and staff of an entire Parisian restaurant imported to do the catering, the affair was a complete triumph for the young couple. As to the Procession itself, Alfred believed it to be 'the most magnificent spectacle I have ever seen!'

So sat Alfred at the centre of the hoop-la, the pageantry and colour of the Queen's sixtieth year on the throne, orchestrating the enthusiasm of a nation; indeed of the globe. The leader slogan for the *Daily Mail* would soon read 'The Largest Circulation in the World'. At every level, Alfred had succeeded. And yet there appeared an unexpected little notation in his diary for the year. It had been, he wrote, 'a very tiring season'. Society, and perhaps success, had been more demanding than expected.

With every public reason to be the happiest of men, Alfred had discovered inexplicably and profoundly that he was not.

Alfred's fear of illness – his childhood alarm at colds, toothaches, eye trouble and sore throats – had hardened into full-blown hypochondria. At every turn, his obsession with his health prevented him enjoying life to the full. And yet it seemed very much as if this concern about his physical well-being was only one aspect of the mental punishment he irrationally thrust upon himself, for what reasons it was impossible to determine. Few knew how much his energetic foray into politics had cost in terms of mental health. Amongst the family, it was known the election had nearly broken him. He had escaped a complete nervous breakdown by inches.

Again, after the launch of the *Daily Mail* – a complete and utter triumph – he suddenly collapsed. A trip to India was hastily assembled, his wife Mary accompanying him. Even that far away from the centre of his universe, however, he found himself unable to stop working. He wrote a tract called 'Hard Facts from India', a description of plague and famine in that country and his ideas for ending the suffering. Less than two years later, his doctor ordered another trip, this time to Egypt, for rest and relaxation.

Not only was his health a source of worry, there was also the question of Alfred's marriage. Once Alfred was established in the field of publications, Mary Harmsworth began to earn a reputation as a poised and able social hostess. Her taste, Society determined, was exquisite; Alfred, on the other hand, possessed 'a quite sincere bad taste'. In one telling incident, Mary completely redecorated Elmwood in Alfred's absence; when he returned, he ordered everything, from wallpaper to carpets, to be restored exactly as it had been.

Then, of course, the marriage had produced no children, a source of continuing disappointment to Alfred. Doctors could find no medical reason why Mary could not bear children. Alfred, according to the style of the time, sought to resurrect a family for himself elsewhere: the illegitimate son of his youth, forgotten by family and intimates, was whisked away from his home in Essex. Alfred Benjamin Smith had been raised by his grandmother and apprenticed to a carpenter, but now he found himself with a tutor and resources. He was to become 'a gentleman', and with this in mind he was sent on a continental tour in order to learn about the finer things in life. He regularly attended concerts and the theatre. Later, the boy and his teacher took a house in Hampstead, where Alfred sometimes visited. In Mary's absence, young Alfred was at least once invited to Berkeley Square to eat dinner with his father. Such covert conduct was part and parcel of the age.

Sex was everywhere – in the drawing-rooms of respectable Society and in the flourishing red-light districts. And, despite the restrictions of the age, men and women found their way into one another's arms. Convention dictated a certain regimen for conducting affairs of the heart, and most especially for those reaching the dizzy heights of Alfred and Mary. Everything was possible if one adhered to the rather complex procedures demanded by Society. Late in her life, Mary claimed, rather foolishly, that she had had lovers – as early as 1894. Sadly, in her world, where Alfred exercised the actual power and her function remained largely ornamental, it was doubtless the only claim she could assert to any sort of achievement. As defined by the age she and Alfred lived in, her main duty was to provide an heir for the empire Alfred was building, and in this she had failed.

It was said that by 1900 Alfred had acquired an Irish mistress, Mrs Kathleen Wrohan. In the same way that Mrs Keppel shadowed Edward VII's movements, Mrs Wrohan shadowed Alfred's. Indeed, Mrs Wrohan herself was a shadowy character, for no one ever succeeded in determining who she was or where she came from. She nevertheless bore Alfred three children, two sons and a daughter, all of whom he left well provided for. Whatever their material comforts, however, the children were, of necessity, forced to remain isolated from the family at large. An aged relative recalled the eldest of Alfred's children playing along the beach near Broadstairs;

he was alone, and it was understood he was quite different from the rest of the family. There can be no doubt that one of the great griefs of Alfred's life was this social necessity of keeping his children well in the background.

Alfred loved children, and went to the trouble of founding a summer camp at Joss Farm, next to Elmwood, for underprivileged boys from the East End of London. To make sure they availed themselves of the opportunity to eat nourishing foods, he invented an annual award for the boy who gained the most weight. Alfred would have enjoyed the pleasure of publicly embracing a family, and many of his mysterious 'nervous ailments' might well have disappeared had he been anchored in an environment where the needs of others diverted attention away from his own.

Instead, Alfred became increasingly self-absorbed, worrying more and more about himself and, from thence, about his control over others. What began as an elder brother's bossiness over younger siblings turned less pleasant as he gained more prominence and power.

No one seemed able to curb his actions, save one, his mother. And although he was obsessed with pleasing her and providing for her comfort – the Harmsworth brothers bought her a thirty-five-acre estate in Totteridge, Hertfordshire, called Poynters Hall, which she occupied from 1897 onwards – Alfred was often far from the reach of her hard-headed, commonsensical, tough-minded advice. Rushing headlong into that old power-fame game, he had no idea there would be a price to pay, and a high one at that. He became a willing party to all the little corruptions that accompany power, the supplications of his employees, the machinations of opportunists; along with it, he showed increasing bitterness, because, at heart, he was an intelligent man who could see as well as anyone what was happening to him.

Amongst his staff, it became fashionable to name a newborn son after Alfred – in the hope he would pay for his education. More often than not, Alfred did. It is impossible to calculate how many of these namesakes there were, but there were several.

The rich, famous and powerful besieged him for help with their special and sometimes eccentric projects. Arthur Conan Doyle wrote asking Alfred to underwrite an 'automatic sculpture machine' he believed would aid in creating memorable works of art. Rudyard Kipling made a personal plea for money to help support a young woman abandoned by her soldier husband. Nellie Melba, Ellen Terry, Lord Curzon, H.W. Massingham, Cecil Rhodes, the list goes on, all contributed to the steady stream of requests for money, publicity or personal endorsement from Alfred Harmsworth. An entry in Alfred's diary, made after meeting Sir Douglas Straight, editor of the *Pall Mall Gazette*, shows how inured Alfred became to all this. 'He is one of the first friends of my father I have met', Alfred wrote, 'who did not want anything.'

Many of those soliciting held him in contempt, perhaps because he occupied the seat of power they envisioned for themselves. The twenty-four-year-old Winston Churchill sent the *Daily Mail* one of his early literary efforts, a short story entitled 'Overboard – An Episode of the Red Sea'. It contained a rather silly verse: 'Then I say boys / Who's for a jolly spree? / Rum-tum-tiddley-um / Who'll have a drink with me? / Fond of a glass now and then / Fond of row and noise; / Hi! hi! clear the way / For the Rowdy-Dowdy Boys!'

'It is a pushing age,' Churchill had earlier explained to his mother, 'and we must shove with the best.' Obligingly, in August 1898, Lady Randolph Churchill wrote a follow-up to enquire whether Alfred had received the story, and indeed whether he planned to publish it. Alfred had, and the story appeared the following year in the *Harmsworth Magazine*.

Winston Churchill, though nine years younger than Alfred, sensed his advantage and made it his business to get to know the press baron personally, meeting him socially several times in the latter half of the year. By 1899, the *Daily Mail* was supporting Churchill in his first and unsuccessful attempt at getting into Parliament under the Conservative banner. Afterwards, Churchill was quick to write thanking Alfred for his help.

At the same time, Churchill wrote to his mother chiding her for wanting to start a new, quality magazine, the *Anglo Saxon*, with the proposed motto, 'Blood is thicker than water'. '[It] only needs the Union Jack and Star Spangled Banner crossed on the cover to be suited to one of Harmsworth's cheap Imperialist productions. I don't say that these have not done good and paid but they are produced for thousands of vulgar people at a popular price. People don't pay a guinea for such stuff. And besides there is a falling market as regards Imperialism now.'

Winston, it turned out, had got it wrong; the 'market' for Imperialism was definitely up, and rising. Alfred, as usual, was right. More than any other quality, he had an uncanny ability to translate his environment into another medium, just as a painter recreates the appearance of reality on a flat canvas; in Alfred's case, the medium was newsprint. A strange corollary of this was a kind of clairvoyance he claimed he had. He kept saying, to anyone who would listen and believe, that he could see into the future. Certainly, at times, it seemed as if he could.

In the autumn of 1897, Alfred sent his gifted descriptive writer, G.W. Steevens, into Germany to write his impressions of events in that country.

The resulting sixteen-part series, 'Under the Iron Heel', identified 'hostility to England [as] the mission of young Germany'.

> The German army is the most perfectly adapted, perfectly running machine. Never can there have been a more signal triumph of organization over complexity. The armies of other nations to-day are not so completely organized. The German army is the finest thing of its kind in the world; it is the finest thing in Germany of any kind. Briefly, the difference between the German and, for instance, the English armies is a simple one. The German army is organized with a view to war, with the cold, hard, practical, business-like purpose of winning victories. The question what show it makes in the eyes of Germany or the world comes a long way second; absolute efficiency is its one and only test....
>
> In the German army the men are ready, and the planes, the railway-carriages, the gas for the war-balloons, and the nails for the horseshoes are all ready too ... Nothing overlooked, nothing neglected, everything practised, everything welded together, and yet everything alive and fighting. The highest unity with the most strenuous individuality. The army is a machine, yet the men remain men. And what should we ever do if 100,000 of this kind of army got loose in England? Volunteers? Good Lord!

If Alfred Harmsworth had offended those whom he could not directly benefit with his entertainments and 'talking points', if his quickly made fortune and rapid social ascension had irked the Establishment, how much more did his political commentaries increase the suspicion he was up to no good? Perhaps the masses had a right to entertainment, and even to information, so long as it didn't lead to the formation of independent opinions. But a sustained series describing the military preparedness of a European country? Either one thing or the other was true of the man: he had something to gain, or he was out of his depth. Whichever the case, he was overstepping the boundaries of the popular press – even if he *had* invented it himself.

There was no end to the lengths Alfred would go in the protection of his publications empire. Apprised of the information that the *Telegraph* was launching a Sunday version of its daily newspaper, Alfred also hastily assembled a Sunday *Daily Mail*. Both papers came out on 9 April 1899 – to the uproar of what seemed an entire nation. Methodists, Presbyterians and Baptists alike condemned the move. One evening newspaper, the *Echo*, took care to point out that the *Sunday Telegraph*, which was owned by the powerful Lawson family, was founded by 'one who belonged to a race that does not recognize our Sunday'.

Faced with this kind of unreasoning disapproval, Alfred put out the order to knife the paper after only six editions, replacing it with the far less successful *Illustrated Mail*. His compositors wrote a memorial verse in the wake of the paper's short existence: 'No more sorrow / No more woe / The *Sunday Mail* has had to go. / Other papers needn't laugh / Presently the *Telegraph*.' Indeed, the *Telegraph* lasted only one week longer before it, too, folded. In the aftermath of one of the shortest newspaper wars in history, the *Mail* received over twenty thousand letters approving the decision.

In the meantime, Alfred got into hot water with the police over his reconstruction of the 1899 Shamrock–Columbia boat race. In the vacant lot behind the newspaper's offices, the *Daily Mail* constructed a hoarding with the Sandy Hook course painted on it, and operated two movable false-fronted yachts. Called the *Evening News* Cineyachtograph, the promotion attracted large crowds considered unruly by the police, who shut it down.

Thus did Alfred alternate between profit, promotion, entertainment and news, a strange amalgamation for the time. Seemingly directionless and sometimes inchoate, the thrust was eclectic and, so far as competitors were concerned, unpredictable.

In an article published by Joseph Pulitzer, the greatest of New York's press barons, one aspect of Alfred's *modus operandi* for entertaining the public was explained. How did Alfred select his serialized stories? Victorian melodrama, Alfred said, had long been a subject of serious study for him. What he sought in one of his serials were the most dramatic incidents of the genre. If these were missing, then he would suggest powerful events which were combined and then incorporated into the story to increase suspense. He cited the work *East Lynne* by Mrs Henry Wood, probably the most famous melodrama of all time. The stage version had the line: 'Dead! and ... never called me mother!' He had floated many a publication on that line, he explained, his cynicism so bland it was difficult to fathom.

The magazine page for women – the same feature that had been condemned and finally accepted by K.J. – was also unlike anything else in the London press. Alfred's theory that you could never lose out by writing about your betters informed the entire page. In 'Women's Realm', which comprised one half of his 'page for leisure moments', a line-drawing of a woman with a fashionable hour-glass figure appeared at the top, with 'To-Day's Dinner' just below. On one day it was 'Oyster soup, Crimped salmon, Roast black cock, Green peas, Potatoes, Strawberry water ice' and 'Wafers'. Woe betide the housewife who actually tried to prepare the meal; hers would be a task of almost unending drudgery. The pleasure of this menu was strictly vicarious.

'Fashionable Stationery' might be a topic for discussion on the magazine page, or 'Dainty Embroidery'. For the general reader, each day had its selection of hopelessly corny jokes, genuine 'ouch' fodder. Under the heading 'Regardless of Expense', for example: 'Is your town lighted by electricity yet?' 'Yes,' comes the answer, 'when there's a thunderstorm.'

A typical serial was 'Married in June', the morning's episode, 'A loving woman finds heaven or hell on the day she is made a bride.' Another morning, another serial: 'The 4.10 from Euston, Chapter III. – Continued. "Cheer up, Banks, there is something good in store for you that will keep you in comfort and make you happy again." ' Or 'Greater Love Hath No Man: "My Dear young lady, I congratulate you. [The will] has made you a very well-to-do young lady indeed." ' Or, 'Are Veils Injurious? Men Doctors Say Yes; Women Doctors Say No.'

The net result of all this was that the *Daily Mail* led the way in advertising slanted towards women readers, and since women did the shopping, advertising revenues went up. The *Mail*'s first drapery advertisement was published in 1897, a 'White Sale' at D.H. Evans. Thereafter, the *Mail* quickly became known as 'The Nation's Shop-Window'. By 1899, seventeen drapers had combined to advertise 'autumn attractions', and winter sales became commonplace. This, despite a serious error on the part of the *Mail* – the depiction of a woman discreetly clad in winter underwear. Known as the 'winter-undies' scandal, the advertisement drew thousands of letters of protest – 'immodest and unseemly', most of them complained.

Alfred Harmsworth, it was said, had 'the common mind to an uncommon degree', and his popular approach – often hit or miss – confirmed this observation. What seemed surprising was such a man's determination to provide something more. Alfred, successful beyond most men's ability to imagine, was dissatisfied with the *Tit-Bits* approach to journalism, as described by George Newnes in his letter to W.T. Stead. And, as Steevens's 'Under the Iron Heel' had presaged, he decided to chart his way into W.T. Stead territory. No longer content 'to plod on, year after year, giving wholesome and harmless entertainments', Alfred began publishing the more serious type of journalism described by Newnes. He would 'direct the affairs of nations, make and unmake Cabinets, upset governments and build up navies . . .'

An early attempt to influence public opinion on a matter of serious public interest was the Mary Ansell case, led by the *Daily Mail*. 'A poor demented maid-servant', Mary Ansell had been convicted and sentenced to hang for poisoning her sister, an inmate of Leavesden Asylum, by preparing and sending her a poisoned cake. Her sister was 'a certified imbecile', and most of Mary Ansell's female relatives had been declared insane, facts unknown at the time of the girl's trial.

> She admitted purchasing four to five bottles of phosphor paste – to kill the rats in the kitchen where she slept. She had purchased insurance against her sister to 'give her a decent funeral'. The policy was worth £11 5s. After an hour of deliberation, the representative for the jury came out and asked the judge if they could have refreshments. The judge replied 'No ... you must go back and come to some decision.' An hour after that, the jury came back with a guilty verdict. The judge sentenced her to death.

In the three weeks between the conviction and the hanging, Mary Ansell's own normality was called into question, and she herself was identified as an imbecile. The *Mail* led the call for a new inquiry into the mental state of the girl, but, although a hundred Members of Parliament signed a petition in support, Mary Ansell went to the gallows at St Albans – the object of almost universal public sympathy. The case, the *Mail* opined in the aftermath, indicated a need for a Court of Criminal Appeal and brought into question the practice of capital punishment.

But, for all the respect such a campaign might bring the newspaper, the *Mail*'s reputation suffered a crushing blow from its report on the Boxer Rebellion. In China, a fanatical secret order called the Society of the Righteous Harmonious Fists (I-ho Ch'uah, or the Boxers) were organizing widespread rebellion against any foreign elements in their midst. Against a background of increasing violence, reports of the murder of the chancellor of the Japanese legation, followed closely by the murder of the German Ambassador, Baron von Ketteler, issued forth from Peking. It was correctly reported that Chinese converts to Christianity had been burned alive as they worshipped in a church, and railways and telegraph lines surrounding Peking were cut.

On 6 July 1900, the *Daily Mail* published a report that the Boxers had taken control of Peking, saying 'The tension of anxiety is becoming more acute every hour. We have not yet been informed definitely of the exact state of affairs at Peking, but news of the complete massacre of all the Ministers and the entire European population is hourly expected.' It was afterwards claimed that the report that followed was held for three days while checking of the facts took place. But, at last, the horrific headline appeared: 'The Peking Massacre; All White Men, Women, and Children Put to the Sword; Awful Story of the 6th and 7th July, A Night of Awful Horror'.

> There can now no longer be any doubt about the date on which this, the greatest

tragedy of the century, was consummated . . . the British Legation was destroyed. The Boxers had poisoned the Legation's sources of water supply. With famine staring them in the face, the gallant band of defenders appear to have made one desperate attempt to beat their enemies off. Hundreds of Boxers were slain . . . Then the carnage commenced . . . The destruction was complete and every European, we are told, was put to the sword.

The source of the report was said to be Reuter's Shanghai and St Petersburg correspondent, and papers as august as *The Times* picked up the story from the *Mail*.

On the same day, the leader in the *Mail* whipped up a state of hysteria in London at the news of the report. 'If the tale is true,' it said, 'white men allowed none of their women and children to fall alive into the hands of the Chinese. The Chinese, as we know them, are capable of inflicting every horrible torment upon their victims . . .'

It was brilliant reporting, editorializing – and a brilliant scoop – if only it had turned out to be true. Amidst the confusion of denials and scapegoating that followed, Alfred Harmsworth's credibility evaporated, and mistrust of the *Mail*, its motives and the ever-present possibility of sensationalizing for profit became a matter of public debate. For Alfred, there followed horrendous public humiliation as everything he had striven to achieve vanished in the wake of this false report.

Fleet Street at last saw its worst accusations vindicated, and with no small amount of glee newsmen coined a new term. For some time to come, the *Daily Mail* was referred to as the *'Daily Liar'*.

4

'Duke's Son, Cook's Son, Son of a Hundred Kings'

The Boer War started 'at tea time', as *The Times* put it, with British forces numbering not more than 25,000 men. It ended two years and eight months later, with the British suffering casualties of 5,774 dead and 22,829 wounded. Britain had been forced to assemble an army of half a million before she could subdue an enemy who had no more than 40,000 in the field at any given time.

The first Boer advance against the British was on 13 October 1899. By 18 October, the *Daily Mail* had chartered a special express train from London to Manchester, at a cost of over £200 per week for each train, thus getting the *Mail* on to the streets some four hours ahead of its rivals and thereby giving credence to the paper's claim that it was Britain's first truly national newspaper. By the end of the year, the *Daily Mail* had opened an editorial office in Cape Town and installed the expensive system of news cables that on one night alone cost £600.*

At the heart of the war was the discovery in 1886 of gold in the Boer republic of Transvaal. For years, Britain's two self-governing South African colonies had been at odds with the two republics, peopled mainly by farmers of Dutch descent called Boers. In several striking ways, the Boers resembled the cowboys of the Wild West. Accustomed to hard riding and shooting, they knew the veldt intimately and were capable of attacking from concealed points, thus sustaining few casualties. They were stubborn fighters who didn't take defeat easily. Nearly a decade before the discovery of gold, the British had managed to annex Transvaal, but in a bloody battle at Majuba Hill the Boers had won back their independence.

Now, with a get-rich-quick mentality reminiscent of the California Gold Rush, the British began to flow back into the republic, and the Boers, ever suspicious of their motives, denied this influx of foreigners, whom they called Uitlanders, the right to settle or to vote. The ill-fated Jameson Raid in 1895 did much to confirm the Boers' suspicions about the British, and

---

* Alfred Harmsworth, *The Romance of the Daily Mail*, p. 26; G. Ward Price, unpublished MS, 1949, Chap. XVIII, pp. 140–1.

soon after, the President of the Transvaal, Paul Kruger, began organizing armies and preparing for war. For the British, the rights of the Uitlanders became a rallying point, and when talks between the two sides broke down in 1899, war became inevitable.

The *Mail* claimed an army of at least 100,000 would be needed to defeat these tough new opponents. It would, they wrote, be a war wherein 'the man from the city was confronted by the man whose life had been spent in the saddle'. This fact alone, the paper predicted, indicated high casualties for the British. With the publication of these figures, the *Mail* found itself in hot water; the Government disputed the number of troops needed in South Africa, implying it was a mop-up operation. More importantly, it could see no point in the *Mail*'s interference in what was, from the Government's point of view, purely a military matter. The *Mail*'s competitors also disagreed, many predicting the boys would be home by Christmas.

On 17 November, the *Daily Mail* announced the 'foundation stone' for its wartime public appeal fund – 'the most wonderful poem in the world!' Well, the staff agreed amongst themselves, perhaps the poem was a bit less than that. The *Mail* had commissioned Rudyard Kipling to write the poem for a hundred guineas – which he immediately donated to the war fund – and he came up with a piece of doggerel called 'The Absent-Minded Beggar'. Because of the unconventional, if not bizarre, cadence of the poem, the composer Sir Arthur Sullivan could think of nothing in song to match it.

At last, according to legend, an inspired Kennedy Jones hummed a little of 'Private Tommy Atkins', which Sullivan forced to fit the poem. At this point, a second brilliant idea was conceived. The *Mail* would offer the poem to other newspapers for five guineas, after lauding it in its own pages as the poem of the decade.* It was in this way that the poem hit the streets of London:

When you've shouted 'Rule Britannia' – when you've sung 'God Save the Queen' –
When you've finished killing Kruger with your mouth –
Will you kindly drop a shilling in my little tambourine
For a gentleman in *kharki* ordered South?

* See Kennedy Jones, *Fleet Street and Downing Street*, pp. 255–7; Hamilton Fyfe, *Northcliffe: An Intimate Biography*, p. 89; letter from Rudyard Kipling to Alfred Harmsworth, 22 Oct. 1899, British Library, Add. MS 62292A, Vol. cxl, p. 40. Amounts said to have been raised by the poem vary according to the source. Also, in some accounts, the song the poem was set to was 'Soldiers of the Queen.' I have taken the account from Kennedy Jones because it is first-hand.

He's an absent-minded beggar and his weaknesses are great –
But we and Paul must take him as we find him –
He is out on active service, wiping something off a slate –
And he's left a lot o' little things behind him!

Duke's son – Cook's son – son of a hundred kings,
(Fifty thousand horse and foot going to Table Bay!)
Each of 'em doing his country's work (and who's to look after his things?)
Pass the hat for your credit's sake, and pay–pay–pay!*

It may not have been, as *Mail* staffers secretly acknowledged, the poem of the *decade*, but it did have something, and 'The Absent-Minded Beggar' actually caught on. It helped to raise £100,000 in three months, and by the end of the war, over £250,000. At the final count, the *Mail* was able to pay for the original buildings of the Treloar Cripples' Hospital at Alton. Reprinted on silk as special souvenirs as well as on handkerchiefs, pillowcases, plates, tobacco jars, ashtrays and other objects, the poem was also a musical hit, sung at the Palace Theatre by such well-known performers as John Coates. Even an 'Absent-Minded Beggar Competition' for brass bands was held at the Albert Hall in London. The poem could constantly be heard, in pubs, music-halls and theatres, until everyone, especially those on the *Daily Mail*, was heartily sick of it.

Said Kennedy Jones, 'Mr. Kipling himself declared that if it were not suicide, he would gladly shoot the man who wrote the jingle.'

So it went at home. At the Front, Alfred Harmsworth had assembled a highly talented group of correspondents, each of whom followed the unpredictable tangle of troop movements in a new kind of war – one using the tactics of the guerrilla. In this new fighting arena, 'battles' turned out mainly to be hit-and-run attacks by the canny Boers upon the British, who continued to use outmoded formations against an enemy who refused to stand and fight.

An early dispatch by Julian Ralph caught the spirit of the Boer War. 'You hear the guns of the enemy cough far in front of you ... The rifle-firing sounds like the frying of fat or like the crackling and snapping of green wood in a bonfire.' Anyone within two miles of the Front was likely to face gunfire, and hear the song of the bullets, 'like the magnified note of a mosquito'.

From a distance, the battlefield looked 'as methodical as a chess-board'. It was only when you came close to the range of fire

* The first stanza of 'The Absent-Minded Beggar', by Rudyard Kipling, from the pamphlet published by the *Daily Mail*, in the hand of Kipling.

that the wounded crawl and stagger by you; it is there that they spend their final output of energy and fall down to lie until assistance comes; it is there that you see the stretchers, laden with their mangled freight, and the sound ones bearing the wounded on their backs and in their arms ... There is no writhing, and the groans are few and faint. There was one man who was simply chewed up by a shell at Magersfontein, and his sufferings must have been awful. Another begged to be killed, and the first wounded man I saw in this war kept saying, in ever so low a voice, 'Oh dear, dear, dear!'

Then, Ralph continued, the ambulances approached, loaded up the wounded and pulled out, 'all day continually, as in a ceaseless train'. The soldiers carried out wounded comrades, then rushed back to the battle. 'At last the cheer of British victory is heard, and the whole Army rushes forward, or darkness falls upon an unfinished fight, and we grope about the veldt seeking our camps and the food and drink that most of us have gone without too long.'

Julian Ralph set the tone for the *Mail*'s coverage of what came to be known as 'Black Week', a series of losses during 10–17 December 1899. An attack against the Boer trenches at Magersfontein resulted in the loss of some 650 officers and men, who were forced to fall back to the Modder River camp. Ralph wrote how the British troops were unable to catch sight of the enemy at all, even as they were riddled with bullets. Wrote Ralph, 'Our men fell just as ripe fruit does from a shaken tree.' It was the first time anyone had actually written of the British boys' defeat, and at home the public plunged into grief.

On the same day, a misinformed British general marched his troops into ambush at Stormberg, losing 700, 600 of whom were marched away to prison camps in Pretoria. Finally, General Sir Redvers Buller led 21,000 men into the city of Ladysmith, but they were hit by small-arms fire and defeated by the Boers at Colenso. With losses of 143 killed, 756 wounded and 220 men captured, Buller called for the surrender of Ladysmith. He was immediately relieved of supreme command and in his place Lord Roberts and General Kitchener as his chief of staff were installed. Roberts's son had died at Colenso after making a desperate attempt to save the guns from the Boers, only days before his father took over command.

Incensed by British losses which it believed could have been prevented, the *Mail* launched a bitter attack on what it called 'War Office mis-management', dismissing claims by *The Times* that Britain's field and horse artillery had 'no superiors in Europe'.

Unfortunately, as has been pointed out by independent experts again and again during the past few years, it is not true. Both Krupp and Canet turn out guns which ... are able to fire a projectile of equal weight more accurately and at greater range. The Boers are in possession of these weapons ... For want of these guns, the Ordnance Department, in order to save its own skin, is prepared to greatly prolong our campaign in South Africa, to risk the lives of men and the morale of our Army, and, it is quite possible, to bring about the fall of the present Government.

By now, the *Mail* had begun a campaign, signified by the call to alarm, 'Guns! More guns! Better guns!' The announcement by the Government of a new rearmament scheme was greeted by the swift condemnation of the *Daily Mail*. The new scheme would, 'unless carefully watched, be marred by the same military authorities who have bungled the question of our field guns and other artillery. What are wanted are more guns and better guns.' The paper began publishing illustrations comparing the British Lee-Metford and Boer Mauser rifles, showing the obvious superiority of the latter. The Mauser was lighter and boasted a higher velocity; the range and penetration were also greater. The rifle could be loaded by a 'clip' containing five cartridges, while the British rifle was a single loader after the magazine was emptied. At the same time, the *Mail* also published detailed line-drawings of British and Boer field artillery, with detailed explanations of how each worked.

A systematic attack like this upon the War Office was unprecedented, and by early January the *Mail* was facing popular demonstrations against its reports of munitions shortages. These did nothing to slow the *Mail*. On 8 January, the editorial leader listed the name of each Government Minister beside his age, calling the Government 'The Oldest on Record'.

> The birthday book of our War Cabinet shows that nearly all its important members are past the prime of life. At an age when in every other kind of enterprise men are laying down their work, a number of men approaching or past their three score and ten are embarking upon one of the largest military and political enterprises in history...
>
> Yet the superabundance of age is not the most serious charge that can be brought against our Government...
>
> Careful observers of the work of our Cabinet have noticed that it is subject to three phases – firstly, optimistic speechmaking; secondly, official silence and inaction; thirdly, panic, including lavish expenditure, chaos, and the discovery of a thousand and one unexpected deficiencies.

Stung by this uninhibited and unprecedented criticism from the press, the Government paused to consider a powerful new voice of opposition, led by a man only thirty-five years old. Before the South African War was over, Parliament would try to find a way to silence the *Mail*, and Alfred Harmsworth would suffer public censure himself.

Harmsworth had sent his best people to cover the war – not only Julian Ralph and George Warrington Steevens, but also the well-known Charles Hands; and by default, simply because she happened to be at the wrong place at the right time, Lady Sarah Wilson.

Julian Ralph wrote the series, 'Through Yankee Glasses: The War as an American Cousin Sees It: The Boer as a Fighting Man', in which he tried to explain what the British were up against. The Boers were haggard and desperate men, Ralph believed, willing to break with convention in order to defend their homeland. From the point of view of the British, who were unaccustomed to guerrilla tactics, these soldiers were unprincipled because they refused to show proper respect for the rules of war: 'To look into [their bunkers], with their rude bedding, scattered food, and general debris, was as if one viewed the nests of so many hawks ... Their dead, whose untidy and neglected bodies I saw seated as the British bullets and bayonets found them, confirmed this theory, for they were poorly clad, unshaven, unclean, and hungry-looking.' These were men who would falsely use the white flag in order to attack unprepared men, mocking the rules of the Geneva Convention. 'The Boers', Ralph wrote, 'had done what damage they could to us and now that their own lives were endangered, they commanded their subordinates to remain, and sought their own safety.'

According to Ralph, the enemy were forced to fight 'at the point of the revolver'. They relied on gin to keep going: 'Empty gin-bottles, bottles still containing gin, and one full bottle ... were to be seen stuck in the loose dirt of the trenches.'

His colleague, G.W. Steevens, who at thirty-three* had already written a bestselling novel, *Monologues of the Dead*, and was considered the best of Harmsworth's writers, was meanwhile at the siege of Ladysmith. He picked up where Ralph left off, amazed at the unconventionality of the opponent. They waged war, Steevens wrote, 'like gentlemen of leisure', restricting the hours of their work with the punctuality of a trade unionist. If they had wished, they could immediately have taken Ladysmith. 'But the Boers have the great defect of all amateur soldiers: they love their ease, and do not mean to be killed.'

Steevens was fascinated by what it felt like to be bombarded. He seemed riveted by the possibility of random death – and his own lack of courage

---

* Steevens's age is variously listed in different sources as thirty-one and thirty-three.

in the face of constant shelling. If you concentrated on the danger, Steevens concluded, you became a coward:

> You hear the squeal of the things all above, the crash and pop all about, and wonder when your turn will come. Perhaps one falls quite near you, swooping irresistibly, as if the devil had kicked it. You come to watch for shells – to listen to the deafening rattle of the big guns, the shrilling whistle of the small, to guess at their pace and their direction. You see now a house smashed in, a heap of chips and rubble; now you see a splinter kicking up a fountain of clinking stone-shivers. This is your dangerous time. If you have nothing else to do, you get shells on the brain, think and talk of nothing else, and finish by going into a hole in the ground before daylight, and hiring better men than yourself to bring you down your meals.

If, on the other hand, Steevens wrote, you were able to hold to your regular daily schedule, doing your chores and thinking nothing about what was going on around you, 'your confidence revived immediately'. So Steevens learned to become blasé about falling shells, and by the middle of the morning of a new round of bombardment he no longer bothered 'even to turn [his] head to see where the bang came from'.

He called the sound of rifle-fire 'the devil's tintacks' and remembered a battle when he hurried from his bed one morning after hearing 'the bubble of distant musketry'.

> The sun warmed the air to an oven, painted butterflies, azure and crimson, came flitting over the stones; still the devil went on hammering nails into the hills . . . We were playing with them – playing with them at their own game.

It was a game that went on for six hours, and at the end three were killed and seventeen wounded.

Steevens's preoccupation with death was only natural, since he stood at the centre of a siege. To get these dispatches out of Ladysmith, they had been 'written in a microscopic hand' and rolled up in a tube to be smuggled to London. Yet, even as the reports made their way to be published in the *Mail*, Steevens himself lay dying, not as a result of bombardment but as one of many victims of an epidemic of enteric fever.

At home, Alfred Harmsworth rushed to the home of Steevens's widow, as devastated almost as she was. This was the first man to die who had started with the *Mail*; Alfred had acted as Steevens's mentor; they were particular friends. He blamed himself, he told Mrs Steevens. The staff were satisfied when he settled £500 per year for life on her as a pension and founded a journalistic scholarship in Steevens's name. But, for Alfred, it was a turning-point. Until now, his good luck had led him to believe in his own immortality, and certainly, along with this, the immortality of his men. There had been nothing to be sorry for in Alfred's climb to the top. Now, Steevens was dead, and Alfred was stricken. Henceforth, there was a grimness about him; less amiability; a new-found seriousness of purpose.

The full impact of his own power began to dawn on him, and the effect of it would not be wholly pleasing.

There were as many stories about Charlie Hands as you cared to listen to. Known as the Laughing Cavalier of the new journalism, he was 'one of the last Bohemians' and certainly without fear in the face of office politics. One story had the *Mail* sending telegram after telegram sacking Hands after he failed to deliver an assigned story. At long last, he replied, 'Cease firing, Hands.' Another had him, again threatened with the sack, crawling into Alfred's office on his hands and knees. 'Is it safe now, Chief?' he asks. Still another sees him bringing his son in to see Alfred and saying to him, 'That's the kind gentleman, my boy, who buys all your lovely suits.' It was said that Alfred retaliated to this kind of flippancy by actually paying the boy's way through Cambridge.

In popular legend, Hands was present at the 'death watch' when Queen Victoria lay dying at Osborne House on the Isle of Wight. Hands failed to turn in his story, so the editor at the *Mail* sent a young man over to Hands's hotel where he discovered him sitting at his desk, near to tears and knee-deep in crumpled balls of paper. The young reporter picked up several of these and found the same sentence: 'Never since the death of Jesus Christ...'

It was in character for Charlie Hands to see the irony of the Boer War, and in one dispatch, 'The Soldier and Death', he talked about 'that wonderful train which starts from Capetown at nine o'clock every night for the front, and nightly carries away a full load of healthy, high-spirited, sanguine Englishmen ... They take only single tickets, because – well, you see, though the reduced fare for the double journey seems at first sight a considerable saving, still, when we come to think of it, there is no certainty that the return half would not be wasted.'

Such a man would not be likely to take the question of his own mortality very seriously, and indeed, when Hands was wounded, he shrugged it off in his typical manner, even though the wound was a serious one and, in the days before antibiotics, extremely dangerous. The *Mail* learned of Hands's injury from correspondents Colonel F. Rhodes and John Stuart, of the *Morning Post*, who sent the telegram informing the newspaper of the event.

Assigned to Colonel Mahon's relief force, Hands had left the encampment on a Sunday at sunrise on the way to Mafeking, when he and his party were ambushed by the Boers in dense bush. 'There was a short, sharp struggle,' said the telegram. 'Hands, who was with the advance guard, was among the first wounded. He sustained a compound fracture of the thigh, but is most cheerful and plucky. The bone was set easily, and Hands is now with the main ambulance at Brady's Farm, where he is receiving every care and attention ... Our casualties were six killed and twenty-one wounded. The Boers left thirty dead.'

Stuart had worked with Hands on the *Pall Mall Gazette*, and the battlefield in South Africa was the first time the pair had met in the six years since then. Hands was in great pain, but promised Stuart, 'Give me a cigarette and I will be happy.' To another correspondent from the *Daily Telegraph*, who asked if he could do anything to help, Hands responded, 'No thanks, old man, unless you care about doing three or four columns for me.'

It fell to news editor Lincoln Springfield to inform Mrs Hands of her husband's injury. He knew Hands was, in the words of General Roberts, 'dangerously wounded', but on the way to her house made the decision to minimize the injury. So he invented a fanciful sophistry to tell her: had Roberts's telegram said 'seriously wounded', he explained, there would be something to worry about. But the word 'dangerous' meant she need have no concern. Thus did Hands lie ill for the duration of the war while his wife remained, if not lighthearted, then at least hopeful.

Meanwhile, another correspondent for the *Mail*, Ralph Hellawell, was intended to represent the paper at Mafeking – another city under siege. Arrested by the Boers as he cut his way out of the city to send a dispatch, Hellawell shortly escaped his captors and reached Vryburg, only to be arrested again and sent to a prisoner-of-war camp at Pretoria. His release was prevented by Paul Kruger, President of the Transvaal, now called the South African Republic, who believed him to be dangerous. Thus it happened that the *Mail* enlisted Lady Sarah Wilson to cover the siege of that city; the wife of an officer serving at Mafeking, she became the first woman war correspondent and one of the most celebrated figures of the war.

Lady Sarah Wilson was the sixth daughter of the seventh Duke of Marlborough. The same age as Alfred Harmsworth, Lady Sarah married Lieutenant-Colonel Gordon Chesney Wilson in 1891, and at the start of the war accompanied him to his station on the western borders where he was aide-de-camp to Colonel Robert Baden-Powell, commanding officer at Mafeking. A true daughter of the Empire, Lady Sarah whiled away her time with ambulance-driving lessons and practising her bandaging on the arms and legs of a small black boy. She and her husband had the use of a tiny cottage in Mafeking, and they took their meals at the Dixon Hotel, 'where the food was weird, but where certainly no depression of spirits reigned'. Although Baden-Powell didn't want her in Mafeking, Lady Sarah nurtured hopes she would be allowed to stay.

The Mafeking garrison contained 700 to 800 trained soldiers. The artillery consisted of four muzzle-loading seven-pounder guns with a short range, a one-pound Hotchkiss, one Nordenfeldt and about seven .303 Maxim machine-guns. A hastily assembled town guard of mixed nationality raised a total of 441 to assist the troops against what was thought to be a Boer force of three to four thousand.

But one evening Lady Sarah received a message from Colonel Baden-Powell that no fewer than 8,000 Boers were expected to storm the garrison the next day, and he requested that she leave immediately in the interest of her own safety. False reports appeared in newspapers in London that she had been forced to flee on horseback, riding some two hundred miles into the night. One of the *Mail*'s competitors was unable to resist the gibe, 'all very well for Lady Sarah, who doubtless was accustomed to violent exercise, but we commiserate with her poor maid'.

In actual fact, Lady Sarah and her maid left early in the morning, in a Cape cart and in the middle of a sandstorm, with a store and hotel run by a neutral Scottish couple as their first destination. They no sooner arrived, however, than word that some Boers were descending sent them scurrying to another place. Thus began a mad adventure wherein Lady Sarah travelled uncertainly in British Bechuanaland until, finally, she was captured by the Boers and at last, some two months and four days after leaving Mafeking, was returned there. Her homecoming was somewhat ignominious, since the Boers insisted they must have the famous horse-thief, Viljoen, in return. The Boer attack Baden-Powell had predicted, Lady Sarah discovered when she re-entered Mafeking, had never occurred, and all that had happened to her in her mad scramble had been completely unnecessary.

The city of Mafeking had changed. To Lady Sarah, it now looked like 'a gigantic rabbit-warren'. Over four miles of trenches had been dug to protect pedestrians from bullets, and some eight hundred 'bomb-proofs' had been built. These dug-out shelters were necessary to protect inhabitants from the constant shell-fire that fell on the town.

From rough holes, hastily dug and covered over with deal boards and earth, which were at first constructed at the arrival of the monster 'Creusot' Boer gun, which fires a projectile of 94-lb., these refuges have been improved upon till they are now luxurious chambers, roofed over with best steel rails and sand-bags, ventilated and lighted by round windows and large drain pipes. Mine, for instance, measures 18 ft. by 15 ft., and is 8 ft. high with a boarded floor covered with matting and panelled wood walls painted white. With three large port-holes for windows, it much resembles the cabin of a yacht, and its efficacy has been thoroughly tested, as it is, I think, the only shelter in the town on the top of which a 94 lb. shell actually exploded – without even making the glasses jingle, or disturbing various war trophies hung on the walls inside.

Despite this addition to the community, each day claimed new casualties from the non-stop bombardment by a high-velocity Krupp gun that gave no warning, since 'flash and explosion are practically simultaneous, and the poisonous little 1-pounder Maxim shells, which seem to come every-where, are generally fired in threes or fours. Death is ever present with us, a stern reality.'

In her dispatches, however, Lady Sarah did not allow herself to dwell too long on the horrors of the siege, but spoke cheerfully of cycling events held on Sundays and the town's celebration of Colonel Baden-Powell's birthday as a holiday.

In this context, stretching dwindling food supplies became a central theme in her stories back to the *Mail*, a problem constantly being solved by the ingenuity of the besieged population. There were 9,000 people in Mafeking, 2,000 whites and 7,000 natives. For the natives, food was an increasing difficulty because of their scruples against eating horsemeat. A soup kitchen, supplied with horses, oxen and stray dogs and cats, was expected to help about a thousand of them overcome their reluctance. In the meantime, the making of shells and powder began to occupy the time of the local workmen, who took the cases of the shells fired by the Boers and melted them down for their own munitions factory. A great triumph was the completion of a five-inch gun and the shells to fire from it.

Though untrained in her new-found profession of reporting, Lady Sarah's writing style was straightforward and matter-of-fact, and she soon enjoyed a huge following amongst *Mail* readers, not only because of her situation but also because of the light, perfunctory way she told of the worst. 'The Boers have been extremely active during the last few days,' she wrote on 26 March 1900. 'Yesterday we were heavily shelled and suffered eight casualties ... Corporal Ironside had his thigh smashed the day before, and Private Webbe, of the Cape Police, had his head blown off in the brickfields trenches.'

A new hardship was the rainy season which made walking in the trenches a muddy slog and which, by dampening the earth, made the 'bomb-proofs' dangerous to their inhabitants. Both Lady Sarah and her husband became infected with fever and had to be taken to the Convent to be cared for. The Convent, although a hospital, was equally subject to bombing by the Boers, and had been hit by shells some ten to twelve times. In the middle of the building's wall were 'large gaping apertures' and 'shattered doors and broken windows', but since the bombings had recently decreased, the nuns in charge believed it to be safe. Eventually, 'the splendid air blowing straight from the free north and from the Kalahari Desert on the west' began to restore the couple's health, and they moved back into their 'bomb-proof'.

One night, because of a visit they received from the Commandant of the Town Guard, the couple were late to their supper. As they chatted with their friend, they suddenly heard the big gun's report. 'The next instant,' Lady Sarah wrote, 'I was aware that masses of falling brick and masonry were pushing me out of my chair, and that heavy substances were falling on my head; then all was darkness and suffocating dust.' Within a few minutes, Lady Sarah's husband and their companion made themselves known, their faces appearing 'through the gloom, as dense as the thickest London yellow fog'.

The six-inch, hundred-pound shell had entered from the front of the Convent, travelled along the attic until it reached the wall next to them and exploded. When they returned the next day, they found they had missed death by inches, since two big fragments of shell were found touching the chair where Lady Sarah had been sitting.

Not everyone was so lucky. Soon after Lady Sarah and her husband had their close escape, she nursed a young man who had been shot close to the heart as he carried a message to a nearby fort. He didn't know that the Boers had taken possession of the garrison, and so was a sitting duck for the expert marksmen. She sat with him the last few hours of his life, brushing the flies away. Just before he died, he suddenly awoke from his silence and said to her, 'Tell the Colonel, Lady Sarah, I did my best to give the message, but they got me first.' The boy died the next morning at dawn.

Then, in mid-April, Mafeking was blessed by the good fortune of having a swarm of locusts descend on it.

There was a remarkable decrease in the applications at the soup kitchen to-day, yesterday, and the day before, thanks to the arrival of enormous clouds of locusts, which in ordinary times are unwelcome visitors, but in our present condition were hailed with joy. The natives gathered a hundred sacks full, and feed on them till their stomachs project in prominence of plenitude.

Soon after, she cabled her sister in London the following message: 'Breakfast to-day, horse sausages; lunch, minced mule, curried locusts. All well.'

Meanwhile, the natives took delight in stealing Boer cattle – 'a work of great risk and danger but attended lately with great success' – since they recently succeeded in taking eighty from under the noses of the Boers. Otherwise, all were on 'strict and somewhat reduced rations', notwithstanding the latest in a long list of ingenious methods of making their supplies last.

Oats are ground to mix with the bread-meal, and the rejected husks still do for the horses ... Of meat we are allowed 1 lb. daily, and of bread 6 oz., and never have I realized before how little this seems to a hungry man, and how closely one can speculate on how much one is eating ... After the rains we get fresh vegetables, carrots, tomatoes, French beans, potatoes, and delicious melons, while sometimes, as a delicacy, plovers and locust birds, shot on the veldt, find their way to our table. So while we pine for England, and our spirits go up and down like a thermometer, we fully realize things might be very much worse; we live in the knowledge that we are not forgotten, either at home or by our gallant generals out here, and that no lane is so long but that at length it has a turning.

But by the end of April it looked very much as if the turning was a bad one. The garrison had been hit with malarial typhoid, and a good many of the population had begun to suffer from nervous prostration. Food supplies were dwindling, and the bread was 'now made entirely of oats and is full of husks, which causes a good deal of illness'.

By the time two hundred days of siege had been completed, on 2 May, the whites in the garrison were down to a ration of one quart of 'sowan porridge' and a pound of horse-sausage each day. Now even they had to go to the soup kitchen, as well as the natives, and the major source of food in Mafeking became 'horse-hide brawn'. So valuable did this new recipe turn out to be that the Government bestowed a £5 bonus on the person who invented it. 'It is not bad, though somewhat "gluey",' wrote Lady Sarah, 'and its sustaining qualities will stand us in good stead.'

At last, despite its weakened state, Mafeking was attacked in the middle of the night 'by a furious fusillade from the eastern face'. The night was moonless, with only a little light from the stars, when the alarm bugle sounded, alerting the inhabitants that an attack by the Boers was in progress. With bullets flying in the streets and in the town square, it became obvious that the Boers had penetrated the periphery of the town and were now in the city. Lady Sarah made her way to the hospital under a hail of bullets after it became clear to her no fewer than five hundred Boers were actually inside Mafeking, and she might be needed. Nevertheless, the men of the garrison stood firm, and at the end of the fight they had captured 110 of the enemy. 'The town', Lady Sarah wrote, 'is wild with delight. It is impossible not to admire the daring attack of the Boers and the way in which it was executed. Our men also deserve unqualified praise, and the dogged pluck of the garrison on short rations is hard to beat.'

The artillery defence of Mafeking had been carried out with 'four old muzzle-loading 7-pounders, which were constantly in the blacksmith's shop undergoing repairs, four Maxims, one Hotchkiss, one Nordenfeldt, one old ship gun firing cannon-balls, and a home-made howitzer'. For eight months, Lady Sarah wrote, the town had been subject to bombardment from the Boers, and there was little she could do to express the delight of the townspeople when they saw the Royal Horse and Canadian Artillery gallop into the city, after covering three hundred miles in twelve days.

At the end of the day, the celebration of the long-awaited relief of Mafeking included only a few people standing in the dusty road singing, 'Rule Britannia'. There were, in all,

> eight or nine dust-begrimed figures, each holding a tired and jaded horse, and a few women on the outskirts of the circle with tears of joy in their eyes. Needless to say, no one thought of sleep that night. At 3:30 a.m. someone came and fetched me in a pony-cart, and we drove out to the polo-ground, where we saw the column come into camp. Strings and strings of wagons were soon drawn up; next to them black masses, which were the guns, and beyond these, men, lying down anywhere, dead tired, beside their horses.

In London, it was otherwise. It was well after nine o'clock on a Friday night when word reached the capital that the tiny garrison had been relieved. Lady Sarah's dispatches and the desperate situation of the outpost, which during the last eight months had often seemed hopeless, had made Mafeking a symbol of Empire and of 'bulldog spirit'. The news was passed from omnibus to omnibus by cheering people who yelled 'Mafeking is relieved', and the city was plunged into mad celebration. Crowds of over twenty thousand quickly formed in front of the home of the Lord Mayor, all of them cheering for the Queen and for 'Bobs'.* Next

---

* Field Marshal Frederick Roberts, Commander-in-Chief of the British Forces in South Africa.

came Trafalgar Square where men climbed out on to the top of cabs waving Union Jacks. The *Evening News* was sold out the minute it hit the streets, and by eleven o'clock all traffic in the city was at a standstill. At the Alhambra Theatre in Leicester Square, a *Daily Mail* reporter stood up to make the announcement, and the audience immediately rose to sing 'God Save the Queen', before bursting into wild jubilation. After that night, a new verb entered the English language, 'to maffick'.

In the *Daily Mail* the next morning, the headlines were of the 'Relief of Mafeking; The besiegers' cordon broken by the flying column; Heavy bombardment and flight of the Boers: The unknown British force triumphantly enters the town: Unparalleled scenes of rejoicing'. In the same issue appeared the lines, 'London's roar of jubilation; Wild frenzy that surpasses description; Lord Mayor speaks to a vast shouting multitude; Thousands serenade Mrs Baden-Powell'. The lead paragraph of the story read, 'Mafeking is free! No more doubt, no more anxiety, no more hours of weary waiting for the glad news. It has come.'

Charles Hands lay several months in the hospital, after having the Mauser bullet dug from his thigh. At last, many months later, he was permitted to come home. News editor Lincoln Springfield was given the responsibility of taking Mrs Hands to meet her husband, having been told by Alfred Harmsworth 'to treat her like a princess'. The two travelled down to Southampton where Hands's ship came in. Both feared he would be in a wheelchair or on a stretcher, but in fact he was standing in clear view as the ship sailed in, leaning on a cane, to be sure, but standing on his own.

At the celebration of his return held by Fleet Street, the champagne was served in jeroboams that were wheeled up and down the banquet tables on miniature gun-carriages; this because Hands had always said his favourite drink was champagne. After the speeches and songs in his honour were finished, at last someone asked him why he had been so foolish as to be at the front of the advancing columns when he was hit by the Boer bullet.

Hands answered that, ever since he had been a reporter, he had always been given tickets in the stalls of the theatre whenever he was assigned to review a play. The way he figured it, since he led the stalls in peacetime, it was up to him to be in the front seat during wartime as well. It was a simple, homespun philosophy, typical of Hands, his way of thinking and his way of writing; but, so far as the men of Fleet Street were concerned, it was an eloquent statement of the responsibility of a journalist.

After the relief of Mafeking, the British quickly overran Johannesburg, and then Pretoria. By 4 July, Generals Roberts and Buller had joined forces at Vlakfontein, bringing to an end all formal resistance. Nevertheless, the war was far from over. Guerrilla warfare continued, fuelled by minor Boer generals who, revitalizing disbanded Boer forces, played havoc with British communications. General Kitchener was left in command after General Roberts returned to Britain, and he faced a guerrilla force that still numbered 25,000 in the field. This led him to take the unprecedented steps of erecting blockhouses as garrisons for his troops, and, imitating Spanish procedure in Cuba, of interning Boer women and children in so-called 'concentration camps'. This was, as Germans would later remind the British, the first extensive implementation of such camps in history.

Conditions there were appalling and, as the deaths began to mount, amidst much opposition the English Quaker and social worker Emily Hobhouse travelled to South Africa to examine for herself the conditions being endured by the Boer women and children. Her reports resulted in the formation in Britain of 'ladies' committees' who together co-ordinated a national outcry against the inhumane and degrading conditions in Kitchener's concentration camps. Despite their efforts, the camps eventually would lead to the deaths of 20,000 Boer women and children. Kitchener himself dismissed Hobhouse as 'that damned woman'.

Unsurprisingly, the *Daily Mail* also attacked Emily Hobhouse, dismissing her as an interfering woman, who was 'not impartial, has no balance in her judgments, and does not know anything of war or its history.' This was the low point in the *Mail*'s coverage of the Boer War. But, most especially, it demonstrated what was to become more and more true of Alfred Harmsworth's character as he grew older. His tight grasp on popular reaction to an event often limited his ability to understand its wider implications; as with his readers, his thrust was and always would be to protect hearth and home, wherever that impulse might lead him. He was, moreover, assured of his own invincibility in such matters, at once his best and worst trait. Nowhere was this more true than in his reaction to Emily Hobhouse.

His competitors nevertheless chalked this single-mindedness down to a slavish and illogical adherence to popular appeal and accused him of chasing a high circulation. J.A. Spender, editor of the *Westminster Gazette*, told a typical anecdote about Alfred. According to the story, Spender was taking him to task about his warmongering when Alfred interrupted him, calling for the circulation ledger: 'Look, Spender,' he said, 'here we began our campaign. See, up, up, up. No Spender, we are right.'

Where was the truth on the question of Alfred Harmsworth's integrity? One could hardly accuse him of mindlessly supporting government policy.

On the contrary, the Government viewed Alfred as a gadfly they would just as soon be rid of. During Kitchener's command, Alfred sent Edgar Wallace, formerly a soldier in the Royal Army Medical Corps, into South Africa to report on the progress of the lengthening guerrilla war. In June 1901, Wallace and his colleagues sent back a dispatch charging that the Boers had shot wounded British soldiers held in their prisoner-of-war camps. After the publication of the story in the *Daily Mail*, the War Minister, William St John Brodrick, later Earl of Midleton, informed the House of Commons that Kitchener had denied the atrocities had taken place, saying, 'there was no foundation whatever for the report'. Four days later, however, Kitchener retracted his statement, saying that one of his lieutenants had stated in writing he had personally witnessed wounded men being shot by the Boers. The Government suppressed Kitchener's telegram.

Again on 8 July, the *Daily Mail* published letters from Edgar Wallace alleging that wounded men had been shot. Letters from soldiers received at the same time also confirmed that reports of the atrocities were true. Once more, the Government denied that the events had taken place.

At last, Kitchener himself said that no fewer than seven men had testified to the accuracy of the reports. The *Daily Mail* published his statement. The Government retaliated by accusing the *Mail* of 'unpatriotically' publishing information that the public had no right to know and retaliated by silencing all of the *Mail*'s correspondents in South Africa. The newspaper was further forbidden access to all official War Office news on the basis that the newspaper had habitually offered bribes to War Office clerks on low income who were not in a position to refuse the offer. For its part, the *Mail* counter-attacked, accusing the War Office of 'suppressing facts and prevarication'. Other journals, frightened of a general news black-out, now rallied to the side of the *Mail*, offering to share their own news and information with the newspaper. In the meantime, Alfred Harmsworth himself challenged Brodrick to 'express definitely on a public platform, where we could proceed against him for libel, that the *Daily Mail* has purloined public documents'.

In the final result, the House voted on the issue, concluding that the challenge to Brodrick was a breach of privilege, but by a vote of 222 to 128, members declined to summon the editor of the *Mail* to the bar of the House of Commons. Against this, the *Mail* countered by saying, 'We resent strongly the suggestion which Mr. Brodrick has made that we have held out temptations to officials of small income to betray official secrets. We have never sought this kind of information, and we do not intend to seek it.'

Then, as if in defiance of the Government and perhaps peevishly, the *Daily Mail* began to print daily accounts of the highly secret negotiations between Lord Milner, British High Commissioner for South Africa, and the Boer delegates at the Treaty of Peace, held at Vereeniging in 1902. By 16 May that year, the *Mail* predicted that 'peace was absolutely assured' even though this statement was not confirmed by Parliament until 2 June.

It was later revealed that the *Daily Mail* had enlisted a spy in the form of a corporal who, riding in the train with the important officials at the end of each day of negotiating, would casually look out the window or, standing on the steps, give signals as the train passed a certain point. Once the *Mail* correspondent got the news, he cabled to a private address in London numerically coded messages which appeared to deal with gold mining and Stock Exchange transactions. Since literally hundreds of similar messages were everyday transmitted from Johannesburg to London in the natural course of business, these messages were able to pass the Censor unsuspected and untouched.

Such open defiance of secrecy in government has rankled establishmentarians from Alfred Harmsworth's day to this, and in official histories Alfred's role in the reportage of the Boer War has gone down ill. Nevertheless, it is hard to credit Harmsworth with the base motive of publishing reports of the murder of wounded Englishmen simply to increase his circulation. Similarly, it is difficult to interpret his cantankerous attitude towards officialdom as a method of furthering his own motives. Quite the contrary. He was growing, albeit unevenly, into the power and responsibility his own position entailed.

But whatever his motives, and these were increasingly contradictory and difficult to discern as time went by, it was beginning to come clear to his opponents that Alfred Harmsworth, despite his growing social prominence, was not always a gentleman.

And he wasn't going to go quietly.

5

'Mr Alfred Worship'

America was divided on 'Al' Harmsworth. Either he was a genius or a huckster – so went the opinions. To most Americans, it didn't much matter which, because in twenty-four short hours Alfred had become a national celebrity, and by American standards that was all that counted.

Alfred had been invited by press baron Joseph Pulitzer to edit his New York *World* on the first day of the twentieth century – 1 January 1901.* Pulitzer had been impressed by Alfred's article in the *North American Review* predicting the eventuality of 'the simultaneous newspaper', a global newspaper that would one day be published simultaneously in all the capitals of the world. It was an idea whose time wouldn't come until satellite transmission caught up with Alfred's futuristic imaginings. But for Pulitzer, whose preoccupation with technology matched Alfred's own, the idea was intriguing. He now promised Alfred a free hand, with 'no interference', to produce 'the newspaper of the future'.

As always, Alfred rose to the occasion, cutting in half the usual size of the *World* and taking as his format the 'small, portable and neatly indexed publication' he frequently touted as the most convenient size for a newspaper. Alfred gave this new miniature the name 'tabloid', meaning compressed, which he appropriated from a British chemist's manufacturing term for a large effervescent pill. He then quickly adapted the typography of the *World* to the tabloid format and added two 'dog ears' at the top: 'the Busy Man's Paper', said one; 'all the news in sixty seconds', said the other. Dressed in black tie as Pulitzer had decreed, Alfred strode through the newsroom the night before the dawn of the new century, warning reporters not to submit a story longer than 250 words. Outside, a pyrotechnical display of coloured lights was splashed across the *World* building. As his final act, Alfred scribbled his own challenge across the top of the paper, 'I ask America for an impartial verdict of this 20th Century newspaper – Alfred Harmsworth.' America obliged, with practically every

* There was considerable debate on what was the actual first day of the century, most scholars holding that 1900 was the last year of the nineteenth century.

paper in the country giving their opinion on 'the Harmsworth experiment'.

By nine o'clock the following morning, Alfred's newspaper had sold out, and another 100,000 copies were ordered to be printed and rushed on to the streets. Alfred was suddenly a hot item who had joined the ranks of America's great press barons: Joseph Pulitzer, James Gordon Bennett, Frank Munsey and William Randolph Hearst. Julian Ralph, who had reported for Alfred during the Boer War, wrote that amongst all these names, 'Harmsworth stands out easily, well-controlled and polished in manner, the most pre-possessing and picturesque figure in journalism on either side of the Atlantic.' Still only thirty-five, Alfred cut a youthful figure at odds with his reputation. After giving Alfred a quick once-over, the clerk at his hotel asked what time his father would be checking in.

Alfred was no stranger to America; he once told Hearst that he had used the old New York *Sun* as the model for his *Daily Mail*. He was no stranger to American reporting practices either. He once said,

> When I come here, as I am happy to say that I do very often, I read the pages of cablegrams, and especially Sunday cablegrams, from London, and I see that England is chiefly peopled by suffragettes, impecunious aristocrats, and four or five amazing society ladies, 'Fashionable Beauties', whose names and antics are recorded, and whose photographs, taken over twenty-five years ago, do steady service very regularly. I wonder if it ever occurred to the gentlemen who send these Sunday cables that there must be some other people over there to conduct the gigantic export trade of Great Britain, to manage her cotton mills, to maintain her mercantile fleet carrying seven-tenths of the world's goods, her shipping-yards, and a navy that has been heard of at times?

Alfred didn't exempt himself from his frank scepticism of American newspaper reports. He wrote to his mother, 'Should any articles about us appear in any English papers, reprinted from here, don't believe one word. All are invented.'

New York was cynical but dynamic, and it was inevitable that Alfred would be caught up in the whirlwind of his own fame. He met Thomas Edison, became friends with Mark Twain; he was at the top of his form. As always, in the wake of triumph, Alfred reacted belatedly to the risk of failure with his whole body, and, predictably, his health gave way. He became one of the victims of an epidemic of influenza then sweeping through the city. He and his wife travelled to Florida for rest and recovery, but there Alfred quickly succumbed to malaria and, just as quickly, to the depression that accompanies the disease.

By now, Alfred's fixation on his health had hardened into classic hypochondria – although he *did* suffer endlessly from actual sickness. At one time or another, he was diagnosed with nervous exhaustion, liver illness, inflammation of the pancreas, attacks of fatigue; his doctor would eventually find valvular damage to his heart. He had frequent 'breakdowns' which his wife grew to dread. His diary was filled with pathetic self-directives he believed would help. He told himself to 'procure fresh butcher's meat', take deep breathing exercises, sweep leaves. He repaired to 'famous sleeping places' and to Paris and to Pau in search of rest. He gorged, he starved, he alternated between vegetarian and carnivore, he jumped from hot to cold baths – all in search of good health. His weight worried him: 'There is no fool like a fat fool,' he said. And, as he descended into the spiral of self-fulfilling prophecy, his health deteriorated further and further, almost in direct response to his own fears.

In the meantime, his reputation and that of the *Daily Mail* became the stuff of legend, as often symbols of evil as of good. Music-hall stars sang a satirical ditty entitled 'By Kind Permission of the Daily Mail', Liberal papers called Alfred 'an enemy of the human race', and young men dreamed of slaying the dragon who had become one of the 'Men Who Are Ruining the Empire, No. I: Alfred Harmsworth'. Rival newspapers jumped in as well, saying of the *Mail*, 'Today it's a fact, tomorrow it'll be a rumour.' And all of this because Alfred possessed one singular ability. 'Somehow,' he said, in trying to describe what it was, 'I knew from the first just what people wanted to read – at least, that is a fair assumption, I think.'

He had learned to accept the tiresome but deadly competition amongst his employees; he jokingly called Carmelite House and his magazine empire 'the dogfight'. Perhaps he came to enjoy it. It was said he kept an aquarium in his bathroom in which two fighting fish were separated by a movable pane of glass. Legend has it he lifted the glass from time to time to 'study the results'.

Whether or not it was true, the story paralleled events taking place at the *Daily Mail* office. S.J. Pryor was editor of the paper at the outset of the Boer War. Transferred to Cape Town for the duration, Pryor was temporarily replaced by Thomas Marlowe, who became managing editor. But when Pryor returned he found his chair occupied, and he and Marlowe fell into competition for it, each in turn arriving earlier and earlier to get into the seat and, once secured, refusing to leave it. It was Tom Marlowe whose claim succeeded because, it was conjectured, he had the stronger bladder. Such shoot-outs were inevitable because Alfred tended to surround himself with tough men 'who had come up from the bottom by sheer hard work; and that had left an indelible hardness to their character.'

These rough-and-tumble characters were encouraged to 'stay at the best hotels' and to travel always with a valet. Never one to underestimate the snobbery of the British, Alfred intended in every way to give the impression that the *Mail* was produced 'for the Best People'.

He gained a reputation for placing staff where they would succeed. When one young sub-editor failed at his job, Alfred asked him what he could do. 'I can write short stories.' 'Well, go ahead then.' The writer did so and made a success of it. When another member of the staff, mistaking Alfred for a colleague, slapped him on the back and said, 'Thank God the Old Man has gone to the Continent; now we shall have peace,' Alfred countered by saying, 'Oh no, he hasn't.' And after a moment spent enjoying the man's confusion, Alfred invited him to dinner to show his sportsmanship. As a result of moments like these, workers tended to give themselves over to 'Mr Alfred worship', calling him Alfred the Great. They often bowed in front of his office, succumbing to the modes of adulation that cost them little but would eventually do Alfred irreparable harm.

Power made him whimsical, and it was nothing for Alfred to award the 'very fine piece of work' by Montague Smith £10 at the beginning of the week, and by the end condemn a report by the same man as muddled and 'completely [missing] the real point'. He complained bitterly of 'shameless puffs', 'company promoters', bad headings, errors in grammar, typos, proof-reading. There was never any let-up.

He did not suffer fools gladly, and any braggarts were dismissed out of hand, sometimes in mid-sentence. A young man who made the mistake of calling him 'My Dear Alfred' was soon sacked. A pair of reporters whose articles he disliked were just as quickly ousted: 'Get rid of both at the first possible date,' he wrote to Marlowe. Of one reporter he might say, 'Does his job very well. Not much education. Father a cab-driver.' Of another: 'His stuff is tosh. Don't use it.' Of still another: 'No brains there, have you noticed how close together his eyes are?' They might be too fat, too thin, too loud, too quiet; the editors did what they could to hide their employees from Alfred's eye after a death decree went out. In one case, an editor renamed the condemned man and in that way managed to keep him on the staff.

A few staffers themselves managed to outsmart Alfred. One whom Alfred had fired had a photograph of himself taken, along with his wife and eight children, whom he lined up in a row. He sent it along to Alfred, asking whether 'the boss could allow him to be sacked and plunge into poverty this many people'. Alfred relented, and the man was rehired. But henceforth, Alfred instructed his editors, they were to determine discreetly the size of the family of any potential new employee. The firm could afford to carry no more than one 'unsinkable' in any given department, he said.

Alfred went over the top – all too often – but he was losing the ability to detect, or indeed to care, when that occurred. Once, before one of his directors entered his office, Alfred told a guest, 'Now you're going to see how I treat a man when I'm angry.' He removed the man's hat, then he kicked it out the door and down the hall. This done, he resumed casual conversation with the guest, who was flabbergasted. He fired one man in a singularly cruel way. He rang him on the telephone and asked who was on the other end of the line. When the man answered, 'Editor, *Weekly Dispatch*', Alfred countered with, 'You *were* the editor.' The numbers he eliminated became legion: he once said to a colleague who happened to be walking with him on the street, 'We'd do best to keep to the byways. We might meet some of the men I've sacked. They lie in wait for me here.'

And yet his acts of generosity were overwhelming. If a foreign correspondent turned in a good piece of work, he sent the man's wife fruit or jewellery or flowers – or simply a cheque. 'Your husband's delightful article this morning gave me great pleasure,' he would say. He educated the children of his staff, Thomas Marlowe's boy, Alfred Harmsworth Marlowe, among them. He provided for former employees down on their luck, paid a pension to their widows, lent money to men he had sacked and sent cash to his father's friends who were in need. Each summer, he held bachelor parties for his staff, providing French cuisine, games, fruits, fine wines and brandy – which he himself didn't drink.

He paid his brothers' way through university, and for the numerous children of his family he sent lavish Christmas gifts. For one of his godsons, he sent a complete little shop, with a counter, miniature jars and packs of groceries, scales and paper bags. One year his brother Leicester's family received one of the first gramophones to be manufactured, along with six records. Whenever he visited a relative's home, he kept his pockets full of gold sovereigns for the children.

By now, Alfred had elected to a style of dress that never changed. He wore dark-blue suits made by Poole, shirts with soft collars and a spotted red tie. His Homburg hat was always pulled down rakishly over his eyes, and he carried a German cigar which he smoked with the band on. He was alternately described by men and women as 'casual versus noble' in appearance. To the former, he seemed pleasantly unconcerned about his appearance; to the latter, he appeared as a screen idol might today. Both sexes characterized his forelock, the single lock of golden hair he wore on his forehead, as Napoleonic, although it was the prevailing style of the day.

The comparison with Napoleon started from an incident when he and his mother travelled to the Continent, and Alfred, trying on one of Napoleon's hats on display in a museum, exclaimed to her, 'It fits!' Thenceforth, it was thought, he tried to emulate the great French dictator, and those who wished to flatter him exaggerated the similarities between the two men.

In fact, it wasn't long before the expectations of Alfred's employees became as demanding and unrealistic as Napoleon's troops had been towards the great dictator himself, ascribing to Alfred the characteristics of a minor god. Even those who hated what they believed Alfred symbolized – and this changed according to the perceptions of whoever was doing the telling – more and more drew comparisons between Alfred and great men of the past. Whatever else might be true about the growing myth of Alfred Harmsworth, it had become apparent that he was both blessed and cursed by the same traits as these men.

In 1902, Alfred at last established his long-planned Manchester office in Deansgate, bringing to an end the high-cost railway distribution system he had used during the Boer War. In its own way, this was an outgrowth of his idea for a simultaneous newspaper, for it permitted the *Daily Mail* to be printed at two centres simultaneously, the paper produced at London serving the southern half of the country, the one at Manchester serving the northern provinces, including Scotland and Ireland.

Kennedy Jones was sent up to the new office where he and an employee named Macrae invented a practical system of coding that permitted them to telegraph from London to Manchester letterpress, headings and positions. In so doing, they managed to keep the London character of the paper while outpacing competitors. Besides setting up the code, K.J. established three telephone wires and rented out an empty schoolhouse in the suburbs where he set up two printing presses and twelve linotype machines, doing away with the need for hand compositors.

In the same year, the offices at the Victorian Gothic Carmelite House were completed at a cost of half a million pounds, and the *Evening News* and *Daily Mail* were installed there. The new address read, Daily Mail, 1, Carmelite House, Tallis Street EC. For the *Evening News*, Alfred now installed eight more linotypes and three small rotary presses in the basement of the building. It was one more example of how the *Daily Mail* and its sister publications led the way in the introduction of new technology. Early on, the *Mail* had consolidated its ascendancy in international reporting. Only a year after the *Mail* was founded, a telegraphic connection between New York and London had been established, a first on Fleet Street; by the following year a wire was laid from Carmelite Street to the end of the ocean cable at Valencia Island off the Irish coast. Now, with the updating of the printing facilities, the *Mail* soared ahead of its competitors.

Inside Carmelite House, Room One was established as Alfred's office, and he shared it with the editor of the *Mail* and the runner who carried his messages. Wainscoted in mahogany, the lower door panels of the bookcase were decorated with a gilt pattern of ornate leaf and flower, and with a symbolic quill, and bore the gilded names of ancient writers and philosophers from Aristophanes to Xenophon. Coal fires were installed at either end of the room, and eventually Philip de Laszlo was commissioned to paint a portrait of Alfred, who appears in it with his arms folded over one another, bound copies of the *Daily Mail* beneath his right elbow. A bust of Napoleon was kept on the mantel. Green marble and dark-grey colouring was accentuated by a richly coloured upholstery for chairs and drapery. In reference to this grandiose room, Alfred was fond of making the pronouncement, 'Big rooms for big ideas'; this before permanently taking over his secretary's small annexe to carry out his serious work.

But most of his work was conducted at home from his Broadstairs estate, Elmwood – the uniquely personalized retreat where, even as Alfred readied himself for his morning assault, a pair of Florida alligators lay wallowing in mud in the purpose-built heated greenhouse he had ordered for them. Picture Alfred then at six a.m. in his white silk pyjamas, lying in bed, reading the morning's newspapers closely and making notes in his bold, jaunty handwriting. Beside him are supplies of freshly sharpened blue and black pencils for just that purpose. At the ready is his telephone, the chosen instrument for his attack. At eight a.m. he begins.

'Ha,' he says, 'do you see that? No one else had the gumption to go after the story behind that question in Parliament. We got it. I told them it was there. I always have to keep prodding them.' Or, if the editor has failed: 'I warned them, I warned them. They will not listen. Here is the very thing in *The Times* that I was talking about yesterday. The *Mail* could have got it – by worrying. We could have made far more of it. Get me the news editor. What? Won't be up! Why not? I'm up, or at any rate I'm at work. Pull him out of bed if necessary.'

Death could be swift, but a man was often spared if his courage held. Those who spoke back, explaining they had been up until well past midnight putting the paper to bed, scored points. Alfred might send a car to carry them to Elmwood, or ask them out for dinner. Others might find themselves badly nicked.

Alfred had a telephone in every room, and he boasted he had been able to speak personally with as many as twenty people without making a single move. His day was 'marked out in minutes', he would explain to intimates, 'and I have to see my friends when I can. It has practically come to this, those who have no telephone I never see.' But the wave of telephone calls he initiated during the early hours brought back wave upon wave throughout the remainder of his day, and there were those who thought he had made himself a prisoner of the very technology he believed freed him.

Certainly, he was not above using the technology he loved for his own purposes. Early on, he paid spies to bug the switchboard of the *Daily Mail*, ostensibly to make sure no personal use was being made of the *Mail*'s innovations. Private reports of what was overheard, however, made their way to Alfred and influenced his staffing decisions.

No doubt it added to the staff's impression that Alfred was omniscient. But, sadly, Alfred himself grew to share their view, forgetting the mechanics of his clairvoyance and more and more attributing to himself an ability to see into the hearts and minds of others. It was inevitable, but it was a shame; an object lesson in the nature of the gradual decline of the great and the good.

The death of Queen Victoria in January 1901 betokened a new era; it delineated a significant breaking-point between the past and the future. On 24 January, the *Daily Mail* wrote of 'Two Londons': those who stayed in their homes, marking the passing of the monarch with respect and decorum, and those who were out on the streets, celebrating the coming of King Edward VII. For those attuned to new streams of thought, it now seemed as if the rigid class stratification that had always defined English society would give way to the rising tide of self-made men. At the same time, ideas about the proper province of women were changing, with the promise of new freedoms for the fairer sex.

Alfred had always championed the rights of women – in his own peculiar way. He had pioneered their mass readership of newspapers, and he continued to define the market. But the topics his women readers were asked to consider remained more stylish than challenging. There was 'The Fashionable Weekend: A Disturbing Habit Much Discussed over Teacups'. Or what about the marriage mart? 'Are Marriages Made in London?' the *Mail* asked. Still another query thought suitable for feminine debate: 'Has the Telephone Killed the Love Letter?' Otherwise, it was the safe harbour of new coiffures, sewing patterns, walking sticks for women, precious gems and dinner recipes. For the *Daily Mail*, as it charted its way from Victorian to Edwardian, the operative word, borrowed from Alfred's magazines *Home Chat* and *Home Sweet Home*, was 'dainty'. In Alfred's publications, any advance made by women must always be tempered by the aura of sweetness and innocence they retained in his fantasies.

On the flip side, Alfred's directives could often sound cynical: his newspapers and magazines must give the impression they were 'high-class' publications, reinforcing his contention they were produced for 'the best people in Society'. 'Nine women out of ten', he said with his customary confidence, 'would rather read about an evening dress costing a great deal of money – the sort of dress they will never in their lives have a chance of wearing – than about a simple frock such as they could afford. A recipe for a dish requiring a pint of cream, a dozen eggs, and the breasts of three chickens pleases them better than being told how to make Irish stew.' This patronizing and somewhat sententious attitude towards women was to lead Alfred to make the most serious miscalculation in his career – not to mention its effect on his personal life.

Exactly where Alfred picked up his idea to publish a woman's newspaper is unknown, but Kennedy Jones believed Alfred lifted it from *La Fronde*, a French newspaper edited by women for women. By now confident his touch alone ensured success for any new publication, Alfred neglected to do the careful spadework that had made the *Mail* the biggest success story on Fleet Street, plunging into the launch of the *Daily Mirror* with more speed than sense. It was essentially a stunt – an all-woman staff for an all-woman readership – but, as the ethos for a daily newspaper with a mass readership, it couldn't work.

Mary Howarth, who had been in charge of features on the *Daily Mail*, was named as the first editor, and the title was preserved for the weeks leading up to publication on small tearsheets six by eight inches. There the all-woman staff sharpened their skills on the short pieces upon which Alfred's empire had been built. One told the tale of a savage fight between two women, and a clever detective who produced a bitten-off ear as evidence in court. Another, headlined 'Mother's Tragic Fate', chronicled the swift death of a woman who, leaning too far over her window-box to watch her husband return from work, plunged to her death when the box gave way. Other grisly topics were 'Baby in a Dustbin', 'Cut Off by Tide' and 'Divorce by Dagger'. Juxtaposed to these were the feminine features of 'Beauty and the Bath – Spartan Ways of Cultivating Comeliness', 'A Page of Interesting Books' and the inevitable 'Dainty Frocks for Children and a Useful Pattern'. This unholy alliance of crime, bathos and self-improvement was an early indication of the schizoid character the new newspaper would assume. And Alfred himself had fostered the split by promising a newspaper that would deal equally 'with flowers on the dinner table to the disposition of forces in the Far East'.

The resulting *Daily Mirror* was an unmitigated disaster. On the first day of publication, 2 November 1903, it was said the women staff suffered fits of fainting from the pressure, with several bursting into tears. Alfred gallantly sent in champagne to revive them. Meanwhile, Kennedy Jones was in despair. Much of the copy was passing through his hands, and K.J. wrote later of being astounded 'at the gulf that is fixed between the male and the female mind'. He quickly renamed 'Our French Letter' as 'Yesterday in Paris', and set a group of male sub-editors to work taking out the smoking-room terms unintentionally included in the issue by the female staff. The men demonstrated something less than romantic chivalry about their women colleagues. Said one, the whole thing resembled a French farce; said another, 'In a French farce, they would be beautiful.' From a first-day circulation of 276,000, sales plunged to an eventual low of 24,801 – another first for Fleet Street, but not the kind to which Alfred Harmsworth had become accustomed. Thus quickly passed from the London scene Alfred's idea for the 'first daily newspaper for gentle-women'.

A Scotsman, Hamilton Fyfe, was quickly named editor, and it fell to him to sack the entire female staff. The women resisted, leaving little presents and notes on his desk begging to be retained. But Fyfe grimly carried out his task, reckoning the experience to be something akin to drowning kittens. Ironically, Fyfe himself was unable to effect the quick-fix Alfred required, and he found himself next on the chopping block. A kind of panic ensued, with Harold, as always, strongly in favour of knifing the paper and Alfred determined to save it – although his losses were mounting. In desperation he turned to one of his technicians, a man with the unlikely name of Arkas Sapt.

Sapt was an unconventional character, careless about money and rumoured to be heavily in debt. One improbable anecdote has him trying to escape from his creditors by running into Cannon Street railway station, checking himself into the lost property office, and sending the ticket to the office with the message, 'Come and get me out.' Sapt now boasted to Alfred, 'I can fill a daily newspaper with photographs printed on high-speed rotary presses.' At the time, the *Daily Graphic* was doing 10,000 copies per hour, and Sapt assured Alfred he could double or treble that speed, printing on an ordinary Hoe press.

He succeeded in producing 24,000 copies per hour, good enough for Alfred to relaunch the paper at a reduced price in January 1904 as the *Illustrated Daily Mirror*. Readers were astounded, although the first photographs were anything but perfect, and sales picked up. By April, the *Mirror* had become London's first tabloid newspaper, and, soon after, it sailed

Alfred Harmsworth snr, father of Northcliffe and Rothermere, c 1865: 'He had long, lanky legs, the languid air of a man of the world, a literary bent and the eyes of a visionary.' Geraldine Maffett, mother. The Irish maiden, aged about 21, who would become matriarch of one of the most powerful families in England.

(Below) Alfred, with his family at his father's funeral, 1888. He is wearing the grey travelling suit his brothers and sisters helped him buy; now everything depended upon him.

Alfred Harmsworth jnr with his pennyfarthing, 1881. He raced from London to Bournemouth in driving rain, without once dismounting, and then collapsed into a fever.

Alfred, the 'young Apollo'
c 1890: 'He had golden hair
and blue eyes and carried
himself in a commanding
way. People often turned to
look at him in the street.'

Mary (or 'Molly') Harmsworth, Alfred's helpmate
on *Answers to Correspondents*, in about 1890,
when the couple lived in modest lodgings in
West Hampstead. Money, power and social
eminence would change her.

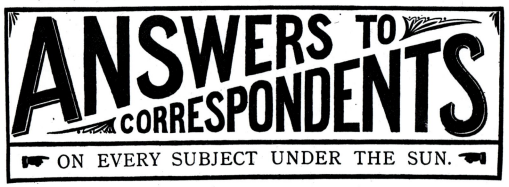

INTERESTING.   EXTRAORDINARY.   AMUSING.

ANSWERS TO CORRESPONDENTS

ON EVERY SUBJECT UNDER THE SUN.

The masthead for Alfred's flagship, launched on 16 June 1888: 'A weekly storehouse of
interesting knowledge; a weekly paper of surpassing interest; praised by the Clergy, the
Press and the Public.'

4 May 1896, the first issue of the *Daily Mail*. Inset: Alfred as seen by 'Spy' on the cover of *Vanity Fair* a year earlier.

(Above) London rejoices after Mafeking is saved.

MAFEKING PICTURES.

Colonel Baines-Powell and Lord Edward Cecil on the look-out in Mafeking. [From a snapshot.]

Colonel Baden-Powell's bomb-proof shelter in Mafeking. [From a snap-shot.

LADY SARAH WILSON,
One of the "Daily Mail's" Correspondents in Mafeking.
[Photo by Elliot and Fry.

COLONEL PLUMER,
Who led the Rhodesian column operating from the north of Mafeking. [Photo by Elliot and Fry.

"B.-P."
This is undoubtedly the public's favourite photograph of Colonel Baden-Powell. It has had an enormous sale.
[Photo by Elliot and Fry.

HIS MOTHER'S FAVOURITE PHOTOGRAPH.
"B.-P." in the uniform of the 13th Hussars, his first regiment.

LORD EDWARD CECIL.
Colonel Baden-Powell's right-hand man in Mafeking.
[Photo by Lafayette.

HOW MAFEKING WAS SURROUNDED AND DEFENDED.
A Plan made by a British officer, and sent by native runner to Bulawayo.

Daily Mail line drawing of the principals in the relief of Mafeking, 19 May 1900. The first woman war correspondent, Lady Sarah Wilson (upper right-hand corner) became a national heroine through her crisp, matter-of-fact reporting of the siege.

(Right) Northcliffe in Newfoundland, pictured beside a Micmac Indian, c 1910. It would be a native of the region, Matty Mitchell, who saved the paper-making venture by discovering a rich ore deposit nearby.

A log-drive on the Exploits River, Grand Falls, Newfoundland, c 1911: 'I take it upon myself to enter heartily upon the watching of the enterprise,' Northcliffe wrote to one of his subordinates, 'because I know that if anything does go wrong the whole blame will fall on me.'

"To preserve sinister & the like to make a considerable longer life a difficult..."

(Left) Mrs Wrohan, Northcliffe's Irish mistress from about 1900, here pictured with one of the couple's three children.

Northcliffe, as he himself has written on the photograph, in 'the first Mercedes in England'. An early promoter of the motorcar, he commissioned Rudyard Kipling to write a series of parodies for the *Daily Mail* in the style of famous poets. After Wordsworth: 'He wandered down the mounting grade/ Beyond the speed assigned –/ A youth whom justice often stayed/ And generally fined./ He went alone, and none might know/ If he could drive or steer:/ Now he is in the ditch, and Oh!/ The differential gear.'

The first Mercedes in England   *Northcliffe.*

Northcliffe, an early promoter of 'aereal motorcars', as he called them, in Pau with Orville Wright, 1907. Just before his ascent before a cheering crowd, Richard Wright was told by his sister that he must wear gloves.

(Above) Blériot flies the Channel, 25 July 1909, proving Northcliffe's assertion that 'Britain is no longer an island'. Within twenty-four hours, Northcliffe, seated on Blériot's left, had organised a celebration luncheon at the Savoy Hotel for 'all the important people in the country'.

Winston Churchill and Northcliffe at the Hendon Aviation Meeting, 12 May 1911. Only two months later, Northcliffe would stage his 1,010-mile Great Air Race, with thirteen staging posts across Britain.

past the danger point. Alfred had once more snatched victory from the jaws of defeat.

Later, trying to patch over a major failure with braggadocio, he would write an article entitled 'How I lost £100,000 on the *Daily Mirror'*. It set off a series of satirical responses, the most notable a parody published in the *Star* – 'How I Dropped £1,000,000 Behind the Piano'. Maybe Alfred was asking for it. He was driven by different devils: on the one hand, the *Mirror* was only one venture of many for the insatiable publisher; on the other, he took any failure as a direct hit, and an effort of this kind inevitably cost him more than money.

His mother, emerging from the shadows, took a hand. The *Mirror* was too demanding, she maintained; Alfred must get rid of it.* There was the implication that she had found the original model for the newspaper distasteful. And truly, it wasn't her cup of tea. Alfred's prototypical woman reader was based more on his wife than his mother, and as much on his mistress as his wife. Mary Harmsworth, self-styled as Molly according to the fashion of the day, was a social butterfly; all entertainments, social life, theatre and Parisian frocks. Mrs Wrohan was the tall, dark, imperious type; all mystery, drama and ostrich-feather fans. Both women were widely acquainted with the aristocracy, or 'the Best People', if you will; both were ambitious; both spent money like water. They customarily adorned themselves in the very frocks Alfred's women readers would 'never in their lives have a chance of wearing'. It was all a bit much for one man, just as the *Mirror* had all been a bit much for his mother. The market-place had demonstrated it was all a bit much for the readers as well.

Alfred, overwrought by the complications of his current love life, turned to the simpler charms of a newly hired secretary, Louise Owen. Owen's motivations were airtight: she had taken the job in order to support the orphan children of her dead sister. She was wholesome, and she was loyal. If not cut from the same durable cloth as Alfred's mother, she was durable enough. She began her workday at six a.m., reading all the morning newspapers and clipping stories missed in Alfred's papers. She tested recipes, sewed her own dresses from the patterns in the paper and criticized the serials on the magazine page. She also gladly rewrote history for Alfred's sake.

From Owen's viewpoint, Alfred all too often fell victim to the designs of women, most of them unworthy of his notice. These were predators who came up with unexpected stratagems to attract his attention: one

* According to Sir Evelyn Wrench, *Uphill: The First Stage in a Strenuous Life*, p. 141, Alfred sold controlling shares to his brother Harold.

sent sandwiches daily that Owen thought a perk of her job. It was not for many months that she discovered they were from one of Alfred's admirers. The secretary good-naturedly accused Alfred of playing for safety by calling all his ladyfriends 'My Dear'. His answer: 'Indeed, My Dear, you don't know them as I do. I have to be careful.'

About Mrs Wrohan, Owen wove a plausible if deeply mundane tale. She was a temp whom Alfred had once paid £25 for some typing. From time to time, he provided her with much-needed employment; later on, he educated her son at Cambridge. Later still, he would give the boy work on the *Daily Mail*. About Alfred's other two children, Owen made no comment. Perhaps she didn't know about them. For his part, Alfred probably needed Owen to do some mythologizing so far as his relationships went. He didn't handle his women well.

Alfred's wife, caught *in flagrante* with Reginald Nicholson, the manager of *The Times*, by a trusted but shocked employee, depended upon Alfred to cover up her indiscretion. Alfred did so, threatening to sack his assistant, the young Evelyn Wrench, if he ever told anyone what he had seen. But Wrench, who later became the editor of the *Overseas Daily Mail*, was highly ethical, and he condemned Alfred, not his wife, for what he adjudged a sorry state of affairs. Thus began a rift that would end with Wrench, loyal in his own way, maintaining his silence for the duration of his life, but cryptically condemning Alfred for trying 'to live his life in compartments'. It was rough medicine for Alfred: he had heretofore treated Wrench like a son, providing him with countless opportunities for lavish trips abroad and showering jobs like sugar plums upon the young man. But Wrench was no longer prepared 'to give Alfred that devotion to which he was accustomed', and he eventually left Alfred's employ, finally praising Harold more heartily than the legendary Alfred Harmsworth.

But Harold had troubles of his own – the same sort as Alfred, if Wrench had only known it. Within the family, it was acknowledged that Harold's wife, Lilian, was having an affair with Harold's younger brother St John; indeed, St John was several years younger than Lilian herself. One evening in July 1906, he was on his way home from Horsey Hall, Norfolk, Harold's country home, when St John turned the wheel of his car over to his chauffeur and went to sleep in the backseat. His driver, following the telegraph posts beside the Great North Road near Lemsford, failed to notice that they were veering away from the main thoroughfare and overturned the car in a grassy ditch, throwing St John from the car and knocking him out. When he came to, St John found he couldn't move; he couldn't even close his eyes. A passing motor-cyclist stopped to help, and eventually managed to get him to a nearby cottage. It was many months before St John was able to be moved and then only by packing him in sand.

The family rallied, Harold, Leicester and Cecil making all the necessary arrangements for his care and Lilian personally supervising his nursing. Alfred rushed back from a trip abroad badly shaken. St John's spine was broken, and he was condemned to a wheelchair for the rest of his life, a paraplegic whose arms weren't quite right either.*

Nobody spoke of retribution or the toils of sin; it would have been absurd to do so. Besides, the family were in the habit of putting the best possible face on any tragedy, and they did so now, even down to Harold, who, befuddled by the complexities of life, nevertheless acted the part expected of him in exemplary fashion. As to Alfred, he was beginning to understand that fortune and power were nothing in the face of fate, and not even the most indomitable will in the world could stand up to the ordinary vicissitudes of life.

Still, he would do what he could.

In his public life, Alfred flourished, engendering, as always, envy as much as admiration. He was offered a knighthood, and he turned it down, certain he would be offered more. Sure enough, in the Birthday Honours List for 23 June 1904, and despite the mixed feelings of the Establishment towards him, Alfred was among those listed as a baronet. Characteristically, he made a joke of it: he was tired, he said, of being called 'Mr 'Armsworth'; it was a welcome change to hear himself addressed 'Sir *H*alfred'. Yet, before the dust had settled on this title, Alfred had another. A short year and a half later, on 9 December 1905, Sir Alfred became a peer of the realm, the youngest ever created, much to the chagrin of his enemies.

'Lord Answers of Home Chat,' they chided, accusing Alfred of buying his title. Perhaps it was his own fault. He had earlier said, 'When I want a peerage I will buy one, like an honest man.' The statement showed a basic want of respect for so exalted a state. But Alfred certainly did know the value of a title in a rigidly ranked society, and he had often spoken of his intention to put 'a handle to his name'.† He later boasted he had achieved it by buying the Manchester *Courier*, 'especially to act as propagandist for the re-election of Balfour at the next general election'. But this story also

* Paul Ferris, *The House of Northcliffe: The Harmsworths of Fleet Street*, p. 136; see also Cecil, Lord Harmsworth, *St John Harmsworth: A Brave Life (1876–1932)*, p. 7; also Reginald Pound and Geoffrey Harmsworth, *Northcliffe*, p. 299; mention is also made by Daphne Macneile Dixon in her interview in South Godstone, 22 Mar. 1992.

† Reginald Pound and Geoffrey Harmsworth, *Northcliffe*, London, baronetcy, pp. 282–4, peerage, p. 295; see also Hamilton Fyfe, *Northcliffe: An Intimate Biography*, p. 121.

had a typical disclaimer: although he got his peerage, Alfred was wont to say, Balfour lost his seat. In the end, it was impossible to determine whether Alfred engineered his own ascension, an act he was eminently capable of, or whether it was thrust upon him. Once in hand, though, he took his peerage quite seriously, settling on a coast near his estate for the title – North Cliff – and rejecting the more obvious Broadstairs and Elmwood ('Goodness, no – it's the wood they use for coffins').

He added an imposing 'e' to the end and emerged as Lord Northcliffe, henceforth styling his 'N' after Napoleon's and deliberately feeding the myth that he viewed himself as the rightful descendant of the French dictator. The whole Napoleon thing had probably begun as one of his jokes, escalating in direct proportion to others' willingness to buy into it. It would eventually backfire on Alfred, after he had begun to believe his own publicity. But there were similarities between the two men, in situation if not in character. Like Napoleon, many hated Alfred and sought to construe his every action as sinister and self-serving. More dangerous still were his worshippers, who were just as numerous, most of them as imaginative as his detractors. Typical of the adulation he received was a speech made by one of his employees, J.A. Hammerton, at a select entertainment held at the Café Royal to celebrate Alfred's new title.

'While there might be those among us', Hammerton intoned, 'who were more at their ease when the Chief was absent from the office, in my own case when I knew him to be in his room I felt like a passenger on a ship in dirty weather who took courage from the fact that the captain was on the bridge.' Even a newly named Northcliffe couldn't let this one go by, and staff and proprietor alike howled in derision of such blatant flattery.

That was the public Northcliffe. Privately, he had to admit that the year had been one of continuous triumph, so much so it was hard not to believe himself a genius. Not only had Northcliffe risen to the most eminent rank of English Society, but he had also consolidated his newspaper dynasty. Like Amalgamated Press, founded in 1901 to manage the periodical business, Associated Newspapers Ltd had been formed in April 1905 in order to manage the *Daily Mail*, the *Evening News*, an increasing number of subsidiaries and provincial papers as well as the *Weekly Dispatch*, earlier purchased for £25,000 and now enjoying an increased circulation under Northcliffe's supervision. A month after the incorporation, he added the *Observer* to the list, buying the 150-year-old Sunday newspaper, the oldest in Britain, and quickly entering into negotiations with J.L. Garvin, thought by many, Northcliffe among them, to be the foremost political journalist in the country.

The relationship between Northcliffe and Garvin was not untypical of the way in which gifted men succumbed to Northcliffe's power. Garvin sincerely wrote to Northcliffe,

> Does my future then lie with you? ... They tell me you tire of men and throw them over and would tire of me and throw me. At my time of life, I cannot afford to make a mistake or leave anything to chance. In spite of all they say, I am personally drawn to you and your creative genius fills me with amazement. I have dreamed for hours often and often of what might be done if I were your political right hand.

Northcliffe welcomed such an alliance, soon securing Garvin as the editor of the *Observer* and adding him to his entourage. He entertained him in Pau, his hideaway near the Pyrenees; he carried him across America aboard his private railway car, the *Independence*. In the end, they fell out because, without warning, Garvin disagreed with Northcliffe in print, an intolerable state of affairs from one of his own editors in his own newspaper (not to mention what Northcliffe viewed as a betrayal of personal friendship). Even at that, he gave Garvin time to enlist William Waldorf Astor as a buyer for the *Observer* – 'a triumph of editor over owner', Fleet Street gleefully proclaimed – as if Northcliffe couldn't have crushed his friend and editor if he had pleased. Instead, he preserved the friendship with his 'dear Garvino' until his death.*

But the *Observer* was only a small part of it. The year after he bought that paper, Northcliffe started a braille edition of the *Daily Mail*, a limited daily edition of 40,000 to be sold at a loss for only a penny each. The Braille edition was introduced with a flourish: the regular edition of the *Mail* ran a feature with a photograph explaining how the new paper would be produced through 'the well-known Braille system of the raised dots in groups of six'. There was also the *Overseas Daily Mail*, created by Northcliffe 'to serve as a kind of weekly letter from the old country to British-born settlers throughout the Empire', which had supplanted the moderately successful *Illustrated Daily Mail*. Northcliffe's personal brainchild for the year, however, was the *Continental Daily Mail*, a Parisian edition tailored to the needs of the British expatriate abroad.

His enlistment of Norman Angell as editor entailed the usual abrupt reversal of the thinking man who, suddenly faced with the opportunity to work for Northcliffe, quickly overcomes any contempt he might have had and falls into line. In Angell's case, he had already met Northcliffe when he sought to persuade the press baron to buy the *Daily Messenger*,

---

* See Alfred Gollin, *The Observer and J.L. Garvin*, for a full discussion of the relationship between the two men.

an English-language paper published in Paris that Angell was editing. Angell was badly in need of an infusion of cash, but it had only taken Northcliffe one quick glance at the balance sheet to send Angell reeling from his singular point of view. The *Messenger* had taken on more advertisers than its circulation could justify, Northcliffe charged. 'It is of course a fraud on your advertisers,' he said. 'They are not getting their money's worth and I'm surprised that a man of your scruples should be concerned in that kind of business.' The *Messenger* needed something in the region of £5,000 to survive, and Northcliffe declined to provide it.

Instead, he ended up offering Angell the editorship of the *Continental Daily Mail*, with seed money of ten times that amount, and the same again if Angell should need it. Angell was far 'too literary' and 'too viewy' for the press baron's taste, and he didn't look the sort of man to read the *Daily Mail*. But Northcliffe nevertheless believed in him and knew him to be the right man for his expatriate crowd. He promised Angell a completely free hand, and it was Angell, not Northcliffe, who broke the bargain first. One of his first acts as editor was to ask Northcliffe: 'Are you prepared to take on a twenty-five year lease for a printing and editorial building and spend five thousand pounds altering it?' And Northcliffe replied: 'I thought the arrangement between us was that you should decide these things and take the consequences. If you make a mistake in a decision of that character it will be a very black mark against you. Decide it.'

Angell did so, and also got the trial issue up and running within a month – to Northcliffe's delight. Henceforth, he became, like Garvin, one of Northcliffe's favoured ones. He might be invited to come along as a guest to a beautiful Spanish house Northcliffe had rented, with a marble patio that was 'open to the sky, and with a garden of roses in full bloom clustering up the walls'. Or he might tag along on 'a long motor tour exploring northern Italy and staying at all sorts of out-of-the-way places'. Or he might stay on the French Riviera and breakfast on croissants, scrambled eggs 'and bacon cut in shavings the thickness of a Gillette razor blade'.

But Angell soon became familiar with Northcliffe's dictatorial side. What amazed him was the attention to detail of the Chief's observations; indeed, nothing was beneath his notice. A policeman depicted in the comics must always be fat; the public expected it. A henpecked husband must always be thin; his wife shouldn't feed him too well. Angell once found himself in hot water because he had criticized a reporter named Mildred for sending him a feature about nose-blowing. Northcliffe immediately remonstrated, 'You were quite wrong to pull up Mildred about sending the nose-blowing story over the wire. It is quite important. Don't you know that the three things which are always news are health things, sex things, and money things. Health and sex and money always; and quickly. Some other paper might have picked it up and you would not have been able to use it.'

Men like Angell believed themselves above such stuff; in fact, Angell had sprung, like Northcliffe, from a typically hard-up Victorian family, with nothing that elevated him above the 'nose-blowing' status except his own self-regard. He had travelled to America, worked for a time as a migrant farm labourer, then as a cowboy and at last as a journalist on America's western frontier. He would, however, later become a winner of the Nobel Peace Prize. His book, *The Great Illusion*, was destined to become one of the most influential of the age. It was an anti-war tract, and Angell himself was one of the first to support a League of Nations. But by then he would have made his peace with the press baron.

Another man who began with contempt for Northcliffe, until it became expedient to think otherwise, was Moberly Bell, manager of *The Times*. Bell was born in Egypt of English parentage and went into business there, at last turning to journalism by becoming *The Times*'s Egyptian correspondent. Since its founding in 1785 as the *Daily Universal Register*, the newspaper had enjoyed cult status amongst the intelligentsia in British society, probably because men of the stature of John Delane had edited it. Indeed, by the first decade of the twentieth century, a mere association with *The Times* had the cachet to confer high status upon any individual. So it was with Bell.

Bell originally agreed with the Walter family, who controlled *The Times*, that it should never be 'trampled in the dirt by men of the Tit-Bits school', referring not to Sir George Newnes who never showed an interest in owning the paper, but to Northcliffe, who did. As early as 1901, when American reporters attributed to the young Alfred Harmsworth a desire to own *The Times*, he had seemed interested, even going so far as to make a visit to Printing House Square where the paper was produced – only to suffer public insult from Arthur Walter. Later, there were rumours Northcliffe had offered £1 million for it, no doubt a false report since the paper had been a notorious loss-maker for years, and putting it in order would have taken still more money. As Northcliffe's reputation on Fleet Street grew, he was considered even more of a threat than ever within the hallowed offices of *The Times*. Despite the straightforward nature of his intentions, he continued to be vilified as an ogre, so much so that the management of *The Times*, sinking further and further into insolvency, struck a secret deal with another newspaper proprietor – C. Arthur Pearson. Pearson had founded the *Daily Express* in 1900, and it was slowly succeeding, but his *Evening Standard* was rumoured to be in trouble. All things considered, there was little to recommend him as the man who would lead *The Times* out of its difficulties, except, of course, the fact that he wasn't Northcliffe. When Northcliffe was made aware of the deal between the Walter family and Pearson from dinner-party gossip, he became enraged.

So was Moberly Bell. Like the editor, G.E. Buckle, Bell had been left entirely out of negotiations that were about to put Pearson in charge of *The Times*, and Pearson made no secret of the fact that he intended to eliminate Moberly Bell from the staff as quickly as possible. Thus, even as Northcliffe, out of exasperation, was making the decision to proceed through secrecy and indirection to obtain *The Times*, so was Moberly Bell independently vowing that he would smash the deal himself.

On 5 January 1908, Northcliffe ordered a small paragraph inserted into the *Observer* that *The Times* was about to be taken over by a new proprietor, alerting Fleet Street that a secret deal was afoot. The conclusion of the pundits was just what Northcliffe would have wished: they thought it was him. This plunged *The Times* men into confusion, at last forcing them to reveal the truth. Two days later, in the *Daily Mail*, Northcliffe published an article lauding Pearson as a young dynamo. In it, Joseph Chamberlain was quoted as saying that Pearson was 'the greatest hustler I have ever known', damning him, if not with faint praise, then with tongue firmly in cheek. In a follow-up, the *Mail* continued in much the same vein, saying, 'Mr. Pearson is to be warmly congratulated upon his great success in securing control of *The Times* at a point comparatively early in his career. Our best wishes will follow Mr. C. Arthur Pearson in his newest and greatest enterprise.'

For his part, Pearson remained sublimely unaware he was being broad-sided, sending Northcliffe a telegram of thanks for his interest and cele-brating his imminent takeover of *The Times* at a dinner at the Savoy, for which, ironically as it turned out, the chef had fashioned as the centrepiece an ice carving of *The Times*'s clock.

In the meantime, Moberly Bell, who only days earlier had declared that Northcliffe would become proprietor of *The Times* over his dead body, now entered into negotiations with him. Northcliffe's offer was terse: 'I am going to buy *The Times*. With your help, if you will give it to me. In spite of you, if you don't.' Bell's answer was equally brief: 'I will help you.' As Northcliffe's worm from within, Bell immediately began tunnelling outwards as Northcliffe's men worked inwards. While Northcliffe hol-idayed in France, far away from the fray in London, Bell convinced the Walter family that he had a more suitable buyer than the now dubious

Pearson, and for £320,000 he secured for 'Mr X' control of *The Times* on 16 March 1908.*

The deal struck, Northcliffe demonstrated his special confidence in Bell by depositing the entire amount for the sale in his name in the Bank of England in order that Bell could close the deal himself. 'A splendid fellow!' Bell exclaimed of his old enemy, thus cementing a relationship that would last for years. As one of Northcliffe's new adjutants, he now joined in the general jubilation that accompanied his triumph.

Were these the best years of Northcliffe's life, those in which he achieved every prize and accolade a man can gain? And what if he attained his every goal by the age of forty-two? His mother had a strange reaction. 'I'm sorry, Alfred,' she said. 'You have lost your horizon.' Henceforth, the only sounds Northcliffe would hear were echoes of his own pronouncements. His photographs would undergo a change. There would be no more portraits of Alfred, almost virginal in their youthful optimism. Instead, a sign of changing times, there would be snapshots, taken as if under protest, Northcliffe's face registering a tired acquiescence.

A grim look about his eyes reflected acceptance of a yoke of his own making.

---

* A full discussion of the takeover of *The Times* can be found in pp. 512–70 in the *History of The Times, Vol. III: The Twentieth Century Test 1884–1912*.

6

'Paper!'

Northcliffe needed paper, he needed prodigious amounts of it. A single issue of the *Daily Mail* required 352 miles of newsprint, fifty-five tons each day. Beyond its ability to astonish, this stark fact carried heavy significance for the newspaper business.

Northcliffe had seen his bill for paper, supplied by Scandinavia, increase to £180,000 a year – up a third from transport costs and inflation caused by the Boer War. 'What would happen to our publications', Northcliffe asked his brother Harold, knowing the answer already, 'if war broke out in Europe?'

Harold understood the gravity of the question. His brother had been haunted by the spectre of war with Germany for several years. Northcliffe was convinced the Germans intended to control the flow of raw materials to all the nations of Europe; he believed they were systematically preparing for war in order to achieve that aim. Harold, with characteristic pessimism, was not inclined to disagree. It seemed vital to the pair that they find a supply of newsprint from within Britain's Empire. What Northcliffe now proposed was for Harold to go to Newfoundland to investigate the possibility of building a paper mill there.

Newfoundland was the oldest colony in the Empire – and the poorest. It had wide tracts of virgin timberland, thickly populated by regenerative spruce, hundreds of lakes and powerful rivers that could easily be harnessed for electrical power. It also had fierce winters and long periods when its ports were impassable because of ice and snow. One of them, Placentia Bay, was held by local legend to be the place where fog was manufactured.

No one had ever dared to develop the interior of the island, although politicians were forever debating the feasibility of such a project. Meanwhile, the population huddled on the outer rim, supporting themselves as best they could by fishing and living in circumstances so desperate as to be almost unbearable. They were plagued by tuberculosis and beriberi, scurvy and rickets. From time to time, an epidemic of typhoid or diphtheria would sweep through a town, taking whole families at a stroke since hygiene and medical care were primitive and inadequate. Weakened as they were by disease and malnutrition, poorly educated and wracked by grinding poverty, the local people were considered too backward to provide a reliable work-force.

As Northcliffe requested, Harold left for Newfoundland within the week, taking with him a young man named Mayson Beeton. Beeton, the son of Mrs Beeton who wrote the well-known cookery book, had just returned from the West Indies where he had written a series of articles on the sugar industry for the *Daily Mail*. He was thought by Northcliffe to have a good grasp of economic geography.

In Newfoundland, Beeton camped out in a tent along the banks of the Exploits River, whilst Harold continued on to Canada where, after examining what seemed to him the most commercially viable propositions, he secured an option to build a mill at Three Rivers in Quebec. Between Northcliffe and Harold, there rarely passed a cross word, despite their differing natures. True, Northcliffe was expansive, emotional by nature and given to flamboyant gestures without considering the cost. Harold, on the other hand, was shy, painfully so, and prosaically practical in matters of finance. Although he always took the back seat to his more creative brother, showing familial loyalty to an endearing degree, when it came to money Harold's vision was like a spotlight showing in sharp relief what was most advantageous. Now, the usually acquiescent Harold felt compelled to make his viewpoint known, and untypically the brothers fell into an enormous row over the location of this proposed paper mill.

Beeton's report on the Exploits River had been most encouraging, and Northcliffe had set his heart on Newfoundland. He believed whole-heartedly in the Imperialist ethos of King and Country; more than that, he subscribed to the view that Britain was under a moral imperative to develop the colonies. Most irresistibly, he had succumbed to an almost irrational belief that his personal destiny was linked to developing the interior of Newfoundland. For his part, Harold saw no reason to brook such unfavourable odds as weather and work-force, arguing strongly in favour of Quebec. In this one thing, he was certain he was right. Predictably, Northcliffe swept aside Harold's objections, lost as always in his own enthusiasms.

But Harold wasn't the only one who opposed Northcliffe's plan. From Newfoundland itself came virulent attacks on the Harmsworths and their intentions, vilifying the brothers as opportunistic capitalists who planned to reap untold wealth from the willingness of Newfoundland's corrupt politicians to sell the birthright of their fellow countrymen. The original agreement, signed on 12 January 1905, provided for the ninety-nine-year renewable lease of 2,000 square miles of woodland – an area larger than Sussex, Surrey and Kent combined – with full water and mineral rights, at an annual ground rent of $2 per square mile. In exchange, the leaseholders were required to invest $1 million – $250,000 on one or more paper mills within the following four years, and a further sum of $750,000 over the next twenty.

From this basic agreement, those in the Newfoundland legislature who opposed the plan deduced that the Harmsworth brothers planned to build 'a ring fence around the interior excluding Newfoundlanders'. The local press was even more virulent: 'Surely,' charged one local newspaper,

> it is not true that the Government contemplates giving Harmsworth power to corral all the deer; also exclusive water power. The land and fullness thereof belong to Harmsworth. Henceforth, no Newfoundlander need apply...
>
> The facts are that during twenty years, one million will be spent and two thousand square miles of land are to be given away. The taxpayers have been bled to pay in hard cash millions of dollars for bungling legislators. We are plunging a large part of this country back at a single stroke to three hundred years ago ... Let us have a public meeting. Awake Countrymen and protest against these despoilers of our native land!

As public meetings go, however, this one turned out to be a flop. It soon became apparent that what the people wanted was the right to hunt and fish on the land the Harmsworths leased. As soon as this concession was made, the opposition fell away, and the hall hired to accommodate hundreds of angry Newfoundlanders was scarcely half full. As one newspaper report put it, the opposition had 'died in their tracks'. Northcliffe, kept abreast of these attacks by his local managers, made no effort to defend himself. 'Our only policy', he said, 'must be to treat them with the silent contempt they deserve.'

Two years later, on 3 June 1907, under the auspices of the newly formed Anglo-Newfoundland Development Company, called the AND-Co. for short, construction of the mill began. The plan called for three machines that could produce some 30,000 tonnes of paper each year, and completion, it was thought, would take three years. By now the AND-Co. had expanded its holdings to 3,100 square miles. Over the next five years, to the delight of the colony and Harold's growing dismay, he and his brother would sink, not $1 million but $6 million in pulp and paper operations, $4 million more than all other revenue sources of the government combined.* Northcliffe saw to it that the wages they offered were the best in

---

* The sums given are in David Macfarlane's *The Danger Tree*, p. 99.

the colony, and workers flooded in to take advantage of what promised to become the highest standard of living on the island. Northcliffe, under the auspices of the AND-Co., would develop townships, railways, mines, harbours and even a line of steamships, not to mention the originally planned pulp mill. As he jubilantly put it, 'Grand Falls is equal to all we have done put together.'

Northcliffe's men moved into formation like a military squadron, subjecting the native Newfoundlanders to a discipline they had never before experienced. Mayson Beeton was named president of the company, moving permanently to Grand Falls, while Carmelite House became 'GHQ' for the newly appointed directors of the AND-Co.

Over and above the daily attention he lavished on his newspaper operations, Northcliffe took an active role in every facet of the development of the town. Requests went out for full reports – due immediately – of any changes in the population of Grand Falls or nearby Millertown. What were the plans for farming operations? he wanted to know. And for the health needs of the settlement? (Would the chief doctor immediately file a report?) A list of goods sold at the company store, both quantities and prices, was requested. And as soon as possible, he ordered, managers were to prepare and send a full summary of the politics of the workers, their religious preferences and proposals for their secular education. Was suitable clothing available for all? Was the drinking water pure? (Send specimens for analysis.) Proper playing fields for cricket, football and baseball should be measured out and teams organized.

What were the estimated coal costs for the winter? And what plans existed for the erection of new boarding houses? Provision should be made for adequate sanitation and the installation of sewers. The city planners were instructed to dig wells and install lighting. And, most particularly, had arrangements been made to present brides with appropriate souvenirs of the company?*

Out of the blue, in January 1908, Northcliffe issued the whimsical directive to buy a herd of fifty reindeer from distant St Anthony, at $10.57 per head, and drive them to Millertown to populate his woodlands. Henceforth called 'the reindeer experiment', this showed more than anything the extent of Northcliffe's intentions. Grand Falls had taken over his imagination, becoming his little Hameau, but unlike Marie Antoinette he didn't erect the village in order to indulge his pastoral pleasures and

---

* All details of the development of the AND-Co. in Newfoundland, unless otherwise specified, come from the British Library's holdings of company records. Wherever possible, these are documented and dated.

fantasies. Behind his vigilance was a commitment of conscience, a fervent belief in the aims of Empire – his own singular version of 'the white man's burden'.

In the world that Northcliffe intended to create, all needs would be met, all treatment would be equitable and all ills would be remedied.

Thus did Northcliffe reach and overreach himself.

By 12 May 1908, 911 men were on the pay-roll of the AND-Co., and work had begun upon the building of the dam. Experienced engineers from Scotland, England, America and Scandinavia were hired, but, except for this small specialized work-force, Northcliffe declined to import his workers. He strongly supported the view that Newfoundlanders were as good 'axe-men' as anyone, including the highly regarded Norwegians and Swedes, and he committed himself and the success of his enterprise to the skills of local workmen. They came from Millertown, Placentia Bay, St John's and places less well known – a 'transient' labour-force of men who had never before held down paid employment.

The new workers, wrote Mayson Beeton to Northcliffe, were 'sadly lacking in any knowledge of the most elementary laws of health and sanitation'. They showed no understanding of the need to dispose of domestic refuse in an orderly way, nor 'any sort of cleanliness as regards the latrines'. Northcliffe's reply came by way of his immediately dispatching a sanitation expert, who recommended 'pail closets' for most dwellings and the installation of cesspools in three locations in the settlement.

'A Catechism (An Instruction to be Learned by Every Person)' was laid down, and all who came to work had to learn it by heart.* In it, workers were instructed to wash their bodies every day in cold water and open the windows of their dwellings for fresh air. The proper treatment of wounds was explained, and prohibition against spitting, important in the control of tuberculosis, went into force. 'Is it wrong to spit in the house?' the pamphlet asked. 'Yes, and on the ground outside. It is dirty and dangerous and cruel.'

Still undismayed by the overwhelming nature of the task he had under-taken, Northcliffe wrote to Beeton, 'It is obvious that the people will have to be educated on the ordinary decencies of life ... Meanwhile, when the time arrives, good pedigree cattle, poultry and farm horses should be introduced for the purpose of farming and farm work.' He reaffirmed his

---

* British Library, Add. MS 62230, vol. lxxviii. The pamphlet was written by Wilfred T. Grenfell, MD, CMG. A note pencilled into the holdings of the British Library indicates 500 were distributed in Grand Falls.

aim to run the town 'on lines which will not only ensure a profit, but will also promote the welfare and well-being of the staff and work people engaged in this large undertaking...'

A one-room schoolhouse, accommodating some hundred or so school-age children, was erected from the profits of the company store. Mr Hicks, the schoolmaster hired by the company, taught Alphabet (for beginners), Reading, Recitation, Writing, Arithmetic, English Grammar, French, Hygiene, Geometry, Algebra, Geography, Freehand and Geometrical Drawing. The children were encouraged to participate in sports, and equipment was dispatched from England for the purpose.

The town itself was divided between 'Shacktown' and the 'Village'. The former comprised some hundred temporary huts built of rough lumber and covered with tar paper; in each of them, six to ten men ate, slept and lived in the same room. This was where the transient labour-force were housed until they could return home, where their earnings would inevitably provide support for a large number of relations. In the 'Village' were some seventy wooden houses, 'laid out in blocks and forming the town proper'. Here the landmark Log House was built, a dwelling that duplicated Mark Twain's New England house where Northcliffe had been a guest. Close by, Northcliffe commissioned Grand Falls House to be built. Located about a mile above the dam and paper mill, Grand Falls House faced the Exploits River, and from its living-room visitors would one day view the logs being driven down to the mill where they would be pulped and cooked into paper for the *Daily Mail* and Northcliffe's other papers. The house, with its orchard and English garden where hollyhocks and marigolds bloomed, was a replica of a Suffolk farmhouse Northcliffe and his wife had liked. This is where he intended to stay when the day arrived for the formal opening of all that he had initiated over the past four years.

On 4 September 1908, a Trans-Atlantic Cablegram arrived at Carmelite House: 'LORD N LDN,' it began, 'GATES CLOSED AND RIVER TURNED OVER DAM THIS AFTERNOON COMPLETE SUCCESS BEETON.' This signalled the beginning of logging operations, and by the end of the month 1,456 men had been employed and 120 horses bought for winter log-driving. Beeton requested 600 more men for cutting pulpwood and sawing logs, and by January of the following year he had them. With 2,067 men employed, the settlement swung into action.

Almost immediately, a crisis arose. Reid Newfoundland Railway, the only means of transporting finished paper to Lewisport, where ships waited to carry the massive rolls to Britain, 'refused to agree to a reasonable scale of freight rates'. Northcliffe quickly undertook the construction of his own railroad line to the closer port at Botwood, and by 15 January 267 men had been employed to start work on this unanticipated task. Soon a gigantic snowplough that looked, if anything, like the prow of a mighty Viking ship was purchased to clear the railroad track owned by AND-Co.

The winter was one of the coldest on record, with temperatures of twenty degrees below zero. The Exploits River was totally frozen over, providing an opportunity for ice-skating, but little else. Smallpox had broken out in adjoining territories, and as a result the four doctors at Grand Falls vaccinated everyone in the settlement against the disease. A man fell off a boiler and broke his thigh, calling attention to the unsatisfactory nature of the employer's liability insurance purchased by AND-Co. After a lengthy and unsuccessful tangle with the insurance company, AND-Co. chose not to renew the policy, instead setting up its own fund. In future, Beeton decided, AND-Co. would handle all its own claims in order to keep employees happy. By accepting its own risk, the company could 'settle any claims promptly and thus prevent any kind of complaint'.

By now, Beeton and the newly hired company secretary, E.A. Sursham, had begun to understand just what Northcliffe expected, and regular reports began flowing into Carmelite House to satisfy his endless demands. On an early visit, Northcliffe had presented Grand Falls with an electric lantern for use in the regular Wednesday-night Amusement Club meetings. Sursham reported that a slide-show entitled, 'London', given on New Year's Eve, with two separate showings, had been a great success. The lantern, he wrote, stood up to three solid hours of use, 'giving every satisfaction'. Later in the week, the presentation of a lecture on Labrador, comprising slides shown on the lantern 'and interspersed with music', had 'proved very successful'.

Dances had been added to the entertainment agenda for Wednesday nights, and on 15 January 1909 'a well-attended concert' had been held. As Northcliffe had instructed, the meeting-hall had been fitted up with electric lights, 'thus rendering the atmosphere healthier and greatly improving general conditions'. Twenty had enrolled in the newly organized adult night school, and a lecture entitled 'Keep your mouth shut' had provided 'a pleasantly instructive evening', wrote Sursham. He was happy also to report a Grand Falls first: 'a theatrical company from the outside world has made its appearance.' To the delight of the children attending the show, one of the fourteen-member performing team was a ventriloquist, and the performers staged a wrestling match as well, not to mention a dance on roller-skates set to music. Soon to follow was a minstrel entertainment performed in black face and entitled 'Arctic Minstrels'.*

---

* British Library, Add. MS 62231, vol. lxxix. All the entertainments took place in January and February of 1909.

So, Northcliffe was given to understand, all was well in Grand Falls and proceeding according to plan. Soon construction would be at an end, and the time would arrive to put the paper mill to its test.

On 28 August 1909, fifty-four cases of sumptuous goods arrived in Grand Falls, preceding the imminent arrival of Lord and Lady Northcliffe for the grand autumnal celebration of the opening of the newly completed paper mill. Sent from Harrods in London, the boxes contained special foods and gifts costing £216 for employees of the AND-Co., honoured guests and residents of the young township that had been so recently hewn out of the rugged interior of Newfoundland.

Earlier in the month, Northcliffe had written to Mayson Beeton, instructing him to purchase in St John's 'properly printed souvenirs' with illustrations of 'the mills, local scenery, houses, hotels, Botwood, Millertown, yourself, her ladyship, myself and all the leading people'. Beeton was instructed to prepare a 'Who's Who' of every important citizen and engineer for Northcliffe to commit to memory so he would be able to congratulate each in his turn without having to ask what he had done. Also in Beeton's hands was the planning of a formal ceremony, 'a torchlight procession, I suppose,' wrote Northcliffe. 'I want this to be the great event in the modern history of Newfoundland.'

The morning of 8 October 1909 kicked off the first of two days of celebration. Colourful flags from many nations flew from the newly erected wooden buildings of Grand Falls, and the words 'WELCOME TO THE CHIEF' were spelled out overhead in electric lights.

The workmen of the township, dapper in their 'store-bought' suits, lined up to watch the procession pass. The women wore ankle-length Edwardian dresses, covered by dark, three-quarter-length coats with stout lace-up walking boots. Their children raced about in sailor suits, holding wooden toys and eating sweets.

Before the wooden buildings of the town, a sidewalk built of planks provided a thoroughfare above the dirt road. An electric light on top of a pylon, wires loosely strung across it, represented the march of progress. The stark absence of trees in the town represented the triumph of the inhabitants over the dark, encroaching forests that surrounded their settlement.

The special guests of honour, Lord and Lady Northcliffe, walked under an archway made of spruce boughs that had been suspended by ropes from the entrance to the new Finishing Mill. Inside, 427 guests of the Anglo-Newfoundland Development Company gathered for a banquet attended by fifty waiters brought in from the coastal city of St John's. The menu was sufficiently impressive to warrant being reprinted in most of the newspapers of Newfoundland.

MENU

Soup: Julienne
Fish: Boiled Fresh Salmon
Lobster Mayonnaise
Entrée: Vol-au-vent of Chicken
Joints: Roast Turkey, Oxford Sausage, Roast Beef, Horseradish,
Glazed Tongue
Vegetables: Boiled Potatoes, Green Peas
Relieve: Partridge
Sweet: Iced Pudding
Savoury: Anchovies on Toast
Dessert: Fruit, Chocolates, Nuts and Raisins, Cake
Drinks: Tea, Coffee, Aerated Waters

The Church Lads' Brigade Band and the Highlanders' Band provided music for the occasion, and the president of AND-Co., Mayson Beeton, 'proposed a toast to "The Guests" ', extolling the virtues of 'all classes and conditions of people in the country' who had helped bring the Company's great experiment to success. The Governor of the colony, Sir Ralph Williams, spoke of the advantages such industries brought to Newfoundland, and the new premier, Sir Edward Morris, spoke of the vindication of the railway across Newfoundland and his hope for agricultural development as well as other industries.

At last, Northcliffe himself rose from his table to speak, praising 'the truly British pluck and tenacity' of his 'patient shareholders' back in London. 'For as many years as I can remember,' he continued,

> this country has been regarded in Europe and America as a land of industrial misfortune. We read in our newspapers of the failure of the fishery or the failure of sealing. I remember, as a young man, gloomy reports about the Banks, and a great fire. Well, Newfoundland has had some better times in late years, and I believe that Grand Falls will help.

The banquet closed at 1.30 a.m. with the singing of the National Anthem, and the following day a similar dinner was given at lunchtime for the thousand workmen who had helped to build the mill, the houses, four stores, two hotels, staff lodgings, the Log House and Grand Falls House. At the conclusion of the meal, each man was given a plug of Beaver tobacco, before adjourning to a playing field located below the Log House where afternoon sports contests were scheduled to take place, with prizes personally carried from London by Lord and Lady Northcliffe. At 8.30 p.m., Lady Williams, the Governor's wife, pressed the levers to start the machinery. It would not be until four months later, on 22 December, that the first shipments of paper would begin to make their way to London.

So powerful was the myth Northcliffe created in Grand Falls that the children of the town called him 'the fairy godfather'. A pair of young schoolboys, who stood that day to watch the torchlight procession make its way down the central thoroughfare of Grand Falls, imagined they smelled rosewater as he passed.

At almost the same time Northcliffe and his wife were making their grand entrance into the township he had built, financial experts in London were predicting the worst. Silently, Harold listened in despair. The Exploits River, they said, had too much ice in winter, and the atmosphere of almost ceaseless fog and rain made conditions too humid for paper making. Even worse was the backwardness of the inhabitants, who were far too slow to grasp the complexity of modern machinery. A cartoon ridiculing North- cliffe had just appeared in the London press; in it, he was dressed as Robinson Crusoe astride a map of Newfoundland. The caption read: 'I am the monarch of all I survey.' But even then, the experts had missed the greatest potential threat to the long-term success of the colony, and that was Northcliffe's personal determination to change the destiny of the town's inhabitants, at whatever the cost.

Now, triumphant after the successful opening of the mill, Northcliffe wrote to Kennedy Jones, also a heavy investor in Grand Falls, that whatever criticism the project had attracted he remained confident 'that this invest- ment of ours out here is the best we could possibly make'. The mill itself, he reassured K.J., was 'perfection', and any delays in delivery were the same sort of 'teething troubles' that they had encountered so many times before in the past. To Harold, who still resented his brother's decision to override his advice, Northcliffe wrote a placatory letter, steeped in a kind of cynicism he hoped would hide how manic his actual feelings were towards the city he had built. 'The opening ceremonies were a magnificent success and did us a world of good in this very suspicious island. We are now in a position to get any concessions out of this country that we wish. The more I investigate the property, the more convinced I am that we have a magnificent investment.' A few days later, he followed up his letter with a proposal for the reconstruction of the Anglo-Newfoundland Development Company, with an investment of new capital totalling £3 million.

Above the all-too-familiar enthusiasm in his brother's message, Harold thought he heard the siren's song. 'I abhor the issue of vast amounts of capital,' he cabled back in short order. 'That way disaster lies.'

But Northcliffe, careering along a decade of phenomenal success, could scarcely grasp his brother's words. He had slipped past reason into that frenetic state that would so often precede nervous exhaustion. Soon he would be home, and sick, and worried once again about the future. Amongst his concerns, which now included nearly half the titles in Fleet Street, not to mention a host of lesser holdings and his magazines as well, Grand Falls would become a constant drain on what Northcliffe still secretly believed to be his limitless energy, and its costs would escalate beyond his furthest dreams – and Harold's worst nightmares.

The genealogy of North American Indians is particularly difficult for white men to trace, but it is thought somewhere in Matty Mitchell's background was the inter-marriage of early French explorers and trappers with the Micmac Indians of Nova Scotia. Local tradition has a name for these half-breeds – 'Jackitar' – which may or may not bear the traces of the casual racial slurs so prevalent in the history of the white man's dominance over the Native American Indian.

Matty Mitchell could not read or write. But within the ranks of Indians his family held the high position of a 'hereditary chieftancy', giving Mitchell, ever since the days of his youth, full hunting rights on all the lands on either side of the Exploits River. He therefore knew by heart every feature of the terrain that Northcliffe and Harold, through the AND-Co., were later to acquire. Immediately after the signing of the leasing agreement in January 1905, mining engineers were engaged by the Company to determine whether the land had any mineral deposits worth exploiting.

Thus it was that William Canning hired Matty Mitchell to go out prospecting for precious metals across the wide expanse of land he knew so well. The pay was $18 a month, plus food and camping equipment, and Mitchell's job was to traverse the streams and lakes and rivers, by foot or in canoe, randomly searching for any outcroppings that might denote the presence of valuable ores. Primitive as the method may seem today, it was the means used to locate many of the early mining sites in the Canadian wilderness.

Not long after he was hired, Mitchell decided to camp at Old Buchans, a site on the prospect of the Buchans River, not far from Red Indian Lake, and started the fire to boil his kettle for coffee. As the water heated, the fire melted lead beneath it, causing it to flow across the ground. When the metal cooled, Mitchell picked it up, together with other ore samples he found nearby, and carried it back for Canning to examine. Canning dispatched all the samples collected by Mitchell to London for analysis, and it turned out the Buchans River find was an unusually rich ore deposit. For this, Matty Mitchell was paid a bonus of $2.50 for the year, in those days about enough to purchase a barrel of flour.

A modest mining operation was now set up on the site, and what came to be called the Buchan River Mine was established. Engineers sank an inclined shaft, mining some of the ore stored deep beneath the surface. It turned out to be a complex ore, rich in copper, lead and zinc, with a tracing of gold as well, but after much experimentation, it was found to be impossible to separate, so the mine was reluctantly abandoned – for the moment. But then again, in 1911, AND-Co. made an attempt to find a way to separate these metals, and a sample was sent to one of the top New York engineering firms. By now, such an operation was possible but far too expensive to make the exploitation of the Buchan River Mine practicable.

The mine was located in uninhabited wilderness, the nearest settlers sixty Swedish lumbermen and their families at Millertown, located on the opposite side of Red Indian Lake. After all was said and done, it was only one of thirty-two mining locations on the south side of the lake for which the AND-Co. held Crown licences, and none of these had turned out to be of any value. The mine was shut down in 1911, and all but forgotten. Above the shaft, the spruce trees multiplied in profusion, covering over the entrance, until the only way of knowing it was there was from an ancient map fashioned by an employee of the Company, over which Mitchell had made his crude 'X' marking the spot.

Of Matty Mitchell, little more is known. Later, he became an assistant on the 'kerosene boats' that hauled booms of pulpwood down the lakes to the Exploits River. Once, he drove a team of horses over Red Indian Lake when it was frozen, a feat no one else would attempt, in order to transport supplies to hungry men in logging camps.

In his years of service to the AND-Co., Mitchell carried out only one other task of note for the Company, and a strange one at that. During the winter of 1908, remarkable even by Newfoundland standards for the cruelty of its weather, Mitchell made a harrowing 400-mile trek in January from St Anthony's to Millertown. He guided the herd of fifty reindeer with their Laplander caretakers that Northcliffe had so whimsically commissioned.

Orders for newsprint from Grand Falls would proliferate, from North and South America as well as London; and yet the Company never recovered from the extravagance of Northcliffe's dream. His 'reindeer experiment' would fail, the animals dying out in only a couple of generations. What finally saved Grand Falls, and all the workers who stood to benefit from Northcliffe's relentless commitment to their way of life, was Matty Mitchell: his Buchans River find, successfully exploited decades after its discovery, turned out to be one of the richest mineral deposits in all of North America. He died aged seventy-five, the same year as Northcliffe, the great press baron never once having heard his name.

On the night of 27 January 1910, the first of Northcliffe's newspapers to use paper manufactured in Grand Falls rolled off the presses – the 6.30 p.m. edition of the *Evening News*. Northcliffe himself was not permitted to see it since he had been sent to a nursing home by his doctor for a 'complete rest', and one of the conditions of his confinement was that he could read only the *Daily Mail* and the *Observer*. The year was destined to be a good one for Grand Falls. Five steam-driven Bagley and Sewell paper machines would set a world record for paper production, and most operations at the mill would go off without a hitch. But Northcliffe, as exhausted by his success as most men are by failure, was nevertheless hardening his attitude towards the settlement.

Part of the problem was a rising expectation on the part of the townspeople. An anonymous report, possibly filed by Northcliffe himself after one of his trips to Grand Falls, had condemned the native inhabitants for 'their deplorably filthy habits', and the report catalogued a rising tide of resentment amongst the very people he had tried to help. Having been well cared for until now, many expected the Company to do even more. One woman refused to clean her front yard unless the Company put up wallpaper in her house; another believed the Company should pay for funerals; all believed the Company should care for widows and orphans. 'In regard to the company store,' the report continued, 'no one in the Island believes that we are not making a large profit out of it.'

Though recognizing the problem was largely one of attitude and expectations, Northcliffe nevertheless irrationally placed the blame on management. Scarcely having returned home, he fired off a furious letter to Sursham, charging him with what he perceived as the failure of Grand Falls. He demanded that Sursham examine the store's pricing policy and determine whether the townsfolk were being cheated. He criticized the amusements on offer. And, with regard to a recent accident in which a man had been electrocuted, Northcliffe roundly condemned the safety measures being taken at the mill.

Sursham answered defensively, insisting, amongst other things, that safety standards had been more than adequate at the time of the man's death. But, despite that, even more stringent measures were adopted at the mill. About entertainment for the workers, he reminded Northcliffe that a salary of $1,200 a year had been allotted for the hire of a good man to run the Amusement Club, someone 'who would, without bringing in any religiosity, introduce a good tone and esprit de corps'. At the moment, cinematograph shows were being put on weekly, as well as dances – and yes, he agreed with Northcliffe the town was badly in need of a skating rink. But, he ventured to say, men working twelve hours a day 'don't always want entertaining', and as for the essentials, such as lodgings, brick houses were being built for single men currently lodging with families. As to pricing practices at the Company Store, he was in the process of determining whether items on sale could be procured at lower cost. And most bravely in the face of Northcliffe's truculence, Sursham told the Chief that he should remember Grand Falls was making the best paper on the market and their work-force enjoyed the highest standard of living on the island.

But Northcliffe's ire was up, and he turned his wrath next upon Mayson Beeton. 'I take it upon myself to enter heartily upon the watching of the enterprise,' he wrote angrily, 'because I know that if anything does go wrong, the whole blame will fall on me. I have always kept as much out of the public eye as possible, but that does not prevent the Newspapers and Public always calling it "Lord Northcliffe's Enterprise".'

Harold, sensing disaster, asked to spend a few days with his brother, in the meantime warning him against overwork. 'Business', he wrote, 'does not matter a rap when your own health is concerned.' Harold intended to hire a manager for Grand Falls, someone to deal with the problems pressing in so gravely upon his brother, and in the days the two brothers spent together he put forth the name of Vincent Jones, a man whom he had spent several hours questioning closely.

When at last Northcliffe made room in his schedule to interview Jones, in fact during his morning shave, Jones managed to antagonize him, and Northcliffe wrote to Harold saying so. 'Jones asks for a dog,' he said in a terse note to his brother. 'It is against the rules.' The Company had already been forced to turn down too many petitions for pets to allow Jones any special privileges in this regard, he said. More infuriating still was Jones's request to live in Grand Falls House, Northcliffe's own home – which struck Northcliffe as an impertinence. Jones also refused the position of foreman, instead insisting on being named the director of the paper mill. In the end, however, Northcliffe reluctantly relented. 'Do not think that I am prejudiced against Vincent Jones,' he wrote to Harold, rather gracelessly. 'I would have preferred an Englishman to any nationality. They do not steal.'

Jones's demands, had Northcliffe but known it, were inspired by a secret flame of desire, revealed in a single sentence in his letter of acceptance for the position. 'I am very keen to go,' he wrote Northcliffe, 'along with a lady I hope to take with me.' This was Mary Bagot, an eighteen-year-old, dark-haired beauty whose elevated social position was such that Jones could never have secured her hand in marriage had he not wrung from Northcliffe all the concessions he did.

Mary Bagot had grown up in the Lake District, in the stately home of Levens Hall near Kendal; Vincent Jones, son of the Rector of Ambleside and eighteen years her senior, sang in her mother's choir. Now, with the prestigious position at the Anglo-Newfoundland Development Company securely within his grasp, Jones spun a tale of privilege and comfort in the settlement of Grand Falls to convince Mary Bagot's father he should be allowed to marry his daughter. Mary, he said, should bring her saddles for riding, along with her fishing gear, and her evening clothes as well for the frequent dances and entertainments in her new home, assuring her family that the girl's life would be one of measured ease.

Vincent Jones thus carried his young bride across the Atlantic to North Sydney, Nova Scotia; from there they travelled by ferry to Port-aux-Basques, an eight-hour trip that stretched out to nineteen in the icy northern waters. From there, the couple travelled by train to St John's; and from St John's to Grand Falls – the final leg of the journey lasting what seemed a lifetime because of unscheduled stops along the line. These were caused by drivers who paused to fill their kettles for making tea and were overrun by local people who came to hear any news they might have of the outside world.

From the window of the railway car, the young and privileged girl witnessed her first terrible sight of the poverty of Newfoundland: of women wearing rags, their children dressed in sacks with string around their necks; of crippled men, born with legs but no bones in them, the result of malnutrition and neglect. Outside the parameters of Northcliffe's settlement, the people survived as best they could on potatoes and cabbage. But by March, when these had disappeared, they fell upon hard tack, salt cod and a few wild seabirds that they trapped along the coast. Seaweed, newspaper, mud and straw filled the wide gaps in their axe-hewn cabins; the large, sickly families all lived in one small room – the air within fetid and unhealthy. You came by chance into such a place, just as Vincent Jones's young bride, and so along the railway line to Grand Falls was the town of Come by Chance, then Halfway There and where it ended, That's It.

Grand Falls, for all the starkness of its raw wooden buildings, cinder roads and clouds of sulphur emanating from the paper mill, was like a centre of promise and hope. From the picture-window in Grand Falls House, Mary Vincent-Jones could watch the Northern Lights swirling in the wintertime, a sign of bad weather on its way. And on the fine nights,

> there was skating, tobogganing and sliding … the best run being over the Log House steps down to the River, and crowds could be seen on moonlit or bright nights dashing over icy ground, causing clouds of fine snow to fly behind, accompanied by their gleeful shouts and laughter. There are also evenings when a half dozen men or so gather round camp stove or on doorstep, depending on the season, and swap tales of the past. The sea is the never failing and ever-engrossing theme … By and by an accordion or fiddle or mouth organ is produced, and the evening merges into night, while their thoughts wander away back in the past, led on by some old, old ditty trolled forth by the lusty throat of a comrade.

And in the summertime, as if by way of compensation for the difficulty of the life there, the sky filled with dark-red sunsets that covered the entire sky, called 'Raspberry Fool' by the local people. Mary Vincent-Jones was all alone in such a place, with no one from her class or station to keep her company. What could she have thought of this new life she had elected? And how could she adapt?

When Northcliffe next arrived, accompanied by his wife, personally to inspect the work of Vincent Jones, he and Lady Northcliffe were surprised to find this lovely young English girl inviting them to tea. They spoke of England, which she dearly missed, and Mary Vincent-Jones told Lord and Lady Northcliffe how different she found the landscape of Newfoundland and how she missed the topiary gardens back at Levens Hall. And with customary civility Northcliffe asked if he could send her anything from home. From this display of kindness, and without warning even to herself, the young girl suddenly burst into tears, telling Lord and Lady Northcliffe she was so lonely she didn't know what to do or how she could continue to live, and could he send newspapers please? She lived in a town, she said, that manufactured paper for newspapers, and yet there was none for her to read, and so she felt excluded from the outside world. Vincent Jones, alarmed by his wife's unexpected outburst, said, 'You really don't need any newspapers.' But she insisted, yes, she did!

Thereafter, Northcliffe made arrangements for every newspaper he produced to be sent personally to Mary Vincent-Jones, and in return she wrote her own accounts of what was happening in Grand Falls, at last meeting his insatiable need to know what life there was really like.

'We have, I think, begun our winter here,' she wrote to him in November 1910.*

> it has snowed alot this week, but it did not freeze so is very filthy and wet, though it is a good thing so far as the logs are concerned, which are, as I expect you know, a bit behind, owing to these huge floods, which are at last stopping. I wish you could have seen the falls there is no word to discribe how magnificent they looked, with 5 feet of water going over the dam.
>
> Yesterday the governor made a raid; he is going to Millertown to see a camp there, so stopped the night at the siding by the log house and goes on today. Dr. Price gave a dinner for him at the log house and Vin & I went: He is indeed a terrible man ... vulgar and swaggering, he ate and drank everything he got a hold off [here Mary Jones strikes out her second 'f'] ... & talked of himself & how sought after he is as a governor: his poor A.D.C.'s sat silently exchanging hot glances, as he swaggered more and more...

She wrote of the farmers in the settlement and how they looked forward to the planting season, 'full of keenness and hope ... I hope all this does not bore you.' And now the heifers had arrived. One of the farmers had sent for the girl he was going to marry, and 'We are going to have a great wedding feast here. Vin is going to give her away!' Within only a day of receiving this letter, Northcliffe cabled Mary Vincent-Jones, with many thanks 'for your good letter'. Somehow, in Mary's ingenuous and heart-felt enthusiasm, he saw himself at the age of nineteen to twenty-four, and sent a letter to her husband saying that he knew 'very much of what you two people are going through'. But even with all the difficulties the young couple were facing, he wrote, he still believed 'the Grand Falls scheme is the best opportunity I know for any young man in England.'

Between the young Mary Vincent-Jones and the imposing press baron, there developed a singular relationship, one of life's strange under-standings between two people separate but alike, that others couldn't hope to comprehend. When parcelling out the silver plaques and souvenirs of thanks, tokens of regard for those who helped him build his city, Northcliffe omitted Mary Vincent-Jones.

Instead, one day in spring, a ship arrived, then another and another, each loaded with rich soil from Devon, and finally a gardener Northcliffe

---

* Mary Vincent-Jones's letters are reproduced as she wrote them, retaining her several errors without the usual scholarly indication of [sic].

had sent to help her plant her English gardens in Newfoundland.

With the distant support that Northcliffe lent then, Mary Vincent-Jones found her way and adapted to this rough new land. She sent him a fuzzy photograph taken by 'Vin' of newborn lambs,

> which are the farmer's pride, for they came 2 months too early, in the bitterest cold, and they are surprisingly well, especially the youngest one which is much the largest. They are perfectly sweet little things & bound around in spite of being indoors all the time...
>
> We have been very happy here and would'nt like to be failures – this life is so interesting to both of us...
>
> Every single person here can either give this place a help on, or throw it back & in ready made places one does not generally see results so clearly, nor do individual efforts count so much – Much love, Mary.

When the typhoid epidemic came to Grand Falls late in 1910, Mary Vincent-Jones pitched in alongside the nurse, Miss Gilmour, and two young doctors. She had already had the disease when she was fourteen, and so helped to nurse the many patients in the hospital that Lady Northcliffe had donated to the city.

Thus did Mary Vincent-Jones grow into her own person, increasingly tough and distant, a surprisingly strong-willed and solitary figure in the town. Later, she would travel to outposts outside Northcliffe's territory, seeing as she could to the needs of those whose lives he hadn't touched. There is a story told of her in her later years, caring for a woman sick with typhoid who had eight children. When she saw the family were wrapped in newspapers to keep warm, Mary Vincent-Jones took off her own clothes, and ordered her young daughter to do the same, and gave them to the woman.

She never knew that Northcliffe's mother had once wrapped her children in newspapers to keep them warm in wintertime.

7

'Those Magnificent Men in Their Flying Machines'

Between those who wished him ill and those who wished him well, Northcliffe never had a chance. His astounding rise from the lower echelons of society was unimaginable to those whose lives were privileged from the start. Harold knew, his mother knew; the rest of the family could just about imagine. His genius made him rich and powerful, and all the world believed that there but for the malice of God went they.

Each saw a single facet of Northcliffe's personality and believed they understood the man. Madman, demagogue, manipulator of the common weal – his enemies despised him, and why? For those in power, he was like a shark in water, cruising, watching for the chance to savage their ambitions. Most unpleasant of all was the accuracy of his presentiments and the damnable ethics he applied. He loved his country; he understood the common man. His integrity was, literally, above reproach. Beneath these troublesome attributes lay the certain knowledge he usually did know better than the bumblers in government and elsewhere what should next be done; and this enraged them. They sought to neutralize this force and searched for weaknesses to exploit.

Those who worshipped at the font were more dangerous still. Northcliffe saw reflected in their eyes a sort of Godhead, and, on bad days, tended to believe it himself. 'A man as powerful as I am', he once mused, 'shouldn't lose his temper.' Right, as usual, but difficult to enforce. Despite the fantasies of friend and foe alike, the man was only human.

The source of his power was stamina, drive, a singular neurosis that both impelled and consumed him, like the flame that eats the wood. A personality like Northcliffe's had constantly to be guided and from a trusted and benign source – he couldn't manage it himself; thus the deep attachment to his mother. It was just as well. Both his wife and his mistress, like his admirers and detractors, were in it for themselves. What could he do for them? 'He gave me *everything*,' his wife said, and then pursued her own delights. So it was with others who attracted his largesse.

Northcliffe overworked.

He drove himself relentlessly and inevitably to complete collapse. From there to self-pity was only a short jump. He felt equally sorry for himself over a slight toothache or a serious bout of influenza. His holidays, he wailed, were spoilt by crises:

> my best attempt was spoiled by *Times* friction ... just as by Amalgamated Press friction. Before that it was Beeton and Newfoundland and so on and so on and so on *indefinitely*. The business is a Frankenstein. *It gives me no peace whatever.**

His mind wandered, his nerves were frayed, he couldn't sleep. Now and again, he gave in to crazy and childish temper tantrums, 'brainstorms' the staff called them euphemistically. In one of them, he forced a man to kneel to him as a peer of the realm. How was it done? Lower still and lower still and lower still, the story goes. 'You see,' he said to a horrified companion, 'I can make them do whatever I like.' In another of his fits, he spied a messenger boy going into the editor's office with his cap on and, in front of the entire staff, angrily snatched it from his head – only to find the boy was bald from a skin infection.† A lesser man would have suffered the censure of his peers and thus found some salvation.

Northcliffe worried about his eyesight – and it became generally known. He worried about ptomaine poisoning – and it became generally known. He jumped in one of the *Evening Standard* vans and caught a ride to the railway station, from thence to travel to Sutton Place, his opulent Tudor home in Guildford, Surrey – and even his brother Harold worried that he had lost his mind. Here at last, his enemies sensed, was an Achilles' heel that could be exploited. The rumour-mill obligingly ground out the heresy that Northcliffe had suffered a complete nervous breakdown. And, whether or not that was true, his judgment did at times seem seriously impaired.

There was, as a case in point, the disastrous Lever libel suit, orchestrated by the Chief himself, with no one else to blame. It began on 18 October 1906, with a letter from the *Daily Mail* to William Lever, MP, the well-known soap manufacturer of Lever Brothers, whose products Lux and Vim were known throughout the land. In it, Lever was promised that a new *Daily Mail* campaign, aimed at halting a combination of soap manufacturers organized by Lever and known as the Soap Trust, would be conducted with 'the strictest impartiality'. From this point on, Northcliffe,

---

* The quote in full: 'my best attempt at a holiday was spoiled by *Times* friction (of which you did not hear) just as by Amalgamated Press friction. Before that it was Beeton and Newfoundland and so on and so on and so on *indefinitely*,' etc. (Northcliffe's italics). Paul Ferris, *The House of Northcliffe: The Harmsworths of Fleet Street*, p. 179.

† Later that afternoon, Northcliffe sent the boy an apology, 'I'm sorry I insulted you,' with two half crowns. Reginald Pound and Geoffrey Harmsworth, *Northcliffe*, pp. 341–2.

perhaps inspired by Theodore Roosevelt's energetic 'trust-busting', proceeded with vehemence approaching spite to bring an end to the Trust, in the process costing Lever some sixty per cent of their business. His instincts were right in that monopolistic practices and price-fixing inevitably have a disastrous effect on the market-place; it was his methods that were specious.

At the heart of the case was a story written by Edgar Wallace, the same reporter whose scoop during the recent war about the shooting of sick British prisoners-of-war by the Boers had caused such a public outcry. In this case, though, Northcliffe personally instructed Wallace to write a story that portrayed the hardships of the poor resulting from Lever's decision to reduce the size of a one-pound tablet of Sunlight Soap. Unable to justify a rise to the next possible fraction, Lever had kept the price at threepence, reducing the size from sixteen to fifteen ounces.

'How Fifteen Ounces Make a Pound,' cried the *Mail*; 'Squeezing the Public' blared another headline; 'Trust Soap Already Dearer', said still another.

But the story at the heart of the case was the one written by Wallace at Northcliffe's behest under the heading 'Cruel Blow to the Poor'. It told of a poor widow who supported her children by taking in washing. Lever's reduction in the size of a washing tablet, the story said, made the difference between buttered or dry bread for her family. This sad tale was the turning-point for Lever. He was forced to restore the sixteen-ounce tablet to the shelves, and the Soap Trust he had attempted to organize was disbanded. In desperation, Lever turned to the flamboyant F.E. Smith, a brilliant young lawyer recently elected Member of Parliament for the Walton division of Liverpool. Legend has it that Smith took the papers in the case and sat up all night poring over them, in the process consuming two-dozen oysters and an unspecified number of bottles of champagne. Over breakfast Lever got his answer: 'There is no answer to this action for libel and the damages must be enormous.'

By the following summer, when the case came to court, Northcliffe himself did what any upright, God-fearing capitalist would have done in his place. He fled the country. As he left, he dashed off a note warning that Kennedy Jones should follow suit:

I urge K.J. to stop soap on score that I cannot carry increasing burden of work, unless free from all complications. Told him none of us can be cross-examined on motives of soap cases and if I am examined should be obliged to tell truth and that therefore Sir G. L. [Sir George Lewis, solicitor] had from outset decided that I could not be put into box. Nor could, in my view, he [K.J.].

Edgar Wallace was dispatched to Narbonne to cover wine riots just as Lever's leading counsel, the esteemed barrister Sir Edward Carson, moved in for the kill. Carson read out the story in the court, allowing as to how the poor widow-woman of the tale 'lost 1s. 6d. a week through the increase in the price of soap'. This, said Sir Edward, put her use of soap at ninety-six tablets per week; that is, ninety-six pounds. He rested his case.

The damages, including costs and payments to Lever Brothers and the smaller manufacturers involved, came to £151,000 – if not a ruinous sum, sufficient to heap humiliation upon Northcliffe's head. Whatever his reputation, he was not infallible, and especially in his choice of lawyers. Later, over drinks, Northcliffe confronted Sir Edward Carson. 'You're the biggest enemy I ever had,' said the press baron.

Said Carson, 'Why didn't you employ me, then? I dare say you'd have won.'

Northcliffe had become acquainted with Sir Edward, and indeed the fabulous 'F.E.' himself, through Winston Churchill. This was despite, as he wrote to the young politician, some feeling of reluctance since both barristers had acted against the *Mail* on behalf of 'a number of dealers in a commodity of which I have heard enough in the last twelve months'.

But Churchill had wanted the press baron to meet Smith in particular, and Northcliffe was inclined to grant Churchill's requests. A special and secret relationship had grown up between the two men. For Northcliffe, at least, the bond was of genuine substance, one in which the older man, for reasons difficult to fathom, acted to further the career of the younger. From the outside, the pair appeared to be little more than superficial acquaintances who met amicably for dinner from time to time; from the inside, Northcliffe's commitment was nothing less than parental.

In the same way that he had assisted his personal secretary Evelyn Wrench, Northcliffe made available to Churchill every means at his disposal. As early as 1899, he instructed the *Daily Mail* to support Churchill when he made his first and unsuccessful bid to serve in Parliament.

Then, at the start of the Boer War, Northcliffe offered Churchill a plum job as war correspondent. With this offer firmly in hand, Churchill hastened to the offices of Oliver Borthwick of the *Morning Post*, where he used the *Mail* offer to get an even better deal – an unprecedented £250 per month for each of his first four months and £200 per month afterwards, plus expenses and copyright. By the following year, he and Northcliffe were again exchanging cordial regards and arranging to meet one another abroad, unbeknownst to society at large.

Churchill's early letters to Northcliffe were flattering, perhaps even servile; he was quick to thank Northcliffe for his help, taking him into his confidence on political intrigues and asking his advice on how to effect the changes he sought. And in April 1904, when Churchill, debating the Trade Union and Trade Disputes Bill in Parliament, forgot his text and, humiliated, sat down with his face in his hands, lamely thanking everyone for listening to him, Northcliffe had been one of those who stood by the young politician, urging him to put the incident behind him and carry on.

Later, Churchill felt sufficiently secure in Northcliffe's good offices to write, 'I wish we had a Manchester paper!', the 'we' signifying how far the alliance between himself and the press baron had come. As if by magic, the Manchester *Courier* was procured, according to one version, in order to secure Balfour's seat and thus Northcliffe's peerage. Or was buying the paper a covert attempt on Northcliffe's part to help Churchill in his political ambitions? Perhaps it was a single stone intended to elect two birds. By now, Churchill had crossed the floor of the Commons, joining up with the Liberals. It was certainly not too complex a situation for Northcliffe to support two opposing parties; quite the opposite, he liked to keep people guessing.

Whatever the case, there seemed no end in sight to the favourable press the young Churchill was able to extract from Northcliffe's newspapers. The pair became chummy and met regularly in the mornings to go for walks together. In November 1905, Churchill practically instructed Northcliffe to puff his biography of his father, *Lord Randolph Churchill*. And by January of the following year, when Churchill stood for the North-West division of Manchester, the veteran reporter Charles Hands, the same who had been wounded in South Africa during the Boer War, was sent to cover the election. Despite his Conservative bias, Hands gave Churchill a terrific boost. '*Winston*', one of his stories was headlined, 'More Interesting than Free Trade; Manchester Fascinated; His Ju-Jitsu; He Sets a Fashion in Hats'. The story contended,

There is no question about it; the public interest of Manchester in the General Election is centred and focused on the personality of Mr. Winston Churchill. You can hardly see the rest of the political landscape for this dominant figure. You hear more talk in Manchester of 'Winston' than of Free Trade ... He appeals to their sporting sense. 'It isn't so much his politics, it's his Ju-Jitsu that I like,' said a citizen today...

They discuss his various attributes; his mammoth posters with 'Winston Churchill' in letters five feet high, his alliterative habit, his looks, his clothes. He is wearing a new old-fashioned hat, a flat-topped sort of felt hat, and already the hatters are having inquiries for articles of that pattern.

For his part, Churchill referred to Charles Hands as 'a gallant little man', whom he invited to join in his celebration supper at the Midland Hotel. What did the reporter think of Churchill's victory? he couldn't help asking Hands. 'It is', Hands replied, 'a grand slam in doubled no trumps.'

Thus was Churchill intoxicated by the support of the great press baron.

It wasn't very long, however, before Churchill found it politically expedient to turn on his benefactor. The *Daily Mail* reported that the premier of Newfoundland, attending a conference of the Premiers of the Colonies of the British Empire, had become angry at what he interpreted as his colony's neglect and stormed out in protest. The premier himself denied the event even took place, and Churchill, now working in the Colonial Office, chimed in in his defence. He expressed surprise that 'a person lately created a Peer should allow newspapers under his control to employ methods of such transparent mendacity for political ends'. And later on, at an Edinburgh meeting held on 18 May 1907, he said, 'A mischief-making Press, eavesdropping, misrepresenting, dealing in word-pictures and dissolving views, tale-bearing, not shrinking from wilful and persistent falsehood, have done their best to sow ill-feeling between the Mother Country and the Colonies, to make ill-feeling between Colonial representatives and Ministers of the Crown.' It was nothing short of 'machine-made, linotype calumny'.

Northcliffe accepted all this with equanimity. But when in 1908 Churchill sued the Manchester *Courier*, the very newspaper he had encouraged Northcliffe to buy, for libel for saying he had broken his parole while a prisoner of the Boers, Northcliffe balked. 'I was amazed to hear', Northcliffe wrote to Churchill on 11 May, 'that you considered our criticisms a personal matter.'

> There was a well understood agreement between us that we should use our stage thunder in the furtherance of our mutual interests.
>
> You have criticized me very hotly in and out of Parliament and I have never felt the least bit about it...
>
> As we have got to live together more or less in public life in more ways than you know, for, I hope, a great many years, I propose that we take a walk in St. James's Park some morning this week and thrash the matter out.

But two days later Northcliffe was in a darker, more threatening mood. Any endeavour to connect him with 'something over which I have no control ...,' he wrote, 'would be an act of grave injustice, and I shall personally consider it an act of hostility'. If Churchill thought Northcliffe was against him, he should think again. Quite the opposite was true. Northcliffe invited Churchill to investigate his intentions for himself by surveying their mutual friends, but warned him to pay no attention to a particular busybody who had tried to come between them. Meanwhile, Northcliffe said, when Churchill finally managed to 'get the annoyances of electioneering out of his brain', he would find that his irritation would come to an end.

By the next day's post, Churchill had promised to leave Northcliffe's name out of any proceedings that might arise. He went on to say that he hoped his friendship with Northcliffe would be 'all the better for this misunderstanding'. But Northcliffe's response was terse: 'I do not propose to discuss the Manchester *Courier* matter further,' he answered, and communication between the two men ceased.

Some six weeks later, the matter was settled, Churchill writing to inform Northcliffe how glad he was to have the incident – which he called 'an embarrassment and a nuisance' – behind him. Now the pair could resume their 'exercise or nourishment together'.

On the same day, Northcliffe eagerly replied, saying he too was 'delighted to think that the only cause of friction between us has been cleared away'.

> My feelings towards you have always been of admiration and esteem, and I shall look forward to a long, if somewhat critical friendship.
> I will call one morning next week on the chance of finding you ready for a walk about 11 o'clock.

The next month, after receiving a walking-stick from Northcliffe as 'a token of peace and amity', Churchill felt free once more to request newspaper coverage from his old friend. Northcliffe, he wrote baldly, was to tell his 'old paper' to continue reporting Churchill 'verbatim'.

> I have not many public engagements, and if I knew *beforehand* that I was going to be decently reported, I would take pains to produce something worth printing. But what always seems to happen is that when I have something important to say no one takes any notice of it, and when I deliver an ordinary party impromptu it is reported in the first person. The uncertainty about reporting prevents politicians from taking trouble about speeches. In consequence they deliver perfectly idiotic speeches and the newspapers are still further choked reporting them. You tell your 'old paper' to report me *verbatim*, at Dundee, at Manchester, and at Newcastle – that is, three times in the next six months: and I will see that they get good copy from any point of view.

The 'young paper', Churchill went on to say rather grandly, was taking a satisfactory interest in his plans to get married.

Northcliffe was not at all annoyed by Churchill's presumption; in fact, by the next spring, he wrote to inform Churchill he had missed a trick. He had noticed in that morning's press that Churchill had submitted a letter to all the London newspapers. He advised him in future to confine any serious missive to *The Times* alone as that paper was more likely to feature it in large print and in a prominent place than if it were submitted to the newspaper's competitors. This encouraged Churchill to press still further; he informed Northcliffe he was planning to make a speech in Manchester, and in order to facilitate *The Times* he had scheduled it for a Saturday. 'A telegraphed report will not be necessary,' Churchill wrote blithely, 'as the reporters can travel back on Saturday evening in plenty of time for Monday's papers.'

By now, as the head of the Board of Trade, Churchill's demands were becoming more and more insistent. He complained of any criticism his remarks received in Northcliffe's papers, and it was clear the *Mail*'s treatment suited him better than *The Times*'s. With regards to an unfavourable leader in *The Times* about Churchill's stand on Daylight Savings Time, he reminded Northcliffe that an entire paragraph of 'gratuitously offensive remarks' had been devoted to criticizing him on the basis of one sentence. And, moreover, his views on the subject were the same as Northcliffe's himself! 'I do not believe there is another newspaper in the country which would have behaved in such a way,' he complained.

Northcliffe's usual ploy for such peevishness was to deflect Churchill's anger with a humorous remark. On one occasion when they failed to cover Churchill for a speech, Northcliffe wrote, by way of consolation, 'My own papers were much too busy reporting my own speeches to take notice of mere Cabinet Ministers.' At last, though, Northcliffe had had enough. The fact was, he told Churchill, that 'outside speeches during the parliamentary session' were impossible to report: 'With the best will in the world, the newspapers are unable to do it.' And he reminded Churchill that there was 'a great pressure of foreign and other news, as you may notice'.

But this line did no good at all; Churchill remained insatiable. He asked whether Northcliffe planned to cover a rally he was to address in a week's time, because 'otherwise I shall spare myself the labour of making a new speech ... When I cannot be fully reported,' he whinged, 'I would prefer not to be reported at all.'

Northcliffe accepted this in good part. Like a typical father, he continued to give. And, like a typical son, Churchill continued to take. But willing as Northcliffe was to help Churchill, wishing him 'all joy in politics and knavish tricks', he managed nevertheless to remain aloof from Churchill's political machinations. When in 1911 Churchill and F.E. Smith formed The Other Club – dedicated 'to fierce political argument across party lines' – one of Churchill's first acts was to invite Northcliffe to join. But the wary press baron preferred to remain independent. Long ago, he told Churchill, he had concluded that a man who owned newspapers had no business belonging to any clubs whatsoever, and with this in mind he had resigned from every club he belonged to.

What he failed to mention was his determination to keep out of government as well. To become a member of the ruling classes, either socially or politically, would ruin his role as gadfly, and he had begun to understand that. And inwardly he still nursed a natural aversion towards politicians, remembering how his own early experience trying to become a Member of Parliament had been like wading through 'a sea of filth'.

What these choices and inclinations betokened was a growing estrangement from the community outside Northcliffe's self-made world of newspapers. As the years passed, Northcliffe would seem more and more alone. His cordial relations with Churchill, his willing support of Churchill's schemes and ambitions, would diminish. He would go only so far. With Churchill as with most of those on the outside, the day would come when he would have to gun for them. And, although he gave little indication this was the case, there can be no doubt Northcliffe knew it.

Meanwhile, Northcliffe continued to campaign for progress, pushing aside satirical broadsides and likewise any sign of obstructionism. An early *Daily Mail* crusade called for a telephone to be installed in every police station in London. No! cried the Police Commissioner, the stations might then be plagued by unnecessary calls.

Then again, Northcliffe was proved right with regard to a proposed London tramway system. The London Traffic Commission recommended to the London County Council the installation of the costly system of electric traction, heralded to ratepayers as a potential profit-maker. The *Daily Mail* objected, predicting deficits and pointing to the coming omnibus. On both counts, the *Mail*'s prediction came true.

But most important of all was the need to modernize the fire-fighting equipment of the Fire Brigade, a measure stiffly resisted by obstructionist thinking on the part of local officials. Northcliffe called for 'motorized engines, hook ladders, long extension ladders and other desirable equipment', but his advice was totally ignored until the needless deaths of eight young girls in a horrific fire in Queen Victoria Street. Even after that, the practical uses to which the new advances in technology were applied remained limited and unimaginative – despite Northcliffe's constant hectoring.

His fixation with 'gadgetry' was thought by those in power to be frivolous, and in the early days of the motor car Northcliffe had indeed had his fun. Before the turn of the century, a poet had dedicated a series of poems about the motor car to the young press baron, 'Song of Speed'.* Then in February 1904, the *Mail* published a jovial set of poems by Rudyard Kipling about this strange new method of travel. These were clever parodies that imitated the style of various famous poets: 'The Advertisement', written in Anglo-Saxon; 'To a Lady Persuading Her to a Car', after Ben Jonson; 'The Progress of a Spark', after John Donne.

'The Idiot Boy', after William Wordsworth, set the tone of the send-up:

He wandered down the mounting grade
Beyond the speed assigned—
A youth whom justice often stayed
And generally fined.

He went alone, and none might know
If he could drive or steer:
Now he is in the ditch, and Oh!
The differential gear.

Aside from this bit of fun, however, Northcliffe had been involved early on in a serious accident, a sinister foreshadowing of the one that left his brother St John in a wheelchair, causing the Chief to call for safety measures and regulation of the roads. But, despite his own near miss and later his brother's accident, he accepted the risks of progress, understanding rightly the importance of the automobile's convenience and speed.

It was only a short jump from the motor car to 'the motor car of the air', or 'aerial motor car', as the *Daily Mail* was wont to call the strange new contraption that, despite being heavier than air, was able to climb into the skies and proceed at heretofore unimaginable speeds. At first, Northcliffe believed the airship little more than an extension of the motor car, but in only a short time the *Daily Mail* was predicting that the skyways surrounding London and other capitals of the world would be 'darkened by the flight of aeroplanes', and there would come a time 'when aerial power will be an even more important thing than sea power'.

* The poet was W.E. Henley, and the poem turned out to be the last he wrote before his death. Reginald Pound and Geoffrey Harmsworth, *Northcliffe*, p. 225.

Northcliffe's serious interest had begun on 19 December 1903, when a short newsclip under the title 'Balloonless Airship' appeared in the pages of the *Daily Mail*:

Messrs. Wilbur and Orville Wright, of Ohio, yesterday successfully experimented with a flying machine at Kittyhawk, North Carolina. The machine has no balloon attachment, and derives its force from propellers worked by a small engine. In the face of a wind blowing twenty-one miles an hour the machine flew three miles at the rate of eight miles an hour, and descended at a point selected in advance. The idea of the box-kite was used in the construction of the airship.

Unrecognized by *Mail* staff for what it was, the story appeared 'down page', as it then was called, and two days late, but it nevertheless heralded, as no other story has, the coming of the modern age.

By the autumn of 1906 when, in the first recorded European air flight, Alberto Santos-Dumont flew two hundred yards in twenty-one seconds, Northcliffe was yelling down the telephone at Walter Fish. The usually astute news editor had buried the story because of the short amount of time Santos-Dumont had been in the air. 'A man with a heavier-than-air machine has flown,' said an exasperated Northcliffe:

It does not matter how far he has flown. He has shown what can be done. In a year's time, mark my words, that fellow will be flying over here from France. Britain is no longer an island. Nothing so important has happened for a very long time. We must get hold of this thing, and make it our own. I will think out what is best to be done.*

It is questionable whether anyone in the newspaper business has ever succeeded so thoroughly in making a thing his own as Northcliffe did the conquest of the air.

He soon announced a £1,000 prize for the first airman to cross the English Channel from Calais to Dover, and, in what seemed a genuine flight of fancy, a £10,000 prize for the first completed flight from London to Manchester. The satirical magazine *Punch* immediately offered three of its own prizes: £10,000 for a flight to Mars and back in a week, the same again for a trip to the centre of the earth in a fortnight, and again, for a swim across the Atlantic before the end of the year. In the event, Northcliffe was to give both of his prizes within five years; *Punch* was still waiting to present its own when it went out of business in 1992.

But Northcliffe was far from satisfied simply to put out a little seed

---

* Bernard Falk, *He Laughed in Fleet Street*, p. 290; see also Reginald Pound and Geoffrey Harmsworth, *Northcliffe*, pp. 300–1.

money. The subject of air travel became an obsession of the *Daily Mail* and, in turn, of the public, who demanded more and more news of it. Rolls of Rolls-Royce was interviewed on the topic, and the twenty-four-mile circular flight of the American air adventurers, the Wright brothers, that ended only because they ran out of petrol, became the focus for a time. Northcliffe set them up as rivals to Santos-Dumont, thus giving the story a dramatic element. The public went wild.

These phenomenal experiments in the air, the *Mail* editorialized,

> have startled the world, and have brought mankind face to face with new and remarkable possibilities – the aeroplane – the name generally given to a flying machine heavier than the air and rising by the force of the wind or air pressure generated by rapid movements. It is a feat so novel as to constitute a starting point in aeronautics and enable us to affirm that the aeroplane has now reached its practical stage.

Soon, the *Mail* speculated, 'aerial motor cars' would become 'the playthings of the rich', and the very roads themselves were destined to disappear 'when it is possible to voyage through space'.

As to the Wright brothers, secretive to the point of paranoia owing to the sustained indifference of the United States Government and their constant fear of industrial espionage, they refused to compete for Northcliffe's prizes – although had they done so, they surely would have won. It was only after they finally secured their contracts in Europe, and the United States Army had at last come round, that they would even speak to the press. Then, of course, it was the *Daily Mail* that got the first interview. In it, Richard Wright described the sensation of flying as 'infinitely more exhilarating than motoring, easier and smoother with a movement of added dimensions'. President Theodore Roosevelt said that the prizes offered by the *Mail* had helped the cause of aviation by focusing public attention on the practical uses of aerodynamics.

The following year, in 1907, Wilbur and Orville Wright were the private guests of Northcliffe at Pau, where they performed their experiments for a select viewing audience, including Edward VII. Kennedy Jones also attended, along with a few other trusted employees from Associated Newspapers. Wilbur Wright was flying, and his sister, keenly aware of the King's presence, instructed him, 'Of course, Wilbur, you must wear gloves.'* By 1909, another visit by the famous brothers was more generally attended,

---

* The datings of a number of news cuttings, plus those documented in Fyfe, indicate that a visit to Pau by the Wright brothers took place in 1907; and another in 1909, this one with local residents present. Hamilton Fyfe, *Northcliffe: An Intimate Biography*, p. 146; and Reginald Pound and Geoffrey Harmsworth, *Northcliffe*, p. 352.

with A.J. Balfour as one of Northcliffe's guests, as well as Evelyn Wrench, who made note of the event in his diary:

> After lunch we motored down to the Champs D'Aviation and drove up to Wilbur Wright's shed. The whole thing is so wonderful that words are useless. We watched Wilbur carefully test every nut, wire and bolt. He usually spends half an hour testing everything himself before going up. When he was ready his pupil took his seat alongside him. He soars up with absolute ease and certainly the air has no longer any mystery as far as he is concerned. For twenty-two minutes they flew round and across the flying ground. The aeroplane looks wonderfully graceful in the air and especially so with the snow-covered Pyrenees in the background.

A crowd of local people had assembled, and the general tone of the group was one of scepticism. They began jeering when Wilbur started his countdown. To his one, they sang out, *'un'*; two, *'deux'*; three, *'trois'*; and then, to their total amazement, he ascended into the air. Their jeering turned into frenzied cheering as his aircraft flew 'into the middle distance'.

Northcliffe was jubilant. But he was also furious. As early as 1903, he had been discussing with his more astute correspondents the uses to which airships were likely to be put. W.F. Bullock, the *Mail*'s New York correspondent, had been privileged to observe one of the Wright brothers' earliest flights and had cabled Northcliffe: 'AEROPLANE PRIMARILY INTENDED WAR MACHINE STOP . . . SHOULD HAVE NO DIFFICULTY DROPPING BOMB GREATEST NICETY ON ANY OBJECT ATTACK STOP.'

Now, with that condescension of manner designed to *infuriate* government officials, Northcliffe shot off a letter to Richard Haldane, Secretary of State for War:

> I wonder if I may bore you on the subject of aeroplanes? I notice that the Germans and French have military representatives here, watching the Wrights' machine, which Mr. Balfour came to see. As I am constantly being chaffed by these foreign gentlemen with regard to the British army aeroplane, which they have nicknamed 'the steamroller', it occurs to me that, if it is worth the while of France and Germany to be on the spot, one of your young men might be sent down here to find out why it is that this aeroplane gets off the ground, and can fly for ten minutes or ten hours, if it chooses, and your Aldershot aeroplane, which is a very bad copy of the very bad French aeroplanes, is unable to leave the ground . . . Pray pardon this effusion.

He sent a second letter to Lord Esher, the courtier and public servant, speaking of Britain's 'national muddleheadedness'. He spoke of what an efficient bomber the aeroplane would make, being almost 'unhittable' from the ground, and its practical application as a means of scouting enemy positions. His anger was clearly evident. From the eminent politeness of the replies to his letters from War Office officials, it was easy to detect how very much they must have hated Northcliffe!

The position Northcliffe found himself in was nothing short of wondrous. He had full knowledge of obstructionists and blunderers, the intelligence to assess them, the literary style to belittle them and the means of exposing them – and all of this in a country whose government officials expected, above all, allegiance and discretion on the basis of social class alone, a distinction Northcliffe could afford to discard since he had come up the hard way, through his own efforts, owing nothing to privilege.

In his kennel, Northcliffe kept a variety of dogs, and once he started a thing it was well-nigh impossible to persuade him to call them off. He had got a hold on this phenomenon of air travel, and he wasn't about to let go. He immediately sent a strange letter to a subordinate, about trees, in which he enquired as to whether Brooklands had any – as 'aeroplanists' did not like them. He was planning in his mind an event that would take place some two and a half years later, but for now he kept his ideas to himself.

Meanwhile, a bare six months later, a few moments after the ungodly hour of 4.30, on a cloudy morning near Calais, a dapper little Frenchman with a limp pushed his monoplane from the shed where he was storing it and asked his friend, 'Où est Douvres?' 'C'est là-bas,' his friend answered, with a languid flip of the wrist in the general direction of England. Twenty-five minutes later, Louis Blériot became the first man to cross the English Channel by air. Such an event, Northcliffe decided instantly, called for a celebration, and within twenty-four hours two hundred guests, including aristocrats, government officials, businessmen, newsmen and, of course, advertisers – or in Northcliffe's words, 'all the important people in the country' – were assembling at the Savoy for a luncheon in Blériot's honour.

By June 1910, when Louis Paulhan, another French aviator, won the £10,000 prize for the once ridiculed flight from London to Manchester, Northcliffe was ready. The *Daily Mail* at once announced a second £10,000 prize for the first flyer to complete a 1,010-mile course set for June the following year. On the same day this announcement was being published, the youngest correspondent on the *Mail*'s staff, G. Ward Price, was getting one of the most impressive scoops of the year, also about air travel but, this time, by dirigible instead of aeroplane.

Ward Price had been sent to Germany to travel aboard the *Deutschland*, *Zeppelin VII*, piloted by the seventy-two-year-old Count Zeppelin. Ward Price had already been up once, less than a week before, on the maiden flight of the gigantic airship. Along with eleven other passengers, he had enjoyed the graceful experience of floating on air through mountain gorges, eating caviare and drinking champagne, 'as delightful and comfortable an experience as one could imagine', Price wrote in his dispatch describing the trip for *Mail* readers. In the air for some nine hours, the passengers soon got used to 'the buzzing of the motors'. Two days later, twenty-one passengers had climbed aboard the motorized balloon, including ten ladies who had paid £10 each for a three-hour trip. 'From the window of the saloon cabins,' Ward Price wrote, 'the passengers could peer down on the tall chimneys of the Krupp works.'

But on the second passenger flight of the *Deutschland*, something went wrong: 'Wreck of the Air Liner; Helpless in a Gale; Fall in a Forest', read the *Mail*'s headlines. Not far from Elberfeld, the Zeppelin's propellers stopped because of a technical failure. By the time they were repaired, the aircraft had run into a storm. Ward Price was actually aboard and had been dropping news bulletins to awe-struck German peasants below in small cardboard tubes. By this method, he alerted those on the ground that something had gone amiss. Caught up in the storm's powerful winds, he later wrote,

> the swerving, diving, rain-beaten airship fought on inch by inch, sloping steeply first forward and then aft as we rose and fell in the storm. It was very cold. Icy showers fell in torrents round us. Often we hung motionless for a quarter of an hour with the propellors revolving at full speed, powerless against the resistance of the wind.

Miraculously, the Zeppelin was brought down without loss of life, and immediately plans for a new one were put into action.

But, despite the bloated magnificence of the Zeppelin, Northcliffe understood instinctively its air-life would be short and limited. He poured all the resources of the *Daily Mail* into the promotion of the motorized aeroplane, not only for the glory of the newspaper and the airmen themselves, but for what he believed would one day be the linchpin of Britain's national defence.

The contest sponsored by the *Daily Mail* in 1911, he had decided, would be the decisive event in the country's understanding of the importance of the aeroplane, and towards this goal he employed every publicity device of which the modern, twentieth-century newspaper was capable. Some six weeks before the actual race, 'the most important of all aerial contests' was being lauded by the *Mail* as 'the first great cross-country contest between the champions of various nations'.

Barred from the race were 'freak machines' and 'inexperienced airmen'. Indeed, the ones assembled were the world's most serious competitors; and now, at Northcliffe's behest, they would become international celebrities, the *Daily Mail* assuring its readers that 'personality is the secret of success in an aerial contest'. These bold adventurers who chose to conquer the air, the *Mail* told its readers, were men 'of a new type, these merry, careless, cigarette-smoking airmen'. Of the two thousand men worldwide who had by one method or another entered air space, 'the great champions' of the airways were few – only twenty-four were judged eligible to enter the *Daily Mail's* contest. Now, the newspaper published a 'Who's Who of Competitors', complete with photo-portraits of the airmen accompanied by punchy one-paragraph descriptions. The 'chief characteristics' of the favourite to win, André Beaumont, were said to be his 'extra-sound judgment, and an ability to fly safely in a thirty-mile-an-hour wind'. Beneath his photograph read the caption, 'Bearded, ever-courteous, unassuming.'

He and the other competitors would take part in a 'fascinating spectacle as aeroplanes of every type whirl away in quick succession'. The rules of the contest, drawn up by the Royal Aero Club, were themselves a year in the making, and the thirteen halting places, each with a control booth, had taken some two years to determine. The race started at Brooklands and took in towns such as Hendon, Harrogate, Newcastle, Edinburgh, Bristol, Exeter, Salisbury and Brighton, thus engaging the interest of the entire nation. The final stop was a return to Brooklands, for a total of 1,010 miles – 'a record in flying competitions'.

The *Daily Mail* published time cards so viewers could keep track of aviators' progress, along with a map of the entire route. And in an article entitled 'How to Recognize the Machines', photographs were published of the aeroplanes themselves, sixteen of which had been built in Great Britain. All across Britain, villages planned to close down on the day competitors were scheduled to fly overhead. And at Brooklands itself the *Daily Mail* set up a press shack, with direct telephone lines to the office and to other points along the race. Since 'no special train or motor car [was] swift enough to keep pace with a sixty-five-mile-an-hour monoplane, an elaborate network [had] to be spread over the entire circuit.' Forty *Daily Mail* reporters would use 'a fleet of 20 Ford motor cars', each 'specially suitable for use over rough ground' and each with a sign across the front of its windshield saying, 'DAILY MAIL CAR'.

These were located at each of the thirteen control points, with other vehicles at vantage points near telephones in order 'to be ready to hasten to any spot where one of the competitors may have had an involuntary descent'; or in other words a crash. Some two hundred local correspondents would then be placed along the entire route to watch and telephone or telegraph back news to the *Daily Mail*'s press shack at Brooklands.

The general public was invited to attend the take-off for an admission charge of 2s. 6d. per person or 5s. for a car. Take-off, the *Mail* explained, was the most important event as this would entail 'the most impressive spectacle of the whole contest: one by one, following each other at intervals of a few moments, the aeroplanes will soar into the air, and fly off in the direction of Hendon.'

On 22 July, the first day of the three-day race, the *Mail* reported that the crowds at take-off 'were vast beyond all reckoning'. Of the twenty-four who began the race, only seventeen completed the first stage. Beaumont brought his aircraft down first, flying the first twenty-mile leg in twenty minutes, three seconds. His landing, wrote a *Mail* correspondent, was 'swift and strong';

> dark against the sky, he comes, making nothing of the wind, devouring the miles between us. The deep and thrilling song of the Gnome* reaches us, the whirling blade casts back the rays of the sun. Downward he dips and rushes, straight to the mark and settles with as little effort as a sparrow on a lawn. The breathless pause of the eastward swoop is followed by a cheer that runs round the circle of the field and comes back faintly from the hillside.

'A spectator' at the race, most probably Northcliffe himself, wrote of the race as 'a great national event'. 'So stupendously vast were the crowds,' went the narrative, 'that one had the impression of an entire people coming together.' Viewed in this context, the air race was more than 'a mere show' or 'exhibition of mechanical skill and agility, more even than a race': 'It was to them the final test of human achievement in a new element.'

Then, two days later, on 24 July, untold thousands attended the final take-off of the last leg of the journey, 'the crowds spreading like a great river from city to city and village to village, widening into lakes at the controls, great everywhere, but greatest of all at the starting point'.

> Gathered before midnight an army of sightseers passed through the black night and grey dawn. Within a mile of the aerodrome, men and women slept by the wayside, heedless of the throng which passed onwards chanting choruses. There were native French too. From one group encamped rose the cry *Vive la France*

---

* The Gnome was the engine used in early aircraft.

whenever the click of tools from a shed punctuated the oft-repeated singing of the Marseillaise.

In London, some three hundred taxi-cabs had lined up, waiting for the huge crowds expected to travel from the city. Those who could afford it paid £1 to be carried out to Hendon where final take-off was scheduled. Those who couldn't had been waiting at Hampstead and Golders Green Underground stations all night long for the first train to Hendon, which came at 2.45 a.m. Tea shops near the stations opened up at 1 a.m., and those who had camped out the night thronged to their doors as police stamped out their illegal campfires. By 4.30 a.m. the thousands of spectators were gathered together, waiting for the great moment.

With the daylight, food and hunger were forgotten. The mouth organs of roystering cockney costermongers were laid aside. The shouting choruses gave place to a murmur of expectation. The world was awake and silent, waiting for the start.

One by one the aeroplanes ascended, on the final push to Brooklands. When André Beaumont brought his aircraft down first, the second contender purposely landed a mile away from the official 'control', far from the crowds, and hastily jumped into a taxi-cab, where he burst into tears. Only half an hour sooner and he would have won the race; instead of £10,000, his prize was only £200, and he had the disappointment of seeing Beaumont carried aloft by the crowds and lionized in the newspapers. During the race, Beaumont had chalked up twenty-two and a half hours in the air.

The great race had ended. Dramatically, and with the assured touch of a great impresario, Northcliffe had staged the most momentous event of the early conquest of the air, proving beyond a doubt that Great Britain was no longer an island.

8

'The Cult of Northcliffe'

To an increasing extent, the idea of Alfred Northcliffe now became public property and, as his fame spread, a full-blown cult emerged. Two major plays – J.B. Fagan's *The Earth* and Arnold Bennett's *What the Public Want* – were staged in the West End, their titles subtly implying sinister ramifications of Northcliffe's awesome power. But those in his innermost circle dismissed these attempts to personify the great press baron. The real man remained a mystery, perhaps even to himself. The interior world of Alfred Northcliffe was a hall of mirrors in which his own image was reflected and refracted through the eyes of those close to him.

There was, for a start, Thomas Marlowe, backseat editor of the *Daily Mail* for a decade. Secretly he blamed Northcliffe for the Lever Brothers fiasco. 'Northcliffe conducted that affair personally,' Marlowe said, absolving himself. 'Everybody concerned in it who published the things he told them, taking their truth for granted, was badly let down.' Was Marlowe blameless, as he himself perceived? Or was Northcliffe right to hold him to account? In the aftermath of the affair, Marlowe had kept his job only through the intervention of the *Mail*'s chief leader writer, who made an impassioned plea to Northcliffe that Marlowe be retained.

Marlowe nursed other grievances as well. He believed Northcliffe's patronage of Winston Churchill was rooted in self-interest. Churchill, he believed, represented a plateau of social eminence to which Northcliffe could only aspire. Or perhaps it was his wife's infatuation with aristocratic connections. One letter from Marlowe to Northcliffe finds him grovelling to the Chief over an insult, real or imagined, suffered by Churchill in the pages of the *Daily Mail*. Marlowe humbly submitted that he was 'extremely sorry Lady Northcliffe should have suffered annoyance on my account', meaning his attack on Churchill had embarrassed her socially. Was this what Northcliffe required of his editors – or what Marlowe *thought* he required? It wasn't what he said he wanted.

Northcliffe to Marlowe: The *Daily Mail* was not made by licking Ministers' boots ... I have a natural horror of that sort of journalism, and suffer a great deal from it at *The Times* ... a Newspaper is meant to publish news, and not to please highly placed people.

Northcliffe to Marlowe: I cannot say what I think of the 'Splash page' this morning. It was certainly the worst in any London paper. It started off with that time honoured 'Don't read me', 'The Powers and Peace', disregarding Lloyd George's very lively speech. What is going on amongst the sub-editors, is going on all round and strangling the paper ... Are we getting middle-aged, or what has happened, that we cannot make changes as we used? If I had been afraid of thrusting responsibility on young people, where would you ... have been? Please give my own methods a trial, after all they have made these various businesses.

Northcliffe to Marlowe: No good printing long articles. People won't read them. They can't fix their attention for more than a short time. Unless there is some piece of news that grips them strongly. Then they will devour the same stuff over and over again.

Northcliffe to Marlowe: In your photographs of the King of Spain, Alfonso is always smiling. His smile is not news. If you got a picture of Alfonso weeping, that would be news.

Northcliffe to Marlowe: My Dear Marlowe, would you see that the social editor keeps his Jews out of the social column. What with his Ecksteins, Sassoons and Mosenthals, we will soon have to set the column in Yiddish.

Northcliffe to Marlowe: An article that I meant to speak of the other day was Coronation Socks. It was admirably done. I wish that we had a little more of that sort of thing in the Paper, as we used to have. Let the writer be encouraged.

Northcliffe to Marlowe: I have not heard a good word for the articles lately. It is a source of constant vexation for me. New writers are no longer found, and members of the staff are unduly worked. You have redundancy and repetition. It now consists of what the Americans call 'flub-dub'.

No wonder Marlowe burned his personal papers. Of the few that survive, one he wrote to Northcliffe when his own son died in a road accident gives his other perception of his proprietor:

23 April 1913 Longmead, Champion Hill

My dear Chief –

I see your hand in so many of the different manifestations of kindness and sympathy that have reached me in the last few days that I must write at once to thank you. The messages ... I can trace directly to your active intervention and I credit them to one of the most wonderful of your qualities – I mean that sympathetic imagination by which you realise even more keenly and 'practically' the feelings and sufferings of others than they do themselves ... Letters are pouring in by every post both here and at Cambridge, but I could have put them all aside if it had not been for the demonstrations of affection from my colleagues – all, I believe, stimulated and stirred up by you. That, I confess, breaks me up ... We are not sending out any invitations for the funeral, but you know that I shall feel it a very great honour if you can spare the time to be there.

> Always gratefully and affectionately,
> Thomas Marlowe

Northcliffe, of course, attended the boy's funeral – along with his wife. But Marlowe wasn't alone in his ambivalence towards the Chief.

There was the classic depiction of the great press baron told by the editor of the Features Page, who used 'to find Northcliffe stretched out on a settee in his panelled room'. According to this version, the great Northcliffe, a genius at trivia, lay staring dozily into space, too jaded even to glance towards the door when it was opened.

> 'Who is that?' he would murmur in a limp voice. He would then take the bundle of proofs from me, and ask which I was going to use next day ... One article of a humorous kind dealt with the boredom caused to barbers by the fact that their customers expect to be talked to. 'Use that one,' ordered the Chief, and asked what heading I was going to put on it. I said I had not thought of one yet. Northcliffe rose from his sofa. 'Give it to me,' he said – and for five minutes the greatest figure in Fleet Street pored over the proof with his breathing growing heavier as his attention became more concentrated. Finally – 'Call it "The Barber's Secret".'

Outside, in the newsroom, a new man noted in his diary the oppressive atmosphere in the *Mail* offices. 'Nobody smiles, nobody goes out for supper – just gobbles it up whenever he can.' Amongst the staff, it was commonly believed that 'Northcliffe will suck your brains and then sack you.' Newcomers, insecure and unencouraged, were customarily ignored by senior staffers. If you could hold on for six months, so went the conventional wisdom, your chances of survival went up dramatically.

Meanwhile, those who couldn't take the heat need not apply. And those who couldn't and did often came to a bad end. One employee blamed Northcliffe for at least two suicides amongst staff members. The first was a news editor who threw himself into the River Kelvin in Glasgow after a nervous breakdown; it was brought on, his colleague believed, 'by the exacting nature of his work'. The other was a quiet man who came to his position as page editor at the *Mail* with quiet optimism. He believed the Chief especially appreciated his work. Two months later, sacked and depressed, he took his own life. Did Northcliffe actually hound men to death?

When Thomas Clarke was promoted to news editor, Northcliffe offered him a yearly £800. But Clarke demanded more, saying Northcliffe would only sack him ten years hence, and 'in the meantime I was going to have every penny I could out of him'. Northcliffe responded by shelling out an extra £200 a year and predicted Clarke would one day become a director of the company. Clarke lasted twelve years instead of ten; then he was sacked.

When Freddie Prince-White joined the editorial staff, Northcliffe called him on the phone, asking 'Who are you? What's your name? Never heard of you. Now tell me, what's the best story in the Mail?' At the end of Prince-White's answers, he dismissed them as nonsense. Writing in his bulletin for the day, Northcliffe then wrote, 'I entirely agree with the new young man in the News Room about the quality and interest of the main stories in today's papers in general, and in the DM in particular.' Forty years later, Prince-White was still on staff at the *Daily Mail*.

The infamous Hannen Swaffer, nicknamed the 'Poet' because he wore his wavy hair cut long, received a cable from Northcliffe: UNDERSTAND PIERRE LOTI ROUGES HIS LIPS, PAINTS HIS FACE STOP SEND GOOD STORY.* To which Swaffer is said to have cabled back: REGRET PIERRE LOTI REFUSES ROUGE LIPS PAINT FACE EVEN FOR ME. Swaffer, who made his name on the *Mirror*, went on to edit one of Northcliffe's several titles on Fleet Street, remaining on the staff long after Northcliffe's death. In fact, he believed ever afterwards he was spiritually in touch with the ghost of the Chief.

Such were the impressions Northcliffe evoked within the offices of the *Daily Mail*. Outside, the invincible Chief was only too human. His mistress, Kathleen Wrohan, gave birth to their first son on 25 August 1910, in her small flat at 2 Brick Court. Apprehensive she would not survive the birth, Wrohan requested a settlement on the child. Northcliffe obliged, instructing his personal lawyer, Henry Arnholz, to set aside £1,000 a year for the first three years of the boy's life and £6,000 a year thereafter. From the beginning of the tempestuous relationship between the fiery Mrs Wrohan and the powerful press baron, money was a point of contention. Northcliffe, who had plenty to spare and was by nature generous, appeared to be resisting the machinations of the hard-core spendaholic.

And indeed Wrohan spent money with the same fearful nonchalance as Northcliffe's wife, Mary. Photographs of each of the two women show

---

* Pierre Loti was a French novelist who wrote romantic fiction featuring Icelandic fishermen.

fashion plates enraptured by the drama of their own images. But, whereas Lady Northcliffe enjoyed carte blanche, Northcliffe's mistress did not. She had received an annuity of £6,000 a year since September 1908, which she overspent shamelessly. As a result, endless rows over Wrohan's bills erupted, to such an extent that it appeared money was probably the means the couple unwittingly settled upon to maintain the furious passion of their relationship. Wrohan wanted Elmwood settled on her son, but Lady Northcliffe had got there already. Never mind, Wrohan wielded her own magical power over Northcliffe, and eventually Elmwood was resettled on the boy.

Wrohan wrote incessantly about the health of Northcliffe, whom she called 'the elder brother' in her letters to Arnholz. Northcliffe's family were called 'the elder brothers', and her newborn son 'the new relation'. There were countless references in the correspondence to appropriate settlement arrangements for her new child – and, more pressingly, to the payment of her own bills.

21 April 1910, Les Roches Rouges

My Dear Mr Arnholz,

I am very greatly distressed that you should have thought it necessary to write to the Chief about Debenham's bill. What is the good of your worrying him about details – when you want more money let me know, and I'll ask him.

If you knew the state of his health and nerves and how we are all working to keep *little* worries away from him you would understand what I mean. Sutton* and I are very angry with you. Please don't write to him about those bills without letting me know beforehand and please believe that I do know what I'm writing about. The Chief's health is very critical – the sudden opening of a door drives him frantic – and your letter yesterday set him back a week. Now this is quite private – we don't want people to know he is so ill.

When more money is required for the bills it will be sent to you, but don't go and write long legal letters that would upset anybody – oh dear! I wish I were near you, the ears of the elder brothers would get boxed – and not on my own account at all, but only because you've gone and upset the Chief about nothing.

Yours very sincerely, Kathleen Wrohan

* One of Northcliffe's top executives; George Sutton began as the press baron's secretary.

Monday, 18 December 1910, Les Roches Rouges

My Dear Mr Arnholz,

Debenham and Freebody will send you a bill for £400 which you will please send them. They are to get that sum quarterly till their bill is paid up, but I'll arrange about it with you later.

The 'elder brother' need not worry about my running up bills – they are only current ones, but under the present circumstance I thought they ought to be taken charge of by all my big brothers and they very kindly consented.

Very sincerely yours, Kathleen Wrohan

According to Wrohan's version of events, Northcliffe was a wretched creature whose frayed nerves could not bear any frustrating news whatsoever, and most especially about Wrohan's expenditures, without his being thrust into a state of near collapse.

Surprisingly, however, Northcliffe's letters to Arnholz on the subject showed considerable sang-froid. It appeared Wrohan's 'current' bills at Debenham's were in the region of £4,000, of which Northcliffe wished at the time to pay only £500. He instructed Arnholz to liquidate her bills 'as slowly as possible', as he had continually instructed her he would not pick up any large expenditure without 'long warning'. She was supposed to have been paying her clothing bills from her allowance, but, as Northcliffe described the situation, she was like 'the lady, who, being told that her bank account was overdrawn, replied "that's all right, I've lots more cheques in my book".' Arnholz, Northcliffe wrote, was 'to be very firm'.

Another of Northcliffe's mistresses, the dull but faithful Louise Owen, pictured the Chief as strong and true as the upright character from Henry James's novel *Portrait of a Lady*, Caspar Goodwood, whose actions always mirrored his name. All-knowing, kindly and generous, according to Owen's version, Northcliffe moved through dooms of love: 'My Chief was no Jekyll or Hyde,' she said. 'I never knew him do anything that I – who was devoted to him – would be ashamed of for the world to know, either in his business or private life.' With all the information available in Owen's position, if Northcliffe had been up to any mischief, *she* would have been privy to the knowledge, so went Owen's version. Most especially, she implied, almost referring to Kathleen Wrohan by name, she would have known if any ill-founded rumours – that is, 'the numerous myths and innuendoes' floating about – were true.

To Owen and those of her colleagues who subscribed to her version of the Chief, Northcliffe was a bit of a crackerbarrel philosopher who used such picturesque expressions as 'Teach your grandmother to suck eggs,' and 'I'll larn you, young fellow!' 'Home with the milk, up with the larks,' was another of his bits of homespun advice. A fun-loving character, he loved to tell stories against himself like the time when he boarded a Channel boat with the day's newspapers tucked under his arm, his cap pulled down over his eyes. Unexpectedly, he found himself being tapped on the shoulder and asked by a formidable elderly gentleman for a *'Times*, please.'

The same sort of mentality informed the Northcliffe who, after complaining day after day that an early-morning van awoke him in his Berkeley Square house, was, after investigation of the nuisance, informed that it was the truck that carried copies of the *Daily Mail* from Whitefriars Street to Paddington. Northcliffe was so amused that it became one of his stock anecdotes.

And this would be the same man who, according to one of his youngest protégés and admirers on the *Daily Mail*, was capable of acts of boundless sentimentality. J.M.N. Jeffries was invited to Elmwood one afternoon as Northcliffe was entertaining a group of thirty or forty orphan girls from a nearby convent. After tea, Jeffries watched as Northcliffe

> shook hands with them, patted their heads, rumpled their hair, called them one and all 'my dear', took part in their games of ring-o'-roses. He beamed at the nuns and chaffed them. He had arranged all manner of prizes for the children to win, but decided soon that every child must have a prize. At least every child was to have chocolates, unlimited chocolates ... Humphrey Davy passed the order to a Broadstairs tradesman, who asked up to what value he might send the desired goods. Lord Northcliffe, present at telephone-side, exclaimed: 'Tut-tut-tut-t-u-t, Davy, what's the matter with the man? Tell him to send up chocolates and other sweets for fifty children ... He doesn't know the base of his own business if he doesn't know children's sweet-capacity. Tell him to rush the sweets in a car; and not a moment's delay.'
>
> When the children went home, Northcliffe stretched far out of a low casement-window, waving his hand loosely from the wrist in 'bye-bye!' fashion to the departing children. They looked back at him and waved and fluttered their handkerchiefs in reply. He stayed in the window and gazed up the empty drive, pensively, with his hand slowed but still waving, up and down, for a minute or more.

Northcliffe was drawn to children, and on several occasions he confided to Arnholz that he and Wrohan wanted a daughter. In the spring of 1912, Northcliffe rang his lawyer to tell him the good news. Wrohan had been safely delivered of a girl, named Geraldine after Northcliffe's mother – although there was never any evidence that the matriarch of the family knew of the existence of her namesake. On 25 May and, later that year, on 21 August, he instructed Arnholz to settle a trust, coded as the 'R' Trust, upon her. When finally his last son, Harold, was born on 14 April 1914, and settlements were made upon him on 28 April and 18 June, Northcliffe's secret family was complete.

His was a double or even a triple life, then, made necessary by the conventions of his day and by his own complex psychological nature. Northcliffe was a man capable of scaling the heights or depths of emotion and intellect; or, more accurately, incapable of not doing so. More alarming still, he covered this range at rapid speed, one moment a terrifying monster, the next a docile lamb. One of his leader writers, E.T. Raymond, later the editor of the *Evening Standard*, wrote that Northcliffe had 'an uncanny way of arriving at the results of thought without thought itself'. Where, amongst all this energy and complexity, was the real man?

His dominant modes were easy to assign. These sprang straight from the nursery, where he had been the eldest sibling. It was only natural for him to take the leadership position. He had done so for as long as he could remember. Not only did he do it better than anyone else, he was always right; only Mother knew better.

But, deep within, a childlike vanity prevailed. He fathered himself in the most naïve way imaginable. There was this secret need for obsessive record-keeping about his own body. He kept a formal Weight Diary, recording any fluctuations meticulously, both 'in pyjamas' and 'without clothes', both in the morning and in the evening. 'Down again, thank goodness,' he would write. Three months later, things were 'not so rosy'. At one point, he chronicled his 'triumph of self-denial', describing himself as a 'good boy' and praising the 'success of [his] regime'. Whenever he put on weight, he counted his failures as 'damnable'. 'There is no fool like a fat fool,' as he once said to his brother.

When, in the summer of 1910, he took up golf at his doctor's orders – he would die young, he was told, if he didn't seriously follow a systematic regimen of exercise – he had beside him one of the greatest teachers of the day, 'Sandy' Thomson, a professional from the Hampstead Golf Club. As Thomson demonstrated, Northcliffe firmly grasped the handle of the club and swung it back, then forward in a perfect arc, driving his first golfball aloft. For the next eight hours, he stood on the sixth tee at Sutton Place and made 284 consecutive drives, until, collapsing from exhaustion, he was led from the course and to his bed to recover.

In that single act was the first, last and best explanation as to who Northcliffe really was.

Northcliffe worried, and that became the galvanizing force behind progress and change on the *Daily Mail*. He worried the newspaper would become less lively, too 'stodgy', a bad read; he feared anything that smacked of old age and the declining generations. And, in this frame of mind, he called for more 'fads' in its pages. There had been the establishment of the Ideal Home Exhibition in 1908, a highly successful venture that had attracted thousands of young home-makers. Then there was the rifle-shooting contest that offered as its prize a two-hundred-guinea cup for teams of young marksmen; one for Britain, another for the rest of the Empire. Behind the promotion was the stated aim of promoting patriotism and 'A Pledge of Brotherhood' amongst the colonies.

But these and similar ventures weren't enough for Northcliffe. He was always on the look-out for more excitement. Thus it was he hired an energetic young innovator by the name of Valentine Smith. Smith had been taken on to the staff of the *Daily Mirror* in its early days and gone swiftly to work thinking up publicity stunts to increase circulation. After Northcliffe bought the *Observer*, Smith moved to that paper, managing to build up sales from 10,000 to 100,000 copies by canvassing communities with sample copies. In 1909, he was promoted to the position of circulation manager of the *Daily Mail*, where he began developing stunts to draw attention to the newspaper, including amongst them jigsaw puzzles, a sand-painting contest, a sky-writing stunt and the most famous of all – the Standard Bread campaign. One of the most remarkable stunts ever taken on by a newspaper, the Standard Bread campaign saw 202 articles published on the topic during one calendar year, 1911.

Several theories have been advanced as to why the *Daily Mail* adopted the improbable cause of promoting wholemeal bread. Predictably, the first was the imputed motive that Northcliffe believed he could force down the throats of an entire nation whatever food he wanted. A second was that his mother had taken a hand. Worried about the nourishment of young children, she encouraged her son to initiate the campaign. Still another cited Northcliffe's determination to draw attention to the *Daily Mail* through any method he could. Then there remained the obvious but oft-overlooked possibility: that brown bread is simply more nutritional than white, and Northcliffe knew it.

The whole thing began when Sir Oswald Mosley, 'stock-breeder and expert agriculturist', had the idea of educating the villagers of Rolleston, who lived near his estate, to the virtues of bread made with wholemeal flour. For the moment at least, Mosley took on the role of village baker, providing a hundred loaves as free samples. With a zeal anticipating that of his grandson, who, two decades later, would found the British Union of Fascists, Mosley announced he was extending his offer to readers of the

Daily Mail. The announcement was made on 12 January 1911; within two days over three thousand requests had flooded in. What happened next was due largely to the efforts of Valentine Smith, who on Northcliffe's orders orchestrated a full-scale promotion of unprecedented proportions.

'Better teeth, stronger bones, steadier nerves and a greater natural immunity against disease, particularly consumption, will be found ... if the people of England will discard the present day white loaf for a more wholemeal bread,' proclaimed the *Mail*. Brown bread was christened the new 'beauty food'. It was said to create a more wholesome complexion and retard the accumulation of fat. Not only that, but scientists at the Liverpool School of Tropical Medicine were quoted as saying that wholemeal bread helped to prevent 'diseases of childhood, notably rickets, scurvy-rickets, tetany and convulsions'. The differing effects of white and brown bread were put to the test on rats, and the *Daily Mail* reported the *British Medical Journal* as saying,

> The result is astonishing. From first to last the rats fed on white bread or flour have done far the worse. Ten of them have died, and five of these were eaten by the others before we could remove their bodies. The white-fed rats are far less lively and less sleek in appearance. It seems clear that children of the poor, who are largely fed on bread and margarine or bread and jam, ought to have the standard and not the white bread.

The same results were observed in pigeons. Put on a diet of white bread, they 'speedily developed marked symptoms of ill-nutrition and serious nerve derangements'. These birds sat 'listless and shivering', many of them developing convulsions. But those pigeons fed on brown bread remained 'healthy and up to normal weight'. Besides these tests, common sense dictated that the chemical content and presence of bleach in white bread posed a positive danger to society.

As to those suffering from 'the dull drab of middle age' with 'no digestive energy to waste', they would find ample benefit by changing their diet to include Standard Bread.

Now prizes were offered to children for the best school essay on the subject, and the *Mail* sponsored a campaign for legislation against white bread. Another competition for the best baked loaf was held at the Confectioners' and Bakers' Exhibition at the Royal Agricultural Hall in Islington where 2,500 loaves from all over Britain were put on display.

On the part of the public at large, however, the net result of Valentine Smith's barrage of publicity was a stunning indifference. Brown bread may have been more nutritional, but white bread was prettier and softer and tasted better. It was also the bread of the rich, and so implied the possibility of upward mobility, an attitude that wouldn't change for some seventy years. In the long run, all the campaign achieved was the predictable but foundless accusation that Northcliffe had investments in the flour-milling industry. Indeed, the Standard Bread campaign represented a forward-looking idea whose time hadn't yet come – that good health and good looks depended upon adequate nutrition.

More popular with the public and certainly more successful was the sweet-pea competition held on 28/29 July 1911. The *Daily Mail* offered £1,000 as the grand prize, along with 100 silver and 900 bronze medals for runner-ups. Held at the Crystal Palace, the Festival of Empire employed more than one hundred boy scouts working from sunrise unpacking the entries. Some fifty to sixty judges participated in the initial judging, with a special panel of ten for the flowers making it into the final competition. In all, there were more than 38,000 entries, 10,000 of which went on display. Children alone represented some 1,000 entries. Amongst the artificial sweet-pea category, there were flowers and stems made of velvet and silk, woven silk threads, paper, and – yes, Standard Bread itself, dyed into pastel shades.

In the wake of this successful promotion, cynical wags dubbed Northcliffe 'King of the Sweet Peas'. Consider then the much ridiculed King of the Sweet Peas as he pursues his next promotion.

Northcliffe to Marlowe: 'Would you please see this Agenda Club man and let him know that if we take up his National Health Week scheme the *Daily Mail* gets full credit or we do not take it up at all? Get something in writing from these people ...'

National Health Week was followed close on its heels by a contest 'for the finest new rose not yet in commerce, to be called the *'Daily Mail* Rose'. Now the 'King of the Roses' moved forward to a 'Too-Old-at-Forty' promotion. Northcliffe's age at the time? Forty-seven.

The man simply had no shame.

Meanwhile, time was taking its inevitable toll. Sir George Newnes, founder of *Tit-Bits* and Northcliffe's original inspiration for *Answers to Correspondents*, had died, aged fifty-nine. Northcliffe himself wrote the obituary. A little over a year later, in 1911, Joseph Pulitzer was dead at sixty-four.

As nothing else could, their deaths made Northcliffe aware of his own mortality. He was directing the publication of almost half the titles on Fleet Street, not to mention a magazine empire. Newfoundland had become a constant thorn in his side, for the very reasons Harold had warned his brother about before the paper-making community had been established.

As Northcliffe viewed it, everywhere he looked, new difficulties and incompetence in others continued to increase his already intolerable workload.

In early February 1913, an entire batch of paper arriving for use on the *Mirror* had to be discarded. Northcliffe's fury could be felt clear across the Atlantic. Vincent Jones was put instantly on the defensive: 'I realise how the *Mirror* lives by its pictures,' he wrote glumly, admitting he knew Grand Falls would lose the order if the quality of paper didn't improve.

More infuriating to Northcliffe, the whole fiasco was a repeat of earlier disasters. A batch sent two years earlier had been ruined by the use of rotten wood. Vincent Jones had sent it anyway, despite the fact he knew it wasn't up to scratch. The excuse he made to Northcliffe at that time was that he couldn't retrieve the better-quality paper out of storage. A worse complication was that the paper lacked the tensile strength of newsprint. It couldn't stand up to high-speed presses. Then, in the coldest months of the winter, there was the problem of ice in the river. If the plant had to be shut down for even as short a time as three days, it killed the month's profit, as had happened in December 1911. And in the previous month of the same year, Vincent Jones had had to shut down for installation of a generator, losing that month's profit as well. Then there was the problem that cropped up each spring: in March, the men just walked off the job to go sealing; they had done so for generations and they weren't about to stop just because they now had steady work.

Neither had the little colony escaped political intrigues. By September 1913, Northcliffe felt compelled to visit Grand Falls in person, in order to make an inspection and investigation of his own. He was appalled to discover what he termed 'the frankly divisive tactics' of Mayson Beeton. And the casual comment of a manager threw him into a frenzy. 'This place just runs itself,' the manager said proudly to his distinguished visitor. 'What did you say?' Northcliffe shot back. 'Don't you know that anything that goes of itself must be going downhill? I never allow that to happen in any part of my businesses.' He later dismissed the visit as 'a very strenuous time'.

As regards Vincent Jones, Northcliffe was especially angry, and for good reason. The sheets of paper London was rejecting and shipping back to Newfoundland were getting worse and worse – 'a regular sand-paper surface'. Jones insisted the paper never left the mills in that condition. By 8 April 1913, he had determined it was a bad batch of American clay that had caused the damage. But that did very little to improve the situation. 'Why not say to yourself,' Northcliffe wrote to his protégé, 'I will not send to England one inch of doubtful paper?' The entire affair was putting Northcliffe 'in the greatest difficulty I have ever been in my business career'. It was Vincent Jones's 'lack of prevision' that was causing the trouble. So far as Northcliffe was concerned, Vincent Jones had better not make the excuse again of bad clay from the United States, or anywhere for that matter. 'Nothing has ever caused me more worry in the whole of my business life than these successive Grand Falls troubles,' he insisted. 'They really begin to affect my control of the parent companies.'

Cutting right through Vincent Jones's backwoods rhetoric, Northcliffe roughly pointed out it was not necessary 'for you to write me nice letters or duty letters'. He preferred Vincent Jones to spend the time seeking recreation, so that in the long run he would be able to produce a better product. In the shortest space of time imaginable, Vincent Jones changed his tune. Instead of the folksy style he and his wife Mary had evolved to address the great press baron, he now organized his letters with headings, the body of each a terse, straight-to-the point report on the topic covered. He was learning to be a businessman. This was more to Northcliffe's liking.

Mayson Beeton was also working his way back into Northcliffe's good graces. He had come within inches of losing his position, but after numerous exchanges and adjustments, by Christmas 1913 it was decided he would stay. Not long afterwards, Northcliffe wrote to say that new shipments of paper for both the *Daily Mail* and the *Daily Mirror* were of 'a highly satisfactory quality', and everything was in a fair way to being settled.

It was just as well. Vincent Jones had become a father only a year before. His son Desmond had been born on 13 February 1913. The baby weighed twelve pounds, and Mary Vincent-Jones had nearly died. Nevertheless, in the months following his birth, her new son completely transformed her life and gave her new impetus to carry on. A little over a year later, a daughter Barbara was born to the couple. Unable to breast-feed the child herself, Mary Vincent-Jones had given the baby milk from the local herd, and unwittingly infected her new baby girl with tuberculosis.

At news of this, panic broke out in the small colony, and Northcliffe, learning of what had happened, sent orders that the entire herd was to be destroyed. It was soon established that the type of cattle least likely to develop tuberculosis was Ayrshire, and Northcliffe immediately sent out a new herd to replace those that had been slaughtered. Perhaps as a result of this episode, Northcliffe, whose special relationship with Mary Vincent-Jones had never really ended, chose to stop goading her husband.

With the Grand Falls problem solved for the moment, Northcliffe made the decision to rid himself of at least one of his responsibilities. At last acceding to his mother's wishes, voiced over a decade before at the founding of the *Daily Mirror*, he sold that paper to his brother Harold for exactly

£100,000 – the sum he originally lost when he launched it.

So, twenty-six years after his dramatic entrance on to the London publishing scene with the launch of *Answers to Correspondents*, Alfred Northcliffe began, in a small but significant way, to lessen his workload, a necessary evil if he was to assure himself of a longer and healthier life. He had sold one of his major newspaper publications, and his magazine empire had also been quietly sidelined by Harold into the hands of capable subordinates. Northcliffe would now be able to take more interest in his shadow-family, perhaps learning to be less of a workaholic. So it might have seemed.

The events of August 1914, however, were about to divert this first, faltering step towards moderation.

For more than a decade, Northcliffe had been predicting war with Germany. As early as 1900, he was warning the nation,

> This is our hour of preparation, tomorrow may be the day of world conflict ... Germany will go slowly and surely; she is not in a hurry; her preparations are quietly and systematically made; it is no part of her object to cause general alarm which might be fatal to her designs.

He had consistently described Germany as Britain's 'secret and insidious enemy', and in October 1909 he had commissioned Robert Blatchford, the brilliant Socialist journalist who edited the *Clarion*, to visit Germany and then write a series of articles setting out the dangers. The Germans, Blatchford wrote, were making 'gigantic preparations' to destroy the British Empire and 'to force German dictatorship upon the whole of Europe'. Britain's policy of 'milk and water' would surely not stand up to the policy of 'blood and iron' that Germany had adopted. He complained of Britain's unpreparedness, pointing to the rising possibility of an 'Armageddon'; in fact, he was probably the first to use the term that would, in too short a space of time, become common currency.

Blatchford immediately fell foul of cries that he was writing for the Tories just as an election was underway. 'Votes?' Blatchford cried out. 'What has the danger to the empire to do with votes? I wrote these articles for men and women, not for votes ... I believe that Germany is deliberately preparing to destroy the British Empire; and because I know that we are not able or ready to defend ourselves against a sudden and formidable attack.'

In the immediate aftermath of the publication of Blatchford's series, Northcliffe found himself being pilloried by the Liberal press. Led by the *Daily Chronicle*, the attackers charged that by constantly reminding the public of the dangers of war Northcliffe was actually in a fair way to causing one. The *Daily Mail* itself was discredited as 'un-British' and accused of 'scaremongering'. The newspaper's attitude towards the Germans was dubbed 'the blue funk school' – a term of derision.

But in fact, behind the scenes, Northcliffe was putting on even more pressure. He was constantly reminding government members of 'the German menace', no one more than the man his editor had believed to be merely a social contact – Winston Churchill. Appointed Home Secretary in 1910, Churchill had, amongst his other duties, assumed responsibility for certain aspects of national security, and, unlike most of his colleagues, he was no stranger to what was happening on the Continent. Upon returning from a trip to Germany, his only comment was, 'I can only thank God that there is a sea between England and that Army.'

In Churchill Northcliffe found his natural ally. Only a month before Churchill became First Lord of the Admiralty, Northcliffe was complaining to him about the ignorance of his colleagues. None of them besides Churchill had bothered even to visit Germany, Northcliffe said. Again, he wrote to Churchill to relate a comment made by one of his relations who lived in Germany. The Germans were like land crabs: 'If we advance, they retreat: if we retreat, they advance: – a very good summary.'

By the following year, July 1912, he was actively gathering intelligence. 'All the new ships of the German lines,' Northcliffe wrote,

> are built practically under Admiralty supervision. That is to say, the Admiralty expresses its wishes in regard to all features of destruction which are bearing on a vessel's future use as a transport or commerce destroyer, and the shipping company orders the builder to make the ship accordingly. This covers, of course, the question of guns too. It is necessary to build gun platforms into a ship while it is under construction, and I am assured that all the fast German liners have these platforms in – invisible to the ordinary ocean passenger's view – but capable of being uncovered and having guns mounted immediately the emergency arises.

Although Northcliffe dismissed his own information as 'not very valuable', he promised more if it should be wanted.

Soon after, he wrote to say that Orville Wright concurred in Churchill's own predictions on dirigibles: 'providing there are sufficient number of dirigibles employed, they might cause annoyance and perhaps some little damage.' Perhaps they might.

Northcliffe was a man who, for well over fourteen years, had believed he was practically clairvoyant on the matter of Germany's intentions. It would prove to be one of those cases where taking credit for accuracy in predicting the future would provide no pleasure.

9

'The March of the Hun'

Lovat Fraser, senior reporter on the *Daily Mail*, was dreaming again – the recurring nightmare that had plagued his sleep for weeks before the advent of the Great War. In it, Germany wages a horrendous attack upon London from the skies, dropping firebombs from gigantic dirigibles and causing terror and chaos below. From the vantage-point of his limitless imagination, Fraser envisioned legions of bloodthirsty German soldiers, who march in perfect unison across the country leaving death and destruction in their wake. In an article he wrote for the *Mail*, Fraser called his terrible vision 'The March of the Hun'; thus at a stroke was created the image of a terrifying, ape-like savage that threatened to rape and plunder all of Europe, and beyond.

It was fitting that a *Mail* reporter was responsible for coining the term 'Hun' since the newspaper's proprietor was credited, or discredited if you will, with almost single-handedly bringing about the First World War. The *Star*, a weak rival with a strong anti-Northcliffe bias, wrote, 'Next to the Kaiser, Lord Northcliffe has done more than any living man to bring about the war.'

Amongst the Germans themselves, the sentiment was not dissimilar:

Exactly what the real cause of the war no one seems to know ... it seems that Europe was thirsting for war, and that the armies and navies were no longer to be restrained. Certainly [in Germany], militarists grew weary of the long lazy peace as they called it, and if the Kaiser had not proclaimed war, he would have been in a precarious position. There are two men at the head of affairs: one is called stupid and the other dangerous. The dangerous one has won the day, and brought the war to a head. Lord Northcliffe seems to be responsible on the other side.

The plaintive *cri de coeur* of the German Secretary for Foreign Affairs summed up the universal hatred felt by the enemy for the irrepressible British press baron: 'But is there nobody who will shoot Lord Northcliffe?' Baron von Jagow asked. 'He is his own country's worst enemy as well as ours. He is more answerable for all this bloodshed and carnage than any other single individual throughout the world.'

According to these avowed enemies, Northcliffe's method was madness; his motive, profit. The customary rumours circulated: one, that he had invested heavily in armaments; another, that he expected to benefit handsomely from a rise in circulation. On 4 August 1914, humorist E.V. Lucas recorded in his journal the following observations: 'War declared. Lord Northcliffe has his teeth sharpened.' Character assassinations aside, the real motivations of Northcliffe were easy enough to discern.

He loved his country with unreasoning passion. He was the living embodiment of patriotism and nationalism, even of chauvinism. He would employ every means at his disposal to halt the German onslaught, or what he came to call 'this massive attempt by the second rate to dominate the world'. Soon, his *Daily Mail* would become the central mouthpiece of the British propaganda machine against the enemy. As to the scathing criticisms of his enemies, Northcliffe mildly remarked, 'I do not in the least mind personal attacks, nor do I care what the public think about me.' Thus was Northcliffe mentally prepared for war.

Strangely, however, when the actual moment arrived, he seemed to falter. The morning after Great Britain entered the war, even as the country prepared to send its first troops abroad, a curious fight took place in the offices of the *Daily Mail* – between Northcliffe and Marlowe. Northcliffe entered the office in a fury, asking brusquely,

> What is this I hear about a British Expeditionary Force for France? It is nonsense. Not a single soldier shall leave this country … What about our own country?

The staff were aghast. To their minds, the pronouncement reeked of cowardice; Thomas Marlowe in particular was scarcely able to contain his revulsion. There followed a most painful clash between editor and owner, one so harrowing that staff members who witnessed it 'wanted nothing less than to fall through the floor to escape seeing any more'. The printers received two separate leaders and two separate news pages, each with a thesis contradicting the other. As the argument raged on upstairs, both Marlowe and Northcliffe instructed the downstairs staff to publish his own pages. In the end and to the surprise of everyone, it was Marlowe who won, and, an unprecedented forty-five minutes late, the pages went to press. What had gone on in Northcliffe's mind? It was as if he had a presentiment of the horrors to come – a vision of the terrible face of war – and had been forced to the realization that, powerful as he was, he was helpless to prevent the catastrophe at hand.

He could rally the forces, he could persuade young men to enlist, he could catalogue atrocities and he could count the dead. But there was nothing he could do to prevent a war that would ultimately cost the lives of millions. This fight with Marlowe had been Northcliffe's last almighty denial before his final capitulation to the act of war. Britain was in, with no way out. Seamlessly, then, and without pause, Northcliffe made his volte-face and turned his whole will towards winning.

'Do you understand?' asked Robert Blatchford in the *Mail* a few days after the terrible argument had taken place. Blatchford was the leader of the Socialist Party who had earlier written dire warnings of the conflict to come. He had recently been to the seaside resorts of Eastbourne and Brighton where he had seen thousands of young people at play. 'Who could realise', he complained, 'that a few hours' journey across that smooth band of sparkling water the troops of four nations were at death grips?'

> We are at war. We are committed to a war that will be desperate and terrible in its action, and in its results appalling. And here are young men flirting, laughing, riding, swimming. Every one of those merry, careless young men ought to have a rifle on his shoulder. Every one of those happy girls ought to be at work preparing for the hardest trial that ever came upon the British nation. This is no time for play. This is a time of war!

To illustrate the dangers the nation was facing, the newspaper published a photograph of the dead and wounded against a line drawing of frolicking young people oblivious to the grim new reality of war.

At the same time, the paper's newly placed war correspondents turned up the heat. 'Reports of German atrocities continue to come in,' wrote G. Ward Price from Paris in August 1914,

> and it now seems that they are not individual acts of savagery but part of a systematic scheme of repression intended to terrify the populace. There are many reports that wounded French soldiers have been shot by Germans...

Other atrocity stories made their way into the pages of the *Mail*. In a story headlined 'The Barbarity of German Troops: Sins Against Civilisation', Hamilton Fyfe wrote, 'I hate to think that any soldiers could be so devilish as to kill unarmed civilians in blind rage, or any officers so wicked as to permit it. But that a large number have acted not like men but like devils is now lamentably put beyond dispute.' He chronicled the tale of random killing in a small French village, where women and children, wild with terror, were lined up against a wall and shot dead. 'Hun Murderers' the Germans were called. 'Wounded Thousands Killed', the *Mail* reported. 'Haystack Furnaces', the headlines blared. These early reports of German atrocities, founded upon hearsay and fed by repressive measures by the Allies who were trying to impede the flow of information from the Front, would all turn out to be false; and eventually, they would disappear from the pages of the *Mail*.

In their place would be stories of the courage and strength of the young men sent over to do the fighting, published as often as not under a banner that said 'Delayed by the Censor' to remind the reading public not only that they were getting an altered version of the truth but also that they were getting it late. News editor Walter Fish earned a reputation as 'a most resourceful and alert newspaper man' as he navigated round the problems of wartime reporting and got the best out of his newly appointed war correspondents. It was Fish who spotted the potential of George C. Curnock's story about soldiers who sang as they marched into battle.

> For two days the finest troops England has ever sent across the sea have been marching through the narrow streets of old Boulogne in solid columns of khaki, thousands upon thousands of them, roaring as they pass that new slogan of Englishmen: 'Are we down-hearted? ... No-o-o-o-o-o!!!' 'Shall we win? ... Ye-e-e-e-e-s-s-s.' Today they are marching to the camps on the hill above Boulogne. Watch them as they pass, every man in the prime of life, not a youth or stripling among them. Their shirts are open at the front, and as they shout you can see the working of the muscles of their throats, their wide-open mouths and rows of dazzling teeth.

They were singing a little-known song from a pantomime that had been staged the winter before. Walter Fish thought the song equivalent to the Frenchman's 'La Marseillaise', and placed Curnock's feature on the front page. 'It's a long way to Tipperary', the men chanted. 'It's a long way to go.'

> It's a long way to Tipperary,
> And the sweetest girl I know!
> Good-bye Piccadilly,
> Farewell Leicester Square,
> It's a long, long way to Tipperary,
> But my heart's right there.

Thus was born the unofficial National Anthem of the British Expeditionary Force.

The *Daily Mail* went swiftly into formation, an orderly response to a conflict anticipated for years. By 6 August, correspondents were in place in Maastricht, Brussels, Paris, Berlin, Antwerp, Ostend and Rome. In constant

THIS WEEK
The leading Drapers of Prestige are
displaying the New Autumn Models of
ROYAL WORCESTER
KIDFITTING CORSETS.
(SEE FRONT PAGE).

Daily Mail
TUESDAY, SEPTEMBER 22, 1914.

WAR NEWS
is telegraphed by "The Daily Mail's"
WAR NEWS BUREAU
(36, Fleet Street, London, E.C.)
TO YOUR OWN HOUSE
(Rate:—24 words for 2/4

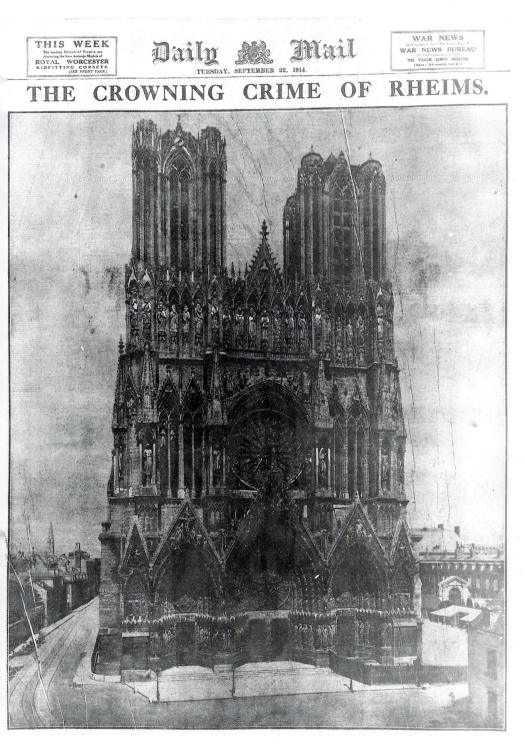

The bombardment of Rheims, the first full-page photograph ever published in the
Daily Mail, 22 September 1914. By showing Rheims as it had been before the bombing, the photograph demonstrated the full extent of the German atrocity.

WEEKLY DISPATCH | BEST OF THE BATCH | **Daily Mail** | LATEST WAR EDITION

Daily Net SALE Six Times as Large as That of Any Penny London Morning Journal Except "THE TIMES."

THURSDAY, MAY 20, 1915.   LONDON.   MANCHESTER.   PARIS   NO. 5,968.   ONE HALFPENNY.

LORD KITCHENER
CALLS FOR MORE MEN

WAR OFFICE
WHITEHALL
S.W.

I have said that I would let the country know when more men were wanted for the war. The time has come and I now call for 300,000 recruits to form new armies—

Those who are engaged on the production of war material of any kind should not leave their work. It is to men who are not performing this duty that I appeal—

Kitchener

NEW CONDITIONS OF ENLISTMENT—Age limit now 40

Age - - 19 to 40.
Height - minimum 5 feet 2 inches.
Chest - - minimum 33½ inches.

Enlistment for general service, for the duration of the War.

God Save the King.

In May 1915, less than a month after the ill-fated Gallipoli landings, Kitchener appeals for more recruits. Northcliffe was about to become the foremost critic of Government policy, facing down the Secretary for War in 'the great shells crisis'.

(Below left) Vyvyan, Vere and
Esmond Harmsworth, with their
mother Lilian; (Right) Vere and
Vyvyan on a sleigh in a posed
studio shot; (Below right) the
three boys with their father.

Vyvyan Harmsworth with his father, 1915. Rothermere, like Northcliffe, was privy to uncensored information about what was actually happening at the Front. He knew what was coming.

Vere at Gallipoli, 1915. The night before his death at the Battle of Ancre, on 13 November 1916, he wrote to his Uncle St John, 'I may have been born just to live my twenty-one years and then fade away … The future seems far away and unreal.'

Vyvyan in the trenches in 1917. He died in Lady Northcliffe's Hospital for Officers in February the following year. His only flash of anger came when he told his Uncle Northcliffe, 'I do not mind having been wounded three times, but I hate to think I have been butchered three times.'

'Evenings in Printing House Square', as viewed by Max Beerbohm. The caption reads:
Northcliffe – 'Help! Again I feel the demons of sensationalism rising in me. Hold me
fast! Curb me, if you love me!' Northcliffe bought *The Times* in March 1908, making it
solvent, but he enraged those who thought he catered too much to the masses.

Northcliffe as Director of Propaganda
in Enemy Countries, as seen through
the eyes of a German cartoonist on the
journal *Simplicissimus*, Munich.

Northcliffe at the height of his powers.

Northcliffe in Sydney on his 'World Whirl', 1921. *Punch* published a send-up: 'Lord Thanet sailed on Saturday the 16th from Tilbury on the *Megalomania* for his great world-pilgrimage, in the course of which he will visit the North and South Poles, ascend Mt Everest and descend to the centre of the earth.' In fact, by then Northcliffe was desperately ill.

Northcliffe's house at 1, Carlton Gardens. It was thought that the dying press lord needed cooling breezes, but the roof of his house proved too weak to support a revolving shelter. His neighbour, the Duke of Devonshire, gave permission for the roof of the adjoining house to be used. There Northcliffe was caged in a small hut until he died in August 1922.

FUNERAL OF LORD NORTHCLIFFE: STRIKING PUBLIC TRIBUTE.

The back page of *The Times* reporting Northcliffe's funeral on 17 August 1922. '...People lined the streets for four hours waiting for the procession to pass. The buses stopped and at a fixed time, thousands stood silent for two minutes out of respect for his passing.'

consultation with these and other war reporters, Northcliffe frequently had eight to ten calls waiting out of the thirty telephone lines that fed into the offices of the *Daily Mail*. The newspaper also maintained a direct line to the Press Bureau in Paris, with a telephone manned twenty-four hours a day. Unable to find a way of setting up telegraph communications from the battlefields, the *Mail* improvised a complex system of communication that found the correspondents wiring their dispatches to New York, from whence they were bounced back again by wire to London for publication.

The *Daily Mail* swiftly became the official newspaper of the British troops, with 10,000 copies of the continental edition delivered to the Front daily by military motor cars. The paper, which carried the latest war cables, special articles and war photos, was condensed to four pages, the only way they could manage to overcome the difficulties of circulation during wartime.

For those at home, there was a special service, offered to the public as an opportunity to have 'War News Wired to You by the *Daily Mail*'. Subscribers could choose a daily wire at five o'clock in the afternoon, or they could elect to receive 'important news only'. It was also possible to receive news by telephone if the subscriber lived within the Metropolitan area.

More importantly, at the end of August 1914, a singular announcement appeared:

> The *Daily Mail* will be glad to receive for publication letters sent to their friends in this country by soldiers serving with the Expeditionary Force. For those letters which we publish we shall be pleased to pay at our usual rates.

It was Northcliffe's revolutionary idea to use the men at the Front as primary news sources. Later on, this simple concept would give him access to information no other newsman could know. But for now, he was, as usual, exposed to ridicule for his idea. *Punch* published a listing in 'Our Personal Column':

> To Officers and Men whose letters contain good vivid accounts of picturesque occurrences at the Front. The Daily Inexactitude places no limit on the writer's imagination.

But 'Inexactitude' was not typically what the *Daily Mail* was known for; the precision of its war operation put the newspaper's coverage ahead again and again for the duration of the war.

Not so at the scene of the actual conflict, however – where chaos and disorder reigned. On 24 August 1914, Hamilton Fyfe's byline appeared over a story that gave the facts:

WAR IN A FOG

Blankville, France, (Department de Never-Mind-Where). I have been motoring about the country and talking to any number of British soldiers, men as well as officers of all ranks. They have no idea where they are going. A general of division left here last night genuinely ignorant of the spot where he was to meet his command. When troops entrain they are told sometimes how long their journey is to be. But about their destination not a word . . . for days and days, horse, foot, and artillery have been pouring through certain French ports . . . Then they disappear. For all that is known of them, they might have been transported to Mars. The fog envelops them. They will not be heard of again until one morning when you open your newspapers and find they have done some splendid fighting.

This was the setting for the Battle of Mons, and when the British public opened their newspapers they found their troops had done some splendid dying as well. The British Expeditionary Force, some four divisions strong and comprising more than 100,000 men, had crossed the Channel and were moving into Belgium. As they marched towards Mons, they were confronted by the full force of Von Kluck's First German Army. The unexpected withdrawal of the French Fifth Army under Lanrezac left the soldiers exposed, and, outnumbered three to one, they suffered appalling casualties. The historic retreat from Mons, recorded by Hamilton Fyfe, began with the words, 'Would to God I had not to tell this story.' Thus began the dispatch that introduced the British public to Armageddon, and the nation was plunged into shock and despair.

The Press Bureau, witnessing the nation's reaction, later that day issued a statement of reassurance to the country, implying that the story had been overstated. Immediately, the *Daily Mail*'s rivals put out the line that the paper was using its old familiar scaremongering techniques. When these charges arose, Northcliffe asked whether the story had been submitted to the Press Bureau for censorship. He was told that yes, not only had it been censored, but in fact F.E. Smith, then head of the Press Bureau, had personally scrutinized the dispatch, even adding in details and writing a note to the effect that the British public had a right to know what had actually taken place.

Northcliffe said, 'Have you that letter?' On being told that it had been kept, he said, 'Print it.' He was told it was private. 'Print it,' he repeated. 'Give it to me.'

There was some demur but he insisted. 'I am not going to be attacked, when I am right, without retaliation.' So the letter is published.*

The *Mail* had begun its formidable task of trying to report the truth in an environment of repression and deceit. Again, in a dispatch written three days later, on 26 August, Fyfe wrote,

> I have just seen the first trainload of British wounded arrive from the Front ... men with their heads bandaged and red stains showing through the white; men with arms in splints, their sleeves hanging empty; men limping, men carried away on stretchers, men with feeble arms round comrades' shoulders only just able to stand upright ... a harrowing impression ...
>
> They had no trenches, no cover of any kind. They had to drop down and lie where they were all day. When it got dark they did their best to make trenches with the shells coming 'as regular as a postal delivery', as one soldier said.

In the meantime, George Curnock had returned to the office from Boulogne where he told the young sub-editor Tom Clarke, 'Good God, Clarke, if you had seen what I have seen, and talked with men who escaped the awful slaughter, you would not be able to sit there.' For his part, Thomas Marlowe dismissed Curnock's words as reckless emotionalism, saying it was obvious he needed a rest.

But a few days after Fyfe wrote his famous story, Asquith admitted the casualties had been more than 2,000 strong; if he had counted the sporadic battles that took place in the five days after the start of Mons, the count would have been closer to 8,000.

A stark appraisal of what was yet to come, the Allied losses, like those of the enemy, began to mount. It was Northcliffe's destiny to chronicle these casualties, and as the full light of their magnitude began to dawn, to call a country to arms. The first photographs from the war – 'A Page of Pictures from the Front' – appeared near the end of August: 'Belgian troops on the way to the Front', 'The Civil Guards at Bruges', 'A Belgian soldier with field telephone', and 'Britain's might – the 13.5 guns of H.M.S. Queen Mary' were amongst the first to be printed. Thereafter, for the duration of the conflict, the back page of the paper would be devoted to these images of war. Typically, the newspaper turned to the troops themselves as a

---

* There appear to be two versions of the story. The first applies to the *Mail*; the other, practically the same account, is attributed to *The Times*. As regards *The Times* version, there are references to the Amiens dispatch in letters between Winston Churchill and Northcliffe. But, since Clarke's version was kept as a diary of daily occurrences at the *Mail* and is therefore a primary source, that is the version used here. Tom Clarke, *My Northcliffe Diary*, p. 68.

source of generating the pictures. A contest was initiated for the best war photographs, with twenty weekly prizes of £100 each.

Picture postcards went into production labelled, 'Daily Mail War Pictures, Official Photograph, Crown Copyright Reserved'. The titles elevated the common events in a soldier's day. 'A "fag" after a fight', ' "Tommy" at home in German dug-outs', 'A gallant rescue under fire', 'Happy "Tommies" wearing hun helmets', 'Loyal North Lancs regiment cheering when ordered to the trenches'; it was stirring propaganda to shore up the morale of those left behind.

But, even as these postcards went to press, Northcliffe and his staff were beginning to understand the lengthening odds against an early end to the war. And just in case they didn't, the Battle of Tannenberg on the Eastern Front amply demonstrated the point. During the last week of August 1914, when the battle was raging, Russian losses mounted to 125,000 men; the Germans lost fewer than 15,000.

The information came to Northcliffe via *The Times*, where a man who had been travelling hard suddenly staggered into the office and gave over the news: 'The Russians have lost a hundred thousand dead and that is the end of Russia in this war.'

On the Western Front, one of the worst atrocities of the war was about to take place – the bombardment of Rheims – and G. Ward Price was there. 'Our Correspondent Sees Rheims Cathedral Burn', the headline blared. Calling it 'the most wanton act of deliberate destruction that the Germans have yet committed ... a monument of German barbarity and sacrilege,' Price watched as German batteries on a hill fired shell after shell upon the Cathedral. The thirteenth-century edifice had taken a hundred and fifty years to build; it was destroyed in an afternoon.

> Avalanche after avalanche of stonework, that had survived the storms of centuries, thundered down into the deserted streets. Burning splinters fell upon the roof, whose old oak timbers caught like tinder. A blazing piece of carved woodwork crashed down to the floor of the Cathedral, where the Germans, during their occupation, had accumulated great piles of straw. Instantly this caught alight; and panelling, altars, confessionals, and chairs were devoured by leaping flames that scorched and cracked the great stone walls.

The dispatch appeared in the pages of the *Daily Mail* on 21 September 1914, and on the next day a picture of the Cathedral, the first full-page photograph ever to appear in the pages of the *Daily Mail*, was published – but not as it was after it had been destroyed. Instead, the photograph pictured Rheims as it had been before the bombing, in order to show the extent of the German atrocity. This was the first war to make full use of photographs to show the advance of the conflict, in large part because of progress made earlier by newspapers owned by Northcliffe.

More than anything else, however, this was a writer's war – a case for poignant observation, with death and mayhem elevated to heroic acts and deeds. G. Ward Price, writing in Paris, took note of how 'men running across the open towards their death have after all very much the same preoccupations as men running to catch a train at home.'

> They are annoyed when they stumble; they pant out little jokes to each other. 'Don't talk. Keep your wind. Don't waste the steam,' gasps out one Zouave to another as they start a bayonet charge at the great distance of 1,000 yards.

The first-person narrative – that is, the actual word-for-word recounting of the experience of a single soldier – was reaching its zenith, and story after story filled the pages of the *Daily Mail* of individual impressions of the battlefield. A Scottish private: 'It was somewhere near Mons. The Germans advanced in great masses four or five deep and as fast as we shot them down another mass came on, simply going over the bodies.' Another Scottish private told Ward Price: 'Yesterday afternoon I was crawling through a mangel-wurzel field with the bullets pinging all round me. I thought my last day had come. Then I got hit in the foot and they fetched me in.'

No aspect of the war went unreported, and amongst the descriptions of various personnel found in the *Daily Mail* were those faced by the regimental surgeons. Always in the midst of the fighting, they had to travel across roads pocked with holes caused by the constant shelling. And, because they followed the troops, they themselves were subject to the same quick death. The noise of an approaching shell, wrote G. Ward Price, could never be forgotten by those who had heard it.

> A shell comes straight for us. It is like the buzzing of a motor-car, the furious bellowing of an animal. In an instant we are on the ground flat on our faces, nose in the mud ... It's a long time to wait. Each of us has time for unpleasant reflections. And often a flood of memories surges through one's head and the future one had dreamed of appears, for a last time, in radiant colour.

Upon reaching the battlefield, the medical personnel discovered an improvised hospital full of casualties, with six German soldiers caring impartially for both the French and German wounded. Ward Price watched as one of the soldiers asked for a drink, and at the moment it was handed to him a stray bullet passed through the shutters, striking him in the head.

He fell back without a sound. 'No one says a word,' wrote Price. 'Each knows it may be his turn next.'

One fine autumn afternoon, Hamilton Fyfe watches as two white coffins are lowered into the ground, a rough wooden cross pounded into the ground as a marker.

> A cart comes slowly up the road. It is full of dead men. In their uniforms. Just as they have been picked up. Sleeping, you would say, save that men do not sleep piled upon one another, all swaying to the motion of the cart.

Their bodies are tenderly placed into a single pit, the earth gently shovelled on top. There are worse things than this, Fyfe reminds his reader: 'Ghastly body wounds' wherein the holes torn in the flesh are as large as a man's two fists, a body rent open with a huge gaping wound or 'an anatomy laid bare'.

In the hospitals men are everywhere, resting outside the makeshift buildings, their heads wrapped in white bandages, their arms in splints. The rotation of bodies is constant; 'as soon as one mangled form is carried away another takes its place.' The surgeons work without cease. This then was the process of war, the systematic organization of a conflict that would continue for four long years.

Hamilton Fyfe, the *Daily Mail* correspondent who wrote these classic descriptions of the suffering endured by men at war, was swiftly rewarded for his efforts. He found himself exiled to Russia, 'virtually a prisoner in Petrograd under an edict of "K's" ', as one correspondent who knew Fyfe well put it. 'K', of course, was the newly appointed Secretary for War, Lord Kitchener, at first strongly supported in this position by Northcliffe. But Fyfe's dramatic exile from the heart of the Allied operations was one of the first signs of how far Kitchener was prepared to go in order to defend the Government's calamitous decision to bring to a halt the publication of any actual news from the Front.

A declaration by Kitchener in the House of Lords that correspondents would no longer be allowed in the field sparked a battle between himself and Northcliffe that was destined to continue up to the very day Kitchener was lost at sea. In defiance of the Secretary's war edict, the very day after the announcement the *Mail* published its most extensive and detailed coverage thus far on the conduct of the war. Kitchener retaliated by threatening to shoot the reporters who turned in the story, whereupon Northcliffe published a facsimile of a dispatch that had been 'mutilated' by the Press Censor; that is, he showed where the copy had been changed or crossed out on official orders. By now, the whole exchange was being described in Parliament as 'a plot' on the part of Northcliffe to discredit the Government. Inside the offices of the *Mail*, Kitchener was dubbed 'K for Chaos', and Northcliffe labelled any publication co-operating with the Government's censorship bureau as 'Hide-the-Truth' newspapers.

The *Mail* meanwhile published a dispatch entitled 'The Press Bureau at Home: Important Work in a Shabby Den'. The Bureau, the article asserted, was nothing less than a 'clearing-house for contemporary history' where 'experts' found themselves in the absurd position of sitting night and day, sorting out information that had been gathered at great personal risk. News literally poured into the agency, a great sea of reportage that cascaded down upon the censors. It trickled out drop by drop. 'Disappointed journalists', the article asserted, 'have facetiously described it as the Suppress Bureau.'

At the Front, the lengths *Mail* correspondents were prepared to go to in order to get round the censors became downright ridiculous. One correspondent caught hiding in an ambulance train was returned to Paris and from thence to London. When he remonstrated, saying he was only trying to gather news, he was told he was acting against the interests of his country. His story? The inadequacy of ambulance trains in the transport of the wounded and dying.

Ferdinand Tuohy described the role of the war correspondent as 'a sorry farce' wherein some two hundred correspondents invaded the Continent masquerading as ambulance drivers or couriers in order surreptitiously to get the news and deliver it back home. Tuohy himself felt he was

> a cross between a spy, a briber and a groveller; forever pursuing underhand methods, and periodically rendezvousing with King Smuggler at Folkestone with stories collected often at one's wits end ... We spent most of our time avoiding personal trouble and 'getting our stuff through' when we should have been trying intelligently to follow the campaign. Nine double Channel crossings were my lot in the first month alone, and the effect of the whole business was that the War passed over most of our heads in a maze of isolated actions, charges, stands, incidents, duly given to you under distorted headings.

Early in the war, when the Germans invaded Brussels, Tuohy had collected firsthand accounts of the action, then travelled 'post-haste' to Folkestone, 'scribbling all the way', meanwhile followed by a Scotland Yard man who was intent on preventing the publication of any news of the event. Putting his dispatches in the lining of his cap, Tuohy carried them straight to London and went back to Ostend that very night. He then joined the stream of refugees fleeing the city, observing how the French women volunteer nurses left wounded Germans to die of gangrene beside the road. As he travelled, Tuohy gave out money, cigarettes and beer to the hordes, listening to their 'thrilling stories' of heroism and taking careful notes. Within two days, he would be at Whitehall with F.E. Smith at the Press Bureau, trying to bargain out the information for publication in the *Daily Mail*. At the time, Tuohy noted with irony, the main subjects on offer to newspapers from official channels were: 'a) mounts, b) batmen and c) underclothes'.

On 7 October 1914, Tuohy became the official correspondent for Associated Newspapers on the Western Front and was with Northcliffe when Kitchener announced his intention to blacklist war correspondents, shipping them home if they could be identified. Northcliffe was in his study in St James's Place, 'pacing, as usual,' wrote Tuohy, 'behind a fat cigar'.

> What's wrong with the man? What does he think I want to do? Wreck my country? Ruin him? Why, it was one of my men, G.W. Steevens, who made him! ... This matter of war correspondents is for French* to decide, and I know he wants them ... They can shoot me if I print anything they don't like. Meanwhile, I shall send out my correspondents as I think fit.

Northcliffe now issued a stinging criticism of the Government over 'the insufficiency of news concerning the British troops at the Front'. No newspaper, he said, wanted to publish information that might give military aid to the enemy. But the truth was that French newspapers had been freely allowed to publish facts that had been suppressed in Great Britain.

And by November a new crisis had arisen. A Cabinet Minister had been criticized by one of Northcliffe's competitors, a newspaper that had been owned by one of his brothers before the war started. As a result of its attack, the *Globe* had been threatened with severe penalties. This prompted Northcliffe in turn to launch his own attack. 'The Government', the *Mail* leader asserted, 'are fast drifting into a sharp and disturbing collision with one of the elementary rights of a British subject – the right to criticise.' Nobody objected to censorship over the movement of troops and ships during wartime; this was a matter of national security. It was one thing for the Government to extend censorship over information; quite another for it to extend it over opinion. 'Liberty of criticism is the very lifeblood of our whole national system,' the article said, 'and the main safeguard we possess against Ministerial autocracy...'

The Government thought otherwise.

And, in the end, it would be one man standing alone who would dare to defy government policy and censorship. That man would be Northcliffe.

*

* General Sir John French, Commander-in-Chief, British Expeditionary Force.

During the Great War, the chief ingredient used to propel bullets from rifles, and high-explosive shells from artillery pieces, was cotton that had been dipped into nitric acid, then lightly washed and dried; or gun-cotton, as it was called. One shot from a Queen Elizabeth fifteen-inch field gun or from a German seventeen-inch Howitzer required a bale of cotton weighing as much as 400 pounds. Similarly, the manufacture of nitroglycerine, the chief ingredient in dynamite, required vast reserves of cotton-seed oil. Despite these facts, by the end of the first year of conflict cotton had not been proclaimed contraband by Britain, nor had it been declared liable to seizure by British or Allied cruisers.

The main sources of Germany's supply of cotton were the southern States of America. The crop was shipped to the neutral ports of Holland, Norway, Denmark and Sweden from whence it was sold to Germany to use in the manufacture of munitions. Since the start of the war, those countries had increased their orders of the staple some seventeen-fold, and still Britain had done nothing to stop the import of cotton into its enemy's hands.

'Killing Our Men by Cotton', read the *Daily Mail* headline. 'Stop the Germans from Getting It.' England was 'already a mass of hospitals', the article asserted,

> and just across the water miles of expensive hospital huts are being erected to contain the future victims of the cotton that is now going into Germany . . .

Were there not widows and orphans enough? the article asked. 'Why do we not issue the proclamation and cut off the raw material of Germany's powder?'

Northcliffe's method had devolved, in his own words, into 'perpetual agitation', because it was the only way he could spur a laggardly Government into action.

> We are told that this is not the time for criticism but for respectful and servile silence. We do not agree, and we rejoice to think that a daily increasing number of people who want to win this war are with us.

It was incumbent upon the Government to declare cotton contraband, compensating exporters in the southern states and informing those neutral European countries who were obviously supplying Germany that they would be permitted to import exactly the amount they had been importing before the war, and no more. This because 'every bale of cotton which reaches Germany means either an Allied cripple or a corpse.'

Was it the dire language of the *Daily Mail*'s appeal that finally galvanized the Government into action? Or was it simply one more case of ineptitude on the part of civil servants at last corrected? The answer was impossible to determine. But by the end of the *Daily Mail*'s determined campaign the Government, in an Allied declaration issued in co-operation with the American Government, at last declared 'raw cotton, cotton linters, cotton waste, and cotton yarns' to be contraband.

Thus was Northcliffe's dilemma defined: if, during wartime, the first casualty is truth, does one report the truth regardless, perhaps contributing to the loss of the war? Or is the proper course of action absolute support of a government whose ineptitude is manifest, in the hope that the nation wins the contest by default? Northcliffe – whose first position had been editor of a lowly bicycling magazine, whose wealth depended upon an empire founded upon 'useless information', a parvenu, an outsider, a half-Irish megalomaniac – decided upon the side of principle.

From 1 January 1915 until the last day of March, General Joseph J.C. Joffre, Commander-in-Chief of the French Army, made his most serious effort yet to regain vast tracts of French territory held by the Germans. But the series of attacks he initiated ended in disaster, and at Neuve Chapelle an initial breakthrough failed after the shell supply ran out. This was on 10 March 1915. By the end of the month, casualties resulting from the three months' thrust were, amongst the French, approaching 400,000. In the two months following, British casualties alone approached 30,000.

Both General Sir John French, Commander-in-Chief of the British Expeditionary Force, and Lord Kitchener himself expressed their concern about the shortage of high-explosive shells. But in a speech made on 20 April in Newcastle the Prime Minister, Herbert Asquith, denied any such shortage. 'I saw a statement the other day,' he said,

> that the operations, not only of our Army but of our Allies, were being crippled, or, at any rate, hampered, by our failure to provide the necessary ammunition. There is not a word of truth in that statement, which is the more mischievous because, if it were believed, it is calculated to dishearten our troops, to discourage our Allies, and to stimulate the hopes and the activities of our enemies.

His statement, Asquith said, had been made only after 'the most careful inquiry of Lord Kitchener', upon whose authority he now spoke.

But Northcliffe held in his possession a substantial number of letters sent to him by soldiers at the Front, contending that the munitions shortage had severely hampered their efforts over the last few months. He did not publish these, but instead sent them on to Government Ministers, amongst them Lloyd George, whom the press baron would soon support as Minister of Munitions, a post he intended to help create. 'These letters',

Northcliffe wrote to Lloyd George, 'will show them how the Press Bureau is keeping the truth from the people.'

Meanwhile, on 14 May, *The Times* published the contents of a telegram from its chief war correspondent Lieutenant-Colonel Repington, who wrote,

> The attacks (on Sunday last in the districts of Fromelles and Richebourg) were well planned and valiantly conducted. The infantry did splendidly, but the conditions were too hard. The want of an unlimited supply of high explosives was a fatal bar to our success at Festubert.

Although the initiative for an attack on governmental incompetence lay with *The Times*, its editor, Geoffrey Robinson,* lacked the heart for what he or any other professional newsman in his position knew was sure to follow. Thus, it was left to Northcliffe and the *Daily Mail* to take the lead in exposing exactly how desperate conditions at the Front had become.

The morning after the telegram from Repington had been published in *The Times*, the *Mail* carried the banner headline, 'British Still Struggling: Send More Shells'. And in its editorial leader the newspaper explained to the public its increasingly difficult position. For, if the paper published 'the truth about the defects of our military preparations', it could always be accused of aiding the enemy; and if it didn't, it was not fulfilling its responsibility to keep the public informed and get the defeats remedied.

At last, on 21 May, Northcliffe published the best-known leader of the First World War: 'The Tragedy of the Shells: Lord Kitchener's Grave Error', ran the headline. Charges of a cover-up at high levels followed on from there: 'The Shells Scandal: Lord Kitchener's Tragic Blunder: Our Terrible Casualties Lists: Cause of the Cabinet Crisis'. The text laid the blame squarely upon the shoulders of the Secretary for War, Lord Kitchener:

> Lord Kitchener has starved the army in France of high-explosive shells. The admitted fact is that Lord Kitchener ordered the wrong kind of shell – the same kind of shell which he used largely against the Boers in 1900. He persisted in sending shrapnel – a useless weapon in trench warfare. He was warned repeatedly that the kind of shell required was a violently explosive bomb which would dynamite its way through the German trenches and entanglements and enable our brave men to advance in safety. The kind of shell our poor soldiers have had has caused the death of thousands of them.

That was the start. On the following day, the *Mail* continued its assault. The paper stood by its original accusation that 'our men at the Front have

---

* Geoffrey Robinson changed his surname to Dawson in 1917.

been supplied with the wrong kind of shell and the result has been a heavy and avoidable loss of life.' A shortage of shells at the beginning of the conflict, the newspaper argued, was understandable and excusable. But the inability of officials to supply adequate munitions after ten months of punishing ordeals for Britain's fighting men was 'proof of grave negligence'.

Now Northcliffe was seen in the offices of *The Times*, a grim and determined expression upon his face. He consulted with no one except his mother, he would later explain, and she approved the course of action he determined upon. At the weekend, he retreated to Buckthorn Hill, Crowborough, there to write the draft for the final volley in the *Daily Mail's* campaign. His secretary, who was present at the time, later wrote, 'His face was white and set.' He wrote in pencil, on writing paper intended for polite correspondence:

We return to the most serious subject before the Nation, the Shells and the Casualties.

The *daily* losses in the war, *on ordinary days*, when there is no attempt to advance, are about two thousand, according to official casualty lists. We are growing callous about the size of the daily lists of killed, wounded and missing. Very few people read even the headings of them, comparatively few grasp the fact that after vast losses we are just where we were six months ago on our little line in the Franco–Belgian Frontier...

No kinds of official hushing can hide those daily recurring losses either from the Germans or ourselves. We *know* that constant appeals for big explosive shells have been made to Lord Kitchener from the Front. We *know* that until the revelation of *The Times* correspondent the Government itself did not know of these appeals. Sir Alfred Mond* often tries to tell us that it is only *now* that the need for these essentials to success and the preservation of our men has become known to our soldiers. That is, in plain English, a lie. Thousands of homes are mourning to-day for men who have been needlessly sacrificed.

As Northcliffe advanced his argument, the slope of his pencil tracing edged higher and higher, until, by the last lines, his dense scrawl was practically at right-angles to the page.

The war, he continued, had grown more and more serious; more and more men had been drafted into service. And thus had arisen the appalling circumstance 'that whole regiments of the flower of the Empire have been blotted out of existence.'

'That is why', he wrote finally, 'we criticize Lord Kitchener.'

*

* Sir Alfred Mond, Liberal MP for Swansea.

'He is no longer a jest,' wrote a rival paper after the publication of North-cliffe's attack on Kitchener. 'He is the most deadly enemy that this country or this Empire has to face. He is ready to set either in a blaze to light a placard.'

Overnight, circulation of the *Daily Mail* dropped from 1,386,000 to 238,000. And in Throgmorton Street a placard was hung across the name-plate of the newspaper, 'The Allies of the Huns'. On the Stock Exchange, members crowded onto the Floor, some 1,500 of them. A resolution was passed against the 'venomous attacks' of the Harmsworth Press. On the floor, a bonfire was kindled with copies of the newspaper, and the blaze grew bright as more and more copies were piled on top.

On Monday afternoon at four o'clock, the day of the publication of his pencilled editorial leader, Northcliffe walked into the offices of the *Daily Mail* in Carmelite House, the staff standing as they always did to show respect. He put on the big horn-rimmed glasses he always wore when reading, and took a seat in an armchair beside the desk of the editor, Thomas Marlowe.

'Have you seen the *Star*, Chief?' Marlowe asked him.

'No, I never read those racing papers,' Northcliffe replied.

'You had better look at it.'

And Marlowe threw over the latest edition of the evening paper, at the top of the fourth column on the front page of which were the words, 'Daily Mail Burned on the Stock Exchange . . .'

Informed of the more than one million drop in circulation, Northcliffe read the report carried in the rival newspaper. He then looked up at the assembled group of newspapermen. 'I don't know what you men think and I don't care,' he said. 'The *Star* is wrong, and I am right. And the day will come when you will all know that I am right. Now, what's on tomorrow's schedule?'*

---

* His exact words were, 'Fish, what's on the schedule?' Hannen Swaffer, *Northcliffe's Return*, p. 24.

10

'The Remainder Were Not To Be Denied'

Northcliffe, it turned out, was right.

In late May 1915, the Liberal Government collapsed under the pressure of the press baron's unrelenting criticism over the shells crisis. True, Asquith remained to head the new coalition, and the much derided Kitchener was also secured in the same post he had held before the changeover. But David Lloyd George was installed as Minister of Munitions, and it was generally believed his appointment was what Northcliffe had intended all along. Certainly, Lloyd George brought to the newly created position the energy, competence and cynicism it required. He also exhibited a deadly determination to carry out his will at any cost, along with a vaulting ambition that o'erleaped itself.

Between the new Munitions Minister and the press baron, no cordiality was wasted. A continuing correspondence between the two men from 1908 showed that both seemed tacitly inclined to adhere to a code of stiff formality conspicuously absent from the easy intercourse between Northcliffe and, say, Winston Churchill. But the war, and Northcliffe's perceptions of its misconduct during the disastrous spring of 1915, was destined to affect even his long-standing relationship with Churchill. For it was Churchill, as First Lord of the Admiralty, who had originally planned to effect a supply route to the beleaguered Russians through the narrow straits of the Dardanelles, which were held by enemy Turks.

As early as February, the *Daily Mail* made known Northcliffe's opposition to his friend's plan, publishing a leader calling the project 'A Most Dangerous and Difficult Operation'.

> The bombardment of the Dardanelles forts by a powerful Anglo-French Fleet is an enterprise which promises immense results. But German guns and gunners have been poured into Turkey during the last three months. Every device which German ingenuity can suggest for the defence of the waterways has been placed at Turkey's disposal.

At the same time and typically, the *Daily Mail* published maps of the area, highlighted with in-depth details of Turkish fortifications and munitions in order that the public could follow the action in an informed manner. And, just as typically, the *Mail* was again confronted by the Government's determination to keep the flow of information down to a trickle, Churchill foremost amongst those favouring heavy censorship.

At the actual battle scene, after a successful but prematurely aborted naval assault by the British on Turkish fortifications, a number of delays followed, at the cost of the British initiative. This fact, however, went unreported. The raw recruits, cooling their heels in Egypt, were mainly territorials from Australia and New Zealand, the so-called Anzacs (Australian-New Zealand Army Corps). Their fate at Gallipoli would be murderous; but the prose describing the event, written by E. Ashmead-Bartlett of the London *Telegraph* – a bitter and disenchanted alcoholic and the only correspondent allowed to report the event – would be of the epic sort favoured by the powers above, with only a bare hint of the underlying disaster.

Under duress, Bartlett trilled out his 'Memorable Scene at the Dardanelles':

> The great venture has at last been launched, and the entire fleet of warships and transports is now steaming slowly towards the shores of Gallipoli.
>
> As the huge liners steamed through the fleet, their decks yellow with khaki, the crews of the warships cheered them on to victory, while the bands played them out with an unending variety of popular airs. The soldiers in the transports answered this last salutation from the Navy with deafening cheers, and no more inspiring spectacle has ever been seen than this, of the last great crusade setting forth for better or for worse . . .

It was for worse.

Boatloads of the inexperienced young men were wiped out even before reaching the shore, with those who had managed to land on the beach unable to fire because they might have shot their own men. Indeed, their weapons were mainly bayonets, while the well-armed Turks raked across the Anzacs with state-of-the-art machine-guns. In the Gallipoli peninsula, there were no hospitals, and the wounded were loaded some 800 to 1,000 at a time into transport ships with 'only three surgeons and two dressers to attend them'. From the scene of the battle to the safe havens of Malta or Alexandria, many men received no attention for five or six days.*

The commander-in-chief of the Mediterranean Expedition Force, Sir Ian Hamilton, filed his own uncompromising report, which was eventually

---

* These facts have been collated from a series of dispatches written by E. Ashmead Bartlett (7 May to 24 June).

published in the *Daily Mail*.* In it, he was sublimely unaware of the distressing nature of his disclosures: 'It was a touch-and-go struggle,' he wrote dramatically.

> The enemy's machine guns were too scientifically posted. Generally speaking the coast is precipitous, and good landing-places are few. In most of these landing-places the trenches and lines of wire entanglements were plainly visible from on board ship.
>
> Throughout the afternoon and all through the night the Turks made assault after assault upon the British line. They threw bombs into the trenches. The British repeatedly counter-charged with the bayonet and always drove off the enemy for the moment, but the Turks were in a vast superiority and fresh troops took the place of those who temporarily fell back. By 7 a.m. on the first day after the landing, only about half remained to man the entrenchment made for four times their number.
>
> Up to the very last moment it appeared as if the landing was to be unopposed. But a tornado of fire swept over the beach, the incoming boats, and the collier. The Dublin Fusiliers and the naval boats' crews suffered exceedingly heavy losses while still in the boats. [There was] the difficulty of placing the lighters in position between the ship and the shore. A strong current hindered the work and the enemy's fire was so intense that almost every man engaged upon it was immediately shot. [The second company then alighted and] many men who had escaped being shot were drowned by the weight of their equipment in trying to swim from the lighter to the beach. At this time between 10 and 11 a.m., about 1,000 men had left the collier, and of these nearly half had been killed or wounded before they could reach the little cover afforded by the steep, sandy bank at the top of the beach.

What met the men when they reached the shore was 'a broad wire entanglement', with 'a supplementary barbed network' just below the surface of the shallow water. Land and sea mines had been planted liberally throughout the area. Then, although a single group of men had traversed the dangerous waters without a shot being fired,

> as soon as the first boat touched the ground, a hurricane of lead swept over the battalion. A long line of men was at once mown down as by a scythe, but the remainder were not to be denied...

With the release of the first list of casualties at Gallipoli, the *Daily Mail* went wild. 'Every Man Wanted for Flanders', the newspaper's leader proclaimed:

---

* A report by Sir Ian Hamilton, which covered the initial landing between 25 April and 25 May, published on 7 July 1915.

'One Thing at a Time'. Flanders, the editorial asserted, was the place where the peril 'for life and liberty' was 'most menacing'. The men and officers who fought at the Dardanelles were to be lauded, because they had accomplished 'a splendid feat'. But it was too bad, the *Mail* continued, that 'we cannot congratulate the authorities who planned the expedition', and had thus diverted a large fighting force to a secondary aim.

> The most decisive success at the Dardanelles would settle nothing in Flanders and would hardly affect the German resolve. To win this war, the German line must itself be broken and the German masses hurled back. Upon that task we must concentrate all our strength and not dissipate it in half a dozen different directions.

By early summer, Gallipoli had emerged as a disastrous muddle and Churchill had departed the Admiralty under duress. The *Daily Mail* damned the Government outright for the continuing mismanagement of the war. The newspaper charged that Britain was making more mistakes than Germany, and 'still sending our boys into the firing line with rifles and shrapnel to face machine-guns and high explosives'. The Ministers had learned nothing; their continuing ignorance was awesome. 'The expedition', the newspaper wrote, 'was started by politicians who did not even know that the Germans had submarines capable of getting round through the Mediterranean to the Dardanelles.'

> Using the power of the censorship, they have for months hidden the whole story of this vast Dardanelles expedition from the public. They cannot hide it from the Germans, for the German newspapers have had ample descriptions of it.
>
> Yet these same politicians are in their places. We have practically the same people in control who were in control at the beginning, while practical Germany has 'scrapped' her incompetents. Unless the British public takes the matter into its own hands and insists upon the dismissal of inefficient bunglers among the politicians and at the War Office, we shall lose the support of our Allies, the enthusiasm of the Dominions; we shall waste the magnificent efforts of our soldiers and sailors; and, eventually, we shall lose the war.

What was the grim reality that fuelled the *Mail*'s desperate rhetoric? At Gallipoli, three nights of 'desperate hand-to-hand fighting' had won the Allies four lines of trenches. The same four lines were lost the following day. All around, 'the wounded and dead choked the trenches almost to the top', survivors carrying on their combat on top of the 'heaps of corpses'.

At the battles of Sari Bair, Hill Q and Hill 70 – the names of the death-traps bore strange witness to the campaign's lack of logic – the Allies 'were driven from their position by artillery fire and sheer weight of numbers'. The territorial and British troops hurled themselves into enemy trenches, only to be impaled upon the upraised bayonets of the Turks.

> As the huge shells from the ships exploded in their midst, huge chunks of soil were thrown into the air, amid which human bodies were hurled aloft and then thrown to earth or into deep ravines. Generals and colonels fought with rifles and bayonets alongside their troops in the firing line. It was a fierce hand-to-hand struggle among the scrub through broken ground. Many commanding officers were killed. Gradually the enemy was driven back and the ground we had been obliged to abandon regained.

This was footage gained with lives, lost with lives and regained once again with lives. A victory? 'Gallipoli losses,' the *Daily Mail* recorded in September of 1915, '87,630 – 41,000 in a month.' Barely a week later, the newspaper reported, 'Last night's casualties lists: 1,336 from the Dardanelles, 203 of them dead.'

As for Ashmead-Bartlett, he had had it, as the rising voice of doubt behind his dispatches began to reveal. And when a young antipodean reporter for the United Service Cable Company arrived at Gallipoli in September, ostensibly to inspect postal conditions there, Bartlett holed up with him, complaining bitterly about the dire conditions the troops were suffering. The reporter was Keith Murdoch, a winning Australian afflicted with a serious stammer, who was wholly shocked by Ashmead-Bartlett's disclosures. The two men hatched a plot whereby Murdoch would carry to Prime Minister Asquith in London a letter describing the follies of the campaign and charging Sir Ian Hamilton with incompetence. But, before this could be accomplished, Hamilton heard about the plan and dismissed Ashmead-Bartlett out of hand. Arriving in Marseilles, Murdoch found himself divested of the letter by a British intelligence officer who then confiscated the young reporter's personal notes taken at the battlefront. Infuriated, Murdoch composed from memory an impassioned twenty-nine-page letter to the Australian Prime Minister, Andrew Fisher.

His responsibility for the inspection of the Australian postal system was dealt with summarily – 'if you allow the inert mass of congealed incompetency in the Postal Department to keep you from instituting alphabetical sorting by units, 75 percent of our unfortunate homesick men in hospitals and at base depots will continue to receive no home letters.' Murdoch then turned to the campaign itself. It was, he wrote, 'one of the most terrible chapters in our history'. Fisher's worst fears were justified, the estimates of Australian losses fearfully under-reported.

I visited most parts of Anzac and Suvla Bay positions, walked many miles through the trenches, conversed with the leaders ... senior and junior officers ...

Taking Achi Baba by frontal assault ... was always a hopeless scheme ... No one can understand why Hamilton persisted with it. Our men were I found immensely proud of their little progress, but I found that we had paid 2,500 men for 300 yards!

To send raw, young recruits on this perilous enterprise was to court disaster ... One division went ashore without any orders whatsoever ... There were many deaths from thirst ...

You would have wept with Hughes and myself if you had gone with us over the ground where two of our finest Light Horse regiments were wiped out in ten minutes in a brave effort to advance a few yards to Dead Man's Ridge.

Morale, he wrote, was 'seriously shaken': 'Sedition is talked around every tin of bully beef in the peninsula.' At Suvla Bay, the troops showed 'an atrophy of mind and body that is appalling'. The letter went on, fed by anger and indignation.

It was true that Murdoch's estimates of casualties were too high, and his letter contained serious inaccuracies. It nevertheless caught the desperation and hopelessness of the Gallipoli campaign as nothing else had done. In Australia, Fisher read the letter and quietly determined to withdraw the Anzacs from the Dardanelles. In London, the letter fell into the hands of Northcliffe, perhaps sent to him by Murdoch himself.

On 30 September, Northcliffe wrote his response:

If I were in possession of the information you have ... I should not be able to rest until the true story of this lamentable adventure was so well known as to force immediate steps to be taken to remedy the state of affairs ... The matter has haunted me ever since I learned about it.

The only remedy could be to pull the men out, but the consequences of such a course of action were very serious indeed. Privately, however, Northcliffe had determined withdrawal was the only viable option. He told a personal friend,* 'I am concentrating every moment of my time trying to get our poor men out of the Gallipoli trap. If they are not removed in a few weeks, they will be destroyed.' Soon after, the *Daily Mail* introduced the possibility of withdrawal on its editorial page:

The idea that so great and bold an enterprise, upon which such splendid courage and so many invaluable lives have been spent, should be abandoned at the first

---

* The friend was Philip Witham, who leased him Sutton Place.

opportunity as impossible from the outset is enough to make the men who were killed in the Anzac landing turn in their graves. Such a decision would be evidence of gross incompetence somewhere, for which hardly any punishment would be too great.

The theme of this editorial leader – that incompetents must pay, and pay heavily – would be repeated over and over again in the coming weeks. Articles with titles like 'The Conspiracy of Secrecy', 'Peeps at the Truth' and 'Gallipoli Gamble: Mr. Churchill's Explanation' steadily accumulated. Altogether, they amounted to a damning indictment of the Government over its policy in the Dardanelles.

By 15 October, General Sir Ian Hamilton was forced to give up his command. His replacement, General Sir Charles Monro, recommended evacuation, and on 23 November this course of action was approved. Thereafter, the only successful manoeuvre of the Gallipoli campaign – the evacuation of the troops – was accomplished, without the loss of a single man. In the pages of the *Daily Mail*, Churchill, who, along with Lord Kitchener, had been instrumental in initiating the campaign, came under unceasing attack. Behind the scenes, Northcliffe instructed his staff to avoid any favourable mention of his former ally; they had 'got rid of the man with difficulty', he wrote, and didn't want him back.

Perhaps as a result of the loss of his friendship with Churchill, Northcliffe took up a correspondence with the young Australian reporter who had single-handedly turned the tide of opinion concerning Gallipoli. Keith Murdoch and Northcliffe would remain friends until Northcliffe's death, the younger man benefiting from the advice and counsel of the elder as he pursued a career in the newspaper business. With the continuing support of so great an ally as Northcliffe, Murdoch would rise to a position of prominence. At forty-seven, he would be knighted, and by the end of his career he would be viewed as a colossus in the newspaper industry in Australia.

As to Churchill, Northcliffe became increasingly condemnatory. Some fifteen months after the evacuation, the *Daily Mail* published in full the Official Report of the Royal Commission on the Dardanelles. On the same day, the editorial leader assessed the performance of government officials during the disastrous campaign:

> In the swollen War Council the amateurs of the Ministry talked; the experts sat dumb as lay figures; nothing was examined with care. Forty thousand killed, missing, or drowned; three hundred millions of treasury thrown away. It is bitter indeed. The 'main responsibility' is placed by the Commission on the shoulders of Mr Asquith, Mr Churchill, and Lord Kitchener.

Mr Churchill was guilty in the first degree. He misrepresented the experts and interfered in matters of which, as a layman, he knew nothing.

On the back page of the issue, there appeared a large photograph of an open boat of 'wounded and sick and dead Anzac soldiers', lying in a lighter beside the hospital ship from which they were being swung. Beneath the picture, the caption read: 'The twenty-eight burdened stretchers form an infinitesimal group in the total of the British–Anzac casualties in Gallipoli, which in number were more than double those suffered in the whole Boer War.'

Plan for a Published Book

by Lt. Hon. V.T. Harmsworth

Royal Naval Volunteer Reserve

Plain bound lined notebook such as you might buy at a stationers. [Illustration.] Colour dark blue, lettering gold, medium-sized. Lines on back in gold also. Title only on back and not on sides of cover. [Illustration.] Title Page: 'With the Hawke Battalion in Gallipoli.' Frontispiece: A full-page reproduction of a print of Admiral Lord Hawke with the following inscription: [The inscription is omitted.]

A Diary

Dedicated to the Memory of the Officers and the Men of the Hawke Battalion Who Fell in Action at Gallipoli.

From Vere to his Father, Harold

PREFACE

Perhaps it may be as well by way of a preface to give a short outline of the history of the Royal Naval Division.

On the outbreak of war, the First Lord of the Admiralty, Winston Churchill, bethought himself of a scheme by which he would bring renoun [*sic*] both to the Lords of the Admiralty and himself. In most previous wars in which England had been engaged there had been a Naval Brigade fighting on land with the Army. In addition to about six thousand Marines there was a surplus of officers and men left over from the Fleet, together with the greater proportion of the Royal Naval Volunteer Reserve. By amalgamating them into one unit for service ashore, the Admiralty would have at its disposal a useful force with which to embark on small enterprises. It was decided to form a division, similar in organisation and administration to an army division. It was to be known as the Royal Naval Division ...

Men who had been officers in the Navy and had been forced to leave on medical grounds, and who, on the outbreak of hostilities, had offered their services to the Admiralty, were roped in . . .

This was the book planned by Vere Harmsworth, middle son of Lilian and Harold Harmsworth – a thoughtful and introspective young man, twenty years of age, who had been educated at Osborne and the Royal Naval College at Dartmouth and who had subsequently entered the Royal Navy as a midshipman. Vere had planned a career in the Navy but was forced to abandon the idea after he was deafened by gunfire. Now fit only for the infantry, Vere volunteered for service in the Royal Naval Reserve, or 'was roped in', as he had put it in his unfinished diary.

In the autumn of 1914, his extemporized Naval division was rushed to Antwerp during its bombardment, and he thus learned at firsthand about the military 'muddle' complained about so bitterly by his Uncle Alfred in the *Daily Mail*. Perhaps the letter Vere wrote to his younger brother Esmond had been seen by Northcliffe, helping to fuel the awful contempt the press lord held for 'the bunglers' in government, whom he held responsible for misadventures like the one Vere described.

'The Germans', Vere wrote to his young brother, 'had some huge guns which they brought up about two miles from us, hidden away behind some trees.' They then proceeded for some time to rain shells on Antwerp. The shells 'whistled' over the heads of the troops, falling all around them and leaving great circular holes in the ground as they 'shattered everything near to pieces'. One of the division's colonels had his head blown off by one.

> The best part of it was that you could hear them coming and immediately flung yourself on the ground. But this precaution does little good if the shell pitches anywhere near you. I can tell you it was exciting work, and at night it was ten times worse. One imagined the whole time that the German infantry were attacking us, and the men of course blazed off their rifles into the barbed wire entailments ahead of the trenches.

'By our second day,' he continued, 'practically everyone had left Antwerp and the Belgians were in full retreat.' Thus, against the background of a city in flames, Vere's Naval division began their own 'awful retreat'.

> On Thursday night we marched till 3.30 a.m. without more than one stop – a distance of about 12 miles. We then had an hour and a half stop in a cow field which was soaking wet besides smelling like the devil.
>
> We then pushed off again. No one had the vaguest idea where we were making for.

The general plan was to reach a railway station and thereby be carried to Bruges or Ostend, but before his brigade could reach it the Germans blew it up.

By the time Vere and his comrades discovered this, it was five o'clock in the afternoon, and they had marched twenty-five miles since ten p.m. the night before 'and all on cobbled roads too'.

The unevenness of the cobbles hurt the feet awfully, and I can tell you most of us were fairly done on arrival. The Germans then started closing in on us and we went towards the frontier where we hoped to find some supplies of food and ammunition awaiting us in buses. You would have laughed to have seen the old London buses all over the place. Some were in the firing line bringing supplies, etc. The board of roads and routes had been removed from the front and: 'LONDON TO BERLIN' chalked in its place. All the old advertisements were still in them, and one saw 'Potash and Parliament',* the hit of the season, and notices such as 'Join the Army Today'. Most of them were still driven by their old bus drivers but some by Belgians...

I lost everything I brought out except what I stood up in. I lost my valise, sleeping bag, overcoat, sword, binoculars, Burberry and everything in the way of spare clothes that I had in my valise and sleeping bag.

On the retreat we threw everything away that hampered us at all and that was when I threw away my great coat. Oh, how I wanted it afterwards.

To continue my narrative. We found no food or ammunition awaiting us in the frontier. It was awful bad luck to think that we had been left in the lurch like that.

Interned for a time in Holland, Vere managed to escape just in time to serve in the action at Gallipoli thought by Northcliffe to be so futile an exercise. Here, the wealth of his father was put to good use providing necessities for Vere's men, the soldiers of the Drake battalion. 'We only get the service rations here,' he wrote to his father from the trenches, 'and want dainties like anything.' He longed for 'a little tinned pheasant and fowl', but later told him not to bother 'as it is not a success. The meat falls off.'

A little over three weeks later, he wrote to his father again, concerning the matter closest to his heart:

Dearest Pater,

Your welcome letter just received. You say you can't think of any food to send me. *Well I can!* I gave a long list of tinned and bottled foods that I wanted to

---

* The play's title was actually *Potash and Perlmutter*.

have sent out to Edward. Nothing has arrived here yet – not a single bit of food for me. I enclose a cutting of sample food from Fortnum & Mason's that I want. You *can't* send too much of it. Our food here is scanty and at no times *good*. We can't buy any. So send out plenty of tins of cocoa and milk (combined) *cakes of all kinds* – chocolate biscuits – Oxo cubes – potted meats – plum pudding. Tinned chicken and pheasant, etc. Good tinned cheese – lemonade and other drink powders – tins of assorted sweet biscuits. Plenty of cake of all kinds. Sweets of all kinds and plenty of cocoa and milk (all ready to cook). So that you have plenty to send and do send it as we have no food here and are so far from home. Tinned fruits (pineapple, etc.) pots of honey – orange marmalade – strawberry jam and all kinds of jelly. Have them all well packed in not too large wooden boxes. They must be well *packed*.

He later wrote that he had received two parcels of food from Fortnum and Mason's – 'They arrived when we were up in the trenches last time, I sent down here to fetch them.' They were a change after 'machonochi and bad bacon'. A week later, he shot off a quick telegram: 'FIT AND WELL SEND MORE FOOD.'

His father's idea of 'sending cigs to the men' was well received – 'only send Virginians such as Woodbines or Gold Flake', which they much preferred: 'Send as many as you like. I will see that they are distributed alright [*sic*]. The men do not get over many. Only about 10 are served out per week.'

Vere's growing devotion to his men – even if they were recruits of the rawest sort – was reflected in his refusal to take a cushy staff job in order to avoid action and survive the war:

One's loathing of the staff and all that appertains to it increases out here, where officers with red hats dash past infantry in motor cars – either splashing them with mud or covering them with dust. No staff for me *ever*. I am going thro' the mill with my men. They are little more than boys most of them and far too young to fight at all. The officer who recruited for the R.N.D. sadly failed in his duties, with the result that the material we now have, is very poor indeed...

Indeed, Vere's letters told more about the war than any history could. He wanted periscopes – 'They are simply longing for them out here ... as many as you like as it is trench warfare of the worst kind that lies before us'; and in the heat of summer, dustproof motor-goggles – 'They must be absolutely dustproof all round' – with green glass if at all possible. 'The great thing is to get them here without delay. My eyes are very sore from this infernal dust hurricane which never ceases.' The day after he wrote to his father asking for the goggles, he shot off a letter to his younger brother Esmond.

Dear Mondy,

This is only a short line to tell you that I am getting on alright. The wind and dust are awful...

We have spent four days in the fire trench. We had only a few casualties. Sawyer had the tops of two fingers taken off and one doctor was hit in the leg.

We were put up there just after a big attack which had partially failed and the ground between our trench and the Turks was strewn with bodies. It strikes me that they will be there a long time. In this heat the body and face turn quite black in less than 24 hours and the smell is terrific. The flies – which are myriad – also add to the general discomfort.

Every time you write enclose a medium-sized silk handkerchief in your letter. White preferably, but any colour will do. You don't know what a joy a silk handkerchief round the neck here is...

You would laugh if you saw me now, hair cut short, face peeling in places and caked with dust, white silk handkerchief round my neck, tunic on, pair of khaki shorts and gym shoes. Of course when any of us goes up into the trenches again we have to be properly dressed in boots and uniforms as it is hard, even wearing up there. We go up again tomorrow, Sunday and we shall stay there for a whole week. Something should happen in that time. Either we shall attack them or them us. Only I hope it is not a complete charge like my battalion had to do. I enclose a bullet which fell in my trench (fire trench) just close to where I was standing.

Goodbye,
Vere

He sometimes headed his letters, 'From the firing line', pointing out in one written to Esmond that they hadn't taken their clothes off for five days, a real tribulation in the hot days of June.

To his father he wrote to stop sending 'any of those History of War books out here':

We have got quite enough war here without reading about it. But send some cover 6d. novels by people like *Guy Boothby and J.M. Forman*. They pass the time when there is nothing doing up in the trenches and take one's mind away from the work in hand...

What he did want was 'a big golfing umbrella – khaki or green in colour if they make them – otherwise black. It will come in extraordinarily useful for the rain when up in the trenches.' His father was to see it was well packed 'in a wooden box'.

> I suppose it would be impossible to send out a case of well-packed apples. They would have to be very hard and crisp apples and very carefully packed in tissue paper, etc. But, by gad, they would be welcome. In fact all fruit is welcome.

And by the autumn he was asking for a hundred and fifty pairs of strong leather gloves lined with wool, 'with no buttons or clips but with elastic round the wrist and a couple of inches or so of mitten stuff up the wrist'. Also he asked for his gramophone and the best records to keep up the men's spirits.

By now, he and many of his men had lasted out in Gallipoli well into November, and shortly thereafter the campaign was abandoned. Was Northcliffe thinking of his nephew when he told his friend he was trying to do everything he could to get 'our poor men' out of 'the Gallipoli trap'? If so, it was to no avail. For no sooner were Vere and his battalion released from Gallipoli than they were transferred to France where the unimaginable Battle of the Somme was about to begin. When in September he and his men were relieved, he was told it was unlikely he would be sent to the Somme, but he was sure 'to be in the forefront of a big push up here somewhere'.

On 24 October 1916, he sent a letter to his crippled uncle, now permanently confined in a wheelchair and unable to move his body from the waist down. Vere was particularly close to St John, a bit ironically perhaps, since it was now acknowledged by the family that St John had been having an affair with Vere's mother before his accident. He wrote 'From Hawke Battn, B.E.F., 24th October 1916, at 9 p.m.,' noting the hour, no doubt, because now every hour counted:

Dear St. John,

> Your pipe arrived yesterday and is really a beauty and quite unique. I put it into action this morning after keeping the bowl full of rum during the night. It now tastes like a well-seasoned briar.
>
> According to present order we have left the worst behind us for good. We came up into the trenches this morning and we go over the top the morning after to-morrow. It will be about dawn, as the whole day will be required for the very big operations in hand. It is a terrifically big show. Our battalion goes over the 1st of our division and we are to take about the first three lines of enemy trenches. After frequent halts we move on about a mile further before the job is taken out of our hands by someone else. If it goes all right and the artillery does not fail us, it will be an A1 show, but otherwise absolutely bloody...

We had to leave our Company Sgt. Majors behind in addition to two sergeants per company. These will help to form up new companies if we are all wiped out. It has been very wet lately, which naturally cramps operations somewhat. The trenches round here are very bad and knee-deep in water and mud.

We shall move up to our Battle Positions to-morrow evening. We shall be very cramped and uncomfortable until the show starts. Who knows what it will be like! It will be like living in a new world, far removed from this. If one comes thro', one will emerge out of the new world rather dazed, and it will take some time to settle down. The awful nightmare of seeing one's own men – that one has been with so long – being struck down all round one, will never move from one's mind. One gets attached to one's men, and their loss hits one as hard as dear friends.

Whether I am to emerge from this show, I do not know. Fate has not definitely informed me. If there is a shell or bullet with my number on, nothing can stop it eventually finding me. Somehow I have never imagined myself as an old man with infirmities and limitations of old age. At school and in later years I have tried to imagine myself at 50 years or so. I do not seem to fit in.

Surely it is a life fulfilled, if one dies young and healthy fighting for one's country. It cannot be a life wasted . . .

I firmly believe that no man can truthfully say he has done his share until he has made the supreme sacrifice . . . At business in the years to come, I shall never be any good. When attending to one thing my mind will be elsewhere.

I am a very curious specimen and . . . if I get knocked out in this show, no one will lose by it at all . . .

So you see, Bonchi, I may have been born just to live my 21 years and then fade away. It may have been my mission in life. My future has always been rather vague. I do not know what I am going to do after the War. The future seems far away and unreal.

The only person it will matter to is the Pater. He has been so good to me, and he has built up such a position for his three sons, that it will be heartrending for him to have part of his life's work wasted. After all, if he has only to give up one of us three, he will be paying quite a small share compared with other fathers . . .

(You and I have always understood one another.)

If I fall, do not mourn, but be glad and proud. It is not a life wasted, but gloriously fulfilled.

Vere

P.S. I am leaving all I have for the betterment of those who have suffered thro' the War. Most of it for the men of my Battalion.

My whole being is wound up in my men, heart, body and soul. Nothing else seems to matter.

For his mother Lilian, he pasted on a sheet of paper the words to a popular song of the time that he had cut from a magazine:

There's a silver lining
Through the dark cloud shining.
Turn the dark cloud inside out
'Til the boys come home.*

Vere Sidney Tudor Harmsworth was killed on 13 November 1916 in the Battle of Ancre. As he was leading his company in an attack on enemy trenches, he was wounded in the throat. Despite the injury, he rallied a party of another battalion, and continued to lead the attack. Having obtained this aim and cleared the trenches of Germans, he advanced on the second line. At this time, he was again wounded, hit in the right shoulder and knocked to the ground. He arose and led the attack on the third line and, as he did so, he was hit by a shell and immediately killed. He was buried on the battlefield with his men.

Field Marshal Horatio Herbert Kitchener, first Earl Kitchener of Khartoum and of Broome, Secretary of State for War – whose stern visage looked fiercely out from recruitment posters during the early months of the Great War – often sought respite from his cares and duties by restoring, redesigning and beautifying his country estate Broome Park, located in Kent near Canterbury. He had purchased the stately home, once the seat of the Oxenden family and an outstanding example of Caroline architecture, in 1911. Since then, he had completely gutted the building, reconstructing its interior with painstaking attention to detail and decorating its finished rooms with trophies and loot collected during his many years as a soldier.

Such an activity was not inconsistent with Kitchener's natural interest in interior and exterior design. For it would be suggested by later biographers and military historians that the bachelor-warrior was a latent homosexual, and perhaps as a natural concomitant of this proclivity, tended towards the aesthetic.

Although it had been his own correspondent, George W. Steevens, who had created the myth of Lord Kitchener's invincibility as a leader of men, Northcliffe now loathed the man, instructing his staff to keep Kitchener's

---

* The wording is occasionally identical in the memoirs and my own account, since only the bare particulars are recorded in Everard Hamilton's compilation of the *Hamilton Memoirs: A Historical and Genealogical Notice of a Branch of that Family which Settled in Ireland in the Reign of King James I*, 1920, 2nd edn.

name out of his newspapers at all costs. A letter sent by Northcliffe to the editor of *The Times* on 30 December 1915 amply demonstrates the press baron's attitude towards the man he believed responsible for the Allies' woes:

My dear Robin —*

Nearly every day in some part or other of *The Times* appears a puff of Kitchener ... Lloyd George assures me that this man is the curse of the country. He gave me example after example on Sunday night of the loss of life due to this man's ineptitude. Is it not possible to keep his name out of the paper?

Kitchener could not help knowing of and absorbing such hostility, but he could afford to remain well above it. Thus, he spent his leisure hours serenely laying out the gardens of Broome Park.

On 4 June 1916, the Field Marshal spent the entire day tending the sunken rose garden on his estate, where he had only recently installed a miraculous fountain of his own design, adorned with plaster impressions of Neptune and various sea-nymphs and monsters. The next morning, Kitchener set sail on HMS *Hampshire* and, along with all on board except a few of the crew, went down with the ship after it struck a mine off the Orkneys north of Scotland.

Later the same evening, Lord Northcliffe arrived at his mother's house at Tottenham in North London. A relative present when he entered the drawing-room remembered his saying, 'The British Empire has just had the greatest stroke of luck in its history. Kitchener is dead – drowned at sea.'

Thus was Britain rid at a stroke of the man Northcliffe reckoned to be its greatest liability. But it wasn't that easy. This was a war of attrition that witnessed battles accounting for countless casualties. Four times Northcliffe visited the Front; each time, he returned with an altered vision of the inner circle of hell. His book *At the War*, the proceeds of which he donated to the Red Cross, recounted incident after incident of heroism and bravery, of epic sacrifice on a battlefield covered with the blood of British soldiers. It was a collection of the dispatches he sent back to be published in the *Daily Mail*. His companion, Wickham Steed, later editor of *The Times*, made a note in his diary:

We both saw the same things; but I saw them in a matter-of-fact way while he saw and recorded them, unconsciously I believe, in a form which the public

* Geoffrey Dawson (born Robinson) was editor of *The Times* 1912–19 and again 1923–41.

would readily understand. His impressions were received through a medium which might be called the public eye in miniature.

The pair drove through roads packed thick with ice and snow, going without food for days at a time and recording their stories until the small hours of the morning. Northcliffe was unable to sleep and fell violently ill from the cold.

Travelling hard by rail across France, he lost the toss of a coin and ended up sleeping curled up in a mackintosh on a seat while Steed took the berth. He was brave in prose, but actually witnessing the suffering of the lads made him a nervous wreck. After sending one dispatch of 6,000 words, he literally collapsed; later he roused himself to share the only food of the day, a chunk of stale bread, he and Steed fortifying themselves with a drop of brandy left in Northcliffe's flask. They witnessed 'the effects of German gas attacks, were shelled by German field guns, had a car wreck in the mud'.

Northcliffe stayed at Headquarters with General Sir Douglas Haig just before the Battle of the Somme, where some 660,000 British troops assembled for the greatest battle in the history of warfare. By now, the futility of inciting his readers had come home to Northcliffe and he at last capitulated, the *Daily Mail* descending into the propagandistic prose that came to characterize the reporting of the First World War. It was a style long since adopted by his competitors; stirring phrases, empty words, palpable lies:

Our Eyewitness's Account: Enemy Outgunned

by W. Beach Thomas

A great battle has been fought. Another is being fought, and many more have yet to be fought . . .

We must think of it as a battle of many battles, not to be likened in duration or extent, or perhaps intention, to such affairs as Neuve Chapelle or Loos. It is and for many days will continue to be siege warfare, in which a small territorial gain may be a great strategical gain; and the price we must pay is to be judged by another measure than miles or furlongs or booty. We are laying siege not to a place but to the German Army – that great engine which had at last mounted to its final perfection and utter lust of dominion. In the first battle, we have beaten the Germans by greater dash in the infantry and vastly superior weight in munitions . . . The 'Up-and-at-'em' spirit was strong in our Army this summer morning . . .

The scene at night had been stranger. No minute while I watched was lit by less than some hundred flashes, not reckoning the graceful and abiding star shells, which had all the semblance of a cosmic or celestial calm. Gorgeous as the scene was in itself, it was a pitiful thing beside the immediate human interest. Gallant fellows, they whistled homelike airs, and on the way to the trench kept a merry heart. A most English regiment was on the march at midnight down a country road in the hope of 'bumping the Boche'. A merry heart goes all the way. Finer spirits never deserved a heartier God-speed or merited more of their country.

True enough. It was the greatest single one-day loss ever suffered by the British Army – 60,000 casualties, 19,000 of them dead. This was the first day of the Battle of the Somme, 1 July 1916.

By 1 December, Northcliffe had returned to London a changed man. Besides Vere, he had lost two more nephews; others were to follow. Going up the stairs to his mother's house, Northcliffe encountered the *Mail's* young news editor, Tom Clarke, summoned there for a business meeting.

Northcliffe started at the sight of Clarke, staring at him as if he were a ghost. 'I thought you were dead,' he said. 'I thought there were no young men left.'

For one long moment, Clarke believed the Chief might possibly have lost his mind: it seemed such a strange thing to say.

11

'After the Somme'

Northcliffe, after the Somme, regarding the impending reconstruction of the Government in December 1916: 'Get a smiling picture of Lloyd George and underneath it put the caption "do it now" and get the worst possible picture of Asquith and label it "wait and see". Rough methods are needed if we are not to lose this war.' Lloyd George, anti-Establishment, Welsh, one of the rising breed of 'bold bad men' might very well be distasteful to the ruling classes, but they were nevertheless at last facing up to the reality that Asquith couldn't win the war.

As to Northcliffe – having conceded victory to the Press Bureau for censorship regarding the boys in the field – he now went about changing the focus of his attack to the Government itself. He told his staff, 'I want the word "Government" in quotes all the way through this article . . . That will shake them up. It will make things lively for you tomorrow . . . You understand it is important and must be strongly handled.'

The piece, a full two-column editorial leader, appeared along with the slogan, '*The Daily Mail*: The paper that is combing them out'.

A moment in our struggle for existence has now been reached when 'Government' by some 23 men who can never make up their minds has become a danger to the Empire. The burden of administration in war makes demands on the body and mind which cannot possibly be supported by idle septuagenarians like Mr. Balfour and Lord Lansdowne or by such a semi-invalid as Lord Grey of Fallodon . . . The notorious characteristic of our 'Government' of 23 is indecision . . . It just waits till the Press and the Germans have done something which forces it to decide in a hurry – and too late.

The headline Northcliffe scrawled across the top: 'Asquith – A Limpet'.

Marlowe followed along behind, quietly changing the title to read 'The Limpets', only moments before the piece went to press. In the wake of this article, there followed a literal barrage: 'Germans Fear Lloyd George', 'France Wants Him', 'The Empire Trusts Him'. Over at *The Times*, a less obvious but similarly deadly thrust was underway to unseat Asquith. Would Northcliffe succeed?

Harold Harmsworth, the future Viscount Rothermere, c 1890. Harold was thought not to be handsome, but this must have been a result of his elder brother's remarkable good looks: 'The truth was, the glamour of Alfred made Harold seem a plodder.'

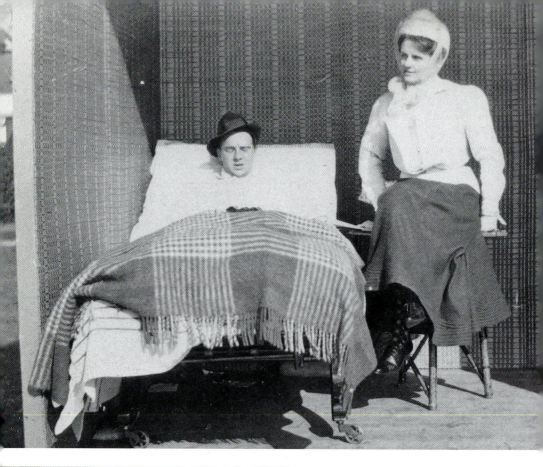

(Above) Lilian with St John Harmsworth, 1907. The beginning of Lilian's tragedy – her early affair with St John was cut short by a freak accident that left him a paraplegic. The death of two of her sons in the war cauterized any feelings that remained.

Despite his separation from Lilian, Rothermere made her a very rich woman. She used her wealth to sponsor André Gide, T.S. Eliot and the mystic Gurdjieff, among others. As to her estranged husband, their cordial relations masked, on Lilian's part at least, burning resentment.

(Above) A surprising display of affection from Hungarian troops in 1927. Rothermere's editorials in the *Daily Mail* condemning the Treaty of Trianon, which ceded land containing over three million Hungarians to Czechoslovakia, Rumania and Jugo-slavia, made him an overnight hero in Hungary.

(Below) Esmond at Szeged University, 1928. Invited to become Hungary's reigning monarch, Rothermere instead sent Esmond to accept an honorary Doctor of Laws degree.

Esmond in Budapest, 1928, where he dedicated a war memorial to his brothers who died in the Great War.

ADOLF HITLER

BERLIN, DEN 20.Mai 1937.

Sehr geehrter Lord R o t h e r m e r e !

Für die mir durch meinen Adjutanten übermittelte
Jadeschale sage ich Ihnen meinen herzlichsten Dank. Ihr wert-
volles Geschenk wird eine Zierde meiner Räume auf dem Ober-
salzberg und für mich eine bleibende Erinnerung an Ihre Freundschaft und Wertschätzung sein.

Ihre Bemühungen zur Herstellung einer wirklichen
deutsch-englischen Freundschaft verfolge ich , lieber Lord,
auf das eingehendste. Ich bin wie Sie wissen, seit je der An-
sicht, daß unsere beiden Völker am Ende doch auf einander
angewiesen sind, und daß es keine bessere Sicherung für den
Weltfrieden gibt als eine dauernde deutsch-englische Verständi-
gung. Ihre in den letzten Wochen veröffentlichten Leitartikel,
die ich mit großem Interesse gelesen habe, enthalten alles,
was auch meinen Gedanken entspricht. Ich weiß, sehr verehrter
Lord Rothermere, daß das Neue Deutschland in England keinen
aufrichtigeren und warmherzigeren Freund hat als Sie.

Der Trauerfall, der Sie betroffen hat, ist mir
erst durch Ihre Mitteilung zur Kenntnis gekommen. Ich darf
Ihnen aus diesem Anlaß meine aufrichtige Teilnahme aussprechen.

Mit der Versicherung meiner besonderen Wertschätzung bin ich

Ihr

One of the many letters sent to Rothermere by the German dictator, 20 May 1937.
Translated by Flowerdew & Co, who had offices in the Strand, they detailed Hitler's
hopes and dreams – among them a united Britain and Germany.

Though Rothermere was informing to the British Government, sending them photo-stats of his correspondence with Herr Hitler, he should have remembered to use a longer-handled spoon.

Press lords converse – Beaverbrook and Rothermere in the summer of 1939.
Rothermere would not long survive the outbreak of war. By the summer of 1940,
Beaverbrook would take on the newly-created Cabinet post of Minister of Aircraft
Production in Churchill's government.

The Blenheim bomber, 1935. Built at Rothermere's expense, a prototype was given to
the Royal Air Force as a 'peace gift'. In the Battle of Britain, it was used as a night fighter.

"Britain First" in Flight.

The first Viscount Rothermere, 1939. In the 1920s, Rothermere's son Esmond had written to him: 'At present you are naturally hated by all three parties, Conservatives naturally, Labour naturally, but also the Liberals, I am afraid'. A wild card, a maverick intellect, an outsider, Harold, like his brother Alfred, suffered a hatred from the Establishment that lasted beyond his lifetime.

On 9 December, the *Daily Mail* announced a new Cabinet with Lloyd George at its head. A rumour immediately made the rounds, that as a condition of support from the Cabinet Lloyd George had agreed to include neither Churchill nor Northcliffe. In the case of the former, the story was true. There was a fateful dinner at the house of F.E. Smith at which Churchill was informed he could not expect to be offered a job in the new Government. It was said he responded with harsh invective, abruptly left the table and the house, and was followed into the street by his host, who beseeched him in vain to return to the party. As for Northcliffe, the reverse was true. The offer of a cabinet post came swiftly, the night before the new coalition government was announced. His reaction was typical: 'Ah-h, wouldn't they like to get me out of Fleet Street! It would ease the pressure on their papers. Would not they like it? *I* prefer to sit in Printing House Square and Carmelite House.' Sit he did, declining an invitation from Lloyd George even to visit Downing Street.

And, as if to demonstrate Northcliffe's continuing independence, the *Mail* next day ran thumbnail photographs of the old Cabinet, headlined 'The passing of the failures'. In the same breath, they ran pictures and short biographies of the new Ministers: 'Cut this out and keep it for reference.'

'For the convenience of readers who have not yet grasped the Government changes,' the *Mail* wrote tellingly, 'we reprint the chief list, with ages and salaries where fixed by statute.' Northcliffe was watching; there would be no let-up.

Perhaps the power was going to his head. In a private telephone conversation with his brother Cecil, Northcliffe asked with glee: 'Who killed cockrobin?' For a single instant, the pair of them were back in the nursery, Cecil singing out the correct response.

'You did.'

Did Northcliffe actually kill cockrobin? Or did someone else take a hand? In 1934, the Canadian-born Max Aitken, by then Lord Beaverbrook, self-made millionaire, creator of trusts, political go-between and eminent press lord, was asked what he believed to be his single greatest achievement. Without hesitation, he answered, '... the destruction of the Asquith Government by an honest intrigue. If the Asquith Government had gone on, the country would have gone down.' Max Aitken, honest intriguer, had abandoned his native shores in the wake of a lucrative but somewhat murky business deal involving cement trusts in Montreal, and emerged in London in July 1910 to see what opportunities might present themselves for a rich man on the make. Few were wanting.

Aitken's first stroke of luck was to make the acquaintance of a promising politician, Andrew Bonar Law. Law had been born in New Brunswick where Aitken had been raised from childhood, and this commonality, plus the attraction of opposites – Aitken was outgoing, Law introspective – formed the basis for what would grow into firm friendship. Law had been uprooted early from his native Canada and raised in Glasgow, eventually rising to become a Unionist Member of Parliament whose mastery over fiscal matters was becoming well known amongst members of government. By nature self-effacing and given over to depression, Law had lost his mother when he was only two years old. In 1909, his wife had died. Desolate, depressed, morbidly self-absorbed, Law was taken in hand by the energetic Max.

The manner in which Max Aitken could detect moments of vulnerability in men of substance was his strong suit; he had done it before, and he would do it again, most notably with a Harmsworth. But for now, he tied his political fortunes to Bonar Law, galvanizing and energizing the political leader, encouraging and advising. Aitken himself had been advised by someone, perhaps Churchill, perhaps F.E. Smith, to read Burke, and he had taken to heart Burke's *Appeal from the Old to the New Whigs*, where, according to Tom Driberg, he found his political *raison d'être*:

> The world is governed by go-betweens. These go-betweens influence the persons with whom they carry on intercourse by stating their own sense to each of them as the sense of the other; and thus they reciprocally master both sides.*

This mastering of both sides had natural appeal for Aitken, and he took the maxim to heart. In 1911, he was instrumental in propelling Bonar Law into position as Leader of the Opposition in the House of Commons. It was said that Aitken had, behind the scenes, managed to place his weaker candidate between two stronger opponents so as to nullify their strengths, and bring his own man to the fore. So went the story, as told by Aitken, and later confirmed by history.

In December 1916, it was generally down to Aitken that Bonar Law and David Lloyd George eventually joined forces, though the pair had many basic disagreements and a history of altercation, in order to oust Asquith. This, Aitken accomplished despite Law's own deep reservations for doing so and Lloyd George's outright denial of any such intentions. There had been scuttlings, back-room dealings, star-crossed liaisons at last con-summated, most of them orchestrated by the 'go-between' Aitken. In what

---

* Driberg is quoting Burke. The thesis that Aitken was a go-between is Driberg's; *see* Tom Driberg, *Beaverbrook: A Study in Power and Frustration*, p. 70.

is considered by many historians to be Aitken's own highly coloured account of the operation, *Politicians and the War*, Lloyd George's eventual emergence as Prime Minister, with Bonar Law as the Chancellor of the Exchequer and Leader of the House of Commons, is recounted in minute detail, each event savoured by Aitken with the same enthusiasm as an old courtesan recounting amorous adventures of her youth. It is said that over the years he refined and re-crafted the text as many as twenty-four times, never tiring of re-examining and amplifying his own role in the coup.

Aitken was ambitious, and his ambitions led him to provide financial backing for the *Daily Express*, the newspaper founded in 1900 by C. Arthur Pearson, who had been forced to abandon the newspaper when he went blind. Bonar Law had told the *Express*'s worried editor, R.D. Blumenfeld,

> I know the man for you. Max Aitken is enormously rich. He knows nothing about newspapers and is not interested in them. But he wants to have a big political career, and he'll be glad of a paper which will back him.

Lloyd George's personal secretary recorded in her diary how, during the most anxious moments of the reconstruction of the Government, Aitken's *Daily Express* – if he did not yet own it, he in fact directed it – lent great aid to Lloyd George's cause. Possibly. At the time Aitken purchased the *Express*, its net sale was 229,344, less than a quarter of the *Mail*'s circulation at the time. And Northcliffe, hammering steadily away upon Asquith in favour of Lloyd George, owned a third of the titles in Fleet Street, his brother Harold several others.

Aitken, who had planned to become President of the Board of Trade, came away instead with only a title – Beaverbrook; he was denied what he regarded as his rightful place in the new Government. In characteristic manner then, he began beavering away to build his *Express* into a mighty organ and thus join the ranks of the Northcliffe and his brother. As for the great Northcliffe, he continued his role as gadfly and irritant to the powers that were.

Who then killed cockrobin?

It was of course Beaverbrook. He recorded the sequence of events that went down as history, exactly how the Asquith Government fell and precisely his part in felling it. Whoever writes the history kills cockrobin.

Northcliffe, less concerned with reputation than winning the war, moved on. 'As regards abuse, I am a pachyderm,' he had more than once asserted, and here suddenly was his chance to prove it. In April 1917, the Foreign Secretary A.J. Balfour visited the United States on a mission to acquaint the American public with the exigencies of the war. Besides the most obvious imperative – to persuade the Americans to enter on the side of the Allies – two other goals lay behind this effort. Britain needed money and Britain needed goods. The United States must be persuaded to extend an overdraft that already stood at $400,000,000 (at a time when five US dollars equalled one pound sterling). And the supply of munitions and goods must be stepped up. A vast sprawling network of British procuring agents, unco-ordinated and uncooperative, had been at work from the start, and their stopgap methods were wreaking havoc, Balfour decided. A central authority should be established to bring order – the British War Mission.

Northcliffe had always said the war would be won or lost in America. For this reason only, he was willing to consider taking on the task of co-ordinating the spending of some £2 million a day as head of the British War Mission, although he had steadfastly refused any other role in government. It meant he would have to go to a country he didn't want to be in, doing work he had no desire to do. As for Lloyd George, his appointment of Northcliffe as the head of the Mission was viewed by many as controversial, if not bizarre. To send as a representative of the interests of the United Kingdom a man whose main appeal was to a 'ha'penny public', as Lloyd George would write years later in his memoirs, came as a shock to more conservative members of the Establishment, and Lloyd George's very phraseology, reductive and demeaning, showed his hidden loathing of the powerful press lord.

Criticism of the appointment grew, as shown by a confidential letter to Lloyd George from Major David Davies, Parliamentary Private Secretary to the Prime Minister. He put his opinion in no uncertain terms:

> If Northcliffe is to go to the U.S.A. as head of the British Mission you will be making a damn bad appointment and you will raise a devil of a storm in the Liberal Party, which is just what you want to avoid just now. Northcliffe is one of the biggest intriguers and most unscrupulous people in this country. It is a gratuitous insult to the Americans to send him there – he will do more harm in a week than Balfour has done good in a month ... If you are sending him there to be rid of him, you are making a huge mistake. It will be said that you are afraid of the Harmsworth Press ... We shall soon have a Government of the Harmsworths, through the Harmsworths, and for the Harmsworth Press!

Besides confidential grumblings like these, Northcliffe suffered a public attack in the House of Lords, where his competency as a businessman came under fire. This was particularly annoying since he had initially resisted Lloyd George's offer on the basis he hadn't the business acumen the job required; on this issue and on Northcliffe's insistence that he had too many enemies to carry out the task efficiently, he had been overridden by the Prime Minister. Now he was being attacked on the very grounds he himself had put forth.

As if the objections of the establishmentarians of Britain weren't enough, the Americans themselves didn't want him. It was thought the United States State Department, at the behest of President Woodrow Wilson, registered its official opposition to the appointment with Lloyd George's office; certainly, Wilson went on record to his personal adviser Colonel House that creating such a position was 'most unwise and still more unwise the choice of person named'. But Lloyd George had acted with such speed that, by the time the State Department's censure reached London, Northcliffe was already on the ship that would carry him through submarine-infested waters to a life he knew he would hate: endless banquets, endless games of golf, endless travel and endless charm.

He wrote to his wife:

I am sent forth literally to *beg* for assistance of all kinds and in colossal quantities and from a people whom certain of our men and journals have attacked up to the last few weeks.

He had his work cut out for him. At the hands of the British Ambassador, Northcliffe met with the kind of rebuff he hadn't experienced for over a decade. No Embassy representative met him when his ship docked. And in fact, when he arrived in Washington, he suffered an extraordinary face-to-face attack from Spring-Rice, the British Ambassador to the United States, who feared Northcliffe might be named to his position, a title which, ironically, Northcliffe had already rejected. The diplomat also believed *The Times* had criticized his work during a time when he was suffering from illness, and he held Northcliffe directly responsible for that. In fact, he told Northcliffe, his wife refused to receive him in Washington. In the face of this implacable rudeness, Northcliffe wrote blithely to the manager of Associated Newspapers, 'There are, fortunately, other charming ladies in Washington!'

As it happened, Northcliffe opted to live near New York, in a rented house on Long Island, travelling frequently to Washington by night train, or 'the flying oven', as he came to call it. No one acquainted with the effects of an American summer can underestimate the power of that sun to flatten the energy of the most energetic man. The will weakens under the oppressive weight of heat and humidity. Northcliffe, sickly by nature and by inclination, entered into the hundred-degree-plus heatwaves of the Midwestern states in the summer of 1917, never once flagging or losing his balance. Accustomed to having his every whim granted, his every order obeyed unthinkingly, he summoned up the old Harms-worthian charm – and lived off it – knowing full well it was the only currency he had with the now all-powerful American businessmen of Chicago, Detroit, Cleveland, St Louis and other Midwestern outposts. He criss-crossed the country, keeping up with a gruelling schedule in blistering heat, and he seldom complained. He was subjected to frequent attacks by pro-German newspapers, one of them depicting him as Satan on its front page.

Secretly he thought of the Americans as 'White Chinese'; their con-formity appalled him. They had managed to standardize their personalities in such a way as to rob themselves of colour:

> They cut their hair the same way, eat exactly the same breakfasts, tie up the small girls' curls with precisely the same kind of ribbon fashioned into bows exactly similar. In every way they all try to look and act as much like each other as they can.

Northcliffe did not believe in it. The blandness of the personalities he met was a constant irritation to him: 'I believe in individuality,' he said. 'I do not believe in standardizing human beings. I believe that one of the reasons why so small a country as Great Britain maintains so vast a place in the world is that we produce individualists.'

There were other problems. On 30 June 1917, he cabled one of his assistants outlining an unexpected aspect of the job:

> NOT ONLY AM I WATCHED BUT EVERY PERSON CONNECTED WITH MISSION WATCHED GOVERNMENT THINK IT NECESSARY THAT I SHOULD NEVER MOVE UNLESS ACCOMPANIED BY SECRET SERVICE AGENTS WHO ARE WITH ME NIGHT AND DAY THAT WILL GIVE YOU SOME IDEA OF THE DIFFERENCE OF LIVING IN LONDON AND IN NEW YORK – NORTHCLIFFE

Northcliffe's mail was pilfered, his car followed; there was at least one assassination attempt. He resented being surrounded by detectives, some-times six at a time, 'and even at golf [had] three of these special Secret Service men with me'.

His office staff had to be imported from Britain. Thus, the most trivial of personnel matters became grist for Northcliffe's mill.

> If we want any more damsels here please hand-pick them yourself from the Fleetway House, and instruct them not to make any shipboard friendships. One who came from the *Times* ... has been a little too much of the eternal feminine this week, and I had to tell her yesterday that if she was naughty again, I would pack her on board and send her home.

If it wasn't romance, it was health. Northcliffe's staff were dropping like flies. If any more workers were sent, he wired his assistant back home, they must be vetted for flexibility and robustness.

ALMOST ALL STAFF UNWELL OWING TO HEAT AND WORK IF I REQUIRE FURTHER ASSISTANCE FROM YOU PLEASE PAY GREAT ATTENTION TO HEALTH AND ADAPTABILITY MY SECRETARY AND PRICE NOT WELL MISS COTTELL NOT WELL MISS GILLON IN BED PRACTICALLY EVER SINCE SHE ARRIVED USHER UNSUITABLE AND SHALL SEND BACK STOP ... I EXCELLENT HEALTH SO FAR MANY THANKS FOR LETTERS AND REPORTS – NORTHCLIFFE

The staffing, the heat, the endless rounds of social activities, the negotiations, the pressures, the travel – all these began to tell. 'But for my implicit belief that the war will be won by the United States,' he wrote to an executive at home, 'I would not stop here twenty-four hours.' A man in such a position impels himself by one means or another, most frequently ego; now Northcliffe, always self-obsessed, permitted his ego to unfold, a buffer against the many criticisms and pressures brought on by this job.

Northcliffe hated public speaking and yet addressed 14,000 at Madison Square Garden, receiving a standing ovation that lasted five minutes after what he himself recognized as a mediocre performance. Proclaimed 'the most powerful man in Britain' in publication after publication, he was subjected to that celebrity status peculiarly American and particularly corrupting. The rapid evolution from public victim to public victor may have been a personal triumph, but it took a different kind of toll. One of his entourage, Hamilton Fyfe, watching the cult of celebrity grow around the Chief, thought Northcliffe had actually begun to believe in it himself. Years later, Fyfe would blame the United States for what he believed to be the beginning of a kind of pernicious self-importance tantamount to megalomania in Northcliffe.

He had been accustomed to absolute authority, and now had the 'curious experience' of possessing only partial authority. He manoeuvred neatly through the pitfalls. But his nerves were beginning to fail.

He told one of his assistants he had never lived through so many 'grave anxieties'. Within the first few days of his arrival a crisis over oil supplies to the Royal Navy claimed his immediate attention. If a major battle were to occur, the Fleet would not have sufficient oil to wage it. Success: he got the oil and at a surprisingly low price – by spectacularly disobeying orders and disclosing the contents of a confidential cable to executives at Standard Oil. A less salutary result: he couldn't help aggrandizing his own resourcefulness. 'I can imagine the panic at No. 10,' he wrote home, enjoying the prospect of his own conjurings, 'if they had known I had disclosed that cable to the oil controllers.' In another letter, he wrote with more than a little pomposity, 'See that this is read to the Prime Minister and that he listens.' There followed an inconsequential account of his situation, highly personalized, as if he were addressing his staff on the *Daily Mail*.

Despite these vanities, he understood exactly what was happening. The balance of world power had shifted, away from Britain and towards the United States. The overdraft was growing. Northcliffe began to call it 'the sea serpent'. He chanted a little jingle he had invented that encapsulated Britain's plight – 'No loan, no war'. It was a frothy way of summing up a hopeless situation. 'I cannot tell you', he said to a friend, 'how weary I am of the headline, "Another Loan to the British".'

Britain was, in his words, 'now second fiddle to Washington'; the nation was living on tick. And so, it might be said, was Northcliffe. The easy charm, the good-natured persuasion applied in crisis after crisis, the affable manner and honest advice – 'Pull yourselves together for a long war. Build ships, save food' – all this was draining his energy. Nowhere in his demeanour could be found the point-blank confrontations suffered by members of his newspaper staff; Northcliffe was docile as a lamb. As he pointed out to himself so many times, beggars could not be choosers. Neither could they ram their will down the throats of another country.

'Duty, duty, duty' was his motto, and he carried out his thrice-woven circle of obligation with apparent ease. Beneath the silken charm, however, was desperation and darkness few could fathom. At home at Elmwood for a short rest after five months of begging and borrowing, Northcliffe startled one of his employees when, suddenly, he picked up a heavy stick and struck at a seagull. Having stunned it, he proceeded to beat it to death before Hamilton Fyfe's disbelieving eyes.

Similarly, Wickham Steed thought Northcliffe's charm masked a serious unravelling of personality. America was the cause, both men speculated separately in their diaries. The months at the British War Mission had been the decisive factor. The job was too much; it undermined Northcliffe's health; it taxed his faculties; it drew on his emotional stability. But there was more. He had advanced from an enthusiastic, fair-minded, almost childlike man to a world figure. Every sentence he uttered was invested with prophetic import and, as often as not, reported worldwide. His pronouncements proliferated; his belief in his own infallibility increased. There is an image of the great Northcliffe at home at Elmwood, reclining on a sofa, dropping correspondence upon the floor for others to retrieve. Behold the thinker: languishing under the weight of his own ideas, allowing them to flutter downwards – flotsam and jetsam floating on top of a thick carpet; most sadly of all, almost all of them were right.

He was feeling poorly. Not yet diagnosed, but suffering from a non-malignant inflammatory growth of the thyroid gland, all he knew was he had a constant sore throat. A photograph made at the time shows a lacklustre Northcliffe, staring stonily into the camera's lens, brow furrowed, puffy eyed, lips grimly set: 'That I should come to this,' he seems to be saying. At long last, a genuine illness and one for which, ironically, he was unprepared. He never returned to America.

It was rumoured he was offered the position of Secretary of State for War. This, it was said, he declined, still adamant he would not become a member of the 'alleged War Cabinet'. Instead, he accepted the post of Director of Propaganda in Enemy Countries, another of the pet projects he had pushed in the pages of the *Daily Mail* and one he believed would contribute directly to the winning of the war.

The day-to-day work went to others. Wickham Steed was there, H.G. Wells for another, the latter spinning out the philosophy of Crewe House in Curzon Street where the propaganda unit was housed and whose name came to signify the project. Campbell Stuart, one of Northcliffe's right-hand men, took over the operating responsibilities, Northcliffe participating only on the level of policy. Northcliffe occasionally made it in from Elmwood to chair a meeting. And he certainly fought the good fight.

The Government resisted the use of aeroplanes in distributing leaflets over enemy territories. Northcliffe took up the cause, calling it 'Case No. 1' against Lloyd George, whose general indecisiveness was driving Northcliffe to the brink. He wrote to Beaverbrook, who had been appointed Minister of Information, that getting Lloyd George to make a decision with any alacrity was an impossible task. Simple decisions were made complex through bureaucratic bungle.

> Now take case No. 2, which I have marked 'B'. This is a very tedious weekly leaflet in the FRENCH language, which not one German in a hundred understands but which is sent over the German lines by balloon. [One government official] has very kindly asked if we should like an ITALIAN edition for the Austrian lines, where at least nine different languages are spoken, Italian being known to perhaps only one percent of the enemy. Why should they not be printed in CHINESE?

As usual, Northcliffe got his way. In June 1918, 1,689,000 leaflets were dropped, and in the right language for the territory; in July 2,172,000. H.G. Wells wrote and designed the contents, although he and Northcliffe had almost come to blows over the question of German immigrants. And indeed, by the time his leaflets were being distributed, Wells had resigned in protest against Northcliffe's unwillingness to employ people of German origin at Crewe House.

It was Northcliffe as well who insisted upon the playing of gramophone recordings of Czech and Serbian national melodies, hitting at the emotions of the half-committed troops and bringing about significant desertions from the ranks of the Austrian Army. And it was Northcliffe's name alone that struck fear into the hearts of the German Headquarters Staff, who referred to Crewe House as 'Northcliffe's Poison Gas Factory'. In German war lore, he became the stuff of legends. Thus, as Ludendorff went down making the last great offensive of the war, the Germans complained:

> The enemy bombards our Front, not only with a drumfire of artillery, but also with a drumfire of printed paper. Besides bombs which kill the body his airmen throw down leaflets which are intended to deaden his spirit.

Many preferred to believe that Northcliffe's paper war hurt them more than General Ferdinand Foch's brilliant defensive tactics: perhaps in the long run defeat was less humiliating from that perspective. By the end of the summer of 1918, nevertheless, four million leaflets had been dropped behind enemy lines, the total cost £31,460 4s. 9d.* – an insignificant amount when compared to its effect upon enemy morale.

Many years later, the Cologne *Gazette* would cite Northcliffe's most notable achievement as 'the moral collapse of the German people'. Another German newspaper pointed out Northcliffe's astounding ability to assess 'the character and intellectual peculiarities of the Germans'. The most telling measure of the power the Germans attributed to the great press baron was the 'Medal of Hate', a bronze badge that depicted a scornful Northcliffe staring hatefully outwards, a quill in his hand, a pot of 'propaganda ink' in the background.† Thus, Northcliffe: evil genius to the Germans, powerful watchdog to the British, dapper impresario to the Americans.

Behind the image, the man. He had been suffering almost constantly from bronchitis and influenza attacks; his system seemed to have no resistance. In his Throat Diary, he systematically recorded every coughing attack, the number of times he spat each day, every instance he brought up phlegm – at doctor's orders, yes, but with the singular self-obsession that characterized every single act he committed. The document seemed

---

* Different sources quote different costs: Steed estimates the total costs for operating Crewe House at something in the region of £70,000; Stuart maintains that of the £31,460 4s. 9d. allocated, Crewe House received only £7,946 2s. 7d. Steed pointed out that daily war costs topped £7,000,000 a day. (See Henry Wickham Steed, *Through Thirty Years, 1892–1922: A Personal Narrative*, Vol. II, p. 227; also Sir Campbell Stuart, *Secrets of Crewe House*, pp. 117–18).

† It is still displayed in Room One of Northcliffe House to commemorate the propaganda coup of the *Daily Mail*'s founder during the Great War.

something more, well, sinister than a mere record of health.

To his gratification, he found that all his family, his employees and his friends mirrored his growing concerns and fears about his health; all this more and more from a distance, since Northcliffe was becoming more and more of a recluse. His life was dwindling to a stream of letters. He rarely went to Crewe House, or to the offices of the *Daily Mail*. Between November 1917 and March 1918, he made only one visit to *The Times*'s offices at Printing House Square.

When he did go out, he was difficult. Arriving at a friend's house at five minutes to one, he complained when the meal was not served exactly on the hour. 'I was asked to luncheon at one o'clock,' he complained. 'I am so sorry,' his host apologized, 'but it really was a quarter past one.'

> Soon the other guests arrived, including the Permanent Secretary in the Food Ministry, Lord Tamworth, Dr. Marion Phillips, chief woman organiser for the Labour party, Mrs. Llewellyn Roberts and Peel's daughter, in her V.A.D. uniform. Even with this guest list, at 2:00 Northcliffe said 'grimly', 'It is time we were at work.'

With this, he abruptly rose and left, leaving his host in some disarray. Northcliffe hadn't eaten a bite because of his strict regimen.

Soon, even this restricted intercourse came to an end, and he became a virtual prisoner at Elmwood because of poor health. 'I have no energy – either bodily or mentally. The doctors say it will come back in good time,' he said, but didn't sound very certain. They had warned him, he explained to staff, friends, virtually everyone who knew him, 'of the necessity for fresh air', but at the same time he was told to beware 'of the danger of east winds'. It was a narrow line.

Meanwhile, at Carmelite House, the order went out to bug telephones. Was this actually a cost-efficient move or something more sinister? There were references in one speech to Fleet Street vampires, later on to medical vampires; was this a particularly apt figure of speech or did the images haunt his psyche?

Wythe Williams, the American war correspondent for the *New York Times*, who also free-lanced for the *Daily Mail*, recorded a telephone conversation he overheard when he was visiting Elmwood.

> What have you done with the moon? (Shouting) I said the moon – the moon! Someone has moved the moon … Well, if it's moved again, whoever does it is fired!

With this, Williams wrote, Northcliffe slammed down the phone, giving what Williams called a peevish explanation: 'Some wretch at Printing

House Square has put the weather report on a different page.' Was this Northcliffe at his most theatrical? Or was the strain really beginning to tell?

Word of his temper tantrums spread. The editor of *The Times* received an enquiry from an old friend of Northcliffe's asking whether he wasn't 'just now a little bit – what shall we say? – affected in the cerebellum … He is a poor turnip.'

Northcliffe mad: the possibility reared its ugly head, and perhaps the evidence of it was accumulating. Alternatively, there was the more prosaic explanation – that Northcliffe was exhausted, that he was genuinely ill. And then there was the other thing. Despite the prevailing mythology of his omnipresence, he was lonely. Night after night at Elmwood, after the entourage had deserted the field, he sat alone in the darkness. He liked 'Alexander's Ragtime Band'; he liked 'How 'ya gonna keep 'em down on the farm, now that they've seen Paree?' He would crank up the gramophone and sit there, listening to the same recordings night after night.

It wasn't exactly what you might have expected of 'the most powerful man in England' – alone in the darkness, tapping his foot to the music. The ideas just kept coming. As much as he tried to stop the flow, there was simply no repose.

So, then, this exterior rumour, told no doubt with all the relish envy could engender: Northcliffe giving way to megalomania, and perhaps worse. Inside the family, another rumour circulated, never surfacing, always suppressed.

Harold Harmsworth was some seven years older than his wife Lilian. He was shy, hopeless at expressing deeply felt emotions except by giving gifts or money generously – or stuffy, if sensibly cast advice. Not surprisingly, his marriage wasn't happy. Lilian had turned to St John, who was closer to her age, a devilishly handsome, dashing young man, carefully groomed and educated by his wealthy elder brothers. Before the terrible motor-car accident in 1906 that had left him in a wheelchair, had St John fathered Esmond, always accounted to be the third of Harold's sons? There would never be an answer. Harold, stolid and reliable, took on the responsibility for Esmond, doing everything that was right and proper, and if there were ever any doubts about Esmond's parentage, Harold never expressed them. He favoured Vyvyan and Vere; that much was known. Of those two, the elder boy, Vyvyan, held the special place in Harold's heart.

In his latter years, Winston Churchill recounted a poignant story of Harold's devotion to this eldest son. One night when Churchill called at the Ritz, where Harold was living at the time, Vyvyan happened to be home on leave. By now he had suffered the first of three wounds on the battlefield. The last one would, after months of suffering in hospital, kill him. Vyvyan, Churchill said, 'had blue eyes and fair hair, he was a good fellow'. Now Harold, he continued, was 'eaten up with love of this boy', and late that night, he had taken Churchill to the room where Vyvyan lay sleeping. The pair of them tiptoed into the room, 'and when Harold opened the door he could see him sleeping like a child'. Harold asked that Vyvyan's leave be extended, and it was, but eventually Vyvyan became restive and asked to rejoin his battalion. 'He went,' said Churchill, remembering ghosts from a war that took place some three decades before. 'He was a good fellow,' Churchill repeated aloud to his friends that night in 1945.

Vyvyan Harmsworth had been at Eton from 1908 until 1912. 'From first to last,' the *Eton College Chronicle* recorded,

> he showed an all-round capacity that marked him out as one that would develop into a man of uncommon endowments, and his steadfastness of purpose that was to be seen both in games and work, his resolution 'to improve the best', in the pursuit of the Poet Laureate's ideal for the sons of Eton, won him the admiration of those that could look a little deeply into the happy life of the place. When he succeeded, one felt that he had richly earned success, though he himself was so modest that he would not allude to it. If he had not succeeded, one would have felt that success was impossible. During his time here he won many prizes, including the Rosebery History Prize; he was Captain of his house in games, and he was a good boxer, afterwards representing Oxford University against Cambridge with his great friend, Charlie Ward. Before going up to Christ Church he put in some valuable months abroad, perfecting himself in foreign languages, and noticing the signs of the gathering storm. He was deeply interested in the new ideas and new outlook in life that Oxford showed him and, while keeping old friends and making new friendships, he was adding to the store of knowledge, both political and economic, for which he had a natural taste.

It was Esmond Harmsworth's lot to follow in the footsteps of his gifted elder brother, entering Eton himself in 1914 when he was sixteen years old. Unlike Vyvyan, he was unhappy there, ill much of the time with mastoiditis, bullied by his fellow students and reminded constantly of his eldest brother's brilliance.

Lady Northcliffe's Hospital
12th December 1914
Irish Guards

4th Guards Brigade
2nd Division
British Expeditionary Force
France

Dear Monde,

How glad I was to get your letter! Such a splendid one too and full of news. Write me like that as often as you get time – letters are very welcome out here...

We are sick of this place. Officers and men. There is nothing to do – we are allowed to go for walks but the men may not leave the village, the ground is very wet and footballs are scarce. The men do nothing but lounge about except for the one parade we have per day...

The men have been refitting – a slow job and it is not finished yet – boots take years to come and then they aren't big enough. (Every man has to have boots big enough to wear 2 socks to stop frost-bite.)...

They say the cold in the trenches is appalling – You don't know what cold is till you get there! There have been several frost-bites, necessitating the amputation of a limb! Poor old circulation...

There are lots of Old Etonian faces out here I recognize and some I know ... Mind you pass M.L.P! [And] tell my tutor I was v. glad to get his letter and will write him when there is more news i.e from the trenches.

Best love,
Vyv.

Irish Guards
January 13th 1915

Dear Monde,

... Hell is the only word descriptive of the weather out here and the state of the ground. It rains every day! The trenches are mud and water up to one's neck, rendering some impassable – but where it is up to the waist we have to make our way along cheerfully. I can tell you – it is no fun getting up to the waist and right through, no fire or anything, as I did last night. You never saw such a muddy mess as I was when I came out! Lots of the men have been sent off with slight frost-bite – the foot swells up and gets too big for the boot. Luckily we get plenty of rest between our goes in the trenches.

Well – I suppose I will write again soon.

Best love,
Vyv.

P.S. *WE WILL DRINK TO*

The downfall of the Kaiser and all the Prussians.
To boys in the trenches.
To Vere in Holland.
To the Mater and Pater at Claridge's.
To Uncle Bonch at Poynter's.
To Cammy's sister...
To Granny at Totteridge...
To the Hero of the Irish Guards.
To Molley & Captain Pam across the high seas.
To Cammy* my only campanian [*sic*]
The campanian of my youth.

'On active service'
Le Havre
7 December 1917

My dear Monde,

I am now well on my way to England and comfort. I have got as far as the base hospital at Staples. Here I am very comfortable and am having a rest after my week in that hectic spot, the Casualty Clearing station.

My wounds are healing very rapidly – in fact I don't worry about them now – but only about the cramp. I keep getting it in the right leg. That is indeed unpleasant.

I have been awfully lucky, no vital or difficult spots, spots such as knees touched, and the wounds free from all dirt and stuff ... I expect it will be 3 or 4 weeks before I can do much more than hobble about...

Of course I have heard nothing but I hope dear Pater was not dreadfully nervous about it all...

Well, Monde – Old Man – I hope you are awfully well yourself and having a good time. Find all news of my whereabouts via the Pater.

Yours with love,
Vyv.

It was Vere who, before his death, had been the organizer, the one who kept things in their place; Vyvyan was careless and easy, slapdash in his brilliance. He was also modest, and he seldom complained, even as he lay dying. The only anger he expressed came down in a comment he made

* It is not known who Molley and Captain Pam are, but Cammy was Mr Cameron, an agent hired by Harold Harmsworth to manage his estate at Hemsted, Benenden.

to his Uncle Alfred a few days before his death: 'I do not mind having been wounded three times, but I hate to think that I have been muddled three times.' Perhaps the word was 'butchered'; there were several versions of the quote, each of them recorded by Northcliffe and reported on to relatives and friends. In his last letter to his uncle, written from Lady Northcliffe's Hospital for Officers, Vyvyan mentioned how kind his aunt had been to him, how lonely he was when she had to go away, how much he liked to face the sunshine as he lay in his bed. Fourteen days later, he was dead.

'Which shattered Harold, absolutely shattered him, he just went wild,' said one relative, a mere wisp of a girl at the time of Vyvyan's death. 'He sort of, oh, I don't know, he didn't take any interest in anything much after that.' To Beaverbrook Northcliffe wrote, 'Only my mother and I know how ill Harold has been. We feared a complete breakdown.'

Every year since his death, on his birthday, the Irish Guards have drunk a toast to Captain Vyvyan Harmsworth, and later, in *The Lost Generation*, A.P. Herbert commemorated his death in 'Beaucourt Revisited':

> I crossed the blood-red ribbon, that once was No Man's Land,
> I saw a misty daybreak, and a creeping minute hand;
> And here the lads went over, and there was Harmsworth shot.
> And here was William lying – but the new man knew them not.
>
> And I said, 'There is still the river, and still the stiff, stark trees;
> 'To treasure here our story but there are only these';
> But under the white wood crosses, the dead men answered low,
> 'The new men knew not Beaucourt, but here we are – we know.'

Now, with Vere and Vyvyan dead, only Esmond remained. It would be his fate, whether he wanted to or not, to be withdrawn from active service, since he was the last living son in Harold Harmsworth's family. It would be left to him, whether he wanted to or not, to run the family business. It would be left to him, in his father's words, to 'inherit all the sacrifices of those great personages your two elder brothers'.

> They would have wished for you a great career and sometimes through my tears I see in your future an ample vindication for what they – and I – have suffered.
>
> Ben* dearest boy there is little or nothing left for me except to watch and help you. My career is closed. I know I have not such measure of health left as will enable me to be more than a speculation of what is passing around us. I would

* Harold always addressed Esmond as Benjamin in his letters.

not choose otherwise. In a solitary life I may find compensation in peace and quietness.

Esmond would carry out his father's wishes, even down to marrying his dead brother Vyvyan's fiancée, whether by his father's design or not was never known.

Thus the sole survivor.

12

'Northcliffe Mad'

Advice from Northcliffe to his top foreign correspondent, F.W. Wile: 'Buy a sixpenny toothbrush and clean your typewriter; take your winkle pin and clean out the d's, a's, o's and other letters.'

Advice from Northcliffe to his news editor, Tom Clarke, embarking, at Northcliffe's expense, on his first trip to the United States: 'Criticise no one or anything. Express delight at everything. You will be told that America won the war. To that you must not demur. Don't wear spats. Goodbye and good luck.'

Advice from Northcliffe to his night editor, C. Robert Mackenzie: 'In future when you write an article for us, you will be known as Crobert Mackenzie. It will not only distinguish you from our other office Mackenzies. It will look fine at the top of an article.'

Advice from Northcliffe to the woman's feature page editor: 'In quite a number of the copies that I have seen this morning, the printing is so faint that you get no idea how these dresses are made. May I say for the hundred thousandth time that women only want to know how the dresses are made.'

Advice from Northcliffe to the artists drawing the popular cartoon 'Teddy Tail': 'I think you are putting in too many animals now. Before you were putting in too few.'

Northcliffe was incorrigible; there was no stopping the man. Despite his constant carping, the staff revered him. At the war's end, he ordered that all his employees be given a two-week 'Armistice Bonus'. Returning veterans found not only that their jobs were waiting for them but also that there would be no lowering of their wages – an unpleasant practice followed by many businesses who realized the former soldiers were practically destitute, with no chance of employment except on terms dictated to them.

As for the politicians, they detested Northcliffe. Armistice Day was 11 November 1918; on the 12th, Northcliffe resigned his Cabinet post. He did not consult Lloyd George. He refused to support Lloyd George in the election of December 1918 unless the Prime Minister submitted to him a list of those who would take part in the new government. Of course, Lloyd George refused, telling Northcliffe he could 'go to hell'. He would later describe his troubled relationship with the press baron thus:

During the War no one could doubt his patriotism. It was sincere and fearless ... But he could not understand comradeship in any enterprise. He only appreciated team work when he was the captain of the team. He resented that co-operation which implied equality and give and take. He had no confidence in any show which he did not run himself. He was too indifferent to anybody else's views to be a good conversationalist. When he visited me on a few occasions at Downing Street he would initiate a topic, sometimes by a question. But you could see that he was not interested in the least in the answer. He had called to tell you and not listen to your reply. The preliminary query was only a matter of form. By this time he had acquired the telephone manner which had degenerated into the telephone mind – the ejaculation of short and sharp orders into a tube which could not question their command. He gave the impression of being bored by the talk of his fellow men. He preferred talking to telephones.

Northcliffe's summation of Lloyd George was more concise: 'It's his big head on a little body that I don't like.'

Said one statesman of the pair: 'Each described the other as impossible and intolerable. They were both very tired men and had been getting on one another's nerves for some time.' Thus were the battle lines drawn.

In every issue of the *Daily Mail*, Northcliffe was insisting on indemnities from Germany. He wanted the Kaiser hanged; he wanted the Germans to pay Britain's loans from America. 'I do not believe in German hard-upness,' Northcliffe wrote to his brother Harold. The slogan of the *Daily Mail* became 'They Will Cheat You Yet, Those Junkers!'*

On 18 January 1919, the Peace Conference assembled in Paris, with President Wilson, Clemenceau, Lloyd George and Orlando in attendance – the so-called 'Big Four'. It was a veritable model of disarray, with Wilson and Lloyd George coming and going, Clemenceau actually shot and severely wounded during the negotiations and Premier Orlando essentially ignored throughout. Harold's son Esmond was aide-de-camp to Lloyd George. Later in life, he would amuse dinner guests with stories of Lloyd George's prodigious amorous adventures during the negotiations, perhaps an unhappy influence on the still impressionable twenty-one-year-old man. But for now, with Harmsworthian alacrity, he reported to his Uncle Alfred. ('According to Esmond,' Northcliffe said, '[Lloyd George] sees far

* The slogan appeared daily in the *Mail* from April to the end of June, 1919.

too many people, and has no time for reflection, talking to people at breakfast, lunch and dinner.'

Besides his young nephew, Northcliffe had others close to the Prime Minister, men long since disenchanted with their leader who were therefore happy enough to report directly to the great press baron. In Northcliffe's collection of informants were historians who understood the significance of each issue better than the statesmen responsible for making policy. 'I have daily a secret report of the "inside" of the Peace conference,' Northcliffe wrote to his mother. 'How different from what the public reads!'

Shadowed, harassed, criticized, his every utterance subject to constant scrutiny from a hostile Harmsworth Press, Lloyd George sought to change the terms of the engagement. He floated an idea: Northcliffe was angry, Lloyd George supposed, because he had intended to take over the Peace Conference himself, and frustrated in this intent, he had withdrawn to the South of France, there to fume impotently. The idea flew. Geoffrey Dawson, recently relieved by Northcliffe of his position as editor of *The Times*, concurred: Northcliffe had earlier told him of his desire to set the terms of peace after the war.

In favour of Lloyd George's theory, Northcliffe certainly showed no signs of letting up on the issue of reparations. He had, in the Prime Minister's own words, attacked him on the basis of a speech he gave in Bristol

which indicated my grave doubts as to the capacity of Germany to pay the Allies the full amount of the damage inflicted upon them. His papers criticised my policy on these lines. When I was addressing an election meeting at Leeds, I received the following telegram from him: 'THE PUBLIC ARE EXPECTING YOU TO SEE DEFINITELY AMOUNT CASH REPARATIONS WE ARE TO GET FROM GERMANY THEY ARE VERY DISSATISFIED WITH THE PHRASE QUOTE LIMIT OF HER CAPACITY UNQUOTE WHICH THEY SAY MAY MEAN ANYTHING OR NOTHING THEY ARE AWARE THAT FRANCE HAS NAMED HER AMOUNT I AM APPREHENSIVE OF SERIOUS TROUBLE IN THE COUNTRY OVER THIS MATTER.' This telegram was evidently intended for publication if I failed to give a satisfactory answer. I replied promptly. 'YOU ARE WRONG ABOUT FRANCE STOP NO ALLY HAS NAMED A FIGURE STOP ALLIES IN COMPLETE AGREEMENT AS TO DEMAND FOR INDEMNITY STOP INTER-ALLIED COMMISSION WILL INVESTIGATE ON BEHALF OF ALL ON IDENTICAL PRINCIPLES STOP DON'T ALWAYS BE MAKING MISCHIEF.' Neither of these two wires was published. I received no answer to my wire, but Northcliffe pursued his campaign to the end.

Lloyd George now brought to bear all his considerable skills at political oratory, and on 16 April, in his speech to the House of Commons on the

Peace Conference, he waged an unprecedented counter-attack on the man he perceived to be his chief persecutor.

He referred to a recent article on German indemnities published and signed by Northcliffe, saying it made no reference to reparations in the wider sense. 'There was no reparation for damaged houses,' the Prime Minister said, 'not even *Broadstairs*.* (Laughter.) Here today – jumping there tomorrow – there the next day. I had as soon rely on a grasshopper ...' He continued that when a man had deluded himself he was the only person who could win the war, but received no call to do so ...

> And then the war is won without him! There must be something wrong! And, of course, it must be the Government! At any rate, he is the only man to make the peace! The only people who get near him tell him so constantly, and so he prepares the peace terms in advance and he waits for the call. It does not come. He retreats to sunny climes – waiting! Not a sound reaches the far-distant shore (laughter) to call him back to his great task of saving the world. What can you expect? He comes back and says, 'Well, now, I cannot see the disease, but I am sure it is there! (Laughter.) It is bound to come!' Under these conditions I am prepared to make allowances, but let me say that when that kind of diseased vanity is carried to the point of sowing dissension between great Allies whose unity is essential to the peace and happiness of the world ... then, I say, not even that kind of disease is a justification for so black a crime against humanity.

At precisely the moment he uttered the words 'diseased vanity', Lloyd George tapped his forehead meaningfully, indicating the obvious derangement of the great press lord.

The speech created, on the one hand, great delight amongst Northcliffe's many enemies and, on the other, dismay amongst those who respected the service he had given his country during the war. By chance, Lloyd George met one of Northcliffe's brothers in the corridor after the attack, and seeing the pained look of incredulity on his face, admitted, 'I went too far.' He nevertheless had accomplished his purpose – the public humiliation of a man who had given his all for his country during a time of great national danger.

Northcliffe's response was predictable: 'We must be careful', he warned staff, 'not to involve ourselves in wrong quarrels with the Prime Minister.'

> I have no personal interest in him either way. When he is vigorous in fighting Germany I support him; when he sings his 'Be kind to poor little Germany song,' I oppose him. I notice a tendency in the staffs of my newspapers to hit back

* Elmwood was in Broadstairs. (Italics mine.)

when the Prime Minister makes foolish remarks about me. I deprecate that attitude. Silence is a more effective and dignified weapon.

To his former mistress Louise Owen, he wrote that he didn't in the least mind attacks of the sort the Prime Minister had delivered against him. 'As you know,' he wrote, 'I am used to them.'

> But what does depress me is that the Prime Minister at a time like this, when every moment is of value in dealing with these world problems, should occupy the attention of the House, even inviting the young Prince to hear him, in abusing me. It shows the mentality of the Premier, and how he lacks all sense of proportion. No ordinary man like myself should at this time figure so prominently before the world.

The strange and perplexing truth was that Northcliffe's claim to be an 'ordinary man' was, for the moment at least, accurate. Far from desiring any kind of public participation in the Peace Conference, he was fighting a battle against serious illness, sometimes with good humour, sometimes with the petulance that accompanies the invalid. During the past ten months, he wrote to Harold, 'I must have coughed at least two hundred times daily, the grand total of which your arithmetical mind can easily assess.'

As to his supposed madness, he agreed at least to being a fool for his continuing support of the medical profession. One doctor's suggestion for solving Northcliffe's health problems – by 'removing the large bowel *in toto*' – was no more radical, Northcliffe wrote to a relative, than many other proposals he had received. 'You may tell me that many people think I have a "kink", but I do not think it is in that part of the anatomy in which he specializes.' He had been prescribed morphine, which had had no effect. Neither had opium, 'asperin' or other 'coal tars'. What did act quickly on him was a special derivative of 'the excellent stuff that Dr. Crippen gave to his nagging wife ...'

As a diversion from this depressing state, Northcliffe had renewed his boyish interest in natural phenomena, and he kept a diary in which he recorded information about local wildlife, including lizards, green frogs, 'a great silver cocoon about as big as an ostrich's egg' and the caterpillars which made them. He was particularly interested in the 'trap-door spider':

> the type that make little clay tubes for themselves, which they line with cobweb that looks like silk. There is a small door at the end of the tube which can be opened or shut. When I tapped the clay cylinder with a pencil, the door was pulled firmly to. These trap-door spider traps are very hard to find.

Meanwhile, he was faithfully using his inhaler, various sprays and a vibrator. He had discovered that, in addition to his sore throat, he was anaemic. A cool wind could put him back for days. His sleeplessness could be relieved only by sleeping on his left side.

Here was the great enemy Lloyd George feared and hated: a sick man regressing naturally to his boyhood interests. Lloyd George would find little difficulty in defeating an exhausted Northcliffe on every issue. Years later, the reparations question would still be unanswered, a source of continuing vexation between Germany and the Allies. Germany would openly defy the Treaty of Versailles. France would become at first disenchanted, then openly cynical about the sacrifices made in the name of war. The League of Nations, fanned into a flame by the idealism of President Wilson during the conference, would burn out when the United States itself refused to join. The Peace Conference had been precisely as significant a resolution to world problems as Northcliffe had predicted. A political document put forth by politicians, its most significant achievement would be to set the stage for the Second World War.

Lloyd George's public attack on Northcliffe, along with the mutterings of men who, for one reason or another, had hated him for years, made a convincing case that the great press baron had gone mad. The idea fired the popular imagination, fuelled by the wisdom of the ages: 'What profiteth a man ...' The inherent irony of such a concept, that a man could rise so high only to be brought so low, was the stuff of well-staged melodrama – and the rumour went like wildfire. Every event seemed to lend credence to the view that Northcliffe had lost his mind.

There followed a *Daily Mail* promotion of the 'Sandringham hat', carried out in the tradition of the earlier sweet-pea contest and the Standard Bread campaign. Winston Churchill, at last back in the good graces of the press baron after several years in the wilderness, took part, wearing the misshapen hat everywhere, but to no avail. The campaign fell flat. This was evidence, it was whispered abroad, that Northcliffe had lost his touch – a sign of failing powers, loss of judgment, even of madness, his critics would assert.

But at the very same time the *Daily Mail* was carrying out one of the most successful campaigns of its history. Dame Nellie Melba, the colourful Australian soprano whose motto – 'Sing 'em muck!' – had, along with the voice of an angel, made her the most famous female singer of the age, agreed, under the sponsorship of the *Daily Mail*, to perform the first wireless concert in history at Marconi Place in Chelmsford. Hailed as

'Melba's 1,000-mile song', 'a concert into space for an all-Europe audience', the *Mail* proclaimed:

> this evening a great singer will hail the world by a long trill into space ... Thousands of people on land and at sea are eagerly looking forward to hearing the glorious voice of 'the Australian nightingale' swelling through space into their instruments. Art, romance, science are all combined in the experiment...

The following day, 16 June 1920, the *Mail* editorialized on the importance of the wireless, not just as a means for business and governmental communication, but as a medium for entertainment.

> It is a new and charming event for a singer to bring pleasure to eager listeners wherever they may be – not only in the country of the song's origin, but also in distant Continental capitals and in ships at sea ... Listeners-in emphasise the delightful clearness of enunciation which reached the world.

In Paris, the French Radio Electric Company amplified the sound by attaching an aluminium trumpet to 'a resonant amplifying apparatus', allowing all Paris to hear the performance. At the same time, the Pathé Film Company filmed the scene for posterity.

> Once before the *Daily Mail* stirred the national imagination to realise the vital importance of flying. It has now taken the lead in private wireless experiments with the object of cultivating national receptivity for the new science and of bringing minds in train for achievements to come ... The appeal of wireless to human interest is that it seems magical and yet is real. In attempting the control of electrical energy we begin to get on terms with the world-force on which the future of mankind – for construction or destruction – will depend. In its practical utilisation, in most forms, this country has lagged behind other nations. The objective of such experiments as the *Daily Mail* has initiated and intends to continue is to enable this country to take the lead. The only safe place is IN FRONT.

As if to illustrate the point, Northcliffe immediately ordered a seven-valve wireless receiving set to be installed in *The Times*'s office, thus making the newspaper the first to rely upon the wireless to speed up news delivery. At the *Mail*, the 1900 slogan, 'From Near and Far: Interesting News by Telephone and Telegraph', was changed to read, 'From Near and Far: News by Air and Wire'.

Northcliffe had always understood the idea of speed as a desirable element in and of itself. The year before Dame Nellie Melba had sung her historic concert, the *Daily Mail* had at last awarded the £10,000 prize for crossing the Atlantic by air that had been on offer since 1913. On 14 June

1919, Captain John Alcock and Lieutenant Arthur Whitten Brown had left St John, Newfoundland at 4.28 p.m.; the pair arrived in Clifton, Ireland at 8.40 a.m. the next morning. It was called the 'biggest news since Armistice', and thousands were there to greet the pair when they arrived at Euston Station, from whence they were escorted to a celebratory lunch-eon at the Savoy. In a letter congratulating the two fliers, Northcliffe wrote,

> Your voyage was made more quickly than the average press messages of 1919. Moreover, I look forward with certainty to the time when London morning newspapers will be selling in New York in the evening, allowing for the difference between British and American time, and vice versa.

Speed was what Northcliffe cared about, new technology and its effect on a rapidly changing world – even as he himself receded from that world. He was unable to attend the luncheon at the Savoy because he was finally undergoing surgery to remove the non-malignant growth on his thyroid gland. The operation was a success, and his symptoms disappeared, but from this time he would venture out less and less. The telephone and the dictated letter – these would be his conduits to the world.

Winston Churchill, as Secretary of State for War and Air, was eager to enlist Northcliffe in a project he was underwriting. He planned to convene an Air Conference in London, one in which 'all the "biggest" people in aviation can come and propound their theories and discuss aviation in all its branches'. He wrote to Northcliffe, asking him to attend and to lend support to the conference in his newspapers. Northcliffe declined, citing ill health. But he wrote a ten-page memorandum on the subject, giving his observations and predictions of what was about to occur in the industry.

He soon expected, he wrote Churchill, 1,000-horsepower single-engine planes, capable of carrying as many as twenty passengers in 'a really luxurious saloon'. He believed air travel would become the most common means of transportation for businessmen, who would soon come to view with disbelief the cripplingly slow methods they had depended upon before the aeroplane. He pointed out that the United States was already using aeroplanes to deliver the mail at no extra charge, and he believed Churchill's Air Conference should give weighty consideration to Britain doing the same. 'Naturally,' he wrote,

> there will be a discussion of recent progress with the wireless telegraph and wireless telephone, which are being applied already in the direction and control of traffic on the airways between London and Paris and London and Holland. It is already clear in fact that, when further improved and adapted to commercial

air traffic, the wireless telegraph and wireless telephone will so combat these enemies mist and fog as to make flying in Europe practicable, and also safe on days when at present it is too hazardous to fly.

Here again the ground should be cleared by a concise report as to the daily cooperation of meteorology in connection with the continental air services. Information should also be obtained as to the aero-meteorology throughout Europe.

It should be borne in mind, as a specially encouraging point, that the use of wireless telephones in aeroplanes now makes it possible for weather-observing stations along a route to communicate direct with machines in flight and inform pilots at any moment of changes which may be taking place in the weather along their path of the airway which the aircraft are approaching.

Finally, he suggested the Air Conference investigate the possibility of vertical aircraft that were lifted from the ground by use of heretofore unimagined propulsion fuels – in other words, the rocket.

Churchill's Air Conference convened on 13 October 1920 without the presence of Northcliffe, who, as the *Daily Mail* reported, was too ill to be present. He nevertheless was quoted at length in a warning to his country about Germany. We now know, he said, that at the outbreak of hostilities in the Great War, when Britain was using at best the seventy-horsepower Gnome engine or the eighty-horsepower Renault, the Germans had been experimenting with 200-horsepower engines. Recent publications in Germany indicated that, in the event of war, they expected most of the battles would take place in the air. He warned that Britain could obtain no accurate figures as to the number of aircraft now in operation in Germany, but he believed these to be greatly in excess of earlier estimates of 15,000.

These warnings, buried on page six, were lost in the welter of words the Air Conference generated. And besides, there was the other matter. As was rapidly becoming known generally, Northcliffe was mad. Lloyd George had said so. No use anymore to listen to ravings from that quarter.

Northcliffe's classic advice on newspaper make-up to Keith Murdoch, now editor of the Melbourne Herald:

The first editorial should be the second thing read every day, the first being the main news ... Smiling pictures make people smile ... I, personally, prefer short leading articles ... People like to read about profiteering. Most of them would like to be profiteers themselves, and would if they had the chance ... The church notes are good. People who drink, smoke and swear have no idea of the interest in church matters ... [Sport] can be overdone, I believe, even in Australia ... The desk habit is, of course, one of the curses of journalism ... Every woman in the world would read about artificial pearls ... The late Gordon Bennett, when his staff could not print pictures, introduced the engineer of his yacht and told him to print pictures. The man did it ... The 'Herald' has a very bad name in Australia. Just as a man is always the last to hear about his wife's sideslips, so is an editor the last to hear about his paper. You have got to live down a past ... I still notice in the 'Herald' an absence of 'items'. Columns of items a day give the reader a great feeling of satisfaction with his three-penny worth ... My young men say you don't have enough stockings in the paper. I am afraid that I am no longer a judge of that.

The friendship that had begun when Murdoch exposed the fiasco at Gallipoli had, by 1920, developed almost into a father–son relationship. Northcliffe had acted as Murdoch's mentor, even to the extent of hiring him to cover the Prince of Wales's tour of Australia and New Zealand for *The Times*. For his part, Murdoch basked in the attention lavished upon him by Northcliffe, his affection obviously genuine, his gratitude sincere: 'You have been the biggest influence and the biggest force over me ... largely from the example I have steadily seen in you and the standard that you have set me.' He actually signed one of his letters with love, and in one touching postscript added: 'I often feel that your eye is on me, and that you insist on great work here.'

In return, Northcliffe studied Murdoch's papers 'everyday', and Murdoch had a standing invitation to visit Northcliffe at Elmwood whenever he visited England.

When Murdoch had the opportunity of buying the controlling interest in a newspaper in Sydney in December 1921, he immediately wired Northcliffe:

FRIENDS AND SELF HAVE EXCELLENT CHANCE BUYING INTO EVENING NEWS SYDNEY STOP I CAN GET CONTROL STOP FEELING THIS MY BIG CHANCE STOP AM WILLING PUT TEN THOUSAND POUNDS INTO SCHEME PROVIDING JUNCTION WITH HERALD WHEN HERALD FREE STOP WOULD YOU JOIN FINANCIALLY WITH FEW THOUSANDS STOP EVENING NEWS MADE 28000 LAST YEAR ON CAPITAL ... FEEL SUCCESS ABSOLUTELY ASSURED ... THIS RARE CHANCE ... IF YOU INTERESTED NAME CONDITIONS.

Northcliffe's response was swift, and, as always, wily. He would support the project, and Murdoch was to publicize that fact:

GLADLYEST INVEST FIVE THOUSAND AS ENCOURAGEMENT TO OTHERS AND PROOF MY COMPLETE CONFIDENCE IN YOU STOP NAME ANY AMOUNT SHOULD BE PUBLISHED

TOGETHER FACT YOU HAVE COMPLETE CONTROL STOP ONE MAN CONTROL ESSENTIAL NEWSPAPER BUSINESS CHIEF

After this show of support, Murdoch wrote to Northcliffe at length about the inside aspects of the deal, touching upon his success on the *Herald*: 'The improved *Herald* is the talk of the town but circulation needs a boost. I am starting the Jarroman serial soon and a beauty competition.'

> We have pulled off three good campaigns – hospitals, police, and tramways. Your notes are my bible. I go to them daily ... Men are not as good here as in Sydney. Subs are specially scarce. I am putting on [Walter] Fish's brother next week ... Whenever I think of you, Chief, which is constantly, I think of big questions and big movements and that's about as great a service a friend can do – it helps me a lot. All the pull here is on to small issues and tuppenny things.

Within a week of sending his cable, Northcliffe had sent the promised £5,000 – 'lose it if you like' – in a statement of complete trust and confidence. Murdoch fired back a long letter saying it was 'wonderful of you to come into the scheme':

> and I know you did it to give me my chance and cannot thank you enough ... The *Evening News* is a wonderful proposition. It is dull, unenterprising, and badly managed. There is no word of a third evening paper in Sydney and we are assured of a good run...

He closed by saying he hoped this explained fully the position of the *Evening News* in the market, and he added the important promise: 'I will not lose your money, Chief.' In the meantime, Murdoch wrote to Northcliffe, he had been accused by the Catholic newspapers and others not only of being a 'yellow journalist' but also of bringing '*Daily Mail* journalism to Australia. I wish I had!'

Linked to Northcliffe to the extent he was popularly known as 'Lord Southcliffe', Murdoch would be one of the first to sense something was seriously amiss when Northcliffe fell ill. There was every reason to believe the press baron was fully responsible for his every action in the early months of 1922, and his letters to Murdoch would indicate this again and again. By late May, however, his tone would change abruptly, and the terror would have begun.

By the time Northcliffe left on what he called his 'world whirl', in the summer of 1921, he was, except to his staff and directors, yesterday's man. He was as adept as ever at fingering faults in his newspapers, and he remained in the strictest control of editorial and of news. But he was slipping. On some days, he was precise and crisp, on others simply childish and self-indulgent. He distanced himself more and more from staff and friends, and, if possible, relied upon his relationship with his mother even more than he had in the past. Too many times, his pronouncements had that strange cast of an echo – of his former self? At fifty-seven, he had aged prematurely, and his timing was often badly off. The truth was, Northcliffe was worn out.

In competing newspapers, he was as often as not a figure of fun. On his departure from England, the *Morning Post* published a piece of not unamusing doggerel, demonstrating Northcliffe was still worthy of a sharp lampoon.

> Alas! Alack! What shall we do?
> Lord Northcliffe's gone on tour.
> Without him even two and two
> How dare we say make four?
>
> Why now the master-hand withdraw
> From Times and Daily Mail,
> That gave the Tables of the Law
> A more than million-sale?
>
> Too late to plead. His sail's unfurled.
> What comfort's to be found?
> For while 'the Chief' goes round the world,
> How will the world go round?

More apt still was *Punch*'s wonderful send-up of the 'Departure of Lord Thanet. Thrilling Scenes. (By our Special Correspondent)'.

> Lord Thanet sailed on Saturday the 16th from Tilbury on the *Megalomania* for his great world-pilgrimage, in the course of which he will visit the North and South Poles, ascend Mt. Everest and descend to the centre of the earth. Incidentally, he will investigate the opportunity for emigration to the Solomon Islands, where, on the news of his impending visit, the inhabitants have given up their anthropophagous practices, embraced vegetarianism and taken to golf.
>
> Subsequently he will enter on a thorough examination of the questions of a Church Disestablishment in Patagonia, the introduction of safety razors amongst the Hairy Ainus, and the construction of a tunnel from the North of Australia to New Guinea...
>
> A series of impressions from Lord Thanet's pen – which originally belonged to Louis XIV – will appear in all the Thanet Press in small pica type from time to time. Purchasers of the issues in which they appear will be entitled to a special

insurance indemnifying them against any deleterious results caused by the ecstasy of perusal...

[T]he demonstrations on the day of his departure surpassed anything recorded in the entire history of the Solar System. Though a man of iron nerve Lord Thanet was deeply muddled. From all corners of the globe came letters, cables and wireless messages wishing him a prosperous and prolonged tour. As he was leaving his home the oldest inhabitant of Thanet, a man of ninety-seven summers, wearing a Sandringham hat, made his way to the door and cried out in tremulous accents, 'Bless you, my Lord, but do not hurry back. The world needs you even more than England.'

It was, alas, all too true. The world loved Northcliffe better than his own country. Wherever he travelled, he was besieged by throngs of admirers. Veterans of the war came to pay homage for what they considered his heroic public defence of their case during the darkest days of their fighting. He was the guest of business magnates, diplomats and world rulers. When he was at sea, he slept – better, he wrote to the editor of the *Daily Mail*, than he had ever slept before.

I have not seen the paper, but my spies report that it is much better than when I was in America in 1917 ... I have had a very remarkable world whirl, so far ... When on shore I work sixteen hours a day. When at sea I sleep twelve ... Give my love to all at Carmelite House. I cannot write to each and every one. I ought to have brought at least two more typists with me.

This was Northcliffe's strange journey round the world – that represented everything he had loved and fought for during his life. Empire, in the waning days of Britain's ascendancy as the most powerful nation on earth; Northcliffe fading; a final farewell. Pathetically, he wrote over and over to his mother how sorry he was he had waited so late, how much he regretted not making the trip before now. It became a plaintive chorus in the background of his spectacular success, where every country welcomed him as a monarch and crowds thronged the streets to see him pass.

And almost everywhere he went, a 'ghost' would suddenly step out of the crowd – a child he had played with as a boy, a printer from the bicycling paper he had edited as a youth, a school friend long since forgotten. Then in late October, word reached Northcliffe that his old partner on the *Evening News* and the *Daily Mail* – Kennedy Jones – had died. K.J. had given up journalism in 1912 after a serious illness. Since then, his career had been uneven: he had spent some time in the furniture business, then in horse-racing. At last he had been elected to the House of Commons, with the help of Northcliffe, with whom he maintained a close relationship. K.J. himself credited his election almost entirely to the efforts of Carmelite House, and 'a great deal of what we managed to do was due to Valentine Smith* and his workers'. During the war, K.J. had provided invaluable information to Northcliffe regarding the ineffectiveness of the blockade formed to prevent Germany from getting cotton for use in the manufacture of munitions.

Considering his genuine closeness to K.J. throughout the years, and the two men's early joining of forces to conquer Fleet Street, Northcliffe's letter of condolence was oddly inadequate: 'His political work and my frequent absences abroad had rendered our meetings rarer of late, but I always preserved and shall always preserve my regard for a colleague of ability, worth and character.'

Such a response was completely unlike Northcliffe. When one of his favourite reporters, Twells Brex, was dying in 1920 of cancer, Northcliffe sat at his bedside whole days at a time. His widow had told one of Northcliffe's reporters she had happened to mention she had been having a hard time getting butter, and Northcliffe 'had gone half over London in his car trying to buy butter for us'. After her husband's death, she wrote to Northcliffe thanking him for all he had done: 'During these first weeks of my widowhood, you have never let me feel the loneliness, distracting my thoughts by every kindness.' For Northcliffe now to dismiss K.J.'s death lightly, never mentioning the matter to his male secretary, was an early sign of serious illness. There were others.

One night, Northcliffe dictated six hours of memories of the trip, until his secretary's hand was cramping from writing shorthand. He never even asked to see the transcript. Then, in Bangkok, as the pair of them were visiting the King's palace, Northcliffe, angry with his secretary for failing to get him a London newspaper, shoved him without warning down a set of stairs. Four of the King's servants, acting as if nothing were amiss, helped him to his feet. Later, the secretary recorded his anguished entry in his diary: 'My birthday – the worst day of the tour so far. The Chief has been most offensive to me in the very worst degree.'

On the last leg of the journey, Northcliffe concentrated with all his might on losing the weight he had been so self-conscious about for nearly two decades, and miraculously it fell off almost effortlessly. He felt young and lithe and light as a feather. That was how he saw himself.

It seemed otherwise to his friends and employees seeing him for the

---

* Valentine Smith, as Northcliffe's great promotions man in charge of the sweet-peas contest, Standard Bread campaign, Sandringham Hat campaign, and many more, was still a key member of the *Mail* staff.

first time since his return. Wrote Hannen Swaffer, one of his most loyal employees, 'His vitality had gone, his face was puffy. His chin was sunk, and his mouth had lost its firmness. He lost his temper during a speech, because someone dropped a plate or something. He was a different man. The fires that burned within him had burned too fiercely all those years. People who heard him knew it was the end.'

13

'Rosebud'

'Let me not be mad.'
King Lear

In March 1922, Northcliffe's former mistress Louise Owen, code-named 'the talkative lady' amongst his closest intimates, wrote to complain of her former lover's tone during a telephone call: 'Your unwarranted telephone abuse is still a mystery to me,' she said. 'It was most Curzon-like, full of your own importance.'

Talkative, tedious, self-absorbed, full of *her own* importance, Owen was nevertheless as loyal to Northcliffe as anyone ever would be. Her letter was that kind of vicious missive that passes between men and women who have loved one another passionately – full of jealousy, bitterness, complaints – and truth. She called her style of writing 'plainspeaking', knowing full well Northcliffe deplored it.

> It is only to your face I am so unpleasantly outspoken. To others – my speeches in America and to the public men I meet – I dwell on those qualities in you which I admire – your patriotism, your devotion to your mother, your courage in dealing with national affairs, your generosity and treatment of your staff (sometimes not), etc., etc. I doubt if I can ever help you as I would like to. On reflection it is palpable that you choose for your surroundings men and women common, mentally, as in every other respect.

How else, she asked, could she have continued to hear 'the most intimate details of your private life' and from at least a dozen sources? With workman-like efficiency, she enumerated the rumours making the rounds about Northcliffe's love-life, each one plausible; the way Owen described them, even probable. But these worried her less than his current entourage, whom she viewed as dangerous.

> Everywhere you are surrounded by sycophants and liars who, while licking the carpet for you to walk over, do not hesitate to cheapen you in every way to their advantage.

I know your influence is on the wane and that you are not master in your own affairs. It is not possible for even a Caesar to thrive only on flattery. Wholesome if unpalatable truth is necessary for the greatest sometimes, and to quote your words 'Royalty so often hear the truth only too late.' Are you aware of the manner in which your instructions are received by the *Times* Editorial staff including the two great S & S?

Here, Owen was referring to Sir Campbell Stuart, the managing director of *The Times*, and to Wickham Steed, the editor. Steed had been a sycophant of long standing; for years he sustained a tone of flattery so consistently pompous as to approach an art-form whenever he addressed the great Northcliffe. Greetings for a recent New Year were typical:

You understand most things but I don't know whether even you recognize all that your health and energy mean to the country and to the *Times*. You must do your utmost to conserve your driving power and your vision.

For Steed, the style had paid off handsomely. When Geoffrey Dawson was forced to resign as editor of *The Times* – 'a child in the hands of skilled intriguers', Northcliffe had called him – the prize went to Steed. And, lest there be any question as to who was the favourite, Northcliffe instructed Marlowe that, if 'a difference of opinion' should arise when he, Northcliffe, were absent, 'the will of Mr. Steed is to prevail'. He had given the power of attorney at Printing House Square to Steed and Stuart in 1920; it would later prove to be a great mistake.

Meanwhile, Steed and Northcliffe were described as 'inseparables', the former careful to eliminate anyone who might have been

working steadily against you, the Paper and me . . . I am determined that no one shall succeed in making bad blood between us, as many people would like to do. I have been loyal to you in deed, in thought and in word. In the *Times* and out of the *Times*, I intend to remain so.

Nothing seemed to faze Steed: not criticism ('Your bulletin helped members of the staff to understand how harassed you've been of late'); not public humiliation (open and posted telegrams criticizing Steed's work); not threatened sackings (Northcliffe put him under notice in May 1921); not undermining his authority (Northcliffe changed key staff members under Steed's authority without consulting him).

Steed stuck. Louise Owen might as well have saved her breath: Northcliffe wasn't listening.

Owen wasn't the only one of Northcliffe's intimates struck by a new coldness in his tone in the spring of 1922. His great friend Keith Murdoch was feeling the chill.

In May, Northcliffe wrote to Murdoch telling him 'too many people are coming by asking for favours. The most valuable thing in my life is time, and I cannot give it except to really important people or matters.' A week later, he was refusing a request to lend Murdoch a printing engineer, referring to 'curious rumours' in London about Murdoch's compromised position. Murdoch had undergone an attempted palace coup, but had emerged unbesmirched and victorious as the chief executive of his new company. To Murdoch's many reassuring and persuasive explanations as to what had happened, Northcliffe remained stonily unresponsive. He referred over and over to 'curious rumours', obviously rejecting any explanations put forth by the successful young entrepreneur. 'WISH YOU WOULD CABLE WHAT IS GOING ON,' Murdoch at last wired Northcliffe wistfully. 'MY POSITION HERE NOW UNDISPUTED CONTROL UNDER SYMPATHETIC BOARD.' Northcliffe wired him back immediately:

MY DEVOTION TO YOU PERSONALLY BUT CANNOT INJURE MY FIFTY THOUSAND SHARE-
HOLDERS ... ALL MATTERS WILL BE DEALT WITH BY [MY MANAGING DIRECTOR] FROM
SHAREHOLDERS POINT OF VIEW.

It was a remarkable response to a close friend of seven years' duration, more remarkable still when one considered that Murdoch had withdrawn his request for the loan of an engineer and was asking only that they maintain the friendship and ongoing business arrangements that were so important to both of them. It was the last time Murdoch would hear personally from his mentor and friend.

Northcliffe was dying.

His blood had become infected with a streptococcus, possibly from a septic infection around the roots of his teeth, and this invaded the bloodstream, eventually affecting the damaged valves of his heart. The very name of the infection – 'malignant endocarditis' – indicates the serious nature of the illness, whose symptoms may include paralysis, lung trouble not unlike the advanced stages of tuberculosis, severe kidney malfunction or the practical paralysis of the brain. In the case of the latter, an organically induced state of psychosis ensues which is indistinguishable from what most people regard as insanity. For an individual with a strong constitution and the will to resist death for many weeks, the symptoms may become enhanced and the subject violent, as they did in the case of Northcliffe.*

In practical terms, this meant that Northcliffe's genius for verbal coherence and the intellectual edifice upon which he pinned his ideas would, in a matter of six short weeks, collapse into a jumble of fragments, not unlike the disconnected pieces of a gigantic, colourful and complex jigsaw puzzle. Since his death, doctors and medical experts of all kinds have speculated that he was infected, certainly for weeks, probably for months and possibly for a year before his death, thus causing moments of incoherence or rudeness or abruptness such as Louise Owen and Keith Murdoch had experienced at his hands during the spring of 1922.

He would die badly, without respite or dignity. And in the wake of this, much of the power of his personality would be lost to history.

Sir Robert Hudson, Lady Northcliffe's long-time companion, to Sir George Sutton, Northcliffe's most trusted chief executive, from Evian-les-Bains on Lake Geneva, Saturday afternoon, 16 June 1922:

> This business is the devil!
>
> I don't know that he is worse, but he is driving everyone round him into a condition which will *soon resemble his own state*! ...
>
> Carlton Gardens ought to be reached about 7.45 tomorrow morning (Sunday). Then he will pass under purely medical control. Telephones will be cut off. No letters or telegrams allowed to pass in or out. No newspapers and no letters allowed! Of course, this will raise hell, but the drs and nurses must face that!
>
> I hope Lady N., *who is on the verge of a breakdown*, will be sent to bed at Crowborough. I think I shall retire to bed ... and pull all the blinds down for a week.

In the margins of a later letter written by Hudson, complaining that Lady Northcliffe was suffering badly from 'the strain of ceaseless anxiety', one of Northcliffe's brothers had pencilled in the comment: 'Bosh she never looked so well.' Another comment concerns Hudson himself: 'Robert Hudson's statements ... cannot be relied upon or credited in any way.'†

---

* This summary of the symptoms of the illness that killed Northcliffe has been prepared from the reports of his attending physicians, Sir Thomas Horder (later Lord Horder) and Dr Seymour Price, along with notes from the *British Medical Journal*, published 19 August 1922, concerning Northcliffe's death. The anguished description of a father whose son died of malignant endocarditis has also been to some extent included.

† The letters were written on 30 June and 4 July 1922. The time the notes were pencilled in is not known. (Harmsworth Archive.)

It is safe to say that Sir Leicester Harmsworth and his brother Cecil, who had taken charge of all the medical arrangements for Northcliffe, viewed Hudson and Mary Northcliffe with the gravest suspicion, and regardless of the civilized relationship Northcliffe himself had always enjoyed with the pair, believed they could not be trusted. Perhaps it was true. It was said, when Northcliffe lay dying, Mary ordered her portrait to be erected before him, and this resulted in Northcliffe's rewriting his will in her favour – although this instrument was later broken because of his legal incapacity to effect such a document.

Certainly, from the moment Northcliffe began his tumble-down descent from the height of his power, factions became immediately discernible: Mary Northcliffe and Robert Hudson, whom she would later marry; the brothers, representing the Harmsworth family, Harold strangely absent from all proceedings; the *Daily Mail* office and parent company Associated Newspapers, headed by the ever loyal Thomas Marlowe; the many other periodical outlets, headed by the tight-lipped Sir George Sutton – and finally, *The Times*'s men at Printing House Square.

By the time the ailing Northcliffe was brought back from the Continent, where he had gone to write several articles on Germany before meeting his wife on Lake Geneva, the acting chief executive of *The Times* had taken the astonishing step of posting a guard at the doors of the offices to prevent Northcliffe entering, just in case he should be able to make his way there. Wickham Steed meanwhile had defied Northcliffe's directive to quit his post, Steed holding the power of attorney for the newspaper and thus being in a position to defy any such order.

By now, the respected specialist in endocarditis, Sir Thomas Horder, had been engaged by the family to supervise the treatment of Northcliffe, and at his suggestion the dying press baron had been more or less caged in a small, specially built hut erected on the top of the Duke of Devonshire's house in Carlton Gardens, his own roof-top next door having been judged too weak to support the construction. There, attended round-the-clock by three males nurses, Northcliffe – insensible, delirious, raving and uncontrollable – spent his final days in terrible isolation.

His mother came once. 'Is it his head?' she asked afterwards of the doctor. She then withdrew again into the shadows, casting no more light upon her own feelings about her son than she had during his lifetime.

For their part, the family tried to halt rumours that Northcliffe was mad – an act of futility that served only to feed the rumour mill. There were reports that a French doctor had certified Northcliffe insane just prior to his journey back to England from the Continent; no such report was ever substantiated. But, as the family set about almost pathologically to prove such certification had never existed, more credibility was cast upon the possibility that it had.

It was Northcliffe himself who had first questioned his own sanity, in three, well-documented instances. The first had been in a letter to Sir Robert Hudson while the latter was still in Evian-les-Bains with North-cliffe's wife. The pair of them had been entertaining Sir Frederick Treves, the famous Harley Street doctor. Wrote Northcliffe:

> You have with you the most distinguished medical man in the world. Will you kindly ask his opinion as to my sanity? I have begun to have doubts whether it is too little work and too much money, or whether it is simply decay of my faculties; I do not know, but I think I am going mad. Please wire me at once to relieve my suspicions.

The second time occurred when he was travelling by train from Paris to Bellegarde, on the way to Evian. He had made some inappropriate remarks to a young woman accompanying his party, and he afterwards asked his companions, 'Don't you think I am mad? Am I mad?'

The third took place in his final days, before he was taken to die in the hut, while he was still in his home in Carlton Gardens. He had found the only telephone in the house left undisconnected by his brothers and immediately called the offices of the *Daily Mail*. There are two versions of what he said to the night editor who happened to answer the phone. The first was that he was being held captive; would the night editor come and rescue him? The second has become the stuff of legend: 'They say that I am mad,' Northcliffe whispered into the telephone. 'Send your best man to cover the story.'

What had occurred since 25 May, when Northcliffe had embarked upon his journey to Germany and to France? A robust and powerful figure had dwindled into a confused and terrified victim of interior disorder and confusion. It was a private act of dying made into public spectacle because of one mercilessly detailed, twelve-page, typed, single-spaced document written by one of Northcliffe's chief lieutenants – Wickham Steed.

Steed's narrative contained everything that could possibly be wished for in a document certain to degrade and sensationalize the final days of a dying press magnate: threats, insults, racism, family squabbles, obscenities, references to homosexuality, revolvers, speeding motor cars, madness and the insinuation of venereal disease.

On Thursday, 8 June, Steed received an invitation to join Lord Northcliffe on the following Sunday at the Hotel Athenée in Paris.* By now, Steed had received a number of disjointed dispatches from Northcliffe, who had travelled to Cologne, there to be entertained by the Commander-in-Chief of the British Army on the Rhine, General Sir Alexander Godley, against the wishes, as it turned out, of the British Foreign Office.† The weather was unseasonably hot, and Northcliffe requested to sit under a tree outside Godley's house, drinking barley water and receiving dignitaries who wished to see him. He travelled under the pseudonym Leonard Brown and carried a pistol, which was taken from him during the visit. At no time did Godley view Northcliffe's actions or talk as unreasonable, although he did note that Northcliffe was obviously feeling unwell throughout the visit.

Back at *The Times*'s office, Steed took the decision to halt publication of Northcliffe's series after noting that the reports were overly long, and indeed, in many places, irrational. He then made for Paris and appeared at the Hotel Athenée a few minutes before 8.00 p.m., the appointed hour. Northcliffe was in bed in his room, 'scantily dressed' and pathetically glad to see Steed, whose hand he grasped 'effusively', complaining of the prolonged time since he had seen *The Times* editor; whether this was for seventeen days or seventeen years he could not remember, and called to his valet to inform him. Northcliffe told Steed he had been threatened by an assassin with a Perrier bottle, but he had saved himself by putting out the man's eye with a walking-stick. Nevertheless, he had sustained an injury to his leg. He asked Steed to hold his hand as he was frightened of falling out of bed.

He complained of a niece who had become engaged to a soldier twice her age and told Steed of his determination that this marriage be prevented. In

* Steed dated the invitation as coming to him on Thursday, 8 June, saying his meeting was for Sunday, 10 June, an inaccuracy in the first line of his narrative.

† The Foreign Office Permanent Secretary, Sir Eyre Crowe, had issued a forceful state-ment condemning Northcliffe's visit to Germany as an attempt to discredit the Govern-ment, implying that General Godley should not receive him. Godley ignored this. A paraphrase of the telegram from Sir Eyre Crowe follows: With regard to Lord Northcliffe's visit I can only express my own private opinion. Lord Balfour is out of town; and Lord Curzon is too ill to be consulted. Northcliffe is merely a British peer and proprietor of a newspaper. In the latter capacity he is carrying on persistently an outrageous campaign against the Government and the Prime Minister and for this purpose he does not hesitate to promote misunderstanding and dissension between the French and ourselves. I have no doubt that his visit to Occupied Territory is intended to serve the same object. I can therefore see no reason for His Majesty's Representative showing him any special civilities or indeed taking any notice of him or consenting to meet him at public places. He is, of course, entitled to such official assistance as he may require as a British peer such as passports, visas, etc.

fact, this appeared to be one of Northcliffe's chief obsessions, since he referred to the matter repeatedly throughout the night. He talked continuously. At one point, he produced a pistol, waving it about in one hand. In the other, he held a book of religious sayings that his mother had given him, and he 'kissed it excitedly, saying that it alone had saved him'. He then burst out fervently that he feared Steed was not a religious man, that Steed did not pray. 'I pray constantly,' Northcliffe said. 'God talks to me . . . You must pray. Promise me.'

Northcliffe was then assisted by his valet in going to the bathroom, and Steed ascertained that the pistol was fully loaded with seven cartridges in a clip. Steed eventually succeeded in removing the cartridges from the clip and managed to return it to the pistol so that Northcliffe would not notice any change in weight of the weapon. Wrote Steed:

> At intervals during his ravings Lord Northcliffe vainly tried to smoke a cigar. Though I lighted it for him dozens of times, using up two full boxes of matches in the attempts, he could not keep it alight.

Northcliffe then spoke obscenely of Sir Robert Hudson and his relationship with his wife Mary, protesting that Steed was his only friend in the world and he must never leave him. He was lonely, he told Steed. Everyone was against him, he complained. He would fire a hundred and fifty at *The Times* – all the 'Lloyd Georgians'.

Now Northcliffe turned on Steed, reminding him of past failures. He then gave his forgiveness: Steed had been 'abominably fooled'; in fact, he 'was a fool', but Northcliffe loved him nevertheless. Northcliffe then abused a long-time companion of Steed's and accused her of making obscene accusations against him. At one moment he accused her of being seventy-four years old; at another sixteen. He then 'denounced her as a Jewess', wrote Steed.

He told *The Times* editor he must go with him to Evian-les-Bains, where he was meeting Lady Northcliffe and Sir Robert Hudson. And indeed they travelled the next morning by rail with a retinue that included the Paris correspondent, Sisley Huddleston, and Miss Rudge, the telephonist. On the platform awaiting the train, Northcliffe announced loudly that God was a homosexual. Once on the train, he denounced Huddleston for having a red silk pocket-handkerchief, breath that stank and rotting teeth. Huddleston left the train at Dijon. Northcliffe next turned on Miss Rudge and made obscene suggestions, driving her from the carriage.

In all, Steed spent nine hours of the ten-and-a-half-hour journey listening to Northcliffe's continuous talk: 'In it were intervals of uncanny lucidity. Part of it was filthy beyond repetition.' At Bellegarde, the party was met by Northcliffe's chauffeur, Pine, who drove them the rest of the way to Evian. On Northcliffe's orders, he drove at breakneck speed – 'over a narrow, winding and uneven road between 45 and 55 miles an hour.' During the trip, Northcliffe had the second of two 'simulated' or real 'coughing, retching and shrieking fits'. At another time, he asked to be let out of the car, so that he could 'lie down and die'.

Once in Evian, Northcliffe verbally abused one of the doctors called in to attend him. He then turned on Sir Robert Hudson, Sir Frederick Treves and finally, Steed himself: 'The malice and concentrated venom of his abuse was such as to command the utmost self-control on my part.'

At last, Steed made reference to Northcliffe's black tongue and a sore on his lip. He wrote of 'a strange squint in an upward diagonal direction' in Northcliffe's left eye. On this evidence, Steed based his unstated but clearly held belief that Northcliffe was dying of General Paralysis of the Insane, that is, the tertiary stage of syphilis. Here then was the written source of the rumour that Northcliffe died of syphilis.*

On 3 June 1954, Steed responded to a letter from a member of the Harmsworth family who was writing an authorized biography of Northcliffe, asking whether he wanted to change or recant any part of the statement he had made in 1922 – that Northcliffe died insane and that he had died of an illness other than 'malignant endocarditis'. Steed was steadfast in his refusal: 'I for my part had no doubt either of his madness or of the nature of the disease that was causing it.' By now, Northcliffe had been dead nearly thirty-two years.

Steed's hatred must have burned bright.

Before he died, Northcliffe left behind only two messages that were lucid. The first was, 'Tell Mother she was the only one!' The second was,

> I wish to be laid as near Mother as possible at North Finchley and I do not wish anything erect from the ground or any words except my name and the year I was born and this year upon the stone.
>
> In the *Times* I should like a page reviewing my life-work by someone who really knows and a leading article by the best man on the night.

In the final summing up of Northcliffe's triumphs and failures, was there nothing that could have saved him from the public scrutiny of the terrible last days of his life – or from the historical obsession with the cause of his death that has continued unabated for decades? No, he himself had created the myth causing the cult of personality that surrounded him. He himself

---

* See Appendix, page 363.

had erected the vast web of communications that spewed out news and rumour relentlessly and with all the speed and amplification twentieth-century technology could deliver.

Northcliffe lived by the sword. And he died by it.

Epilogue

On the day of Northcliffe's funeral, 17 August 1922, people lined the streets for four hours, waiting for the procession to pass. The buses stopped, and at a fixed time thousands stood silent for two minutes out of respect for his passing. Four thousand gathered outside Westminster Abbey where the service was held.

In his will, Northcliffe left three months' salary to each of his six thousand employees, a sum of £533,000, but because of unanticipated death duties, there was a shortfall of £100,000. In one version of the events that followed, staff disbelieved there were insufficient funds and, when settlements were offered, strikes were threatened, with actual notices of stop-work orders posted before agreements were finally reached. In another version, Northcliffe's brother Harold, Lord Rothermere, paid the difference to honour the wishes of 'my great brother'.

Northcliffe's entry in the *Dictionary of National Biography* was written by Geoffrey Dawson, who in 1919 had resigned under duress from his position as editor of *The Times*. This perhaps helps to explain why the entry is curt and dismissive, minimizing Northcliffe's achievements in the newspaper world and his part in exposing folly during the First World War. Many years after Northcliffe's death, Lord Beaverbrook claimed credit in various of his historical writings for overthrowing the ineffectual Asquith Government in December 1916, and that has gone down as history.

It is said that Northcliffe's Schemo Magnifico, written when he was an unproven young man, was kept locked in a safe until a short time before his death, when it was destroyed on his orders. Whether this was because he had greatly outpaced his own ambitions or had failed to achieve all he hoped is not known.

Within a year of Northcliffe's death, Lady Northcliffe married Sir Robert Hudson. Louise Owen remained loyal to Northcliffe, and in her many writings about the press baron she continued to defend his memory from what she considered to be scandalous reports about his personal life. In one bizarre episode, she supported Hannen Swaffer's contention that

Northcliffe had returned from the dead and could be summoned through various spiritualists of the age.

Northcliffe's first son died in Sydney in 1930 – according to legend, in a mental institution. Mrs Wrohan died in a nursing home, presumably of drink, about a year after Northcliffe's death. Northcliffe's personal solicitor, Henry Arnholz, attested in a signed statement given on 7 May 1952 that Mrs Wrohan had shown no signs of alcohol abuse before Northcliffe's death. It is not unreasonable to assume she drank herself to death from grief.

Northcliffe's daughter by Mrs Wrohan died in 1968. Of his other two sons, little is known. It is said their descendants work in one department or another of Associated Newspapers, but this may be just one more instance of the endless flow of Fleet Street gossip that continues to emanate from Northcliffe House.

HAROLD

14

'The River Fleet'

The River Fleet flows underground, deep beneath the surface of the street that takes its name, before it empties, under Blackfriars Bridge, into the Thames. In its course, the river veers in the direction of Carmelite House, where in the basement, not far from the presses, a deep pit was built to trap the rising water that sometimes flooded the lower regions of the building and thereby brought a halt to the production of the *Daily Mail*.

It was Sam Wright's responsibility, after heavy rains or at high tide, to check the pit and, if the water was up, to turn on the pumps. Wright had, as a boy, operated the ancient lift in Carmelite House, but this was before he came back from the Great War with 'half a hundred weight of shrapnel in his head, and one of his eyes shot out'. According to legend, Northcliffe had called Wright to Room One and asked what the young veteran would most prefer to be. Off the top of his head, Wright had replied, 'an electrician', although in fact he had neither formal training nor aptitude for the craft. An electrician nevertheless he became, clambering up and down ladders in the machine room and scribbling into the log book the cause of any misfunction he was sent to investigate as 'zero contact'.

At quitting time, the machine hands queued up to wash at the long troughs in the changing room. More than once, one or another of them would catch Wright just before he left for home. 'Oh, you dropped this, Sam,' they would say, and hand over the glass eye they had spotted in the greasy water at the bottom of the trough.

While downstairs Sam Wright laboured through the various duties and tasks that made up his daily grind, upstairs Harold, brother of Alfred and first Viscount Rothermere, was selling off *The Times*.

A story passed from one member of the Harmsworth family to another – each privately attesting to the likelihood of its truth – that when Northcliffe lay dying in the cramped hut on top of his neighbour's house in Carlton Gardens, the great press lord had suddenly 'started up in bed and said, "Harold will ruin my paper: he will think too much of the money".' Alfred died in August 1922; by October, Harold had completed the deal to sell *The Times* back to John Walter, the original owner. Walter was unable to afford the prestigious newspaper himself, but had managed to convince the American millionaire John Jacob Astor to back him.

The ownership of *The Times* was then, and for many years to come, an issue exciting national interest. For a short time during the complicated negotiations that followed Northcliffe's death, Lloyd George himself had vied, unsuccessfully, to acquire the newspaper; such was its import as a symbol of the Establishment. Rothermere, however, remained typically indifferent.

There were two versions of the way Rothermere went about divesting Northcliffe's estate of *The Times*. In the first, he actually intended to acquire the newspaper for himself, offering £3,250,000, but found he was outbid by the Walter–Astor contingent. In the second, he cleverly planted the amount of his bid in the enemy camp in order to up the ante, thereby benefiting Northcliffe's beneficiaries. Those who knew Rothermere well generally accepted the latter version as the truth; those who didn't, the former. In the event, the most likely scenario was that Rothermere would have willingly paid the sum he bid, but allowed his competitors to know his intentions on the principle he had nothing to lose and everything to gain – whatever the outcome. He was swift to recognize a 'heads-you-win, tails-you-win' situation and so could flip the coin with infuriating *sang-froid*.

Some years later Rothermere said about the transaction, 'I have never had any regrets about losing *The Times*, for common sense dictated that I should decrease, not add to, my worries.' If he had got *The Times*, he wouldn't have had any regrets either, since no doubt he would eventually have contrived to get a decent return on his investment. This was vintage Harold: a newspaper was only a newspaper, an appropriate or inappropriate investment for capital.

He was equally complaisant about selling off Amalgamated Press, amongst whose titles was the wonderfully nostalgic *Answers*, in order to cover the death duties on his brother's estate – an unpleasant, but briskly executed task. Unlike Northcliffe, Rothermere harboured few sentimental notions about the business of gathering and disseminating information. It was said that the only reason he didn't sell the flagship of the business, the *Daily Mail* itself, was that his mother asked him not to.

By 1922, Rothermere was considered a phlegmatic character, stuffy, stolid, utterly without imagination, not unlike the dull husband of Madame Bovary in Flaubert's notorious novel; this was the public image. It was especially satisfying to the national press to portray Rothermere as something of a fool because it had been almost impossible to assail the masterful Northcliffe, whose power of personality and editorial integrity struck envy into the hearts of his Fleet Street competitors. Regardless of his image as the lesser of the two brothers, however, it was Harold Rothermere who had picked up the *Daily Mirror* in 1914 for £100,000, watching its circulation grow as the war created amongst the public a frantic desire for visual images of the events taking place across the Channel. The *Mirror's* circulation eventually overtook that of the *Daily Mail*, its profits outpacing its sister paper dramatically, since Rothermere had sole control of outlay and kept the paper's costs low. A stroke of luck, his competitors asserted: Harold had merely benefited from his brother's genius and from the competence of the *Mirror's* editor, Alexander Kenealy.

But it was Rothermere acting on his own initiative who decided to ride out the trend in March 1914, by putting out a Sunday edition of the *Mirror* – the *Sunday Pictorial*. Within three weeks, its circulation hit 1,840,722. This feat alone would have made him a colossus in Fleet Street had it not been for the genius and flair of Northcliffe, whose combustible talents made shadows of anyone else's accomplishments. Rothermere had to content himself with an uncontested reputation as financial guru, from his careful husbandry of Northcliffe's resources; it was several years before his acumen in investment would be fully recognized, and the same again before his outright wizardry in the world of finance would sink into public consciousness.

Perhaps it was in his nature, from early on, to be overlooked. Shy to the point of backwardness, he would, as a young man, stand near the doorway whenever he and his brothers attended dances, asking how soon they could go home. Then, after he was seconded from his dull job in the Civil Service to help Alfred establish *Answers to Correspondents*, Harold was the paper-and-string man to Alfred's editorial stardom. His contribution was his amazing ability to calculate and organize and predict profit and loss. If he erred, it was always on the side of caution. But mostly he was right. It was Harold who monitored circulation, Harold who told Alfred when he had enough money to purchase Elmwood, Harold again who determined the amount the brothers could afford to set aside in support of their mother, Harold who mastered the stock markets. Always the gatekeeper, his status derived from having facts readily at hand. One had the impression that he was simply happy to be included at all.

All the Harmsworths were handsome, Harold no exception. Beside Alfred's golden countenance, however, Harold's dark good looks seemed ordinary and commonplace. And, while Alfred inherited his father's delicacy of feature, Harold had the heavy lower lip of his mother, which he disguised by wearing a walrus moustache. Then too, as the years caught up with him, he showed a tendency towards corpulence; this plus his military bearing and ponderous manner, no doubt adopted to conceal a natural awkwardness, tended to perpetuate the impression of an over-bearing nature. He was, in manner and speech, almost a parody of the proud, gruff captain of industry – the mighty capitalist envisioned by Karl Marx, exploiting his workers in pursuit of profit.

The only problem with this persona was that it was almost wholly inaccurate. Rothermere dealt evenly with his employees. He didn't inspire in them a sense of purpose; mystique was hardly his strong suit. But he paid well and fairly, and was quick to spot talent; he was much less inclined to be impressed by it than his brother, however. 'You can always buy brains,' was one of his *bons mots*, although it didn't do much to endear him to the brains he was buying. But there were many who preferred him to Northcliffe, less fire no doubt, but less heat as well.

Within the family circle, he was generally adored. At family gatherings, he kept his pockets full of golden sovereigns, giving them away to the many children in the Harmsworth clan. The most touching tribute from any member of the family came from his son Vyvyan, a little less than two years before his death from wounds suffered on the battlefield. It was a bizarre occurrence, the son of a great press baron writing to a Canadian expatriate to try to get a job for his father – presumably because of Sir Max Aitken's close relationship with Andrew Bonar Law.

Dear Sir Max,

I hope you don't mind my writing to you, but I wish you could get the Pater to take some job under the government. He is so modest that he won't do anything himself; then of course the newspapers are against him but then in times of war those things should not count. I am sure you will agree with me that his great experience would be of the greatest value in any department.

Apologising and hoping you won't think me a damned fool

Yrs sincerely,

H. Vyvyan Harmsworth

Harold was duly appointed director-general of the Royal Army Clothing Factory in 1916. Did Sir Max Aitken intercede to arrange his appointment? Aitken was certainly around, and ready to do service, especially of the kind that called into play his new, self-determined role as go-between. Whether it was Aitken's doing or not, the directorship was exactly the kind of position in which Harold was bound to do well. It involved internal organization and carefully planned distribution, both areas where Rothermere excelled. Then, too, there was the suggestion of corruption within the ranks, a situation quickly put to rights by Harold, whose close attention to the books brought a halt to dealings on the blackmarket.

Did Harold's innate ability to sort and cull and get things done make him any less a figure than Northcliffe? His sons, Vere and Vyvyan, the successors to the business, almost perfectly mirrored the abilities of father and uncle – Vere with his careful collecting of comforts for his men; Vyvyan with his dazzling intellect, offhand bravery and subtle intuition. It was an anomaly within the Harmsworth family that the talents were so evenly divided; branches of the same tree splitting into such diverse directions.

The truth was, the glamour of Northcliffe made Harold seem a plodder.

Lloyd George was starting an air force – an entity separate from the air power of the Army and Navy. It was a controversial move, since few in the military believed it necessary. There was, for instance, the argument that a separate air force would duplicate already existing facilities; more to the point, many top officers opposed the move because they didn't want to see any limitations put upon their own power. The man who could stand up to creating a new branch of the military was Northcliffe, Lloyd George believed, and, more importantly, such an appointment would put a muzzle on the press baron, who had begun to dog Lloyd George in the same way that he had his predecessor Asquith.

But Northcliffe publicly declined the post, and in terms most humiliating to Lloyd George. In an open letter to the Prime Minister published in *The Times*, he wrote, 'In present circumstances, I can do better work if I maintain my independence and am not gagged by a loyalty I do not feel towards the whole of your administration.' It was a shocking act of defiance, especially in light of the fact that the President of the Air Board, Lord Cowdray, who had been doing a creditable job and had assumed he would be asked to fill the new position, had not been informed that Northcliffe was under consideration. Infuriated by this piece of political perfidy, Cowdray immediately resigned, and in an attempt to calm troubled waters, it was said, Max Aitken, by now Lord Beaverbrook, put forth Harold's name. In an act of political appeasement, Harold accepted the post, with the immediate goal of creating the Royal Air Force.

Quite reasonably, he selected as his Chief of Air Staff General Sir Hugh Trenchard, then commander of the Royal Flying Corps in France under the direct supervision of General Sir Douglas Haig. Trenchard had done little to distinguish himself in his long career in the military, never advancing beyond the rank of major, until in 1912, at the suggestion of a friend, he learned to pilot an aeroplane. It would lead him to become one of the first strategic bomber pilots of the war, accounting for his rapid rise in the army at an advancing age.

Trenchard was loyal, courageous and strong-willed – almost the ideal of a military man. He had a characteristic way of speaking – slowly and ponderously – that earned him the nickname 'Boom', a term of affection amongst his subordinates. For, despite 'Boom's' stiff, upright manner, he was able to instil in his men a sense of high morale. In fact, except for two characteristics, he was precisely the man to help create a separate air force.

The first was that he was exceedingly dim-witted, having failed all his major examinations as a boy and only scraped through the examination for militia candidates after two failures. The second was more daunting. Although the post had been created in order to form a separate air force, Trenchard accepted the conventional wisdom of the time and did not actually anticipate the importance of air power in battle; this despite his own experience as a pilot. He viewed the creation of the Royal Air Force as an act of treachery against the man he most respected, General Sir Douglas Haig, and indeed the Army itself. With his limited imagination and understanding, he lacked the vision to foresee what the RAF would one day mean to the nation. And, if Trenchard was the ideal of the military man, he was also the epitome of all that was wrong with the war-time mentality – an unoriginal reflection of the rationale that kept the war going.

Summoned by his new superior to a meeting at the Ritz in London, Trenchard crossed the Channel on 16 December 1917, with serious mis-givings about his ability to serve in the position now thrust upon him. At 3.00 p.m., he went up to Harold's room for a perfunctory meeting which should have lasted only a few minutes. Twelve and a half hours later, a shattered Trenchard left the room, having argued ceaselessly and through several meals not only with Rothermere but also with his brother North-cliffe. Disenchanted with Haig, the two brothers attacked Trenchard for his dogged defence of his old superior. His lack of enthusiasm for the task at hand dismayed the two Harmsworths, who nevertheless at last wore him down, convincing him to accept the post in the new ministry he so opposed. And although by 3.30 a.m. the next morning Trenchard was thoroughly defeated, he managed to get in the last word – with what he thought an appropriate riposte: 'Don't forget also that I'm neither a good writer nor a good talker,' he warned.

To Trenchard's way of thinking, Rothermere embodied every evil of the modern-day press lord: unconventional thinking, a lack of respect for hierarchy, an autocratic manner and a determination to effect change. For his part, Rothermere found himself confronted by the entrenched military thinking that his brother Northcliffe had opposed throughout the war. The partnership that began so unpropitiously was destined to degenerate exponentially. Rothermere wanted to build up numbers in the new Ministry; Trenchard preferred to let the Army and Navy determine how many men they could give. Rothermere sought advice from returning pilots; Trenchard preferred to consult their military superiors. Rothermere knew that types of aircraft could be distinguished one from another by their sound; Trenchard thought smell as likely a determinant. And so it went.

The situation, though deteriorating seriously, might have stayed on the level of petty squabbles between one particular mind–set against another, the sort of political infighting that accompanies most attempts at bureaucratic incorporation – except for Harold's failure of nerve. And this resulted from personal tragedy.

Harold's eldest son Vyvyan, who was so like Northcliffe, died from his wounds on 12 February 1918. This, after the death of Vere, who had been killed in action in November 1916, was more than Harold could bear. On 23 April, he tendered his resignation as Secretary of State for Air to the Prime Minister. In it, he cited three reasons for his departure. The first was ill health, a euphemism for what threatened to become a complete nervous collapse. His second reason was his own notoriety which, if he were to continue in his post, would cause public 'comment and criticism' of the new air force, a genuine threat to the fledgling service. The final reason was that the fusion of the Royal Naval Air Service and the Royal Flying Corps had now been accomplished.

Lloyd George accepted Rothermere's resignation, writing swiftly back to him:

> Your sacrifices to the national cause have been so heavy, and the strain imposed on you so cruel that it would be impossible to deny you the right to some repose. Sympathy in these matters is generally best given by silence, but I am sure you know without my telling you how much I sympathise with you in your losses and in the way in which you have continued your public duties in spite of everything.

This token of goodwill and sympathy elicited a second letter from Harold, this time giving the real reason for his departure. 'Every day,' Harold wrote to Lloyd George, 'the burden of work and responsibility seemed crushing and I was suffering much from ill health and insomnia.' It was said behind Harold's back that he was 'drinking sometimes one or two more than he could manage', and, when one of his secretaries went to report this to Northcliffe, he replied, not without relief, 'I was afraid you were going to tell me Harold is going insane. We have had it in the family, you know.'

In fact, Harold *was* close to breaking point, so close that it seemed inevitable. His rescue came not from his brother Northcliffe, however, nor from the family, but from Beaverbrook, who had by now become one of Harold's closest friends. From an early age, Beaverbrook had shown an acute sensitivity to weakness in others, both from the point of view of friend – and of predator. Was there anything he could do for the sufferer? And, after that, was there anything the sufferer could do for him? Beaverbrook now brought all his resources to bear on Harold's condition, actually taking care of him at Cherkley, his country estate just outside Leatherhead, Surrey.

Meanwhile, Trenchard had also tendered his resignation – 'a great thing for the Air Force', Rothermere believed. He wrote to Bonar Law that Trenchard's attitude of 'Je sais tout' had been a danger to the new Royal Air Force and that Trenchard had been 'insisting on the ordering of large numbers of machines for out-of-date purposes'. All that was left was for Trenchard to return to the air fields of France, where his notable courage and ability to inspire men under fire continued to distinguish his career.

Ironically, his achievements in action eventually resulted in his regaining his position as Chief of Air Staff in the Royal Air Force. So, as fate would have it, Trenchard came to direct the very institution whose establishment he had so vigorously opposed. As Rothermere had feared, he would continue there for the next ten years in a lustreless career, perpetuating the outmoded belief that strategic bombing 'could win a war all by itself' and giving little concern to air defences, a view which would follow on into the crucial 1930s when Britain's defences would fall into a pitiable state even as Germany rearmed. Amongst Trenchard's contributions to the RAF would be the design of insignias and uniforms for staff. But, although he would remain as popular as ever amongst his subordinates, his reforms would not last beyond his tenure.

Did Harold ever recover from the deaths of his two eldest sons? And later, from the loss of Northcliffe? These key events would give impetus to the nomadic life style that would come to characterize the last two decades of Harold's life. He would tumble through the dramatic events of the 1920s and 1930s like a leaf before harsh wind, a serious pessimist who, predicting disaster at every turn, almost rejoiced when one or another catastrophe came to be.

Harold had married and, within the interior spheres of family legend, his wife ranked low. Said one Harmsworth, a matriarch of high moral fibre and considerable backbone, 'Harold was shattered by the loss of his sons, ... but when Vyvyan was wounded and in hospital in London, his mother never went to see him at all, didn't bother with him at all. He died.' It was an uncompromising assessment of a woman reckoned to be beyond the pale of decent personal conduct.

Whether or not that was true, Harold's wife Lilian was going to have to be very trivial indeed if she were to overcome her tragic destiny and live her life entirely for pleasure. She managed to measure up to the task. The daughter of a bankrupted City hardware merchant, Lilian Share was a member of the middle class, with a mother ambitious for her to marry well. It was said Lilian herself dreamed of marrying a rich man. Later, after a series of devastating events, her sister was reputed to have warned a young niece to be careful of making wishes; they might, as they had with Lilian, come true.

Lilian was eighteen when she married Harold. By the time she was thirty-two, she would have had a tumultuous affair with his brother – only to see him paralysed for life in a freak motoring accident. By the time she was forty-three, two of her three sons would be dead. These cruel events occurred against the backdrop of Harold's ascent into the highest ranks of society: he was made a baronet in 1910, a baron in 1914 and the first Viscount Rothermere of Hemsted in 1919.

Thus even as money, position and prestige unfolded before Lady Rothermere, the loss of lover and sons took a toll very different from that inflicted upon her husband. Her natural feelings, cauterized by events, left her free to follow whatever fancies she might, and these inclined towards the literary and the mystical – against the age-old backdrop of sexual freedom that so frequently accompanies artistic licence. It was said Lilian first became acquainted with André Gide through St John, whose business interests in Perrier made him an habitué of France.

She had by 1917 acquired a protégé, Paul Meral – a poet who, between two tours of duty at the Front, produced a work of genuine merit, 'The Recitatives'. Not much older than her sons, Meral nevertheless became her close companion, the pair of them translating Gide's *Prometheus Unbound* into English. The book, published in 1919 with Lilian's name as sole translator, was Gide's introduction into the language. It was a significant contribution to the field of literature, but Gide himself reserved his approval: 'The chief difficulty', he wrote, 'comes from the fact that my sentence constantly suggests rather than affirms, and proceeds by insinuations – for which the English language, more direct than the French, feels rather a repugnance.' Gide continued that Meral himself was no doubt intelligent but he lacked 'true greatness', an assessment that has been borne out by history. But, if Lilian had chosen a talented but undistinguished poet as her protégé, her relentless patronage of Gide indicated a superior sensibility – although the great French poet himself remained ungrateful.

And then, considering her imprint on the stylish literary scene in Paris during the early 1920s, few writers felt compelled to make any sort of record of Lilian Rothermere. There was a general belief that she was beautiful – although the few surviving photographs show a rather plain, broad-faced young woman with a heavy jaw and frilly curls. The most comprehensive remembrance of Lilian is the fictionalized character of Lady Lilian Griffiths created by Gide in his masterpiece *The Coiners*. It is less than flattering.

The character is introduced as she lies in bed with one of her young lovers, the Comte de Passavant, waiting for a second lover named Vincent to arrive. The tone of the rendezvous is set when de Passavant says to Lilian,

'Quick, one word before [Vincent] comes in. My father died this evening.'
'Ah,' she said simply.
'You haven't a fancy to become Comtesse de Passavant, have you?'
At this Lilian flung herself back with a burst of laughter.
'Oh, oh, my dear friend! The fact is that I have a vague recollection that I've mislaid a husband somewhere or other in England. What! I never told you?'
'Not that I remember.'
'You might have guessed it; as a rule, a Lady is accompanied by a Lord.'

Lilian then turns the conversation to the lover who will soon arrive. Vincent is a young doctor with an interest in natural science who, because of his overpowering passion for Lilian, has just left his pregnant mistress, who, because of her overpowering passion for Vincent, has just left her husband. Lilian rhapsodizes about fish that fall victim to predators in the deep; some, it appears, are able to live in varying degrees of saline solutions while others are left in a weakened state by a change in environment. At the point where the saline content changes, those unable to adapt are devoured by those who are, a concept that appeals to the character of Lady Lilian Griffiths. Indeed, she will later explain to Vincent:

... Don't imagine that because I have given myself to you, you have won me. Make certain of this – I abominate mediocrity, and I can love no one who isn't a conqueror. If you want me, it must be to help you to victory; if it's only to be pitied and consoled and made much of ... no, my dear boy – I'd better say so at once – I'm not the person you need – it's Laura [his jilted mistress].

How she has arrived at this conclusion, she later reveals to Vincent. It is the result of a trauma she suffered at the age of seventeen, when she was aboard the *Bourgogne* as it sank. Plunged into the freezing cold water, she determined to save a beautiful young girl whose mother had disappeared into the dark waters. This she managed to accomplish. But, once aboard a lifeboat, she witnessed a scene that changed her life:

There were about forty or so of us in the boat all crowded together, for a number of swimmers had been picked up at last gasp like me. The water was almost on a level with the edge of the boat. I was in the stern and I was holding the little girl I had just saved tightly pressed against me to warm her – and to prevent her from seeing what I couldn't help seeing myself – two sailors, one armed with a hatchet and the other with a kitchen chopper. And what do you think they were doing? They were hacking off the fingers and hands of the swimmers who were trying to get into our boat. One of these two sailors (the other was a Negro) turned to me as I sat there, my teeth chattering with cold and fright and horror and said, 'If another single one gets in we shall be bloody well done for. The boat is full.' And he added that it was a thing that had to be done in all shipwrecks, but that naturally one didn't mention it.

At this point, Lilian tells Vincent, she fainted. But, upon coming to, she realized that 'henceforth there would be a whole heap of delicate feelings whose fingers and hands I should hack away to prevent them from climbing into my heart and wrecking it.' Thus Lilian, as Gide saw her.

Later in the book, he condemns her for being a soulless and unfeeling predator who, like the fish that can survive in differing saline solutions, victimizes the others who cannot. Finally, though, Lilian does not survive: she travels to the darkest corner of Africa where she is drowned by her lover Vincent, who by now has been driven mad by her demands.

It is impossible to determine where fact and fiction coincide in Gide's book, but it is undeniable that, regardless of the ways in which Lilian Rothermere benefited him, the writer held her in contempt. In a novelist's aside, he confesses that at first Lilian 'rather took [him] in', but after a while he was able to judge her properly:

People like her are cut out of a cloth which has no thickness. America exports a great many of them, but is not the only country to breed them. Fortune, intelligence, beauty – they seem to possess everything, except a soul ... No past weighs upon them, no constraint; they have neither laws, nor masters, nor scruples; by their freedom and spontaneity, they make the novelist's despair; he can get nothing from them but worthless reactions.

Indeed, Gide's fictionalized assessment of Lady Lilian Griffiths was shared by T.S. Eliot's wife Vivienne about Lilian Rothermere: 'She is unhinged –' Vivienne Eliot wrote to Ezra Pound, 'one of those beastly raving women who are the most dangerous. She is now in that asylum for the insane called La [*sic*] Prieure where she does religious dances naked with Katherine Mansfield.' But perhaps this was unkind.

Lilian had been sighted carrying cups of coffee in the Château du Prieure; she was not, however, unclothed at the time. Nor was there any evidence she took part in the Sacred Dances of Gurdjieff, although she had certainly helped to finance the château where the dances took place.

In referring to the Prieure, Vivienne Eliot, who actually did die insane in an asylum, was speaking of the home of the institute founded by Gurdjieff – mystic, philosopher, cultist, hypnotist, telepathist, practitioner of 'auto-mythology' and choreographer of a hundred Sacred Dances, some of whose practitioners had died in the Gobi Desert while trying to find an appropriate location to carry out the important 'Movements'.

Gurdjieff was born in the Greek quarter of Alexandropol in Armenian Russia, and had been deeply affected when, as a child, one of his teeth had been knocked out in a fight:

> This strange tooth had seven shoots and at the end of each of them stood out in relief a drop of blood, and through each separate drop there shone clearly and definitely one of the seven aspects of the manifestation of the white ray.

This seemed a sign, and Gurdjieff began his endless search for answers to the questions of being, beginning with the Sarmoung Brotherhood, of whose existence he had become aware while reading through a pile of ancient Armenian parchments. And, although this search didn't actually render any of the answers he was seeking, it did help him refine his sense of mission, which was

> an 'irrepressible striving' to understand clearly the precise significance, in general, of the life process on earth of all the outward forms of breathing creatures and, in particular, of the aim of human life in the light of this interpretation.

In this quest, Lilian, 'utilizing her exalted worldly position and vast wealth as a lubricant to living', was able to assist Gurdjieff. For it was Lilian who had originally summoned Gurdjieff to London by telegram – 'deeply impressed by your book ... will pay all expenses' – thus allowing him to explain his philosophy in a public lecture that included sixty-odd of the London intelligentsia who might be interested in 'pre-sand Egypt' or any of the other obsessions of the mysterious, liquid-eyed mystic.

Gurdjieff would eventually achieve his all-embracing definition of God, 'Our Almighty Omni-Loving Common Father Uni-Being Creator Endlessness', abandoning his teachings and recording his interpretation of life in his master work *All and Everything*. But it was all too much.

By now Lilian had lost interest; she returned to her original love of literature, and here, as with the sponsorship of Gide, her patronage played an important part in the development of twentieth-century literature. For the first three years of its existence, Lilian financed the *Criterion*, T.S. Eliot's revolutionary quarterly literary review. The first issue alone, published in October 1922, contained writing by Hermann Hesse, Roger Fry, Ezra Pound, Paul Valéry, Virginia Woolf, W.B. Yeats and E.M. Forster.

Eliot had come into prominence for winning a $2,000 prize for *The Waste Land* from the American literary magazine the *Dial*. Richard Cobden-Sanderson, whose grandfather Richard Cobden had been the great Liberal statesman, and whose father had fostered orphans Frank and Bertrand Russell, was a publisher, a member of the London literary set, who, along with his wife, entertained lavishly in their home in Hammersmith. It was Cobden-Sanderson who brought Eliot into contact with Lilian.

Perhaps the most wonderful description of the literary set of the early 1920s belongs to Alice B. Toklas, the long-time companion of the poet Gertrude Stein who renders, in her own distinctive way, the unfolding of Eliot's fame and Lilian's patronage:

We met Ezra Pound at Grace Lounsbery's house, he came home to dinner with us and he stayed and talked about Japanese prints among other things. Gertrude Stein liked him but did not find him amusing. She said he was a village explainer, excellent if you were a village, but if you were not, not. Ezra also talked about T.S. Eliot. It was the first time anyone had talked about T.S. at the house. Pretty soon everybody talked about T.S. Kitty Buss talked about him and much later Hemingway talked about him as the major. Considerably later Lady Rothermere talked about him and invited Gertrude Stein to come and meet him. They were founding the *Criterion*. We had met Lady Rothermere through Muriel Draper whom we had seen again for the first time after many years. Gertrude Stein was not particularly anxious to go to Lady Rothermere's and meet T.S. Eliot, but we all insisted she should, and she gave a doubtful yes. I had no evening dress to wear for this occasion and started to make one. The bell rang and in walked Lady Rothermere and T.S.

Eliot and Gertrude Stein had a solemn conversation, mostly about split infinitives and other grammatical solecisms and why Gertrude Stein used them. Finally Lady Rothermere and Eliot rose to go and Eliot said that if he printed anything of Gertrude Stein's in the *Criterion* it would have to be her very latest thing. They left and Gertrude Stein said, 'Don't bother to finish your dress, now we don't have to go,' and she began to write a portrait of T.S. Eliot and called it the fifteenth of November, that being the day and so there could be no doubt that it was her latest thing. It was all about wool is wool and silk is silk or wool is woollen and silk is silken. She sent it to T.S. Eliot and he accepted it but naturally he did not print it.

In the context of the magazine, many letters crossed between Eliot and Cobden-Sanderson about how much money Lady Rothermere would 'cough-up'. Although the pair thought otherwise, this amount turned out to be finite, since, after three years, Lilian sold her shares to the publishers Faber & Gwyer, moving permanently to France. It was thought she withdrew her patronage because Eliot refused to publish a work of André Gide, and in this, of course, Lilian, whose faults were many but whose literary taste was impeccable, turned out to be right.

In another matter as well, she would turn out to be right. Several years later, when her last living son Esmond took over the running of the *Daily Mail*, placing his hands, in her words, 'on the wheel of control of a machine having invaluable possibilities for good and evil', she issued him a warning about the rise of Beaverbrook's *Daily Express*.

> I am ... convinced that Beaverbrook has only one dominant aim in life, perhaps a quite natural one, which is to place his papers ahead of ours! Therefore I do *most emphatically warn you against this man* and ask you in full seriousness to weigh up *the reasons* which *prompt* him now and will in the future to make all kinds of overtures to you, believe me none will be prompted by the desire to really help you – of *this I am certain* ...

Lilian said she had been watching the *Daily Mail* sink, ever since 'the time your father entered into a certain collaboration with Beaverbrook and the decline in his prestige ipso-facto and of that of the papers he controlled'. Thus Lilian on Beaverbrook.

Her assessment of her estranged husband's inexplicable relationship with the emerging press lord would not only explain what happened during the 1920s; it would foreshadow the disastrous effect of Beaverbrook on the Rothermere dynasty for decades to come.

Lilian was not the only member of the family to take note of Beaverbrook's machinations. Six months before his death, Northcliffe had directed one of his editors to

> Watch Beaverbrook. He is swallowing Hulton. Hulton will be absorbed. I can see it. Beaverbrook has him hypnotised. Think then of the papers Beaverbrook will control. He is no fool.

There was in fact no end to Max's appetite: he was like the cannibal who believes he absorbs the power of whatever enemy he consumes. But Beaverbrook ate what he loved, he ate his friends.

By 1923, the year after Northcliffe made his prophecy, Beaverbrook's lips were greasy from consuming Hulton's newspaper empire. He kept for himself only the *Evening Standard*, passing along the other newspapers, the *Daily Sketch* and the provincials, to his good friend Harold. Rothermere in turn sold them, making, he said, a £1.8 million profit. This was fine: Max loved making a profit for his friends, and Harold was now amongst his very most intimate circle.

The reasons for Beaverbrook's affection were cumulative. Whereas Northcliffe had from the start viewed Beaverbrook with suspicion, Rothermere always believed in him. He would one day make a great success in the newspaper business, Harold believed, and he told Beaverbrook that. And, although he was not able to invest in Beaverbrook's newspapers out of loyalty to his brother, Rothermere did all he could to help him succeed. It had been Harold who, along with Lord St Audries, sponsored Beaverbrook's introduction into the House of Lords. In the early days as well, when Beaverbrook was learning the trade, Rothermere was his secret guru, writing long letters about the newspaper business and making pessimistic predictions about all that could go wrong. If it happened that his mentor was downhearted, 'wondering how Fleet Street [was] paying its weekly bills', the astute Beaverbrook quickly picked up the theme:

> The situation here is very depressing. The days are cold and the nights are stormy. The wind blows always from the East. When we are not worried about strikes, we are depressed about balance sheets which show losses instead of profits. I refer particularly to the *Daily Express*. Last week's loss amounts to £1,000. I agree with you about the price of newsprint. The Firms will not cut their price of £27; but I am told that in New York paper sells freely at 4 cents a pound.

It was a friendship sparked perhaps by Rothermere's early sponsorship and patronage, but certainly cemented when Beaverbrook cared personally for Rothermere after his sons died. More than that, Rothermere must have felt he was not simply tolerated for his talents but also appreciated for his views, and, with Max parroting his every word, he felt free to exaggerate the worst without incurring ridicule.

'I am not looking forward with pleasurable anticipation to the next two or three years of newspaperdom,' he wrote to Beaverbrook in May 1921,

> We shall require all our wits and energies to make anything at all ... Some London and many Provincial papers will disappear. Wages will have to come

down but the Trade Unions, with their usual blindness, will submit to reductions only after quite a number of newspapers have stopped publication. There will be much less competition in London, especially in Sunday newspapers...

Despite this litany of woes in the industry, however, Rothermere didn't miss out in giving his friend the right advice: Beaverbrook 'should hold on with the *Sunday Express* as after the funerals there will be sufficient "baked meats" for those who survive'. Just as Rothermere predicted, the *Sunday Express* did survive; and shortly after Rothermere gave Beaverbrook his advice, the *Daily Express* was actually in profit for the first time in its history.

As for Rothermere, with Northcliffe gone he brought his financial wizardry into full play, getting his fair share of Fleet Street's 'baked meats'. It was true he had let go of *The Times*, but he purchased the rest of Northcliffe's interests for £1,600,000, recovering £1,440,000 by a public issue of debentures and thus keeping the equity for only £160,000. As a result, he now controlled the *Daily Mail*, the *Evening News*, the *Daily Mirror*, the *Weekly Dispatch* and the *Sunday Pictorial*, as well as several titles in Glasgow. In order to facilitate the deal, he created the Daily Mail Holding Trust, the means whereby Northcliffe's 400,000 shares in Associated Newspapers were transferred, along with all his newspaper holdings, into Rothermere's control. After the formation of the Trust, Rothermere then distributed shares valued at £1 for only two shillings amongst the staff, at a stroke creating a vast reservoir of wealth for them, and, it might be assumed, a sense of loyalty.

It was soon after this, on 18 November 1922, that Rothermere scribbled at the bottom of a letter the important postscript that would have such a long-lasting effect on the *Daily Mail*: 'How would you like me to purchase an interest in your newspapers?' Three days later, Beaverbrook sent his answer:

Replying to the post-script, of course I would like you to purchase an interest in the Express newspapers. Nothing would give me greater pleasure than to work in co-operation with you and, indeed, with the *Daily Mail*.

The Daily Mail Holding Trust then bought forty-nine per cent of Beaverbrook's holding in London Express Newspapers, paying him £200,000 and 80,000 Daily Mail Trust shares.

To his son Rothermere sent the 'very private news' that he was buying half Beaverbrook's interest in London Express Newspapers; to his executives he explained this unusual union by stressing that it would be impossible for Beaverbrook to operate if a forty-nine per cent shareholder were hostile, implying that the purchase was an effective barrier against a too-hot competition between his *Daily Mail* and Max's *Daily Express*. A psychologically important factor, however, must have been the fact that he made the offer to Beaverbrook only three months after his brother Northcliffe's death. He surely was seeking some kind of relationship to replace the one he had just lost.

At the same time Rothermere was completing this deal, Beaverbrook, a man of many parts, was busy in his role as go-between for the politicos of the moment. For, in 1922, as Lloyd George's coalition government was crumbling, Beaverbrook had plumped up the confidence of his good friend Bonar Law, pushing him ahead in the fight to become the new Prime Minister.

Rothermere lost little love on Bonar Law, probably stemming from the fact that Bonar Law had tried, in the early days of his position as Secretary of State for Air, to persuade him to resign in order to quell criticism arising from the press and certain members of the Cabinet. Indeed, at his father's insistence, Esmond had turned down a job under Bonar Law. Now, at what he believed to be Bonar Law's continuing lame performance in office, Rothermere didn't hesitate to state in a letter to his son the basis for his contempt for the rather ineffectual politician:

> The Bonar Law government will be the laughing stock of English political history. A C3 politician cannot grapple with an A1 problem. The important thing is that the B.L. fiasco may consummate the ruin of the Conservative party.
>
> Whichever way B.L. turns now he will only view further unpopularity. This Government will fall sometime about July 1st. How glad I am you did not take office under him. We must HAVE BEEN inspired when we decided you must refuse.

At the surprise news from Beaverbrook that Bonar Law was ill with throat cancer and unable to continue in office, however, Harold nevertheless responded honourably, most probably to save the feelings of his friend Max, whose devotion to Bonar Law had been described by one politician as almost 'feminine' in character. 'If the worst is realised,' Harold wrote to Beaverbrook, 'I wish you to promise the support of the papers to whomsoever Bonar designates as his successor.' Meanwhile, Max, devoted and stricken, nursed his dying friend, just as he had Harold earlier during his near nervous collapse. It was said that at the end he even bought shares in the same concerns as his dying friend, 'so that he could bring him good news of rising prices'.

Ever since Beaverbrook had left his native country, making Britain his permanent home, he had traded on his relationship with Bonar Law; thus had he assured his own entrée into society and provided himself with a little-deserved but integral role in his adopted country's political life – as go-between, yes, but also as powerful manipulator. In essence, though, Beaverbrook did not only eat what he loved, he loved what he ate: as Bonar Law lay dying, he was inconsolable.

Others in Beaverbrook's entourage would come and go, benefiting from the patronage of the press lord as he saw fit and sacrificing up in return what he required. Only one would be as close as his dead friend Bonar Law – Harold Rothermere. The returns would be great, and so would the costs.

15

'Nomad'

HAROLD TO ESMOND, ADVICE: *On Speaking in Parliament*: 'I hope you are preparing your speeches with great care. Except occasionally speak only after preparation. Without preparation speeches tend to become brimful of repetitions. There is no harm in reading the really important part of a speech.'

On the Sale of Property: 'Push along with the sale of Fairlight. In these times and in the times that are coming over-housed people will have a rough time. I do not intend to be caught out as many of the old families of England will be during the next few years.'

On Friendship: 'You will have to get rid of the Arkwrights. They are simply there for what they can get.'

On Associations: 'Middle Classes Union – Don't go into this until you know how much money there is. I think they are after yours.'

On Investments: 'I am selling some Mirror shares. They are $4\frac{1}{2}$. I will talk to you about them, but don't sell any yourself.'

On Investments: 'Don't hurry but sell some Mirrors if opportunity offers. Your Mother has sold 10,000 and so have I. You should sell 10,000 but get Fuller to do it. $4\frac{1}{2}$ is a good price. Don't sell more. They are good but you have too much in them.'

On Stamina: 'It is difficult for me to give attention now to detail and politics. I am swamped with work of all kinds. I don't believe anyone in England has half the important things in hand that I have.'

On Stamina: 'YOU SEEM EXCITABLE AND WORRIED CAN ALWAYS SELL PAPERS AND IN VIEW OF MY FAILING EYESIGHT SHALL PROBABLY DO SO YOU DEAREST BEN COULD NOT STAND MY DAILY STRAIN.'

Esmond was given to understand – in some versions, intuitively; in others, overtly – that his dead brothers had been brighter than he was. He told one friend his father had said to him, 'If only those two were still around he would have nothing to do with the newspapers and the newspapers would be better off.' The rumour that Rothermere 'treated Esmond like dirt' made the rounds. But this was untrue: his father simply unloaded on his last son the hopes and ambitions he had harboured for all three.

This by itself was enough to overburden Esmond, and although he never faltered, he felt pressurized to do better than he imagined he was able.

He dreamed of being a barrister, like his grandfather, and said he would have been had he been able to make his own choices in life. As it was, he had to become a gentleman – hard work, as he chose to portray it. He had to know about silver, about porcelain, about books and art; to play bridge, tennis, hunt and shoot; to converse gracefully. He was Conservative Member of Parliament for the Isle of Thanet from 1920, and grew accustomed in his nine years at Westminster to giving graceful and convincing speeches. His father Harold, on the other hand, was terrified when he had to give a speech and tended to project on to his son his own fear of speaking in public.

In the early years of Esmond's parliamentary career, father and son worked co-operatively on the father's obsession – anti-waste; however much Esmond loved politics, and he did, he couldn't escape from his father's all-embracing views or overpowering manner. A reprint of articles published in the *Sunday Pictorial* between 1919 and 1920 on the subject of waste in government was published under the title *Solvency or Downfall? Squandermania and Its Story*: it was dedicated 'to my son Esmond Harmsworth, the first anti-waste MP and the youngest member of the House of Commons'.

'I know of no precedent', wrote Rothermere in the introduction,

> for the extraordinary prodigality with which our Government, at the close of a war unexampled in its dimensions and its cost, proceeded to scatter broadcast the remaining assets of the nation on a scale which would have been alarming even if we had suddenly been endowed with illimitable riches. The epidemic of squandermania has not yet subsided...
>
> Meanwhile this little volume ... will provide an arsenal of facts and figures ... in the struggle for the restoration of sane and thrifty principles in our public administration...
>
> I find myself still imbued with my original belief that the first step necessary for our economical salvation is a root and branch reduction of Government expenditure ... For more than two years I have waged a rather lonely fight against Squandermania. I have done so in the national interest, and my only object is to serve my countrymen.

Rothermere had founded his Anti-Waste League in 1919 when a politician publicly ridiculed him for insisting the Government could be run for £800 million per year. Taking two manifestos – 'Has the Day of Reckoning Come?' and 'The Seven Lean Years' – the League was headed by Rothermere, who became President, and run by his secretary Ernest Outhwaite and by Esmond, who, as always, did what his father bid. So dedicated was Rothermere to the cause of anti-waste that he moved into a 'modest flat', holding forth at length on 'the coming bankruptcy of Britain' and, much to the chagrin of guests, substituting water for wine at table. He abandoned the League when, three years later, the Government attained an annual budget of £800 million.

The Anti-Waste League had been based, typically, upon one of Rothermere's pessimistic assessments of world trade and economic conditions, about which he wrote passionately to Esmond:

> ... the world's economic edifice is caving in. Italy will follow Germany and then it will be our turn. Neither the Anti-Waste League nor any other organisation can avert the inevitable. We are witnessing the obsequies of international trade and without international trade only self-contained countries like the USA and France can endure at all. They will both be terribly poor but may survive if they are not overtaken by revolution.

What no doubt sparked Rothermere's fears was the Russian Revolution of 1917 and the bloody civil war that arose between the Reds and the Whites when the former separated the latter from their land and belongings. Indeed, the rise of Communism was destined to become Rothermere's *bête noire*.

But beneath all his pessimism lay an audacity at odds with his consistent pessimism on global conditions. 'We are on the threshold of a world slump,' Rothermere wrote to Beaverbrook in November 1921.

> In its momentous consequences it is I am sure going to dwarf even the Great War. In the economic collapse of Russia, Austria, Hungary and the Balkan States, Turkey – Europe and Asia – and the approaching collapse of Germany, we see steadily being unfolded before our eyes a drama fraught with more perilous consequences to the human race than anything recorded in history. As these states disappear one by one they will drag with them to their ruin England, Italy, a great part of South America, Australia, New Zealand, South Africa, and possibly Canada. Would you like six articles by me – price £250 each?

Beaverbrook declined. For once, he disagreed with Rothermere. Newsprint might be high, and profits in Fleet Street under threat. But Harold's depiction of a domino-theory of economic collapse was too much even for Max. It would be left to Esmond to try to moderate his father's strongly felt convictions – a task few would envy.

Esmond to Harold, advice, 17 January 1924

At present you are thoroughly hated by all three parties; Conservatives naturally, Labour naturally, but also the Liberals, I am afraid. The whole House would not be adverse to smash the Newspaper Trust. ... I don't think Labour will attempt to stop the *Daily Mail*. They will be much cleverer. They will break the Trust; in other words, pass legislation that one man can only own or control one morning, one evening and one Sunday paper ... If we are to keep the Trust intact, it can only be done by very skilful guidance. In my opinion this guidance should be as follows:

On Labour coming into power, *go very slow*. Give them a showing. Do not fractiously fulminate against them ... get right behind the Conservative Party ... If you are behind the Conservative Party, the Socialists will not dare to tackle the Trust. But if you are alone, hated by all three parties, they will do so and do so successfully.

From his vantage point in the House of Commons, Esmond was able to assess the political climate with considerable sagacity. Ramsay Mac-Donald's Labour Party, together with the Liberals, had just managed to unseat Baldwin's Conservative administration. Esmond wrote to his father that MacDonald was a first-class speech-maker, who 'spoke with the authority of the office that is hanging over him'. Baldwin, on the other hand, who had briefly and only by default become Prime Minister because of Bonar Law's death, was 'too feeble' a figure. He had 'no fight, no ginger ... nothing'. So far as the determination of several parties to smash the Trust, Esmond was shocked by their bitterness. And, although the young MP believed MacDonald himself would level no threats against the Daily Mail Trust, he still counselled his father to follow his advice.

But such a warning unduly excited Rothermere, and he wired Esmond of his intention not only to order 'EVERYONE GIVE [LABOUR] GOVERNMENT FAIR CHANCE', but also to divest himself of control of his Glasgow and Manchester newspapers. He even planned to distance himself from his London titles. To Esmond, such an extreme reaction seemed like panic, and he advised his father to put off his plans.

Everybody seems to think the Socialists may stay in 12 months – I believe a benevolent attitude on the part of the Press and in the Commons may do them more harm than opposition. Violent opposition tends to make them all hang together and gives them something to complain about ...

For the moment, Esmond wrote to his father, the *Mail* need only 'educate' its readership, avoiding any appearance of bullying and lending its support to the Conservatives – and all would be well.

But by May 1924 Harold had not been able to resist registering an attack on Baldwin and the Conservatives, alienating himself from the man destined to lead the British Government for the next five years, and again during the crucial 1930s. Baldwin's reaction showed his hostility towards the Trust:

> I am attacked by the Trust Press, by Lord Beaverbrook and Lord Rothermere. For myself I do not mind. I care not what they say or think. They are both men that I would not have in my house. I do not respect them. Who are they? ... This Trust Press is breaking up. The *Daily Mail* is dead; it has no soul. Northcliffe, with all his faults, was a great journalist, with a spark of genius. But this man!

Thus Rothermere found himself estranged from the party his son had advised him to support at the very moment it became apparent that Labour's base was eroding and MacDonald would soon be forced to call an election. With Rothermere's natural abhorrence of the philosophy of the left wing and his dislike of the leader of the right wing, he did finally decide to follow Esmond's advice. He threw his support behind the Conservatives, but with the proviso that Esmond would refrain from accepting any office under Baldwin.

> Frankly the man has neither the imagination, decision nor courage necessary in what inevitably will be a great crisis. Stand out. Your time will come. You can only hurt yourself by making an alliance with a fiasco.

MacDonald was destined to win, Rothermere believed, ushering in 'a period of high food prices'.

> The index cost of living may have a very sharp rise. If this is so any government which succeeds Ramsay may have to confront difficulties which will certainly overwhelm them in a few months.

By indulging himself in a pessimism that had actually begun seriously to cloud his judgment, Rothermere twice advised his son badly. The first time occurred when he prohibited Esmond from serving under Bonar Law. For it was only by chance the inexperienced Baldwin, who was not so particular, had been selected to serve as Chancellor of the Exchequer and thus been propelled into the highest office in the land. What opportunities might have presented themselves to Esmond – who truly loved politics and government and who had, even as a young man, displayed sound judgment and a sense of serious purpose in serving his constituency? The second time Rothermere misadvised his son was even more serious. By prohibiting Esmond from accepting office under Baldwin and in effect making a permanent enemy of the politician, Rothermere cut Esmond off from the only possible arena for his political talent. Esmond would have been a very likely appointment to Baldwin's Cabinet.

But who could have predicted the improbable landslide victory in 1924 that would put Baldwin firmly in control of the British Government for the rest of the decade? Not Rothermere – nor anyone else. In fact, that mandate resulted from as bizarre a set of events as ever affected the outcome of an election in the history of the nation.

On 25 October 1924, four days before the General Election, a sensational story broke in the *Daily Mail*:

CIVIL WAR PLOT BY SOCIALISTS' MASTERS

Moscow Order to Our Reds

Great Plot Disclosed Yesterday

Paralyse the Army and Navy

And Mr. MacDonald Would Lend Russia Our Money

Document Issued by Foreign Office

After 'Daily Mail' Had Spread The News

The Foreign Office had announced that they had in their hands a letter marked 'Very Secret', written by the Executive Committee of the Third Communist International, Moscow, to the Central Committee of the British Communist Party. The letter was dated 15 September 1924 and was signed 'ZINOVIEV'.

It urged the British Communist Party 'to strain every nerve' to put pressure on the Labour Party – and thence on the British Parliament – to ratify a proposed treaty between Britain and Russia. This in turn was to prepare a way for a revolution by the British working class. Styled in the customary turgid prose of the Soviet Communists, the letter seemed genuine enough:

> It is indispensable to stir up the masses of the British proletariat to bring into movement the army of British proletarians whose position can be improved only after a loan has been granted to the S.S.S.R. for the restoration of her economics and when British collaboration between the British proletariats has been put in order.

And indeed, no matter how convenient the timely discovery of this letter must have been for Rothermere and the man who got the scoop, *Daily Mail* editor Thomas Marlowe, there was really no basis to believe that either of the pair doubted at all the authenticity of what would come to be known as the Zinoviev Letter.

The *Mail*'s exploitation of the find, however, was masterly. Marlowe not only published his copy of the letter in the *Mail* but also passed it along to the other newspapers. The political consequences were without parallel. For this was the blow destined to bring defeat to Ramsay MacDonald, preventing the first Labour Government from gaining a majority and thus forming the first truly effective Labour Government of the century.

Ironically, MacDonald had himself viewed a copy of the letter some ten days earlier and written on it a minute instructing the Foreign Office that it must be carefully authenticated – but in the meantime a note of protest should be prepared to the Russian chargé d'affaires in case the letter should turn out to be genuine. This decision, made by an exhausted Prime Minister trying to carry out the duties of office while simultaneously running a demanding re-election campaign, would prove disastrous to the continuance of his fledgling government. It carried with it a general impression that MacDonald himself thought the letter genuine, and by the time he began to deny it the election was all but lost. The Conservative press – the *Mail*, the *Express*, *The Times* and the *Telegraph* – all jumped on the letter as the lucky break they had been seeking to defeat the dreaded Socialists, who were, as everybody knew, or ought to know, second cousins to the Soviet Communists. Only the lone voice of the *Daily Herald* suggested that the letter was a forgery, indeed that Zinoviev himself had denied the letter was genuine.

The facts about the Zinoviev letter were to a large extent established within four years by Russian intelligence and were published in 1928. But it wouldn't be until the 1960s that these were confirmed. The letter was indeed a fake, forged by a group of White Russians in Berlin whose success in discrediting the Soviet Union and retarding relations between Britain and their former country exceeded their wildest hopes. That their letter should have succeeded when, in the words of one of Ramsay MacDonald's biographers, there were 'enough "Red letters" fluttering around Whitehall to paper the walls of the Foreign Office' brought about great rejoicing in their camp. For the Conservatives, it was a bold stroke of good luck – nothing short of a miracle. The man thought to be the outsider, Stanley Baldwin, was returned to office with forty-eight per cent of the popular poll and 419 seats in the Commons.

For Rothermere, however, the event evoked only modified rapture; as Beaverbrook was quick to point out in a wire sent on 30 October, 'I CONGRATULATE YOU MOST HEARTILY ON YOUR MAGNIFICENT VICTORY STOP YOU HAVE MADE THE NEW BALDWIN MINISTRY.' There then followed a wise-guy punch line typical of Harold's friend Max: 'NOW CONTROL IT IF YOU CAN.'

Beaverbrook didn't share Rothermere's assessment that up against

MacDonald's Labour Party Baldwin was the lesser of two evils: 'Baldwin is what is known as a scream,' he wrote to his friend.

> He has the Press on what he is pleased to consider his brain. It is our bounden duty to rivet it there ... Some of the young lions on my papers wish to open long range fire on the Baldwin Govt. now but I am holding them back ... I make a prophecy. The Baldwin Govt will look sick before March is out.

If his Government was destined to 'look sick', Stanley Baldwin was not. He may have been ineffectual, or perhaps, according to some, just plain lazy. He may even at times have had what some of his friends reluctantly regarded as a kind of 'porcine stupidity'. But, in an age when the BBC was coming into its own as a national institution and the most effective means of swaying the masses was about to change radically, Baldwin had a secret weapon.

He could talk. He could talk persuasively. And he could talk in a way that made ordinary people identify with him. And, when he talked, it seemed such a simple skill. But it was one that would rout his two mighty press adversaries and send them scurrying in complete disarray.*

There had been glimmerings of Baldwin's command of the spoken language earlier in his career. Perhaps the key moment had occurred in the House of Commons when Baldwin, then Chancellor of the Exchequer and under fire for making an unfavourable agreement with the Americans for repayment of war loans, turned the tables on his critics by shaping a few fine phrases. 'The English language', he said then, 'is the richest in the world in monosyllables.'

> Four words, of one syllable each ... contain salvation for this country and the whole world, and they are Faith, Love, Hope and Work. No Government in this country today which has not faith in the people, hope in the future, love for its fellow-men, and which will not work and work, and work, will bring this country through into better days and better times, or will ever bring Europe through or the world through.

In this way did he advance himself from relative ignominy to relative glory, distinguishing himself as a serious contender.

But it was not until the crisis of the General Strike of 1926 that the full

---

* Baldwin could talk, but he may not have been able to write. A.J.P. Taylor, *English History: 1914–1945*, p. 205, n. 2, points out that the speeches of Baldwin, much admired for their literary quality, 'were largely written for him by Tom Jones, assistant secretary to the cabinet'.

effects of his plain speaking could be gauged. The General Strike was the Revolution that didn't happen – a well-organized, orderly, twelve-day protest that proved once and for all that Britain was not Russia: it could never happen here.

Exports had been dealt a blow when the country, under the direction of Baldwin's new Chancellor of the Exchequer, Winston Churchill, returned to the Gold Standard and thus increased the value of the pound. This, along with growing competition from the Ruhr and Poland, began to weaken Britain's coal industry, and owners saw no alternative to lowering wages and increasing working hours. The miners balked, threatening strike action. The majority of Britain's work-force consisted of veterans of the Great War; no strangers to futile gestures, they determined to stand behind the miners. The tinder-box was ignited when compositors at the *Daily Mail* refused to print an editorial entitled 'For King and Country'. When word of their defiance spread first to government, then to the workers, a national work stoppage began. It was May Day, 1926.

The General Strike revealed a great deal about the country and its politicians for those who cared to look beneath the surface of events. It certainly showed the moderate nature of the left-wing movement in England simply by the peaceful conduct of the action. There was no violence or loss of life. There was a unified atmosphere of co-operation amongst the very parties who might have been shooting at one another. Then again, the strike reminded those critical of Winston Churchill, had they needed reminding, of his mounting ambitions. On Baldwin's orders, he ruthlessly instituted and edited the *British Gazette*, commandeering, or trying to commandeer, all the available newsprint in the capital and taking dictatorial control of what was thought at the time to be the primary means of communication. He urged 'unconditional surrender' of the work-force, generally maintaining a hawkish outlook at odds with the situation. And, finally, the strike presaged the growing importance of road transport as opposed to the railways. The delivery of foodstuffs and other essential supplies was smoothly accomplished by the former, with few hitches, leaving the striking railway workers to consider their future.

But for the reflective – and the calculating – the most important revelation of the General Strike was the remarkable power of radio when used by a gifted rhetorician, such as Stanley Baldwin. He was credited with single-handedly bringing a halt to the General Strike; in some ways, it was his finest hour as leader of the country.

Baldwin broadcast three times. In the first message, he urged the populace to stand behind the Government, who were doing their part by preserving 'the liberties and the privileges of the peoples of these islands';

in the second, he gave his word to revitalize and rebuild the coal industry of the country. 'I am a man of peace,' he told the country.

> I am longing and working and praying for peace. But I will not surrender the safety and the security of the British Constitution. You placed me in power eighteen months ago by the largest majority accorded any party in many, many years. Have I done anything to forfeit that confidence? Cannot you trust me to ensure a square deal for the parties – to secure even justice between man and man?

It was powerful prose, simple and balanced, from the man who was first cousin to Rudyard Kipling. It instilled the common man with confidence, it convinced the sceptical and it promised action. At last, in his final message, Baldwin was able to announce the end of the General Strike.

And then he slid comfortably back into his congenital indolence – and did nothing. No relief for the workers, no arbitration, no action except in 1927 to pass a statute making sympathetic strikes illegal. Nevertheless, he had accomplished what no man had before. He had shown what could be done with the new broadcast medium. Churchill, watching, learned an invaluable lesson that he would put to good use in the future. But he was not the only one. In less reputable quarters, the power of radio to persuade was duly noted. It would be the primary propaganda tool of the tumultuous 1930s – and perhaps the single most decisive factor in the turning of the tide in the Second World War.

But if, in 1926, the importance of radio was little more than a visionary's fantasy, the shadows of future aggression were hardly discernible. Of course, Rothermere, the eternal pessimist, anticipated that hard times lay ahead; his speculation about what these might entail, however, were thrashings in the dark. He worried. He fretted. He made himself seem ridiculous by always anticipating the worst. He appeared to almost everyone to be of a didactic inclination – to some, a bully; to others, a figure of fun. But privately he had a winning way, his own version of the Harmsworth charm. With the family, he remained uninhibited and playful. At reunions, he tended to pay attention to the little ones, taking them round the garden and playing leapfrog when he thought no one was looking. Whereas his brother Northcliffe had had no let-up, no stop-mechanism, no control whatever over his workaholism, Harold was said to 'understand the art of living; he had the gift of combining work and pleasure in a reasonably proportioned whole.'

His recall was surprising. During a conversation with a shipowner, he rattled off a figure he thought might be the population of Northumberland; the shipowner, a cynic, insisted on looking it up. Rothermere, it turned out, was right. A casual remark made by a friend in 1910 sometimes resurfaced fifteen years later with devastating effect. Harold may have looked like a bumbler, but he was not – at least, not nearly so often as his enemies would have wished. In money matters, he was invincible. By 1926, his fortune was estimated as something between £15 and £26 million;* even the lower figure was at the time a vast fortune that ranked Rothermere, so it was said, as the third richest man in Great Britain.

And he was generous to a fault. By four o'clock in the afternoon, he had usually run out of cash, from showering tips on everyone who served him. On walks with his staff, he slipped money into the hands of beggars he encountered. When he lived in Mayfair, he saw two elderly women walking down the street, singing hymns and collecting money for peace. He shocked his companions by opening the window and throwing them half-crowns. Then, to the astonishment of all, he began singing along with them. A little-known fact is that Rothermere actually employed a member of staff for the sole purpose of giving away money.

His *raison d'être* made its way into the diaries of Arnold Bennett; and, with his fine writer's perception, Bennett made a permanent record of what his guest inexplicably revealed about himself:

> Rothermere came to lunch. He had told me at Ciro's that he wanted to have a chat with me, and so I asked him. But I could not divine his purpose and I can't now. He drank water. He said that some years ago he was smoking too much and he said to himself: 'I won't smoke anymore', and he never has done so. He said that while in London he spent most nights at his mother's at Totteridge. She is 86 and gets about a lot. The whole batch of her ancestors was long-lived. She goes out a great deal. He said he didn't believe in the power of the Press. He said it produced a certain 'expectation' and then the mob changed its interest and forgot completely. He said the *Mail* could begin to pay and the *Sunday Pictorial* £15,000 in each issue. He said advertising was very good but that if it dropped the *Mail* might easily begin to run at a loss. I said then: 'How do you spend your income?' This was in answer to his remarks that he hated possessions and had only one house, small, at Cap Martin, and a flat in Savoy Court. He had had a big house in Kent, with 17 bathrooms (10 of which he had put in himself), recently sold for a school.† He had nothing else. His Renaissance pictures were stored.‡ In answer to my question he said that he had made his (separated) wife

---

* Bernard Falk put Rothermere's personal fortune at £15 million in 1926, in *He Laughed in Fleet Street*, p. 229; Cecil King at £26 million in *Strictly Personal*, p. 40.

† Benenden.

‡ A substantial number of these were forgeries.

a very rich woman; and he had given 1¼ millions to his son Esmond and a house in town,* that presents to his sisters and nieces cost him £30,000 a year. I said: 'There's nothing else but women.' He agreed and said he spent 10 to 20,000 pounds a year on them. 'It's worth it,' I said. 'Of course it is,' he said. He was on the whole pessimistic. Full of sense and information about finance. Said he lived 4 months on the Riviera. Travelled a month in Italy, also in Spain, etc. He accounted for 7 or 8 months a year out of England. As regards the *Mail*, he said he left it to staff. His manner has been much impaired by millionairism.

The last statement Bennett made about Rothermere, alas, was all too true. His manner *had* been impaired by his money: he simply had too much of it.

Lady Rothermere, always abreast of whatever was most stylish at the moment, acquainted her estranged husband with Diaghilev's famous ballet company, and he became a patron. He also became fascinated with the delicate beauty of the ballerinas. He fell for several. There was the rather proud Komarova; she was the first. The next was Lydia Sokolova, also known as Hilda Munnings, an Essex girl made good: she studied with Anna Pavlova and was the first English dancer in Diaghilev's company. Known for her loyalty and warmth, she was an open-hearted young woman who made the famous millionaire feel comfortable with his awkward need to be tender and kind.

It had fallen to Sokolova to ask Rothermere to back the company for a début at His Majesty's Theatre in London, and for this purpose Diaghilev gave a sumptuous dinner party with dancing. Sokolova had already been acquainted with Rothermere, but 'had no experience of extracting large sums of money from rich men'. In her own account of what transpired, Sokolova later wrote,

The supper party took place at the Carlton Hotel ... and I was seated between Diaghilev and Lord Rothermere. At what he judged the right moment, the 'Old Man' whispered, 'Now you must go and dance with him.' I was very nervous and it was not until we had had two dances that I summoned the courage to approach the subject. Lord Rothermere did not make it easy for me. Eventually, after a little persuasion, he said 'All right. I will do what you ask. But I want you to make it clear to Diaghilev that I am doing this for you personally.'

Later, when Lydia Sokolova had to have an operation, Rothermere paid her expenses. And, while she was recovering, he sent 'enough flowers for the whole hospital'. Alice Nikitina was also at the same party, placed far

* Warwick House in St James's.

from Rothermere at the banqueting table. But, as Nikitina herself wrote in her memoirs many years later,

> this did not prevent Lord Rothermere leaving his circle and coming to ask me to dance several times … In spite of his tallness and corpulence, Lord Rothermere danced with remarkable lightness and a great deal of rhythm.

What were these young women to Rothermere, except a hobby and a diversion? The only exception was Nikitina, who, in her childlike and admiring way, returned his affection – although the affair, which lasted almost until Rothermere's death, was far from carnal.

When Rothermere first came to see the company perform, Nikitina was, along with the other ballerinas, highly excited because a long row of chairs had been set up for a visiting dignitary and his party: 'We often had such visits, we had the Duke of Connaught, the Kings of Spain, of Egypt, the Prince of Monaco.' This time it was Rothermere, shy and smiling and putting everyone at ease. He stopped Nikitina on her way out and asked whether she would like to dance in London. When she replied 'very much in the affirmative', he said, 'Well, we'll see to it that it is done.'

She was later invited, along with the other members of the company, to La Dragonnière, Rothermere's villa at Cap Martin. In the words of Northcliffe, who had visited the villa when he was ill, La Dragonnière was a 'fairy-like little palace' named from a legend that a dragon had been slain on the site in former times. The villa stood

> in a garden of about two acres of orange groves, and there [was] a rose covered pergola. The house itself [was] also covered with flowers. It [was] some two hundred yards from the sea, overlooking Monte Carlo.

Although the villa was small, the rooms were large, with high ceilings. When the ballerinas entered La Dragonnière for the first time, they saw several 'gigantic silk chocolate-boxes from la Marquise de Sévigné'. These were given to the young women as favours before they took their tour around the orange grove. There, each was given a flower from the garden. 'For me,' wrote Nikitina,

> Lord Rothermere picked a pink camellia, a double flower, like Siamese twins. He walked along with me, showering questions upon me, so as to learn more about me. He wanted again to know whether I would like to dance in London and assured me once more that it was a settled matter. I was flattered, jubilant, grateful. Then Lord R. offered us some tea … after that we were driven back to Monte Carlo.

When at last the company did perform in London, each dancer received 'huge baskets of flowers', the one sent to Nikitina 'a small artificial lake filled with white and yellow water-lilies and roses surrounded with golden ribbon'.

From this point on, Rothermere favoured Nikitina, lavishing gifts on her – Chanel dresses, fine furs and a beige and blue Panhard car. Once she received a five-litre bottle of Chanel No. 5; not knowing what to do with so much of a good thing, she at last simply massaged her entire body with it.

She returned Rothermere's generosity by worshipping him: 'All his gestures, his remarks, were persuasive, quick, and you felt an unusual intelligence behind it all, a charm that emanated from his whole being.' At the time she became involved with Rothermere, he was fifty-eight years old, but, as she perceived him, he seemed a young man. In her memoirs she gave her adoring impression of the press baron:

> His superlative manners, his youthful humour, that came straight from the heart, made me feel very soon at my ease, as with a friend of old standing, when we went to have supper together. In spite of his dazzling personality he knew how to raise you on to a pedestal and make you feel superior to himself. He questioned me on my life, my childhood, and admired my love and devotion to the dance. He wanted me to feel more secure and settled. He said that a great artist should be able to get the utmost pleasure from life in return for what she or he gave to the world.

As for Diaghilev, his motivation in encouraging the affair was strictly commercial. He needed a rich patron for his ballet, and in this, despite constant worry, he succeeded in winning over Rothermere, who for years to come not only donated tens of thousands of pounds to the company but saw to it that, when they performed in London, they had superb publicity.

Was the relationship of the older press baron and the childlike ballerina lascivious? Hardly. Harold wanted someone to love; Nikitina – flattered, undemanding, admiring – accepted what he wanted to give, with as little avarice as was possible considering the discrepancy between their positions. Within the family, it was known Rothermere had a good many women friends throughout his life, some of them mistresses, although Nikitina insisted that their relationship remained platonic throughout its fourteen-year duration. The sad fact was that Harold, shy and diffident, but with a generous nature, never believed that his own value extended beyond what he could give to another person. So more and more, as the years accumulated after the deaths of his sons, the measure of his love was how much he could spend.

*

White Russians were fashionable; Eastern European princesses were fashionable; the French Riviera was fashionable. And a puff or two of opium didn't go amiss. Of course, things could go too far and, amongst the very rich, addiction to the drug was not all that uncommon. One of Rothermere's serious mistresses, less wide-eyed and innocent than his lovely dancers, fell prey to the drug – much to Harold's grief.

Rothermere himself neither smoked nor drank, but he saw a good deal of these and other excesses in the stylish circles he drifted into and out of during his travels. And, as he watched Annabel Cruze wander into that strange half-world of fantasy and reality, he remained as always loyal – and eminently sensible. He advised her husband, James, on the investment of his capital, thus allowing the Cruzes to make an impressive foray into the social milieu of southern France – as a dazzlingly rich couple that would have been at home amongst the pages of a novel by F. Scott Fitzgerald. They lived in Monte Carlo, frequenting the casinos and engendering envy amongst those of their acquaintances who couldn't keep up. Annabel was the sort who had her name embroidered upon all her linens, her undergarments, her silk stockings. And, naturally, like attracted like.

It wasn't long before Annabel became close friends with Princess Stephanie Hohenlohe, a Hungarian beauty with 'a Grecian profile' who had managed to marry and misplace a Hungarian prince. Princess Steph had risen, by virtue of pulchritude and flair, opportunism and cunning, from the ranks of the dull bourgeoisie of Vienna to the heady stratosphere of the super-rich – the blue-bloods of the 1920s. Instinctively, she had rejected her school books in favour of sport; Steph quickly learned 'to swim, to ski, to row, cycle, play tennis – and when she was older – she added riding, fishing, shooting, golfing, bowling and mountaineering to her achievements.'

She had had the good fortune, after she abandoned her husband, of having an early lover poison himself, and although the young man lived, her reputation as a *femme fatale* was thereby assured. Henceforth, she was showered with flowers and silks, gems and furs from wealthy suitors which she accepted with conspicuous egalitarianism. No token of admiration was rejected – although the giver often was.

While other young women languished over their embroidery, Steph took to smoking Havana cigars, learning to cut a dash by striking a match on the sole of her shoe. She allowed her skin to tan in the sun whilst others remained pale white, entered and won a beauty contest and, 'to protect her *décolleté*', commissioned special leather fans to be made from Juchten – the finest Russian leather – which became her trademark at fancy-dress balls. When war came, she volunteered as a nurse and, equally undismayed by gangrene or amputations, won an entirely new round of admirers for her 'devastating chic', wearing uniforms specially tailored to flatter her figure. Princess Stephanie Hohenlohe had been around, so to speak.

And so a powerful English press baron, a viscount, even the third richest man in Britain, would not be too formidable a conquest for such a bold young woman. The meeting, initiated by the Cruzes, was cemented when Princess Steph ran into Rothermere at the gaming tables in Monte Carlo. He seemed depressed, she said. It was a lack of interesting news, he explained. *She* could give him a topic, she said, if he 'weren't so intent on sensationalism'. They chatted, he departed, promising lunch, and Steph went back to her gambling.

The next day, she received a call from Rothermere's assistant Ernest Outhwaite inviting her to the promised lunch at La Dragonnière. But, once she had arrived, instead of identifying himself as a potential suitor, the usual state of affairs for the beautiful princess, Rothermere actually showed no hint of interest in her as a woman. Instead, he seemed genuinely curious about her idea for a news story. So Princess Stephanie acquainted Rothermere with the injustices against Hungary after the Great War – the brutal partitioning of the country, the hacking away of great parcels of land – all the result of the hastily negotiated Treaty of Trianon, an afterthought affecting millions that followed in the wake of the Treaty of Versailles. And after their lunch,

> she showed him the boundaries of Hungary on a small illustration in the Encyclopedia Britannica. He told her: 'You know, my dear, I never realised until today that Budapest and Bucharest were not one and the same city.'

This was the Princess's version of events, as passed down through family folklore, until, in 1976, her son Franz Hohenlohe formalized it in his biography of his mother. Was Princess Stephanie Hohenlohe, then, the genesis of Rothermere's abrupt and unexpected shouldering of the injustices against the Hungarian state? Most probably.

For Rothermere had become a nomad, a wanderer, with no fixed abode or even itinerary. He moved and, as often as not, he moved randomly. In the same way that places had begun to enter his purview, then fade from it, only to be brought once more into focus with a return visit, so had people taken on something of the same quality. And so had ideas. In his travels, whole philosophies, some of them quite exotic, had entered his range of consideration. A genius at finance, he was accustomed to the flux of the market-place, the vying of stocks one against the other for potential investment. He applied the same logic to people and ideas. He was curious, and he listened, at once making himself one of the best-informed men of the age and also one of the most absurd, for most ideas, no matter how far-fetched, received at least a cursory hearing from the press lord. Curious and credulous, he was sifting through the trends of the age looking for clues about the future.

Thus he became acquainted with Germany's cynicism over the Treaty of Versailles and its determination to evade its provisions. Similarly, he was familiar with the injustices created by ill-considered treaties negotiated at the end of the Great War by exhausted, disillusioned diplomats eager to return home – even though he might not have known the specifics of any one of them. Eastern Europe had become one of Rothermere's special interests; he believed it was one of the most important trouble-spots since the end of the war – 'a powder-keg', he called it. But the situation was little understood in Britain, nor did anyone particularly care. Anyone who did care was considered to be either an interested party or a crank. What Princess Stephanie Hohenlohe did was to reinforce Rothermere's interest in Eastern Europe, focusing his attention on Hungary alone, and he believed, despite the apathy of his countrymen, that the matter was worth raising in the *Daily Mail*.

He wrote only two editorials. The first – 'Hungary's Place in the Sun' – was published on 11 June 1927, the second on 30 August. In them, he protested the ceding of land containing over three million Hungarians to Czechoslovakia, to Romania and to Yugoslavia. Particularly offensive was the brutal requisitioning of land owned by Hungarian minorities by the Czechoslovakian Government: these 'land deals', wrote Rothermere, perpetrated 'some of the worst frauds that have ever taken place in the public life of Europe'. This was the gist; who could have foretold the results?

Hungary went crazy with gratitude. Within weeks, Rothermere's office had been flooded with over 200,000 pieces of correspondence from Hungarians effusively thanking him for his interest in their country. The Hungarian press made him into an icon. And wildly – citing a precedent from the Renaissance in which the Hungarians had elected their kings – they invited Rothermere to become the reigning monarch of Hungary. He declined. The idea was absurd, and he would have nothing to do with it. But it did its work: the fate of Hungary would become a lifelong obsession, its destiny a focus of the editorial policy of the *Daily Mail* for the next dozen years – not to mention a continuing source of ridicule in Britain.

It fell to Esmond to accept the gratitude of an entire nation. It was agreed that, instead of the crown, Esmond would accept, on behalf of his father, an honorary Doctor of Laws degree from Szeged University. On 13 May, Esmond duly departed for the ceremonies planned by the Hungarian

Government. At home, even this watered-down honour was met with derision. Typical was Stanley Baldwin's putdown of Rothermere and his son Esmond to Churchill, at that time his Chancellor of the Exchequer: '... And don't worry about Rothermere,' he wrote,

> he has done you all the service he can for the present, and I think you are a little disposed to overrate his influence in the country ... What a fool Rothermere is allowing his boy to make of himself in Hungary! They haven't a ray of humour between them.

If Esmond was a fool in Britain, he was a hero in Hungary. There, the event was viewed as epoch-making. Filmed by a Hungarian movie-maker in clips that somehow were preserved for over six decades, the celebration still resides in the archives of Associated Newspapers.

> Esmond arrives in Budapest in an Imperial Airways bi-plane, received by a party of officials wearing frock coats and top hats. As he waves to them, they take off their hats to welcome him. He rides in an open car through streets lined with cheering Hungarians to the St Gellert Hotel.
>
> Before the window of Esmond's room, an endless parade of troops and bands, floats and vehicles roll by. Thousands of onlookers cheer. Throughout this and the introductions afterwards, Esmond is relaxed, genial and handsome; he appears comfortable with the protocol. Wearing a bowler hat, he leaves his hotel in an official vehicle.
>
> Hands to lapels, Esmond speaks to thousands of enthusiasts in a gigantic stadium. Afterwards, dancers appear on the playing field. They form into a map of Hungary, some in white dress, others in black. All at once, the dancers dressed in black move away from the others, symbolically showing the effects of the Treaty of Trianon.
>
> Twenty-eight trains are needed to carry all those officials wishing to watch the granting of the honorary doctorate to Esmond at Szeged University. When the ceremony ends, Esmond flies away in his bi-plane, literally into the sunset.

And how did Esmond feel about all this pomp and circumstance? In the film clips, he appears slightly embarrassed, somewhat sheepish, but gracefully resigned to the importance his visit signifies to the people themselves. Thus, he appears to accept his accidental but highly symbolic role with good heart.

Once more, he carried out the duties imposed upon him by his position, and, if he resisted at all this rather gratuitously grand celebration, nothing in his manner gave a hint of it. He did what was expected of him.

And what of Harold Rothermere, who by his own estimate spent a quarter of his life aboard trains or ships, in aimless movement from place to place? Was all this movement an attempt to outrun the memories that caused him so much unhappiness – the loss of his sons, the failure of his marriage, the burden of the business? It seemed otherwise. For so many years he had lived under the direction of Northcliffe, or in his shadow, that Rothermere seemed to be searching for a figure or an idea sufficiently compelling to fill out an empty life. Beaverbrook was about to reveal himself as a self-centred character more interested in gaining attention than in effecting positive change in his adopted country.

No, if he was searching for a role-model, Rothermere would have to look elsewhere.

16

'The Glorious Twelfth'

Harold was not a man of the world – despite the money and despite the girlfriends. Unlike Beaverbrook, who was known to bed chorus girls two at a time and who used his newspapers ruthlessly to barter his way into British social and political life, Rothermere was shy and genuine. He worshipped the loveliness of women, and when he became enamoured of one of them he treated her like a princess. He would never have considered divorcing his wife, and so never considered remarrying. The system had the merit of variety, but the demerit of instability. Hence, Harold was a lonely man.

And, at the heart of him, he maintained a solid integrity that made him seem dull but kept him clean and upright. He might be wrong, but he was honestly wrong; there was no trace of corruption about him. This was the influence of his mother Geraldine – for, no matter how rich or powerful her sons became, she retained the whip hand. The power behind the entire family, Geraldine had a vision of ethical behaviour that prevailed amongst her progeny even after her death in 1926.*

Neither was Esmond a man of the world – despite the good looks and despite the privilege. Made wealthy by his father before he reached thirty, he owned an imposing house in St James's, Warwick House, and a castle in Kent, Mereworth, which was built in imitation of Palladio's villa, the Rotunda, at Vicenza in Italy. But, even with his vast fortune and social grace, Esmond remained, all his life, slightly aloof – a surprisingly solitary man despite his dazzling charm. Even though his father continuously questioned the motives of anyone who sought his acquaintance, Esmond's inclination was to be trusting and loyal. There was something heart-breaking about Esmond right from the start: he acted so well, and he fell so short.

Esmond was only twenty-two when he married and, predictably, he

---

* In early April of 1927, Rothermere purchased and then donated a fourteen-acre park – the site of the old Bethlehem Hospital – to Southwark, as a memorial to his mother.

disappointed his father, who wished for a more ambitious match – even though it was Harold himself who had first discovered Margaret Redhead, known as 'Peggy'. Family legend had it that Rothermere had met Peggy's mother coming back on a ship from Canada. Genteel and of good family, she had been married three times, and widowed three times, with four daughters and a son, and was pregnant with a sixth child when her last husband had been killed. Rothermere, hearing her story and with his customary generosity, lent her a house on the Benenden estate, and thus the girls became known to the Harmsworth sons. Peggy had met Vyvyan at Rothermere's instigation when he had invited her and her sister to stay at the Ritz the night before Vyvyan left for his last tour of duty.

> Much later she recalled how she had seen Vyvyan off at the station after they had gone to the theatre together the previous evening. They had sat on a bench, and to pass the time, she said, 'I like your boots.' He replied that no one had said such a nice thing to him before.

Peggy was mischievous and funny and ravishingly beautiful, with high cheekbones and an arresting gaze. They were a beautiful couple, she and Esmond, but there was always the question, had Vyvyan lived, whether she might not have preferred him, and beneath Peggy's gaiety, the other question – whether or not Esmond was a replacement for her irretrievably lost love. They were married on 12 January 1920, and within the year, their first child was born. Within five years, there were three: Lorna, the eldest; Esme, who looked most like Esmond; and, at last, Vere, named after Esmond's brother who had died on the battlefield. All of them had the high cheekbones of their mother, and because of this, the two girls were amazingly beautiful, but only Vere had his mother's disquieting gaze – the propensity to look straight into another person for a very long time, perhaps seeing, perhaps not.

The children lived as in a fairy-tale. Their father was handsome and tall, given over to fun and merriment. Their mother was slender and indulgent, full of affection and good humour. They holidayed on the Isle of Wight, or in Italy, or in the South of France. They had a baby bear to terrify and delight them, along with other wild animals, as was the fashion. Their father was always instigating practical jokes, and soda-siphon fights were not uncommon amongst the family.

As for their grandfather, he was a great believer in 'good air', and so the children were often carried away to his house by the sea. There, in the small village of Dornoch, in Scotland, they were expected to breathe deeply, to take exercise to improve their health and to eat huge quantities of food to keep up their strength. Esme, by now a grandmother herself, remembered what it was like when she was a child:

> Burghfield House was like a Scottish shooting box, arranged with a lot of guest bedrooms, although first you came into a spacious hall and a huge dining room and two double drawing rooms and big principal bedrooms on top of that. Then there would be a wing with ten small bedrooms and that was typical of a lodge for all the people coming out to shoot. There was a big billiard room, and a lovely garden. One went for the month, or for the 12th of August, the Glorious Twelfth, and left at the end of September.
>
> My grandfather used to be called and would go for a long walk and get back into bed and have his breakfast tray, and then read all the newspapers in bed. He would read every single one of them, all the national papers, so many.
>
> Father didn't always have breakfast in bed, he got up for breakfast. There were huge breakfasts, wonderful! with a choice of seven or eight things ... bacon with kidneys, kedgeree, cold pheasant, ham plus all kinds of eggs, the whole choice was there. And very large lunches. If there was a house party, there would be a starter, a second course, main course, pudding, cheese, fruit. And a huge tea with hot scones or muffins and cakes or sandwiches. They ate it but they didn't have very big helpings.
>
> The other thing was that they were active physically. There was always hunting and tennis, always some sport going on every day. They really used up the fuel.

It was an idyllic life for the children, with fun and laughter and lingering afternoons when the shadows of the adults grew long across green lawns.

But Esmond seemed dissatisfied. To the workers on the newspapers, he would say that the happiest he had been was the short time he had spent working on his father's newspaper, the *Sunday Dispatch*; to his friends, it was the time he spent in the House of Commons. To some it seemed he had never been happy at all. Several years later, he admitted to Esme he had been afraid of his father. But afraid of what? Friends of Esmond actually took sides, inventing scenes that never occurred in an attempt to explain Esmond's fear of his father.*

With all the grace and beauty, intelligence and wealth that the world had to bestow, with a family so beautiful it would have been difficult for any magician to conjure it up, Esmond was unhappy. Did he suffer from low self-esteem? It was survivor's guilt – though he himself might have

---

* Aidan Crawley believed inexplicably in a 'wicked father' syndrome, although Rothermere's letters to his son are a model of affection and respect.

been hard put to say so. He loved his father, and the pair of them did work well together, showing one another enormous respect. But, for Esmond, there was always that fear of momentary disapproval, or worse, implicit comparison between himself and the brothers who died.

Thus Esme, not only a grandmother but also the Dowager Countess of Cromer, wife and then widow to Rowley Cromer, Governor of the Bank of England and later Ambassador to the United States of America; Esme, now an author and Lady-in-Waiting to the Queen, speculated upon the devastating effect the break-up of her parents' marriage had upon herself, her brother Vere and her sister Lorna.

All of us were bad at school, all three kids. I don't know why we were stupid, or whether a child psychologist would say it was the divorce when we were young. I think a child psychologist would say that was the root reason. We were not interested at all in learning anything, we had a built-in resentment against all the teachers. It wasn't until I came across a school report of mine that I realised all this. My mother sent it to me with the message, 'This was the best report you ever got in your life.' She had kept it.

I had been threatened with expulsion. I had had a chequered career, and had finally ended up at day school after two boarding schools when I got this threat of being expelled. I was terrified. If I was expelled, I would be sent back to boarding school, so I tried very hard. I hated boarding school. Children of divorced parents often do. They were more like reformatory schools, we weren't allowed to speak certain places or times. So I had got this good report.

Father had custody of us. So he was in charge of us. We lived mainly with him, and then only about two months with my mother, every other Easter and half the summer holidays and otherwise with my father. He was not as strong as my mother who was a very strong personality, and great guts one had to say. My father: Gemini. Two characters in one. A very tough businessman, but not tough in his private life. Being so good looking and women used to fall for him and chase him from pillar to post, he had a weakness as far as women were concerned. My grandfather did too.

But he was quite a severe parent.

The severity of Esmond made it easier for Harold to be generous. If his son was to take on the duties of a stern and responsible parent, Harold could give full vent to his affection, indulging his passion for giving. Not long after Vere's birth, just as the marriage began to slide into trouble, Rothermere set up three separate and distinct trusts, domiciled in Canada. The first two were for Esmond's benefit, the third for the grandchildren, thus ensuring, come what may, that they would be provided for after his death.* It was the start of Rothermere's serious giving. There were stories that he had lost everything in the 1929 crash – he had not;† there were tales he was broken by the provincial newspaper wars with the Berry brothers – he was not.

Rothermere gave his money away. So much so that by the time of his death his vast fortune had dwindled to a mere £300,000.

As for Peggy and Esmond, their divorce took the better part of a decade. Acrimonious at first, the couple's splitting was as passionate as their mating, Peggy fleeing to Claridge's with the children. Later, Esmond seemed to favour the girls; Peggy looked to Vere. The three children worked it out amongst themselves, accepting what had happened and allowing their own relations to settle into harmony – and always an overriding family loyalty.

Esmond would marry twice more, three marriages altogether, two of them ending in the courts, and so would Peggy. But, amongst the three children, the full unhappiness of their parents' parting was always strongly felt, and none of them ever divorced.

In business, as usual, Rothermere prospered – sometimes through simple good luck.

In 1925, he founded 'the largest newsprint factory in the world, known as the Anglo-Canadian Pulp and Paper Mills', locating it in Quebec, where transport was well established and the work-force highly trained.

This was because Northcliffe's dream of developing the interior of Newfoundland had foundered, costs outpacing profits to such an extent that the investment had come literally to nothing. By the time Rothermere decided to build his factory in Quebec, it had been demonstrated conclusively that summer production in Grand Falls, however lucrative this might be, could not compensate for the huge liabilities accrued during the cruel winter months when the Exploits River froze and transport became impossible. This balancing of one season against the other meant that the Anglo-Newfoundland Development Company neither gained nor lost – but stayed in unprofitable equilibrium – exactly as Rothermere had foretold when Northcliffe selected the site.

* Bernard Falk, *Bouquets for Fleet Street: Memories and Musings over Fifty Years*, p. 167. Harold's grandson Vere Rothermere adds that the first trust was set up in 1929, with two more in the 1930s. Interview with Rothermere, London, 21 January 1993.

† Falk insists Rothermere lost nothing in the crash; King speculates in *Strictly Personal* that he did – some $40 million in one month – at p. 78. Vere Rothermere explains Harold did not lose in 1929, but in the second crash in 1933 – although not as badly as many others. Harold wrote to Princess Stephanie that he 'lost heavily in the recent crash', meaning the 1933 crash.

But, just when it looked as if Grand Falls was finished as a going concern, one of those wildly unpredictable strokes of good fortune occurred. The windfall from the trek of Matty Mitchell – the Jackitar Indian who had prospected the land in 1905 – came to fruition. Mitchell had died the same year as Northcliffe, leaving behind only a map with an 'X' pencilled over Buchans Mine, the tattered record of his prospecting trip made over twenty years earlier to ascertain the value of the mineral holdings of the Anglo-Newfoundland Development Company. And, in 1905, mining the complex ore Mitchell had found – a mixture of zinc, lead, copper and a smattering of gold – was impracticable because no one knew how to separate the metals. By 1911, a way to separate them had been discovered, only at too high a price. But by 1926, with advancing technology, not only was it feasible, it was cost-efficient.

A fifty-year concession was awarded to the American Smelting and Refining Company, with fifty per cent of profits going to the Anglo-Newfoundland Development Company, which was owned by Associated Newspapers, which in turn was owned by the Daily Mail Trust Ltd. In January 1928 at the Fifth Ordinary General Meeting of the DMTL, the president of American Smelting, Mr H.A. Guess, made his first report. 'The ore', he wrote,

> is a very fine-grained sulphide complex ... about 7 per cent lead, 16 per cent zinc, 2 per cent copper, 3 per cent silver and 0.03 gold ... Some 3,000,000 tons have been indicated by the considerable diamond-drilling and underground work so far done. The construction programme now under way includes a selective flotation mill of some 600 tons daily capacity, with a hydroelectric plant of 2,000 to 2,500 h.p. on Buchans River alongside. Also included is a 22-mile railway taking off from the Anglo-Newfoundland Development Company's Millertown branch at a point 15 miles west of Millertown Junction.

Within a year, an adjoining site was discovered that would add eight million tons to the original estimate, and in 1951 still another strike would eventually yield comparable tonnage. By the 1980s, the Buchans Mine was recognized as one of the richest finds on the continent of North America, 'accounting', as one authority put it, 'for a total of some 17.5 million tons of ore, equivalent to 6.3 million tons of concentrates produced'.

Alongside the mill, railroad and hydroelectric plant that were being erected, a company town was built. Its population quickly grew to 2,500. Living there was a picturesque experience, one welcomed by many, especially after the stock-market crash of 1929. As one old-timer Edward M. Martin, recorded:

Everything in the town belonged to the company – the houses, the furnishings, the road, everything. We used to live pretty good.

People lived pretty well next to each other all the time. You worked with the same guys as you recreated with ... After a while you got a good group of people who could work together, socialize together, go to church together ... Fridays and Saturday nights in Buchans were always a pretty good night out ... We drank rum and we drank whiskey and we made home brew when we didn't have very much money. There was no liquor store. The company knew everything ... So if you wanted to get a bottle, even in St John's, you could only buy three bottles of liquor a week per person and you had to have a book issued to you by this liquor department.

You had your own entertaining, you'd gather in somebody's house one Friday and probably someone else's house the next Friday. A lot played cards, poker. The fellows were reasonably careful not to let the gambling take over. If you stepped out of line you were fired, if you didn't do the right thing with your house (you signed a lease when you went in), the lease was broken.

In the '30s if you had a job, you never took the chance of looking for another one, you just hung on because there were six other guys just eager to get your job ... Believe me you kept your nose to the grindstone, you were very fortunate to be making any money at all.

Thus Rothermere – because of the Buchans find – managed to keep the Grand Falls project afloat. In money matters at least, Harold was lucky. Even in terms of selling the metal that was mined, there was unanticipated good fortune. Most of it was zinc, used primarily in the automobile industry. When, during the Depression, the bottom fell out of the car market and sales began to plummet, help came from an unexpected quarter.

European brokers sent back word that the sale of the metal was enjoying a sudden surge and that they would be able to sell all the zinc the American Smelting and Refining Company could produce. Germany required the metal, and one way or another, under the leadership of an aggressive new Chancellor, they were managing to find the funds to purchase it.

At the same time Rothermere was prospering on the North American continent, his great friend Beaverbrook was robbing him blind. It was in Beaverbrook's nature to cheat those he cared for, just as he needed to swallow whomever he loved.

It amused him to take advantage of his cross-holdings in the Daily Mail Trust Ltd to finance his own newspapers, using the dividends of

Rothermere's highly profitable operation to fund the development of the *Daily Express*.* By investing fulsomely in staff and equipment, he managed to continue at a loss, even as his circulation rose. His goal, and it wasn't even much of a secret, was to put his best friend's newspaper out of business. As he told one of his cronies, 'I shall go back to New Brunswick and retire a failure if I don't succeed in killing the *Daily Mail*.'†

The method Beaverbrook used must have amused him as well, for it was extremely amusing. Decades after the deaths of both men, Rothermere's grandson Vere most especially saw the humour of it:

> Beaverbrook was a natural journalist and he understood the whole situation instinctively. He hired away from the *Daily Mail* all the top journalists, all trained by Northcliffe, and of course the managers on the *Daily Mail* were, on my grandfather's instructions, cutting this and cutting that and ... pushing down the journalists, and Beaverbrook said essentially, 'What do you want to work there for? Come and work for me, and I'll give you more money ...' and so he got all the best sub-editors, and the best sports writers, and so on, and he got them all over to the *Express* and the *Express* started to get ahead.
>
> Eventually Beaverbrook turned his front page to news; the *Mail* had the advertising all over its front page as was the custom before the first world war. Beaverbrook realised that this was now passé and, besides, he didn't enjoy that kind of revenue so he turned his front page to news, while the *Daily Mail* managers couldn't bring themselves to do that because they would lose all this fat revenue.‡ So the *Express* sales went soaring and the *Mail* started declining, and by the time they caught on, they had lost the battle and the *Express* had overtaken the *Mail*. And Beaverbrook never paid a dividend! Well, not until 1937, and by then, the damage was done!

Thus did Max contrive to cheat his great friend Harold.

---

* See A.J.P. Taylor, *Beaverbrook: A Biography*, p. 214, and Lewis Chester and Jonathan Fenby, *The Fall of the House of Beaverbrook*, p. 67; the fact is generally substantiated in the lore of Fleet Street.

† Beaverbrook made the remark in passing at the races in Newmarket on 30 October 1928, according to A.J.P. Taylor in *Beaverbrook: A Biography*, p. 250.

‡ Rothermere's attitude towards page one was brisk and businesslike: 'This page means a daily revenue of £1400. Once a year the directors religiously discuss whether to put news on the front page, or keep it, as now, a medium for publicity, in my opinion the cheapest in the world, having regard to the wonderful benefits accruing to the advertiser. Admittedly it is a considerable advantage to have news on the front page. Lord Beaverbrook regards it as essential to start the news there, and he is always urging me to take this course. I value his judgment highly, but in this matter I agree with the Associated Newspaper directors in thinking such a development would be a mistake.' Bernard Falk, *Five Years Dead: A Postscript to 'He Laughed in Fleet Street'*, p. 175.

For his part, Harold tried not to be cheated. On 16 October 1926, he proposed to Beaverbrook to sell the shares in the *Daily Express* owned by the Daily Mail Trust for £1.5 million, a sum that Beaverbrook could raise simply by reorganizing his company according to a plan Rothermere had devised. Within five days, Beaverbrook wrote back sweetly, 'I have no interest to acquire the interests held by you in the *Daily Express* or *Evening Standard*. It suits me splendidly to have you for a colleague.' Again in 1927, Rothermere tried to end the partnership, this time offering to pay Beaverbrook £2.5 million for Beaverbrook's majority interest in the *Daily Express* – an 'immense offer', he admitted apologetically to one of his associates, 'for a ... business which has so far never made anything like £100,000 a year profits'.* But Beaverbrook again declined and countered by offering the same for Rothermere's holdings, an offer he knew Rothermere would decline. So it was that Harold ended up footing the bill for the expansion of the greatest rival the *Daily Mail* would ever have – Max Beaverbrook's *Daily Express*.

And even as he did that, Rothermere let himself become entangled in one of the strangest episodes in press history, one orchestrated by Beaverbrook for the glory and ambition of Beaverbrook. For Beaverbrook believed, since he had got this far, that he could go even further. How far? As he told some young contenders in public life, 'the only prize worth anything is the Premiership', and so it could be assumed the Premiership was Beaverbrook's secret goal. Thus began his campaign for Empire Free Trade which would eventually lead to the formation of a separate political party – the United Empire Party.

It is difficult to calculate the folly of the United Empire Party. As Beaverbrook cast about for a way to become a public figure in a country not his own, and Rothermere tried to find a substitute for his brother Northcliffe, the two press barons descended into a political torpor almost impossible to imagine.

The concept of Empire Free Trade, as Beaverbrook later freely admitted, was based upon a lie. In his own words, it was protectionism made palatable to a British public 'addicted to Free Trade and fond of the Empire'. He simply used a little selective phraseology in order to fool some of the people some of the time. The idea was that there was to be free trade amongst all the countries of the Empire, and a tariff upon everyone else, most especially the great competitors, the United States and Europe. And

* Rothermere to Pomeroy Burton, n.d. (Harmsworth Archives). A.J.P. Taylor offers differing timings and figures from those found in the letters held in Rothermere's archive, but the aim of both men was the same – for Rothermere, to get out of the agreement; for Beaverbrook, to hold on. *Beaverbrook: A Biography*, p. 249.

most especially, there was to be a food tax upon staples not produced in Britain or countries within the Empire.

This irritated Rothermere, who had, along with Northcliffe when he was alive, opposed any kind of 'stomach tax'. The question was why Rothermere ended up supporting a campaign which he had for decades firmly opposed and, at the same time, backing a man who had no real chance of gaining office. When Stanley Baldwin posed the question to one of his aides, the answer came back, 'I fancy it is Lord B's restless ambition temporarily combined with Lord R's detestation of you.' The remark was flippant, it was memorable, it was *almost* true.

The missing element was Rothermere's affection for Beaverbrook and his gratitude to Max for taking care of him after the deaths of Vyvyan and Vere. Harold had no defences against Max: he loved him, well, like a brother. And so much as he loved Beaverbrook, that much did he dislike Stanley Baldwin – and mostly on merit. There was a rumour this dislike stemmed from Baldwin having refused to grant him an earldom and to give Esmond a place in the Cabinet, but this was unlikely since Rothermere had expressly forbidden Esmond to serve under a man he considered to be a second-rater – a political miscalculation that cost his son dearly. But there was another reason. Rothermere blamed Baldwin and his uninspired 1929 campaign slogan of 'Safety First' for losing the election to Ramsay MacDonald's Labour Party. He believed Baldwin had betrayed the Conservative Party and indeed the nation by letting in the Socialists with so little fight.

Meanwhile, Rothermere himself was growing ever more nationalistic. He had always been patriotic. Of late, however, exempting the Empire, he felt more and more protectionist. His feelings were reflected in an editorial that kicked off his support of Beaverbrook's Empire Free Trade Campaign, which appeared under the headline, 'We Have the Goods':

> British manufacturers and British work people are turning out the best goods to be bought in the world. They are far ahead of their competitors in two of the most important factors – quality and durability. The achievement of our industrialists and workers is the more impressive because they are handicapped in so many ways. Whereas in foreign countries politicians are considerate of industry and do all that is in their power to aid it, here the politicians will not even condescend to tell those few trades which have some slight vestige of tariff protection whether that protection is going to be continued or abolished.

Thus did Beaverbrook's new party and its notions of fiscal unity within the Empire fit Rothermere's notions of the proper balance of business, trade and government for Great Britain.

But Beaverbrook's approach was more sensational, more Northcliffian, or at least it tried to be. The *Express* called the movement a 'Crusade', and readers were urged to 'Join the Empire Crusade Today'. 'First Marching Orders' were given to the 'Crusaders', who were entreated to urge their friends to enrol. And they did enrol, although why they did so remained a puzzle.

Perhaps it was hard times. Beaverbrook's 'Crusade' perfectly intersected the stock-market crash, thus receiving an irresistible impetus upwards. Otherwise, the movement caught the rising tide of nationalism that was already a major force in Italy and about to become one in Germany. It preyed on people's fears, that foreign businessmen were getting the upper hand, that cheap eggs and sausage casings and foreign foodstuffs of all kinds were driving the local farmer out of business, that Britain was on the skids and only draconian measures could stop the slide. And the movement also demonstrated that people often didn't know what to believe – and here at last was *something*.

For those who did believe, the events that followed were to leave them feeling bruised and ridiculous. Beaverbrook's new United Empire Party, formed on 18 February 1930, was, with no explanation, disbanded on 8 March. The excuse *appeared* to be, although no one could be sure, that Baldwin had agreed to a public referendum on food taxes, and so, with this great victory in hand, the Party was no longer necessary. But on 3 April, similarly with no explanation, the United Empire Party was reinstituted, this time with Beaverbrook himself going on the stump, speaking with all the fire and brimstone of an old-time country revivalist. A listener recognized the oratory of the press baron's father, who had been a minister in the Presbyterian Church in Newcastle, New Brunswick. Thus Max, wagging away on the lectern, preaching like his father – a parody of a preacher, a parody of a politician – with Rothermere lending his support.

A pathetic note: the *Daily Express* began to expound the merits of a new 'Imperial Loaf' – 'Empire Wheat, British Milled in British Bread'. It was Beaverbrook's hollow echo of Northcliffe's Standard Bread campaign.

Not unsurprisingly, Rothermere continued his support. On 5 January 1930, G. Ward Price, who by now had become Rothermere's unofficial mouthpiece, wrote in a leader that

> the conviction was fast spreading among Conservatives that their next leader must be found outside the established hierarchy ... There is no man living in this country today with more likelihood of succeeding to the Premiership of Great Britain than Lord Beaverbrook.

Rothermere then endorsed the nomination at a public dinner. For his part,

Beaverbrook announced that Rothermere was 'the greatest trustee of public opinion that we have ever seen in the history of journalism'.

With regard to Beaverbrook's peerage, Ward Price asserted that it 'could only be a temporary handicap since the reconstruction of the Upper House, with the abolition of the heredity principle, must soon make it possible for all Peers to sit in the House of Commons'. 'The proposal', wrote one of Beaverbrook's biographers several years later,

> was greeted with an explosion of almost universal mirth. It was, so to speak, a sitter for the sardonic leader-writers of the *Morning Post.* 'Here, indeed,' they sneered, 'is an argument which might reconcile the Conservative Party to the abolition of the heredity principle – that it might set free Lord Beaverbrook from the only obstacle – the obligations of his caste – which prevents him from becoming their leader. At last we have an adequate reason for reconstructing the House of Lords!

Despite the ridicule, Beaverbrook began putting up candidates for the new Party, and, in the first by-election in East Islington, succeeded in splitting the vote, with the result that the Labour candidate won – a fact Beaverbrook should have deplored but in fact did not. For it caused Baldwin to suffer a temporary failure of nerve, and, as a result, he came close to resigning his position as Leader of the Conservative Party. What brought him back was a personal attack in the *Daily Mail*, the gist of which was that, having lost the immense fortune left him by his father, Baldwin was unfit as leader of the Conservative Party. The article, signed only 'Editor', gave Baldwin the impetus to make his single most famous speech, one that restored his political dignity and laid waste not only the United Empire Party but also the two press barons who had become his habitual foes.

'I have no idea of the name of that gentleman,' said Baldwin, referring to the anonymous author of the article.

> I would only observe that he is well qualified for the post which he holds. The first part of that statement is a lie and the second part of the statement, by its implication, is untrue. The paragraph itself could only have been written by a cad. I have consulted a very high legal authority and I am advised that an action for libel would lie. I shall not move in the matter, and for this reason: I should get an apology and heavy damages. The first is of no value, the second I would not touch with a barge pole. What the proprietorship of these papers is aiming at is power, and power without responsibility – the prerogative of the harlot throughout the ages.

The date was 17 March* and the speech was made on behalf of the Conservative candidate Duff Cooper. On 19 March, Cooper was declared the winner of the St George's by-election, routing Beaverbrook's candidate and effectively destroying the United Empire Party.

The sting in the tail of Baldwin's speech was said to have been written by his famous cousin Rudyard Kipling, writer for Northcliffe and Beaverbrook – and friend of Rothermere.

What the whole Empire Free Trade imbroglio had demonstrated was that Beaverbrook's bullying methods of advancement were useless in the political arena, and he sulked away, having made a public fool of himself. The effect on Rothermere was to reinforce a belief he had long been nurturing. ''Pon my soul,' he later told one of his editors,

> the amount of nonsense talked about the power of the newspaper proprietor is positively nauseating. All manner of people outside the newspaper business persist in crediting us with far more influence than we actually possess, and I have often been amused by the studied pose of those proprietorial colleagues of mine who cannot resist the temptation of subscribing to the fallacy. Of course, I have long since ceased to have any illusions on the point myself ... How could I have any illusions on this score, after the way Baldwin managed to survive years of the most bitter newspaper attacks on his ... muddle-headed policies?

As to the relationship between press lord and press lord, who can say of what real affection consists? Over thirty years later, Max would read through the letters that he and Harold, now many years dead, had written to one another when they campaigned for Max's ill-fated United Empire Party. The pair of them had ripped through the Establishment, shaken people up, upset the apple-cart. Old and ailing, Max wrote plaintively to Esmond that going through the old correspondence with Harold had reminded him 'once more of how much I miss him'. There was no reason to doubt his sentiments: Harold had been his greatest ally and his best friend – and the only competitor whose company and whose newspapers, despite all Max's wiles, won out in the end.

Beaverbrook's United Empire Party had been based upon the proposition that any highly motivated individual with political ambition could more or less concoct a platform that would propel him into high office – had he sufficient means at his disposal to manage the climb and the charisma

---

* The date is alternately reported to be 17 March by Martin Gilbert, *Winston S. Churchill, Vol. V., 1922–1939*, p. 398 and 18 March by Tom Driberg in *Beaverbrook: A Study in Power and Frustration*, p. 213.

to attract a following. The other essential ingredient, it appeared, was a *common cause*, as Vladimir Ilyich Ulyanov had earlier shown. And to Ulyanov, better known as N. Lenin, that common cause was a newspaper. Beaverbrook had a newspaper – several in fact – and the support of Rothermere, who had even more. Together, they commanded a readership that would have made the Bolshevik revolutionary green with envy. They had nevertheless been unable to attract more than 200,000 members, a mere one per cent of the vote.

It was otherwise with Lenin.

By the time Stanley Baldwin had, with a few fine phrases, routed the two mighty press lords, Lenin – with his legendary five followers – had managed to create a unified nation of adherents who all subscribed, willingly or not, to a single philosophy: 'From each according to his ability; to each according to his needs.'

Lenin's success in single-handedly imposing his will upon a diverse and unruly nation had shaken the world, and from the moment it became apparent he would prevail, there were the questions whether such a State was desirable and whether it could happen elsewhere. A further debate arose about the nature of Communism itself: was it a good thing, or a bad?

To Rothermere's mind, the rise of Communism was catastrophic, and the avowed goal of the Bolsheviks to export their revolution to foreign shores struck terror into his heart. Perhaps his early hatred of the Soviets sprang from their immediate decision, upon seizing power, to withdraw from the war, making them, as one commentator put it, 'enemies of God and man – and sold to Germany – a loathsome union of anti-Christ and Judas'. Or perhaps Rothermere hated the Soviets because of their requisitioning of the belongings of the upper classes for the benefit of all. Rothermere's watering-holes were filled with White Russian aristocrats who had had to flee their native land, to live out their lives as idle and discontented vagabonds in foreign climes.

Or perhaps it was simply the natural instinct of one of the world's foremost proponents of capitalism to despise a creed that gave no quarter to personal initiative, substituting in its place the common weal. Whatever the case, Rothermere never wavered in his belief that Communism was the root cause of evil in the modern world, and he and others began to search for some means of halting its spread.

It came in the form of a handsome young Italian Socialist, who had, as early as 1914, invented a term – *fascio* – to describe an entirely new political philosophy. 'Fascio' means 'bundle' or group, and it was used not in the first instance by Benito Mussolini, as he claimed, but by a left-wing splinter group who wished to abandon the conventional Socialist creed and embrace a more native version. By the time Mussolini had taken over as editor of *Popolo d'Italia*, however, he had made the term his own and, as such, it represented a strange amalgam of socialism and nationalism based on purity of language and race. Mussolini was scornful of Lenin, calling him 'a man of straw'. 'Only a Tartar and Mongolian people could fall for such a programme as his,' he wrote in his newspaper, expatiating upon his theme of Italian supremacy. Nevertheless, when spinning out a suitable programme for the Fascist Party, what he came up with sounded suspiciously like that of Lenin's Bolshevik movement: 'land to the peasants' was one of Mussolini's slogans, lifted straight from Russian revolutionary prose, along with programmes for progressive taxation, the expropriation of factories, the establishment of a minimum wage, and so on and so forth, with what was fast becoming the obligatory jargon of the twentieth-century revolutionary.

This was 1919. By 1922, when the Fascists made their famous 'march on Rome', Mussolini had concocted a new platform wholly inconsistent with his earlier beliefs but smartly in step with a rising tide of resistance to the new Soviet regime. There was, he had discovered, considerable cachet attached to being the only bulwark against Communism in Europe, and he now began calling for 'a balanced budget, a smaller bureaucracy, a more stable currency and reduced inflation'.

The Italian Government was weak; Mussolini was strong. He had assembled a loyal band of followers, political hooligans armed with castor oil and propaganda leaflets. And so, by a clever combination of political intrigue, brute force and a certain bravura, Mussolini managed to thrust himself, at the age of only thirty-nine, into the top position of government, becoming Prime Minister of Italy and in the process ushering in the Age of the Dictator.

What was a dictator during those regenerative years that followed on from the terrors of the Great War?

He was a god, an omniscient being, a mystical force; an organizer, a planner, a workaholic who needed no sleep; a friend of school children, protector of the poor, patron saint. He was virile yet gentle, ruthless yet kind, intelligent yet patient. He nurtured, he explained, he disciplined. New-age yet old-fashioned, the dictator of the twentieth century was both macho and photogenic. *And* he could make the trains run on time.

Nobody could have embodied this image better than Mussolini. He affected a masculine persona that reeked of sex and power. Chest thrust outward, lips pooched, he is photographed shirtless on the beach, wearing only swimming trunks; or, ominous and stony-faced, he sits at his desk in the Prime Minister's office, signing new legislation; or, legs astride, in high-top leather boots, his hand tucked neatly into his jacket, he strikes a Napoleonic pose.

Or, at the head of the *bersaglieri*: he is in uniform, he is running.

All over Italy, *mussolinismo* flourishes. Hundreds of towns rename themselves Mussolinia, the young men shave their heads to look like Benito, the brutal stare becomes the latest mating call, the *bersaglieri* appear in every small village: they are in uniform, they are running. Above it all, Mussolini watches. All is well.

In Munich, a little over a year after Mussolini became the twenty-seventh Prime Minister of Italy, still another group of revolutionaries conspired to take the government into their own hands, this time that of the Bavarian State. But for Adolf Hitler and his comrades, the path to power would be a long one. The Beer Hall Putsch on 8 November 1923 would end in fiasco, with a hastily assembled plan to march on Munich the next morning resulting in the deaths of sixteen of Hitler's comrades-in-arms. After a highly publicized trial, he would be imprisoned, high above the River Lech, in the old fortress in Landsberg. There, he dictated his master-work, *Mein Kampf* – Hitler's struggle. What that struggle entailed was the subjugation of an entire nation to the will of '*one man . . .* only he alone may possess the authority and the right to command'.

Democracy, such a philosophy entailed, had failed. The complex problems of the modern world could be solved only by a superhuman leader who knew better than the people themselves what they needed. Mysticism and government were thus wed, and the cult of the dictator was born.

Were the phenomena of Lenin, Mussolini and Hitler isolated events? Or were they a logical outcome of the chaos of the Great War? Even in Britain, the idea of 'one man, one rule' became highly fashionable, and 'the mere word "dictator" caused wide interest'. It was rapidly becoming a buzz-word for efficiency and thrift, surfacing especially amongst the rich and privileged, the intelligentsia and opinion leaders of society. In London, the Methuen series *If I Were Dictator* was launched, with various well-known intellectuals giving their quick-fix plans to remedy the country's ills, much in the spirit of a latter-day radio show that highlights the likes and dislikes of a show-business personality.

The appeal of the idea was not lost on Rothermere, and by 1927 he was suggesting to Lloyd George that, by using the word 'artistically' in his political utterances, he might be able to enliven his campaign to regain power in government. Later, Rothermere would suggest the country needed a 'dictator of the air', by which he meant a strong leader who could cut through the red tape of bureaucracy and get aeroplanes into production.

On a more personal level, it was only natural Rothermere should warm to the concept. His own world had been shattered by the deaths of his sons, and later by the loss of Northcliffe. His mother had died. Except for his link with Esmond and Esmond's children, his affections were splintered and fragmented. He had become a nomad. To such a one, the need for direction and authority in a chaotic world was self-evident.

And indeed, if choice must be made, any well-informed individual might have favoured the rising powers in Italy and Germany. It was a matter of simple arithmetic.

Between November 1917 and January 1934, the Soviet experiment had resulted in a savage civil war, the brutal requisitionings of War Communism, the deportation of the kulaks and two horrific famines. An archipelago of slave-labour camps had been erected in the frozen tundra of Siberia where millions languished – suspended between life and death – in a state of suffering unimaginable to Western sensibilities. Altogether, it was not unrealistic to count some twenty million enslaved or dead as a direct result of the leadership of the Bolshevik regime.

In contrast, during 'the radiant days in October', 1922, when Mussolini seized power, so few had died that a slightly embarrassed *Duce* later made the comment he should have ordered more put against the wall and shot. In the decade that followed, the castor oil, the public beatings, the book burnings and accidental deaths seemed little more than a few isolated incidents carried out by over-zealous enthusiasts, necessary perhaps in keeping Communism at bay. In Germany, Hitler became Chancellor under circumstances so auspicious that Rothermere was moved to comment, 'in comparison with other revolutions ... the Germans have set the world a model of moderation.'

It was true.

Before 'the Night of the Long Knives', 30 June 1934, little concrete evidence existed of the Fascists' aptitude for annihilation. True, the mindless regimentation of the Nazi regime augured ill for independence of mind among the young. But this was Germany, not Britain, where such obsessions with mass conformity and ordered behaviour had always been commonplace. Then too, there were the incoherent ravings of *Mein Kampf* and its emphasis upon masters and slaves, Aryans and Jews, 'pure blood' and 'racial chaff'. But these were only words.

When Hitler was made Chancellor of the German Reich on Monday, 30 January 1933, there were approximately 504,000 Jews living in Germany. Across Europe, their numbers exceeded nine million.*

What was he going to do? Kill all of them?

* Figures supplied by the Holocaust Museum Library, Washington, DC, citing *Encyclopedia Judaica*, Macmillan, 1971.

17

'The Blackshirts Are in the Wash'

For every demagogue who worked his way to the top of the heap, there were dozens of others, each with his own following, vying for power. In Britain during the 1920s and 1930s, the Home Office kept careful watch not only on Communist cells but also on Fascist organizations, of which there were many – the Blue Shirts, the Green Shirts, the British Fascist League, the Imperial Fascist League, the list goes on. Of these, only one group would rise to prominence, and that was the British Union of Fascists, popularly called the Blackshirts, founded by Oswald Mosley, grandson of Sir Oswald Mosley, the fourth baronet who had originated the Standard Bread campaign that Northcliffe backed in 1911. Ironically, Rothermere was destined to support the younger Mosley, thus embroiling the *Daily Mail* in a controversy that would last for decades.

Oswald Mosley, popularly known as Tom and to his intimates as Kit, was a darling of the British Establishment, an 'Old Boy' while still a young man – well born and better married, in 1920, to Lady Cynthia Blanche, second daughter of Lord Curzon and granddaughter of Levi Leiter, the Chicago millionaire.

Mosley had served in the Great War, and like many of the young men who survived the apocalypse, never really got over a vague sense of betrayal by his country and by democracy itself. This appeared to influence his actions ever after.

There was about Mosley a topspin of instability that might have been a facet of his character or a result of the war, it was impossible to say which. Elected to the House of Commons in 1918, he quit the Conservatives to become an Independent, only to join Labour, only to quit again. He had written in 1930 a memorandum – arguably the most innovative and brilliant economic brief of the decade – and when it was rejected, he launched the New Party. When that failed, he loped off to Italy to see how Mussolini fared, coming back in 1932 to found the British Union of Fascists. Through all these swerves and U-turns, he and his wife 'Cimmie' conducted a dazzling and somewhat wicked social life; he tall, handsome and moustached; she comely and warm. Were they 'vile bodies'?

Certainly, Tom was. In the same year he founded his Fascist movement, he became enamoured of Mrs Bryan Guinness, daughter of Lord Redesdale and sister of Jessica, Nancy, Deborah, Pamela and Unity Mitford. 'Eccentric' was the word frequently used to describe the Mitford girls, but that might have been a euphemism. During the Spanish Civil War, Jessica would surprise her family by running off to fight for the Republicans. A destroyer was sent to carry her home. Unity was destined to become the foremost groupie of Adolf Hitler, shooting herself at the onset of the war. She was shipped home via Switzerland on direct orders from the Führer, so goes the story, where she died after great suffering from her wound. Diana, Mrs Bryan Guinness, a much admired social hostess, would become mistress and then wife to Tom Mosley, after the premature death of Cimmie from peritonitis. The happy couple were secretly wed in Berlin; Frau Goebbels gave the wedding luncheon, Hitler attending.

Mosley was a chameleon – adjudged vain, arrogant and ambitious by the closest of his friends; a calculating careerist by others. One quote from his oratory tells all:

> Better the great adventure, better the great attempt for England's sake, better defeat, disaster, better far the end of that trivial thing called a political career than stifling in a uniform of blue and gold, strutting and posturing on the stage of little England . . .

'Better to reign in hell than serve in heaven,' he might have added. For like Satan in *Paradise Lost*, Mosley was a glittering character, brilliant and mercurial, gifted and mad.

Rothermere, like others, became involved for reasons not terribly complex. First, Mosley was and had always been 'one of us'; that is, he was the protégé of F.E. Smith, peer of Winston Churchill, friend of John Strachey, acceptable – even sought after – in the best circles. And in the early days of the British Union of Fascists he stood for all that Rothermere admired: youth, action and, most importantly, rearmament. He brought charisma to politics, a characteristic sadly lacking in both Ramsay Mac-Donald and Stanley Baldwin, who more or less took turns as Prime Minister during the 1920s and 1930s, neither of them distinguishing their terms by any decisive or direct action.

As early as 1931, Rothermere was offering to place 'the whole of the Harmsworth press at [Mosley's] disposal', even as Churchill was urging Mosley to stand, with his full support, for the Westminster by-election. But Mosley remained coy. He had a secret plan – to conquer and rule – but it was as yet too early to reveal these ambitions. Resentful that he had to depend upon the 'prima donnas of the press', he nevertheless needed

Rothermere desperately if his movement was to gain respectability.

To Rothermere, Mosley and his fledgling Fascists represented 'sound, commonsense, Conservative doctrine'. Inspired by 'loyalty to the throne and love of country', they were little more than an energetic wing of the Conservative Party. To this, Mosley responded with private contempt: Rothermere was an 'Albert Hall supporter', a political innocent who was trying to tie him down to the Establishment when Mosley wished to soar.

Typical of Rothermere's approach was the *Daily Mail* article 'Hurrah for the Blackshirts!' that kicked off Rothermere's support on 8 January 1934. It was the United Empire Crusade all over again, and he approached it with a similar 'rah-rah' tone. Another of Rothermere's newspapers, the *Evening News*, secured five hundred seats at a rally at the Royal Albert Hall, offering them as prizes to readers who sent in 'the most interesting and constructive reasons as to why they like the Blackshirts'. Still another Rothermere title, the *Sunday Dispatch*, sponsored a beauty contest for Blackshirt women. There were no entries, and an exasperated Mosley found himself 'embarrassed to explain [to Rothermere] that these were serious young women dedicated to the cause of their country rather than aspirants to the Gaiety Theatre chorus'.*

Meanwhile, G. Ward Price, a close friend of Mosley and chief reporter at the *Daily Mail*, helped to hatch a plan for Mosley and Rothermere to go into business together by forming a cigarette-manufacturing company, New Epoch Products Ltd. The idea was that the Blackshirts, purportedly with some five hundred chapters in the United Kingdom, would use their personnel to distribute cigarettes which Rothermere would manufacture. The plan in fact advanced far enough that Rothermere actually spent £70,000 on a factory and machinery. It was at this point that the relationship, some five months old, came apart at the seams, and many believed this was a result of what is now known as the 'Olympia riot'.

On 7 June 1934, Mosley, after a successful rally at the Albert Hall in May, planned the largest public gathering in the history of British politics – at Olympia. For the first time, instead of his usual polarized following of intelligentsia and working class, members of the British middle classes would be attending, to decide once and for all whether Mosley had anything to offer them.

Fifteen thousand gathered that night to hear the leader of the Blackshirts, and although the proceedings started half an hour late because of

* The two events were recorded by the Home Office; they occurred in May 1934 (Public Record Office, Kew, Home Office File 144 20140/674216). Also Mosley himself describes the incident at p. 344 in his autobiography (*My Life*) written in 1968, from which the above wording is taken.

disturbances outside the building, when at last they did begin it was impressive stuff. Mosley, flanked by his underlings, and 'preceded by a long procession of Union Jacks and Blackshirt banners, advanced down the whole length of the 200-yard central aisle to the high platform at the far end'.

But this brief moment of triumph was destined to end in chaos. The Communists had been able to put two and a half thousand agitators into the hall, seated at different locations, and just as the Blackshirt leader began to speak, an unending round of well-organized harassment started: 'FASCISM MEANS MURDER,' the agitators chanted, 'DOWN WITH MOSLEY!' As soon as one group was quelled, another began.

G. Ward Price, fast becoming an apologist for the Fascist movement, put a brave face on the events of the evening in a story he wrote for the *Daily Mail*:

> If the Blackshirt movement had any need of justification, the Red Hooligans who savagely and systematically tried to wreck Sir Oswald Mosley's huge and magnificently successful meeting at Olympia last night would have supplied it.
>
> They got what they deserved. Olympia has been the scene of many assemblies and many great fights, but never had it offered the spectacle of so many fights mixed up with a meeting.
>
> The Blackshirt stewards had the combination of a first-class Rugby football team.

The stewards apparently expelled the agitators with maximum efficiency, beating them before onlookers and then expelling them brutally from the meeting-hall. The climax came when two infiltrators climbed up the lattice-siding to the girders above and walked across, as if on a tightrope, while the horrified audience watched from below. Had one of them fallen, not only would he have been killed instantly, but so might several below have died or been injured.

The peculiarly Fascist combination of pageantry and violence that might have been interpreted in Italy as *machismo*, or in Germany as might, was in Britain viewed with distaste. The British middle class, witnessing at first hand Fascist tactics, retreated rapidly, and a long debate began in the newspapers as to what it all meant.

In Berlin, Ralph Izzard, a correspondent working for the *Daily Mail*, though not yet twenty years old, was less naïve than most of Britain's population as to the significance of the ongoing contests of strength between Fascist and Communist. There, skirmishes were commonplace.

> Each side had a local pub, the Communists and the Nazis, then one pub would

go and beat up everybody in the other pub, smash the windows, do damage. Then they would all go and play football together afterwards.

We heard Rothermere had started supporting the Blackshirts. Some of the staff agreed with him and started wearing Blackshirts to work. This is what we heard. It was trendy to do so, a fashionable thing. I knows it's true because when that phase ended, I was in Berlin and had a telegram from London, from the news editor, which said 'The Blackshirts are in the wash and the colour is running very fast.'

People stopped wearing their uniforms into the office, it was the end of the fashion and the trendies. What it meant to us in Berlin was we were no longer so friendly with the Nazis as we were before. It was a tip-off for us.

Was it the Olympia riot of 7 June that finished off the relationship between Rothermere and Mosley? Mosley had a different version.

According to Mosley's autobiography, an agitated Rothermere called him to his hotel room one afternoon where he lay, 'an imposing figure of monumental form lying flat on his back on a narrow brass bedstead ... an incongruous setting for one of the richest men in the world'. There, Rothermere informed Mosley he was pulling out. He was having trouble with his Jewish advertisers over his support of the movement, he explained. The cigarette scheme had met with even less approval.

Mosley's response was devilish. He said,

> Do you know what Northcliffe would have done? He would have said, 'One more word from you, and the *Daily Mail* placards tomorrow will carry the words: "Jews threaten British press"'; you will have no further trouble.

But even with an argument as persuasive as Mosley imagined this one to be, Rothermere was not convinced. The Blackshirt leader chalked down his stubbornness to the whimsy of the rich.

But besides Olympia and the Jewish-advertiser thesis, there was still one more version as to why Rothermere wished to distance himself from the Fascist movement, this one more closely aligned with the date of the proprietor's withdrawal. On 30 June 1934, in the Hanslbauer Hotel at Wiessee on the shores of the Tegernsee, an event took place that came alternately to be called the 'Blood Purge' or 'The Night of the Long Knives'. Hitler's long-time colleague and supporter, Ernst Röhm, along with some seventy-seven of his SA followers, had been butchered under the most chilling of circumstances. It was not the first violence perpetrated by the Nazis, but in no way could it be construed as a random act committed by overly enthusiastic underlings. Hitler was implicated. Far from being an inspired campaign for economic and political reform, Fascism was now irrevocably identified as an organization of systemized terror. In the Home Office, there was at least one adherent to the theory that it was the Blood Purge, and not Olympia, that had shaken Rothermere out of Mosley's Blackshirt movement.

In a public exchange of letters, Rothermere and Mosley amicably parted company. Mosley took advantage of the opportunity to reiterate what his movement stood for. Rothermere stated his reasons for withdrawing as four-fold: he deplored the term 'Fascist', he feared the increasing anti-semitism of Mosley's organization and he opposed the substitution of a Corporate State run by officials and industrialists instead of Parliament. Also, by now, he had outlived his interest in a strong-man leadership, emphasizing that he believed a dictatorship wouldn't work, especially in Britain.

Rothermere's brief flirtation with British Fascism had ended. The Black-shirts would henceforth decline in respectability to the extent that, not long after the onset of the war, in May 1940, Tom Mosley and his wife, Diana, were arrested and interned under Regulation 18B. Rothermere's campaign had lasted barely six months. Of all those who looked to the movement for political deliverance, he was the first one out.

Was it because of Rothermere's controversial political views that the cir-culation of the *Daily Mail* began its perilous decline? The editorial staff were convinced of it. Thomas Marlowe, after twenty-seven years as editor of the newspaper, had resigned in 1926 after quarrelling with Rothermere, so went the rumours. After his departure and that of other key staff, it became easier for Rothermere's imprimatur to become the key factor in editorial policy. And Rothermere, who favoured the managers over the journalists, was no Northcliffe. For six years, the news editor who had been trained by Northcliffe, Walter Fish, edited the *Daily Mail*, and the quality of the paper remained high. But there followed a series of men who, perhaps overcome by the power of Rothermere's personality or perhaps simply passive by nature, chose to take a back seat.

To make matters worse, a new and vigorous young editor had taken over at the end of 1933 at the *Daily Express*. Mild-mannered and spectacled, Arthur Christiansen didn't seem the sort who would work a fourteen-hour day, pounding away at the competition as he cajoled and threatened his own staff into creating the classiest and most readable broadsheet on Fleet Street. But he was destined to become one of the Street's great legends, and, in finding him, Beaverbrook had pulled a coup.

At almost the same time, Beaverbrook at last bought back the shares the Daily Mail Trust held in the *Express*, paying 'less than half what he offered five years earlier', according to one of his biographers. He sold his Daily Mail Trust shares at a much higher figure. So, like a canary-swallowing cat, he had the satisfaction of saying, 'Rothermere used to be my brother. But he has no more brotherly love now that the *Express* has passed the *Mail*.' This was the usual self-congratulatory claptrap Max sometimes talked, since Rothermere actually stated in black and white that Max was his greatest friend, and he would brook no criticism of him from anyone. Nevertheless, Beaverbrook, freed from his financial ties with the *Mail*, now permitted the *Express* to attack the other paper openly.

This bothered Rothermere not at all. He had illustrated on a number of occasions his indifference to criticism, and especially from the newspapers. 'Do nothing' was his motto when confronted by calumny. And as for Max getting the better of him in circulation, the *Mail* was primarily a business to Harold, not a calling. Although he deplored losing out to the competition, what mattered to him was that his business prospered. He had no sentimentality about the *Daily Mail*, or indeed any of his other holdings.

Rothermere had sold *The Times* in 1922 without looking back. In 1931, he disassociated himself with equal indifference from the *Mirror* and the *Sunday Pictorial*. He wrote briskly to the managing director of the company:

> Referring to our conversation this morning, I wish you to understand most clearly that, in future, the Mirror and Sunday Pictorial businesses are entirely under your and your colleagues' control. As my responsibility, I am reserving for myself the Associated Newspaper Company, Northcliffe Newspaper Company and the Daily Mail Trust. This is sufficient for a man of my age.

It was. He had founded in 1928 a £3 million company called Northcliffe Newspapers, a chain of provincials to compete with the Berry Brothers who, until then, had enjoyed a primary position in the market. There followed a newspaper war that reached across most of England and Scotland, with Rothermere succeeding in Gloucestershire, Staffordshire, South Wales and Hull. In Bristol and Newcastle, the competition from the Berrys was much stiffer. Both chains resorted to give-away promotions in order to increase circulation, causing ruinous losses to both. At last, an agreement was reached. Rothermere was to leave Newcastle and not to start papers he had planned in Cardiff, Sheffield and Aberdeen. The Berrys left Bristol, and Rothermere took over the Derby *Daily Express*, which he merged with the *Daily Telegraph* to form the Derby *Evening Telegraph & Express*. At last in December 1932, Northcliffe Newspapers was wound up, and its remaining provincial papers passed to the parent company, Associated Newspapers.

The dissolution of the company was viewed in Fleet Street as a complete defeat for Rothermere, and at the time so it had seemed. But it gave Associated Newspapers a foothold in the provinces, and would, decades later, prove to be one of Rothermere's most lucrative and far-seeing investments. But, for now, it was a continuing source of ridicule – as was another of his schemes: for a tunnel beneath the English Channel to connect Britain with France. Churchill agreed with Rothermere that the idea had merit, but efforts to put it into operation were quickly halted by Stanley Baldwin.

It was just as well. Rothermere was facing other stumbling blocks. Inside Northcliffe House, a monument built by Rothermere to his brother in 1927, the atmosphere was rapidly becoming poisonous. A newly hired sub-editor, Arthur Wareham, who would one day become editor of the *Daily Mail*, wryly observed that, instead of being blamed on Rothermere's politics, the *Mail*'s slide in circulation was being blamed on the journalists:

> The day-to-day production of the paper was carried on under the system of bullying and insult ... But there can be no doubt that A.L. Cranfield, my first editor, was under great and constant pressure.

The pressure passed down the line. Wareham now realized why he had been so quickly and easily hired: he could just as quickly and easily be fired. In his first four months on the job, sixteen sub-editors were sacked. Those who stayed were subjected to endless jibes and insults. Meanwhile, competition with the *Express* reached mammoth proportions, with the *Mail* men hastily re-making the late editions to pick up the stories that had run in the earlier editions of the *Express*.

Inevitably, prima donnas appeared, and one of these was Collie Knox. Advised by Christiansen that his days on the *Express* were numbered, Knox put in his resignation and sauntered over to the *Mail* where he proposed to write Fleet Street's first column on the wireless, a criticism on the programming of the BBC. It would turn out to be a popular feature, and Knox emerged as one of the *Mail*'s stars. In a single year, he received 35,000 letters from readers, a fact that did not go unnoticed in the office .

No sub-editor could alter Knox's copy. They handled it only in order to write the headlines. The young Wareham remembered a day when eleven headlines were proposed and discarded for one of Knox's columns. For a big name like Knox, working conditions at the *Mail* were superb – the finest on the Street.

It was an extraordinary experience working in the *Daily Mail* office after the

Express. Here no one worked in shirt sleeves and no one dashed about or shouted . . . The atmosphere was more like that of a cathedral than a newspaper office . . . No fuss, no noise . . . No undue excitement.

In the reporters' room as well, the environment was more like a club than a business office.

There was a large open coal fire and a hanging bell which would bring a boy to carry you tea and toast. The news editor was a safe distance away, twenty yards down the corridor in the news room. The connecting link was an old-fashioned, crook-handled telephone, but sometimes in moments of stress the news editor would scurry down the corridor looking for some reporter.

Six tape machines lined the walls, spewing out miles of the narrow tapes which were then pasted up by boys and taken to the news room.

Reporting was a man's game, but in November 1932 a young woman named Margaret Lane joined the staff. The daughter of Harry Lane, who had edited the *Sketch* and later went on to direct Northcliffe Newspapers, Lane had been educated at Oxford. After leaving university, in an act singularly intrepid for a woman of her generation, she travelled to the United States where she managed to get an interview with the notorious Al Capone. Legend had it that Capone had rejected all requests from journalists, but when he saw Lane, who was very pretty, he changed his mind. From then on, her reputation in the business was secure, and she went from triumph to triumph. In America, she was gratified to discover, journalists were considered very important people. Police officials tended to adopt her, giving her access to 'most-wanted' criminals and even offering her a 'ringside seat' at an electrocution, an invitation she declined.

After Lane came back from America, she free-lanced at the 'line rate', quickly earning more than many of her male colleagues on staff – much to their chagrin. When the R101 went down in flames near Beauvais in France, Lane covered the story, bringing back a grisly account of how one of the women aboard the airship had been wearing pearls that had to be dug out of her brain. Another story that helped to make Lane's reputation was an exclusive interview with Frau Goebbels. Lane was the only British woman on Fleet Street who got near the Nazis.

Margaret Lane was unique. At a time when no one at her professional level lived in the East End of London, she made it her home, commuting into Fleet Street from Wapping. From her experiences there, she wrote a novel, *Faith, Hope, No Charity*, for which she won the Prix Femina-Vie Heureuse for 1935. Recognizing her as a talent, Beaverbrook decided to poach her from the staff and invited her to dinner to make a deal. Perhaps naïvely, she turned him down because she had already made plans. She didn't get a second chance. Her fate nevertheless was not a bad one: she would go on to become one of the star columnists on the *Mail*, she would marry the eldest son of Edgar Wallace and later, after her divorce, go on to marry the Earl of Huntingdon. From that time, she devoted herself to books, including biographies of Edgar Wallace and Beatrix Potter.

Lane paved the way for other women to enter the profession. One of them, who came in some time after Lane, was a young woman named Rhona Churchill. She was hired by the legendary news editor Jimmy Lawrence. Strict, aloof and abrasive, Lawrence nevertheless had a reputation for being fair:

> When I went in one morning, only a few weeks after Mr Lawrence had engaged me, wearing a diamond ring on the third finger of my left hand, he sent for me. 'Miss Churchill,' he said. 'Am I to understand that you have become engaged?' 'Yes, Mr Lawrence,' I said. 'Well, I can only say I'm sorry,' he said. 'I would not have given you a job on my staff had I known you had marriage in mind. I could have trained you to become a great reporter. Now you will be of little use to me.'
>
> He was a wise old owl. His dressing down merely made me more determined than ever to make good on the *Daily Mail*. But doing so did mean that the marriage had to make allowances for the fact, for instance, that I had to work every other Sunday (Fleet Street's daily paper reporters in those days worked an eleven-day fortnight), and that though my hours were 11 a.m. to 6 p.m., the 6 p.m. was an illusion. One stayed on the job until one's day's work was done, even if it meant the last minute cancellation of a dinner or theatre date or staying away overnight. But dear old Jimmy Lawrence must also have adjusted, for he frequently sent me, with two tickets, to cover glittering Establishment or Society functions, such as the Lord Mayor's Banquet or the Queen Charlotte's Ball for the year's debutantes. And when he eventually retired and I, at about the same time, left to have a baby, he left a memo to the editor suggesting I should be given my job back if I ever asked for it.

Rhona Churchill did eventually ask for her job back, and ended up becoming the best-known woman war correspondent of the Second World War.

But the biggest star who wrote for the paper rarely saw the inside of the building. For years, Winston Churchill had been a free-lancer for the *Daily Mail*. Then he suffered the double blow of big losses in the stock-market crash of 1929 and also being passed over for Ramsay MacDonald's 'all-Party Government'. Thus did Churchill's by-line become a familiar presence in the *Daily Mail*. He was awarded a lucrative contract negotiated by Esmond's friend Brendan Bracken in August 1931 that stipulated a reported £8,000 for a series of weekly articles.

Perhaps his most colourful piece was written during a lecture tour that was scheduled to take place in the United States. Churchill's agent had negotiated some forty lectures for £10,000, but he ended up delivering none of them. For, as he was searching for Bernard Baruch's house on Fifth Avenue in New York, he crossed the street, looking the wrong way, and was struck down by a car. Suffering serious blows to the forehead and thighs, Churchill was then carried by a taxi to the hospital, where he developed pleurisy.

He eventually ended up in a room at the Waldorf-Astoria, where he wrote a full account of the accident for the *Daily Mail*. A fine photograph of him appeared in the 5 January issue of the newspaper. In it, he is sitting in a wicker wheelchair bundled up in an overcoat and warm hat, holding his cigar aloft in what was to become his trademark gesture.

The story appeared under the headline, 'My New York Misadventure: I Was Conscious Through It All; How It Feels to be Smashed Up.'

> I certainly suffered every pang, mental and physical, that a street accident or, I suppose, a shell wound can produce. None is unendurable. There is neither the time nor the strength for self-pity. There is no room for remorse or fears. If at any moment in this long series of sensations a grey veil deepening into blackness had descended upon the sanctum I should have felt or feared nothing additional. Nature is merciful and does not try her children, man or beast, beyond their compass. It is only where the cruelty of man intervenes that hellish torments appear. For the rest – live dangerously; take things as they come; dread naught; all will be well.

In the cover letter to Esmond, he wrote, 'Have had horrible bump. Good wishes for New Year and love to your pets Ramsay and Baldwin.'

His stiff upper lip was rewarded fulsomely by his friends. Esmond, along with Lord Burnham, Sir Harry Goschen, Lord Lloyd, Lord Londonderry, Sir Harry McGowan, Sir Archibald Sinclair and Brendan Bracken, conspired to buy him a Daimler to celebrate his recovery. Less well known was the probability that in 1922, when he purchased it, the Rothermeres had contributed heavily towards the cost, and later on, the upkeep of Chartwell, Churchill's country home in Kent. He was moreover a frequent guest at Harold's villa in Monte Carlo, La Dragonnière, where he painted during the day and talked with Rothermere into the night about the rise of Adolf Hitler.

It was no wonder, even in these wilderness years, that Churchill was so self-assured and self-centred. If all else failed, he was still the darling of the *Daily Mail*.

But there was more in the relationship than a bit of chat and a few feature articles. These days Winston and Harold shared the same dark view of the Government as well as the belief that a strong air force was the only power that could protect Britain if war came again.

In an article written as early as November 1932, Churchill had already begun harping on what was to become nothing less than an obsession. He was calling for

measures necessary to place our Air Force in such a condition of power and efficiency that it will not be worth anyone's while to come here and kill our women and children in the hope that they may blackmail us into surrender.

This theme continued, becoming more and more familiar in the pages of the *Mail*. Then, only a few days after the Night of the Long Knives, in early July of 1934, Churchill wrote,

I marvel at the complacency of Ministers in the face of the frightful experiences through which we have all so newly passed. I look with wonder upon our thoughtless crowds disporting themselves in the summer sunshine, and upon this unheeding House of Commons, which seems to have no higher function than to cheer a Minister. A terrible process is astir. Germany is arming.

That August, in a letter to his wife, he pointed to a strange new trend in the *Daily Mail*. 'I was disgusted by the *Daily Mail*'s boosting of Hitler,' he wrote.

[Rothermere] wants us to be very strongly armed and frightfully obsequious at the same time. Thus he hopes to avoid seeing another war. Anyhow, it is a more practical attitude than our socialist politicians. They wish us to remain disarmed and exceedingly abusive.

Churchill, as usual, was right, both about the socialist politicians and about the new leanings inside the *Daily Mail*. The newspaper, always friendly towards Mussolini, seemed these days to have adopted Adolf Hitler as well. Inside the offices of the newspaper, the trend was regarded as chilling – and utterly indefensible.

The first occasion upon which Rothermere chose to write about Adolf Hitler had been in an article, date-lined Munich, that appeared in the *Daily Mail* on 24 September 1930, ten days after the Reichstag Elections in which Hitler's National Socialists emerged as a major party. 'Germany and Inevitability', said the headline: 'A Nation Reborn'; 'Youth Asserting Its Power'; 'New Chapter in Europe's History'.

Rothermere had travelled to Munich 'to examine at close range' what he deemed to be *the* major event of the decade – 'an enduring landmark of this time'. It would stand out in history, he wrote, 'as the beginning of a new epoch in the relations between the German nation and the rest of the world'.

> What are the sources of strength of a party which at the general election of two years ago could win only 12 seats, but now, with 107, has become the second strongest in the Reichstag, and whose national poll has increased in the same time from 809,000 to 6,400,000!
>
> Striking as these figures are, they stand for something far greater than political success. *They represent the rebirth of Germany as a nation.*

The vast majority of those who had voted for the Party, he pointed out, were between the ages of twenty and thirty, showing that the new trend reflected the values of youth. 'To underestimate the importance of these events would be folly,' Rothermere wrote, 'and in my belief, to over-estimate it would be difficult.'

> A new Germany is rising before our eyes. She is strong today; she will be much stronger a few years hence. She is determined now; she may before long be defiant.

It was significant that Harold had actually travelled to Munich to observe the reactions of the German populace at a time when most of the British, and certainly those in charge of government, were indifferent to what was happening there. His interest intersected a seemingly unrelated event taking place in the Dorchester Hotel in London.

The adventurous Princess Stephanie Hohenlohe, invited to live at the fabulous new hotel at a reduced rate, had, despite this useful windfall, found herself distinctly down on her luck. It was a case of too much gambling, too many jewels, too many furs, too many shooting-boxes and, well, far too generous a nature, her son would explain some years later. A close friend of Princess Steph's had dropped in on her at a time when she was fretting over her financial straits.

Her companion had a brainstorm: 'Rothermere owes you a living!' he exclaimed, and ordered her to get in touch with him right away. After all, the great press lord had enjoyed the benefit of her guidance on the unfairness of the Treaty of Trianon, and he had gained international fame because of it. Now that Princess Steph was feeling the pinch, she should become a journalist; indeed, she was a natural-born journalist, if only she would realize it! Reluctantly, the petite Princess allowed that this was true. And after only one request, Princess Steph was able to see Rothermere, who swiftly agreed to use her as a personal courier of sorts, to make contact with persons of importance he might wish to see on the Continent, for as a Hohenlohe, even though she was now divorced from the Prince, she had entrée into the highest circles of European society. Thus, on 29 July 1932, Princess Stephanie entered into a contract to become Rothermere's anonymous ambassador abroad for a period of three years at a remuneration of £5,000 a year, with an extra £2,000 for each assignment.

Her first few assignments were a test of her reliability and her discretion, which on one occasion at least were found wanting. On 1 November 1933, Rothermere sent her a terse note, saying, 'You have been talking about me. If you continue to do this I shall be unable to see you.' Suitably chastened, the Princess calmed down into her duties, and on instruction from Rothermere, began to make inroads with 'her friend in Berlin' on a project he had in mind. The friend would turn out to be Captain F. Wiedemann, one of Hitler's closest adjutants.

In the meantime, articles touting Hitler's rise to power had appeared more frequently in the pages of the *Daily Mail*, the most famous perhaps the leader 'Youth Triumphant' written by Rothermere in July 1933 from 'Somewhere in Naziland'. The editorial praised the Nazi regime 'for its internal accomplishments, both spiritual and material'.

'Something far more than a new government has arisen among the Germans,' Rothermere wrote.

> There has been a sudden expansion of their national spirit like that which took place in England under Queen Elizabeth. *Youth has taken command.*

And if it was true that there had been 'minor misdeeds of individual Nazis', Rothermere added, these would certainly be 'submerged by the immense benefits that the new regime is already bestowing upon Germany'. So complimentary was the article that it was later used by the Nazis for propaganda purposes.

Rothermere's support of the Fascists was attributed to his hatred of the Soviet system, and along with the *Morning Post* and the *Observer*, the *Daily Mail* was accused of becoming 'unbalanced on the issue of Communism'. To an extent this was true, but Rothermere wasn't the only one. Lloyd George believed Hitler represented 'a bulwark against Bolshevism', and J.L. Garvin, the editor of the *Observer*, certainly leaned to the right in order to compensate for his dislike of the left. It was in fact not an easy stance to maintain – 'balance' on the matter of Communism. By now, the excesses of the Bolsheviks were beginning to come to light. Stalin had initiated the first of his Five-Year Plans, one that institutionalized slavery by deporting the kulaks from Ukraine to Siberia and, in the world's first man-made famine, literally starving to death those left behind by requisitioning their grain. This he dumped on international markets, including Great Britain, in order to finance the industrial sector of the Soviet Union and thus build a stronger country. And although the sinister show trials and purges were still in the future, it was increasingly clear to anyone who wished to see that the Reds were awash in a sea of their own blood.

Against this background, Rothermere received on 22 August 1934 a cryptic note from Princess Stephanie Hohenlohe:

> I have seen both your friends and have much of interest to tell you.
>
> Please let me impress upon you that you ought to see H. now. I know he already has some doubts as to your sincerity. I hope you have not forgotten that you assured him in your last letter you would see him the latter part of August.
>
> You surely realise that his position is now legally established for many years to come and he is fully conscious of it, because he knows that no other Government Chancellor or President in any other country in the world has ever received such an overwhelming majority.
>
> He intends to discuss his present and future plans with you and I think it is for the first time more to your interest than to his for you to see him.
>
> Will you ring up on Thursday at 12 noon as you suggested.
>
> Yours,
>
> Stephanie Hohenlohe

Despite the self-importance of her Mata Hari chic – a style destined to characterize Princess Stephanie more and more as she became involved in serious international intrigue – she *had* delivered the goods. This fact would later lay her open to accusations of being 'Hitler's mistress', 'Hitler's henchman', 'Hitler's spy' and 'Germany's paid agent'. As a matter of record, she was Rothermere's paid agent. And although rumours circulated, most strangely of all in the files of the United States Federal Bureau of Investigation, that she was mistress to both Rothermere and to Hitler, the tone of the letters between the press lord and princess remained austere throughout their relationship, clearly a partnership of employer and employee. It was even more dubious the Führer would have become sexually enchanted by anyone so frequently accused as she was of being Jewish.*

No, Princess Stephanie's intimate relationship was with Wiedemann – as a keepsake photograph of her and the darkly handsome Nazi official

---

* German newspapers frequently alluded to her 'non-Aryan origins'.

would later make obvious. The heady mix of double-dealing and sex must have made for exquisitely dense pleasure. Perhaps as a result, Princess Steph was destined to make a lifelong career of 'ambassadorial' work.

As for Harold Rothermere's relations with Adolf Hitler, they quickly became cordial. For Hitler did appear to hold Rothermere in genuine esteem, in some part because of Northcliffe. When Rothermere met him the first time, the Führer had said, 'Lloyd George and your brother ... won the war for Britain.' A great admirer of strength, Hitler would naturally have accorded Northcliffe high respect, and now he was dealing direct with the great propagandist's brother. It was no little thing.

Indeed, by 19 December 1934, the baffling friendship between German tyrant and British press lord had warmed to the extent that Rothermere as well as Esmond, and the ever present G. Ward Price, were three of four foreigners among only two dozen guests who attended Hitler's first dinner party given in his official residence in Berlin. Amongst the others present were Goebbels, Gœring and Ribbentrop.

Rothermere visited Berchtesgaden three times, once in September 1936, again just after Christmas in 1937, and finally the following May. In return for his hospitality, Rothermere gave Hitler two priceless gifts, a Gobelin tapestry and, later, a jade bowl. His accompanying note said he knew Hitler was indifferent to worldly goods but he was 'sending this gift to Hitler the artist'.

As for the *Daily Mail*, at the same time other newspapers were condemning Hitler's regime for its abnormality – 'the most powerful and most brutal machinery of oppression which has ever been created', according to the *Daily Herald* – the *Mail* wrote that Germany was 'in the forefront of nations', and Hitler himself was 'stronger than ever and more popular with his countrymen'.

ADOLF HITLER TO HAROLD ROTHERMERE

22 June 1933 (five months after becoming Chancellor of the Third Reich): Her Serene Highness Princess Hohenlohe has today handed me on your behalf two copies of the *Daily Mail* and drawn my special attention to the articles by you ... I beg your kind acceptance, as a mark of my special thanks, of the enclosed signed photograph of myself. With the expression of my highest esteem, I am, Yours very truly, (signed) A. Hitler

7 December 1933 (seven weeks after withdrawing Germany from the League of Nations): I should like ... to express the appreciation of countless Germans, who regard me as their spokesman, for the wise and beneficial public support which you have given to a policy that we all hope will contribute to the enduring pacification of Europe ... It is my conviction that an Anglo-French understanding directed to the maintenance of genuine peace would serve a useful purpose. Germany herself has no aggressive intentions against France. Just as we are fanatically determined to defend ourselves against attack, so do we reject any idea of taking the initiative in bringing about a war ... I am convinced that no one who fought in the front trenches during the world war, no matter in what European country, desires another conflict!... We are ready to disarm to the limit, but only on condition that other nations do the same.

2 March 1934 (some four months before the failed Nazi Putsch in Vienna; Dollfuss murdered): I have already impressed upon the kind bearer of your letter and gifts how greatly I would be pleased to confide to you personally, Lord Rothermere, if a visit to Germany were possible, much good would surely ensue for the preparation and realization of a sincere understanding between the European nations, which to you, Lord Rothermere – as your important activity as a great publicist has proved – is as dear as it is likewise the objective of my political work.

19 June 1934 (eleven days before the Night of the Long Knives; Ernst Röhm and his followers murdered, end of the SA): To-day, I should merely like to say that the voices from the other side of the frontier ... [saying] Germany, under my leadership, will not last very long, seem to me too absurd for me to deal seriously with them. Those who are spreading such rumours are solely guided by the desire, in the anxiety to mourn over obsolete ideologies, not to allow Europe to be at rest. I am fully convinced that the history of the next few years will teach them differently.

3 May 1935 (six weeks after Hitler denounced disarmament terms of Versailles Treaty): I believe that some day it will be found in a methodical scientific examination of European history during the last 300 years that 1/10th of the blood spilt on the field of battle flowed entirely in vain, that is to say, in vain measured by the most natural interests of the peoples who took part therein ... England opened up the greater part of the world to the white race. An imperishable and unending service ... The security of the British world, position, so important to the whole white race, has been weakened rather than strengthened by concomitant and in part new international power factors ... When will reason at last prevail and the white race draw back from a development which otherwise would inevitably mean its end? I believe, my dear Lord Rothermere, that if it does not come from England and Germany, any hope for the future may well be buried at least within a humanly measurable space of time...

During the last 16 years, I have spoken in Germany at least 4–5000 times before small, large and gigantic audiences. There is, however, no speech of mine in existence, nor does there exist a single line, which I ever wrote in which, in conflict with that realization, I spoke against an Anglo-German understanding. On the contrary, I have fought for it, by the spoken and written word, for a long time . . .

In Germany, we have a wonderful saying: 'That God loves and blesses him who appears to demand the impossible.' I want to believe in that God!

20 December 1935 (six months after the Anglo-German Naval Agreement; Germany rearming): In replying to you now I ask you, dear Lord Rothermere, not to make any public use of my reply because it contains opinions which I would otherwise express in a different wording or probably not express at all. This letter contains only opinions and I have not the slightest doubt that they are entirely unsuited to influence public opinion or to make it change its own views in a world and a time in which public opinion is not always identical with the innermost insight and wisdom . . .

To-day an oil sanction against Germany would be of no avail as our own fuel production and our own oil-fields can produce an annual quantity several times as much as we needed in 1914–1918 during the Great War.

I do not know the conditions in Japan. For it is obvious that the question of existing stocks is also in all these cases of decisive importance . . .

. . . I can say that from the human point of view there is much that attracts us to the English, while on the other hand, from the political point of view, we have a good deal in common with present-day Italy. Obviously the German nation will not today be able to give noisy expression to its enthusiasm for a nation which only a year ago referred in its press to Germany very unfavourably not to say rudely. On the other hand, we cannot forget that years before that Italy and Signor Mussolini in particular have given us many proofs of a reasonable and often more than decent sympathy with our fate. We cannot be ungrateful . . . My Dear Lord Rothermere . . . I haven't taken a single step which cannot be planned long before and which I [would] not have taken otherwise . . .

For a hundred million years this earth has been moving around the sun and during this long period it has always been filled with the struggle of living beings for nourishment and later for dwelling and clothing, etc. It is certain that beings whom we can call men have existed on it for many millions of years. Innumerable influences produced constant changes in the distribution of property. Just as in each nation. The economic structure is constantly changing, changes occur outside the national limits. Climatic changes, discoveries of raw materials more or less strong on the one hand, while other nations become sterile, continually produce tensions which urgently require solutions . . .

You will understand, however, dear Lord Rothermere, that these problems more than others are wholly unsuited to be handled in front of the masses, but that ultimately they can only be discussed in a small and select group.

... I firmly believe that a time will come in which England and Germany will be the solid pillars in a worried and unstable world.

4 April 1936 (one month after Germany denounces Locarno Pact of 1925, reoccupation of the Rhineland): I sincerely thank you for the good wishes sent to me on the occasion of the electoral triumph and couple therewith my best wishes for your personal well-being.

22 April 1936: Warm thanks for your friendly thought and your good wishes on my birthday.

20 May 1937 (six months before Hitler's top-secret meeting with Nazi officials, outlining policy of 'Lebensraum' – territorial expansion): Your leading article published last week, which I have read with great interest, contains everything which coincides with my own ideas.

Undated, January 1938 (three months before the Anschluss): For your friendly thoughts and good wishes at the new year which I cordially reciprocate I express to you my heartfelt thanks.

Undated (Munich): I appreciate your hopes that I should become as popular in England as Frederick the Great was. Your reference of Adolf the Great is also very flattering but I do not aspire to other than plain Adolf Hitler. Thanks kind congratulation.

HAROLD ROTHERMERE TO ADOLF HITLER

29 April 1935: My dear Fuhrer ... No one is more wholeheartedly in favour of an Anglo-German understanding than myself, and if there is any information which Your Excellency can impart which might further this cause I can assure Your Excellency that such information would only be used as you might desire and determine.

I esteem it a great honour and privilege to be in correspondence with Your Excellency. It is not often that anyone has an opportunity of learning the views of one who may occupy the first place in all European history.

I hope Your Excellency is taking great care of yourself. The burden on your shoulders is almost beyond human strength.

Undated: 1. Will Oil Sanctions against Italy stop the Italo-Abyssinian War?

2. How other powerful and highly-armed countries like Germany and Japan, neither of which have oil-producing areas, will regard an oil embargo against Italy in view of the fact that a similar measure may be taken against either of them?

3. Whether now is not the time to raise the question of the return of

the German colonies held under the mandates of Great Britain and France?

4. Whether the return of these colonies can be accomplished by peaceful means?

Undated: 1. Will the Reds win the war in Spain? If so what will be the effect in Europe?

2. Is it possible for to do anything in regard to Hungary's claims for revision . . . ?

3. Does your Excellency see any way by which an agreement in regard to the limitation of armaments can be reached?

4. What are the prospects of peace during the next three or four years?

5. Does your Excellency think it possible for your government to make a definite proposal of the conditions on which Germany would rejoin the League of Nations?

Undated, April 1937: MAY I JOIN THE MYRIADS OF THOSE WHO ON YOUR BIRTHDAY WILL BE WISHING YOU LONG LIFE TO CROWN YOUR EFFORTS TO ACHIEVE GOOD GOVERNMENT LIBERTY AND PEACE.

26 September 1938 (Munich): IN THE NAME OF OUR OLD FRIENDSHIP AND OUR COMMON DESIRE FOR PEACE BETWEEN OUR PEOPLES I DO URGE YOUR EXCELLENCY TO USE YOUR INFLUENCE TO POSTPONE THE DECISIVE MOMENT OF OCTOBER FIRST TO A LATER DATE THAT TIME MAY BE GIVEN TO ALLAY PRESENT PASSIONS AND PROVIDE OPPORTUNITIES FOR REACHING ADJUSTMENTS OF DETAIL.

26 September 1938 (Munich): CONFIDENTIAL MY DEAR FUHRER YOU HAVE HAD PROOFS OF MY FRIENDSHIP TOWARDS GERMANY AND I AM CONFIDENT YOU WILL NOT RESENT IT IF I VENTURE RESPECTFULLY TO APPEAL TO YOU BEFORE YOU SPEAK TONIGHT PEACE AND WAR ARE IN THE BALANCE AND LIKE YOU I KNOW WHAT ARE THE HORRORS OF WAR FOR AS YOU ARE AWARE I LOST TWO OF MY THREE SONS IN THE LAST WAR A HOPEFUL WORD FROM YOU WOULD BRING RELIEF TO MILLIONS.

1 October 1938 (aftermath Munich, Britain rearming): PERSONAL MY DEAR FUHRER EVERYONE IN ENGLAND IS PROFOUNDLY MOVED BY THE BLOODLESS SOLUTION OF THE CZECHOSLOVAKIAN PROBLEM STOP PEOPLE NOT SO MUCH CONCERNED WITH TERRITORIAL READJUSTMENT AS WITH DREAD OF ANOTHER WAR WITH ITS ACCOMPANYING BLOODBATH STOP FREDERICK THE GREAT WAS A GREAT POPULAR FIGURE IN ENGLAND MAY NOT ADOLF THE GREAT BECOME AN EQUALLY POPULAR FIGURE STOP I SALUTE YOUR EXCELLENCYS STAR WHICH RISES HIGHER AND HIGHER.

18

'Butter'

Rothermere, of course, was informing to the British Government.

The Night of the Long Knives was not the determinant of his plan to do so – he had made that decision eight months earlier – but the cold-blooded murder of Hitler's once-close associates acted to renew his personal sense of mission. A little over three months after the annihilation of the SA, on 5 October 1934, he wrote to Neville Chamberlain, then Chancellor of the Exchequer under Ramsay MacDonald:

> The oligarchs of Germany are the most dangerous, ruthless men who have ever been in charge of the fortunes of a people of 67,000,000 in number. They will stop at nothing. Violent as they were on the 30th of June in internal politics, they will be equally or more violent in external politics.

It did not take a visionary to come to this conclusion, but it did require some insight – more, it seemed, than the British Cabinet was able to muster. To the cynical mandarins of Downing Street, observations like Rothermere's were at best alarmist, at worst overbearing. They certainly didn't help get out the vote. There was, moreover, something slightly distasteful about all this sense of purpose. In the minutes of the Foreign Office, the press lord was called 'the craven Lord Rothermere'.

It was this sort of attitude that persuaded Rothermere to take matters into his own hands, as he later explained to Winston Churchill; that, and a chance occurrence that caused Hitler to seek Rothermere out, offering his friendship:

> He has a strange sentimental regard for me, because in the year 1930 I wrote an article in the *Daily Mail*, proclaiming that Hitler would be the eventual ruler of Germany.
>
> Hitler read extracts of this article in German papers. At the moment he was feeling rather down on his luck, but (he says) this article had an immense invigorating influence on him. He really believes that in consequence he is under some debt of gratitude to me.

This was the article written by Rothermere himself from Munich, where he had gone to view 'at close range' what he ambiguously termed 'an enduring landmark of this time'. It was the rebirth of a nation, Rothermere had written, pointing out the number of young voters who had cast their lot with Hitler's National Socialist Party.

But Rothermere remained under no illusion as to the nature of the Nazi Party. In December 1933, he wrote to the British Ambassador to France, Lord Tyrrell, speculating as to what Hitler represented to the future of Europe:

> Personally, I think there is not the least doubt as to what will happen within the next three or four years.
>
> Germany is going to burst her bonds...
>
> I have travelled to Germany repeatedly in the last four or five years. I prophesied Hitler would be the eventual ruler of Germany, years before Germans thought so themselves.
>
> Hitlerism means war. Unlike the last war, the next war will be fought with the entire concurrence and endeavour of every German man, woman and child.

By the following February he admitted to having become obsessed by the idea 'that Germany will spring a surprise war on one or other of her antagonists in the Great War'. This was the reason, he wrote to Lady Vansittart, the wife of the then Permanent Under-Secretary of State for Foreign Affairs, that he was maintaining 'a close communication which I have established with Herr Hitler'.

> I think when the emergency comes this relationship might be of great value to this country.
>
> He tells everyone that I alone among the great newspaper proprietors of the world outside Germany was the only one who gave himself and the Nazi movement a fair deal.
>
> He is quite sentimental on this question.
>
> I do not believe what either he or General Goering say in regard to Germany's war preparations, or really what they say in regard to the specific intentions of their country...
>
> My policy is quite clear. It is to endeavour to keep on friendly terms with Germany, but to say all the time that circumstances and not personalities rule events.
>
> Even if Hitler and Goering were pacifists, which I do not for one moment believe, the present Austrian situation might force Germany into a war.
>
> If we had a Government led by really great statesmen, it would make clear to the people of this country the dangers of aerial warfare, and the necessity of

adequately guarding the country whether there was any immediate chance of a war or no.

And in May 1935 he wrote to Ramsay MacDonald, then Prime Minister, saying that he had been successful in establishing a special relationship with the Nazi dictator, having 'built up a fund of some good will with him'.

> If in the coming emergency days an informal, semi-official conversation between him and me can serve any national purpose, I place my services at the disposal of the Government.

Whether MacDonald would have welcomed Rothermere in such a role remains an unanswered question, because in June the Conservatives, led by Stanley Baldwin, were returned to power for the third time, putting any such possibility out of reach.

By now, Rothermere's pessimism had full rein over his thinking because of Britain's steadfast refusal to rearm even in the face of conclusive evidence that the Nazis were dangerous men bent on fracturing the fragile peace that had existed since the Great War. France was disorganized and weak, Rothermere believed; Mussolini had been side-tracked by his war on Abyssinia. Germany, once she was sufficiently armed, would not hesitate to attack Britain, France or Italy. When that happened, Hitler would have 'an easy win', so Rothermere speculated.

Meanwhile, the press lord's position with the Nazi dictator had improved to the extent that, when Hitler saw *Daily Mail* correspondent G. Ward Price at a tea-party in the hall of the Deutsch Hof, he actually embraced him, holding him 'by the shoulders with both hands'. Ribbentrop later told Ward Price, that when he had dined with the Führer the night before, 'entirely of his own impulse' the Chancellor had remarked,

> Rothermere is one of the very greatest of all Englishmen. He is the only man who sees clearly the magnitude of this Bolshevist danger. His paper is doing an immense amount of good. I have the greatest admiration for him.

For his part, Rothermere believed his British compatriots were dealing tactlessly with Hitler, and when addressing the German dictator he resolved to use 'the language of butter because these dictators live in such an atmosphere of adulation and awe-struck reverence that the language of guns may not go nearly as far...'

Indeed, by now Hitler was rewarding Rothermere with letters as long as seven typewritten pages, written in German – *Verehrter Lord Rothermere!* – that were translated for the press lord by Flowerdew & Co. Ltd, Temple

Bar Chambers, whose offices were located on the Strand. They were signed with Hitler's strange emblematic first initial that, as he wrote it, looked not dissimilar to the Swastika, with the bizarre drop-off signature of his last name that resembled a ribbon flowing more and more narrowly. The mighty thud of Hitler's forced-march prose, with its passing references to masses ruled by 'small, select groups', seems by modern frames of reference very like that of Dr Strangelove. It was more than stolid and boring, more even than German: it was Nazi. Pages and pages of Hitler's autonomic screed worked their way into Rothermere's files.

Hitler loved Rothermere.

His sentiments were not shared by members of the British Government.

HAROLD ROTHERMERE TO GOVERNMENT MINISTERS AND OTHERS. *To Sir Robert Vansittart, Permanent Under-Secretary for Foreign Affairs, 16 February 1934*: Would you return the Hitler letter and my reply?

I think you must expect nothing but disappointment from the Eden Mission.* It was, perhaps, the only thing to do in the circumstances, but when you have a Government which is quite unable to make up its mind, it must be almost impossible for high officials like yourself to know what to do.

I am keeping in active touch with my German friends.

To Sir Robert Vansittart, 3 April 1934: I send you another letter I have received from Hitler ...

Our defenceless condition is an open invitation to attack. We have more loot and less means of defence than any similar people in history.

To Winston Churchill, MP, 31 August 1934: Will you tell Van I entirely disagree with him in regard to his information about Germany's air preparations. The new type of aeroplane on which the Germans are concentrating is a single-seater, single-engine, tremendously high-speed light-bomber with great manoeuvring powers. The Germans are making this machine in series, and it is no more difficult to make than sewing machines or £100–£200 cheap motor cars ...

To Ramsay MacDonald, Prime Minister, 30 September 1934: When one knows the preparations being made by the Germans, the programme of adding 600 aeroplanes to our Air Force within the next five years amounts to little more than a tragic hoax ...

The Junker Works at Dessau, not far from Berlin, will be complete by

---

* On 21 February, Anthony Eden was in Berlin to discuss the disarmament impasse; there, he was told by Hitler he was prepared to reduce the SA by two-thirds. No doubt Hitler made the statement in good faith since, at the end of the following June, the SA was obliterated in the Blood Purge.

the end of November. They are four times the size of the Ford Dagenham Works and the 16,000 present employees are to be increased to 30,000.

Moreover, the Germans are engaged in the intensive manufacture of submarines...

[They] claim they can build a new aerodrome in seven weeks...

To Neville Chamberlain, Chancellor of the Exchequer, 5 October 1934: Today Germany, day and night, week in week out, is building an immense air force with, as many people think, the intention of raiding and ravaging England and France. Yet the National Government, whose first duty is to secure national safety, has apparently nothing more than the most meagre programme for meeting this supreme menace...

Today money is voted for the upkeep and extension of unnecessary war vessels and for the upkeep of Cavalry forces which should be spent solely on the Air Force.

I am quite sure that by redistribution of expenditure – and this is why I am writing to you – the present moneys voted for the fighting services are sufficient provided that of the expenditure not less than 50% is voted in the Air Estimates.

I do beg of you to use your influence to make your colleagues see this matter in its proper perspective.

To J.C. Davidson, Chancellor of the Duchy of Lancaster, 7 October 1934: For some months past I have been seeing numbers of people who have had interviews with [Hitler] and others who, in the course of repeated visits to Germany, have collected much information in regard to that country's armaments...

Personally I have no doubt he and his ruthless associates intend immediately he has a command of 30,000 or 40,000 aeroplanes to wage an aerial war against France and ourselves if we stand with her. Such a war might put our very existence at stake...

We have two alternatives: either we must arm to the teeth in the air or we must follow a policy of neutrality dangerous as it may be. The really dangerous policy is to assure France that we [will] help her in the grave emergency that may lie almost immediately ahead when our fighting resources are quite negligible.

To the Marquess of Londonderry, Secretary of State for Air, 28 October 1934: I do not suppose you expected to have a reply from me to your last official communication.

It was just the kind of communication I expected because your Ministry – and you are in no way to blame – has, in its short life of 20 years, managed to accumulate more red tape than the Admiralty during its record of more than three centuries...

I am not blaming you, although your term of office is rather a long one. With bi-planes and wooden propellors quite apart from other eccentricities of design, it is difficult to make anything of the Air Force. A technical department responsible for R101 is capable of anything...

To Commander Sir Bolton Meredith Eyres-Monsell, First Lord of the Admiralty, 5 November 1934: More than twelve months ago M. Herriot, French Minister at Geneva, told our correspondent, Mr. Cardozo, that according to their information a factory in Germany was manufacturing a great number of periscopes.

This information, he said, was passed on to London but the authorities there did not believe it.

The great firm of Unilever has £6,000,000 or £7,000,000 frozen in Germany. To release some of this money the Directors decided to build cargo steamers at German shipyards, to use the vessels either for their own business or to sell them in the international market. They asked for tenders from the largest German shipyards but were told that no tenders could be submitted as they were full of orders. On further inquiries they found there were no ships on the stocks but under cover there was intense activity in the shipyards and they satisfied themselves that this activity was concerned in the intensive building of a new type of submarine...

It is I think obvious that at the outbreak of Hitler's coming war against the West, German submarines will be found on all the great trade routes and in the vicinity of the warships of Germany's enemies.

Would it not be as well closely to examine the measures for communicating with all British passenger and cargo vessels in the event of a six or twelve hours' ultimatum?

To Eyres-Monsell, 10 May 1935: Hitler states that the figure is nearly 11,000 'planes, all of the latest design and of great speed and range. Unlike other European Air Forces, he says the German Air Force is confined to three designs all of the same pattern. He says other European Air Forces comprise machines of largely varying designs, thus rendering them much less effective. He says an Air Force consisting of many designs is like an army with five or six different kinds of field-guns.

P.S. Germany has been building submarines for more than fifteen months. I understand she has now a flotilla of 80 which is rapidly increasing. She is applying some of the methods of mass production in the manufacture of this kind of craft. You will remember I wrote to you on this question on November 5 of last year.

Copies noted by hand to Baldwin, Vansittart, A. Chamberlain, N. Chamberlain, Lloyd George, Eyres-Monsell, Inskip, Churchill, Duff Cooper, Halifax, Weir, MacDonald, Sankey, Londonderry, 15 March 1936: In the presence of Hitler last Friday, Goering told Ward Price that every half hour Germany adds one new aeroplane to her air fleet and that 80 per cent of German aeroplanes are bombers.

GOVERNMENT MINISTERS AND OTHERS TO HAROLD ROTHERMERE:

From Neville Chamberlain, 30 October 1934: ... You will not expect me to argue the case for the Government's programme in connection with armaments, but I cannot think that it would do to neglect either the Navy or the Army in order to build up a gigantic Air Force. Aeroplanes at present do not bring us food or raw materials, and we must protect the trade routes; while armies are still necessary, if only to ensure us suitable locations for Air Forces...

From B. Eyres-Monsell, 12 November 1934: ... The Admiralty consider that even if the Germans had laid down some submarines it would not be possible for them to construct more than a few without authentic information becoming rapidly available; also, if a few are being constructed secretly, the number would be totally inadequate for any offensive on the trade routes.

It is impossible to operate submarines successfully without a highly trained force of officers and men, and the time required for the efficient training of such personnel is very considerable. As the Germans have no submarines in operation they have been unable to train this personnel.

With regard to the question of periscopes, it is known that Germany has been manufacturing these instruments, the principal firm thus engaged being Messrs. Zeiss and this firm has a branch in Holland from which it is known that periscopes have been exported to foreign countries.

The actual number of periscopes being manufactured in Germany is not known, but we think that the number is small, and that most of them are for export...

From Stanley Baldwin, 13 May 1935: I am much obliged to you for sending me a copy of Hitler's letter to you, together with the translation. I have read it with the greatest interest, etc.

From Neville Chamberlain, 10 May 1935: I am afraid I find the information about German air strength very confusing and contradictory, but a figure of eleven thousand aeroplanes appears to me quite incomprehensible. Even taking in all civil as well as military aircraft, I don't believe this figure can be accurate, [added by hand] unless 'gliders' are included.

From Londonderry, 14 May 1935: I have received your letter for which I am much obliged. I hope you will forgive me for following up what you say. It seems to me that if Hitler is ready to give you a number, he would also be ready to give you a description of the machines. I cannot help thinking that in the 11,000 are included a number of gliders which would of course, make all the difference. Again, importance is attached to gliding pilots and whilst of course, I am ready to believe that gliding pilots may have some value, still the value is a very small one. It is interesting to note that it is an established fact that pilots of engined machines are invariably bad gliders...

From Sir John Simon, 16 May 1935: ... and I must thank you in particular for your courtesy in letting me see the photostatic copy of the autographed letter which you received from Herr Hitler.

I need not assure you that the Government are devoting the most anxious and unremitting attention to the best means of solving ... most grateful to those who, like yourself ... take the trouble ... discharge of our formidable tasks, etc.

From Austen Chamberlain, 17 March 1936: I find it difficult to credit Goering's statement of the rate of production.

From Duff Cooper, 17 March 1936: Even if it were possible, as he says, to produce a new aeroplane every half-an-hour, it undoubtedly takes longer than that to train a pilot.

From Neville Chamberlain, 17 March 1936: ... I am not clear whether this meant day and night, or day only. If the latter, and taking five working days at eight hours a day, this would produce eighty aeroplanes a week, which doesn't seem at all improbable...

One man listened.

Winston Churchill wrote regularly to Rothermere, thanking him for any intelligence he could provide and sending back what he had managed to gather. It was thought that Churchill, isolated from the seat of power, was getting his information from Desmond Morton, the head of the Committee of Imperial Defence's Industrial Intelligence Centre, whose figures were consistently and substantially lower than Rothermere's. The pair of them – Churchill and Rothermere – then speculated together on what the actual figures were likely to be.

For his part, Rothermere admitted to distrusting all 'official sources of information'. 'They are nearly all inaccurate,' he wrote to Churchill, 'and are very often written by people who wish to believe what they state.' He reached his high count of German aircraft by including civilian aeroplanes, which were in any case, he maintained, 'convertible in an hour or two into bombing machines'. And although a good deal of his information came from the Führer and other top-ranking Nazi officials, he had other means of gathering information. In this he was like Northcliffe just before the Great War. But Rothermere was far more systematic in his sweep for information. The spy-cell he set up included correspondents for the *Mail*, carefully nurtured informants and highly placed German officials, none of whom was in his confidence – not even G. Ward Price, who was believed to be Rothermere's mouthpiece not only by the public but by Ward Price himself. Rothermere also made frequent forays into Austria, though he went to some trouble to keep these visits from being known.

In late January 1936, Churchill wrote to his wife Clementine that Rothermere, 'who has long letters and telegrams from Hitler and is in close touch with him', believed some sort of important announcement or military action was imminent. Soon thereafter, on 1 March, Hitler reached his decision to reoccupy the Rhineland, and at dawn on the morning of the 7th a small token force of German troops crossed the Rhine, entering the demilitarized zone. They met with no resistance from the French.

That summer Rothermere wrote to Churchill that he had 'read your gloomy article in the *Evening Standard*. But you are a blazing optimist compared with myself.' He was hoping that the war would not break out before 1938, but 'it could come at any moment'. Churchill wrote back thanking Harold for his letter:

As you will see I keep on trying my best. If as you say we are going to be vassals of Germany I can only hope I shall not live to see it.

You have been wonderfully right in your talks with me:

1. At Christmas predicting the violation of the Rhineland;
2. The collapse of the Abyssinian resistance; and
3. That Mussolini had squared Hitler about Austria.

My information tallies with yours that Czecho-Slovakia will soon be in the news.

But Rothermere had other information to share. At the end of 1937, he wrote to tell Churchill that he had seen from his speech in the House of Commons

that you are still harping on what I suppose is your belief in the invincibility of the French Army. *You are utterly mistaken.*

The French Army is slowly but surely sinking into a condition of chaos and confusion such as is beginning to distinguish the life of France. I hear that in some districts officers' pay is in arrears. There is a loosening of discipline. The artillery ammunition is deficient in quality and quantity ... Anything like a suicidal attempt to come to the aid of Czecho-Slovakia or Austria, in case of German intervention, would expose the fact that the French Government was trying out a policy to which nearly all the fighting men of France are utterly opposed.

The Air Force is beneath contempt. France still has a number of fine pilots but the number of fine aeroplanes is so small as to be almost negligible. Whereas in other countries like Germany new types of aeroplanes are manufactured within three or four months, it takes three or four years in France. Today nearly all the aeroplanes being delivered to the French Air Force are completely out of date ... Corruption in this vital branch of national defence reigns supreme.

Major-General Fuller states that the Maginot Line can be easily pierced. He says the German General Staff are fully aware of this and count in the next war on the defeat of France in the first few weeks at most...

I wish you would keep this letter.

Meanwhile, the British Government had succeeded in resisting rearmament with apparent pride; the policy certainly seemed the most popular course to follow. In a speech to the House of Commons in March 1935, Baldwin had proclaimed:

Our Air Force is fifth among the air forces of the world. We do not seek equality with the largest. We adhere to the position of equality with any Power which may be within striking distance.

At the time Baldwin made this skewed statement of intent, the Air Force had no more than 'a few hundred machines around the coast'. And on the morning that Hitler's handful of troops reoccupied the Rhineland, Britain's air power at home was down 'to about 400 first-line machines...'

Even in the wake of so telling an event, on 4 May 1936, Lord Londonderry wrote to his cousin Churchill what would turn out to be a dramatically premature 'I-told-you-so' letter:

... I never could convince you or Rothermere that there was no imminence of an invasion of Great Britain by Germany from the air. You have both been responsible by your speeches and writings for changing the attitude of the Government towards our defences and I certainly feel that we owe you a debt of gratitude, but your success was due to your being able to frighten the people of this country by giving them wholly exaggerated figures...

This grudging tribute showed the resentment the Establishment felt towards Churchill and Rothermere. Both of them were regarded with suspicion, if not contempt. To Churchill was ascribed the trait of being a 'Die-Hard Warmonger'; to Rothermere, the desire to boost the circulation of the *Daily Mail* – although, if truth be told, Rothermere's relentless hammering for rearmament was having the opposite effect and reducing circulation.

It was against this background of governmental irresponsibility and obstructionism that the press lord decided to take matters into his own hands.

With an investment of £5,000 of his own money, he started in 1935 the National League of Airmen, an organization whose goal was to stimulate 'the air sense in our population and [to foster] a rapid advancement in our Air Force strength'. For two shillings and sixpence, anyone could join. Full membership was awarded to pilots who had a hundred flying hours and associate membership to anyone who hoped one day to pilot a plane. Even Rothermere was surprised to discover how eager young men were 'to get into the air', and arrangements quickly followed to give associates the opportunity to take sufficient flying lessons to make them eligible to take the flying test for only £14. Later, Rothermere donated £10,000 to the RAF to be used for sports and recreational activities.

In addition, in 1936, the *Daily Mail* produced a publication, *Arming in the Air: The Daily Mail Campaign; Warnings of Three Wasted Years*. It consisted of leading articles from the *Mail* and relevant quotes from politicians that argued the case for aerial rearmament.

These projects showed the extent of Rothermere's determination to push through a policy of what he called 'air preparedness'. But he was not satisfied with stopping there. As early as March 1934, Rothermere had made enquiries to the Bristol Aeroplane Co. asking if they would build him an executive plane that was 'faster than anything available elsewhere'. He met with unexpected resistance. The company was frightened that 'a streamlined monoplane might offend their chief customer the RAF by highlighting the outmoded appearance of contemporary British war-planes'. But Rothermere wasn't having it. He had money. He could pay. And in such a test of wills, it was only a matter of time until the press lord prevailed.

Eventually, the Bristol 142 prototype was produced. It flew for the first time on 12 April 1935. Designed originally as a civil transport plane, the aircraft was named Britain First* by Rothermere, who sent immediately to the United States for two Hamilton variable-pitch propellers to replace the wooden units. Once these were installed, the aeroplane, whose original cruising speed was 260 m.p.h., was timed at 307 m.p.h. at 11,800 feet – 80 m.p.h. faster than any fighter in the RAF and 20 m.p.h. faster than anything the United States had. Its range was 1,450 miles.

The Britain First had two 645-horsepower Mercury engines, with a span of fifty-six feet, seven inches; a length of forty-two feet, nine inches; and

* Tom Mosley claimed Rothermere's name for the aeroplane derived from the Black-shirt motto, 'Britain First'.

could carry a three-man crew. On 9 July, the Air Ministry held a conference and, at Rothermere's request, began drafting new specifications in order to convert the aeroplane into a bomber. Eventually, the aircraft would have a bomb load of 1,320 pounds and it had an unusually spacious interior, a unique quirk in the design that was destined to make the plane invaluable in the first days of the coming war.

In August 1935, Rothermere, on behalf of the *Daily Mail*, formally presented the prototype to the RAF as 'a peace gift'. But, he went on to say, he still believed 'that a Britain well armed is the best guarantee of peace'. The Air Force renamed the aeroplane the Blenheim Bomber, placing an initial order for a hundred and fifty of the aircraft, which were delivered to the RAF by March 1937. Predictably, Rothermere was immediately accused of profiteering, but this time he was ahead of his critics, for he had long since taken care to rid himself of all investments which could in any way be construed as increasing in value in the event of the nation's active engagement in warfare.

Through his efforts, he managed to make the point that if an interested individual came up with a high-powered machine the nation badly needed, went to the trouble to have it designed and developed, built it, paid for it and gave it to them, well then, the Government might just accept it.

When then on 26 September 1938 the long-awaited German–Czech Crisis at last came to a head, culminating in the annexation of the Sudetenland by Germany and the controversial Munich Agreement, Rothermere optimistically wired Churchill: 'IF IT HADN'T BEEN FOR YOU AND ME THE COUNTRY WOULDNT BE NEARLY AS WELL PREPARED FOR THE ENCOUNTER AS IT IS TODAY HAROLD.'

That was his first reaction. But as the days passed, his optimism fell away. It was true he had tried, as had Winston – but it hadn't been enough. Rothermere was certain of it.

Four days later, on the 30th, in a follow-up letter marked '*Private and Confidential*', Rothermere predicted to his friend that 'the agreement signed in the early hours of this morning' would last no longer than 'nine or ten months'. When that time was up, he said, the British people would fold. And by the week's end Rothermere had sunk into one of his depressions, completely engulfed by his overriding pessimism.

'Munich in no way surprises me,' he wrote to his friend.

I should have been surprised if there had been any other outcome.

   There you had a struggle between parliamentarian and front-line fighters, between the Parliamentary system and the system of dictatorship.

Such a struggle is decided before it starts.

Britain is passing into the twilight. A moribund people with a moribund system of government cannot stand up to the perils of these times.

He added in a postscript: '... I know because I gave, and as it now appears wasted, five years of my time in an intensive endeavour to open their eyes.' Thus he descended into his own personal slough of despondency.

But typically, within the year, all his pessimism had melted away. In July 1939, he wrote to an old correspondent, Joachim von Ribbentrop, that the past few months had given him 'an opportunity of going through a large number of reports dealing with the outlook of the British people at the present time'.

It is unquestionable that they were never more determined. It is a sober, silent determination; nothing spectacular.

Our people have immense grit ... They are baffling sometimes to understand. They appear to foreigners to be casual and emotional. This they often are but behind this façade is a wonderful spirit.

Of this there is no question whatsoever. We air our minor deficiencies in the newspapers but in all the major factors of rearmament the development and work are splendid.

Moreover our young men are ideal pilots. Flying suits the adventurous spirit of our youngsters...

I do urge you to use all your great influence to prevent any upset over Danzig or Rumania. No one wants another three or four years' war.

Would Ribbentrop be so kind as to show his letter to the Führer? Rothermere asked in a postscript.

Within a fortnight, on 2 August, Rothermere put a follow-up into the mail:

I have never known the British people more warlike than they are today. They are talking as they did at the outbreak of the Great War and the Boer War.

The rearming of the country has been wonderfully well done; worthy of the best periods of British history. And this has given the people much confidence.

Ribbentrop fired back his reply:

... of one thing I am certain: if these two countries should ever clash again, it would this time be a fight to the very end and to the last man. And this time, every German conscious of the tremendous power of these 80 million people behind one man and of Germany's powerful allies, is convinced that this war would end with the German victory.

After receiving this missive, Rothermere bundled it up, along with his letter to Ribbentrop and, one more time, sent it to the Prime Minister and others high in the British Government. Despite everything, he was still informing.

And yet one more idea worth considering occurred to him. He sent the bare bones of it to the Minister of Agriculture at Whitehall, with a copy to the House of Commons:

URGENT AS A WAR MEASURE BEFORE IT IS TOO LATE DO PLEASE ISSUE STRONG RECOMMENDATION TO FARMERS ALLOTMENT HOLDERS AND PERSONS WITH BACK GARDENS TO GROW ALL POTATOES POSSIBLE ROTHERMERE

Viscount Rothermere: to all outward appearances the very epitome of the Capitalist. Of middle height and heavy build; dressed always very smartly, habitually pacing up and down, hands in pockets, expansive; yet with that delayed, clipped step so reminiscent of Empire. Like Northcliffe, he stood outside the magic circle of the Establishment.

Amongst the ruling classes, he was considered dangerous, unpredictable – a wild card. Nothing was overlooked in the tacit conspiracy to discredit him: Blackshirt, collaborator, profiteer, buffoon, alarmist, international busybody, as mad as Northcliffe; all those things and more. Each stroke of the tar brush incarnated a different individual; each offered a simple depiction that diminished the man.

It was said he zigzagged: first this, then the other. He couldn't make up his mind. An exasperated F.E. Smith, always a devoted friend, wrote him an eight-page, typewritten letter quoting back to him his own letters, showing him the inconsistency of his thinking, his changeability, his unreliability. Then, exhausted by the effort, F.E. admitted his profound affection for Harold and the durability of their friendship. But where the devil did Harold *stand*?

Inside Harold was a complicated machinery. Those who knew him well knew enough not to question the mechanism. His heart was good. He was loyal. He liked giving. He didn't zigzag, he simply reasoned by opposites. The duality peculiar to the Harmsworth family was in Harold more pronounced, and he grew accustomed to travelling in two directions at the same time. Perhaps it was the stockbroker in him, making parallel and opposing investments at the same time, hedging his bets, admitting to all possibilities.

Then there were his troubles. After the deaths of his sons, he had changed. One editor, Bernard Falk, said that as Harold grew older his personality and actions 'reflected his bitter disillusionment with life generally'. This contrasted starkly with the man in his mid-thirties; then he was, according to the same editor, 'full of fun, he seemed to extract the utmost enjoyment out of life, his hearty laugh being a thing to remember'.

This unending grief led to a pattern of dejection, depression, helplessness and resurgence that Harold re-enacted again and again. In the first stage, he was open to the extent of being ingenuous. Interviewers were sometimes shocked by the complete 'readiness and frankness' he showed in answering anything they asked, 'even with a most stunning openness and pointedness ...' As on the day he lunched with Arnold Bennett, Rothermere laid himself open for inspection with an honesty that was almost alarming. And what was revealed inside but grief? This he accepted, but desperately, descending into a bottomless well of depression. At times like these, he would retreat to his bed, shaking violently. Then, when the panic passed, he would rise up and act, with energy and conviction, until, exhausted, he fell again into dejection – only to repeat the pattern yet again.

'My father was a gloomy man,' Esmond said of Harold. Not even he was in his father's full confidence, and as Esmond grew older, they fell apart. Esmond left Parliament in 1931 to take over the Company, but behind the scenes he was still subject to his father's will. Now the pair of them would fall into genuine rows over the direction of the *Daily Mail*. Esmond no longer even pretended to understand his father's motives, or took it on faith that he was always right. He viewed him now as others did.

'There is nothing in modern politics – not even in German politics –' one commentator in the *News Chronicle* wrote, 'to match the crude confusion of the Rothermere mentality as revealed in the Rothermere Press. It blesses and encourages every swashbuckler who threatens the peace of Europe – not to mention direct British interests – and then clamours for more and more armaments with which to defend Britain, presumably against his lordship's pet foreign bully.' Beaverbrook's *Daily Express* also harshly criticized the *Mail* for harping on rearmament when it 'has spent the last five years assuring us that "Dolfie" Hitler is a wonderfully good fellow and is very fond of Britain'.

Esmond secretly agreed. In a telling memorandum, he systematically listed all that was wrong with the *Daily Mail*, tracing out its history since his father took over the newspaper from Northcliffe. From 1922 to 1926, he wrote, '*Daily Mail* supreme, 2,000,000 circulation'; from 1926 to 1929, '*Daily Mail* great money maker. All energies bent on this end. Paper crowded with advts. As a newspaper stagnates but impetus still visible.'

At the beginning of 1930, the great decline begins in earnest: 'Boosting of Beaverbrook and campaign against Baldwin.' From there, support of the Mosley Campaign: 'Many affronted,' Esmond wrote. By 1934, the newspaper had begun to defend 'Germany and Hitler at time when England affronted at their excesses ... All these campaigns unpopular and most ended in failure.' The memorandum went on sensibly to outline proposals to improve the newspaper as a commercial venture. If the newspaper were under his editorial control, he confided to a friend, he would discontinue all political campaigns, concentrate on the weather and make the *Mail* 'damned boring'.

But to Rothermere, the *Daily Mail* was of little importance in view of what he believed the future held. 'There is no real incoherence in what appears in my papers,' he wrote to a friend, 'although seemingly there might be.' He made genuine attempts to reconcile Britain with Germany, thereby buying time in which his country could rearm. If reconciliation didn't work, and from 1933 Rothermere had no belief it would, at least his country would be able to meet the menace. Rothermere was a strategist, not a tactician – a strategist who often despaired, a complex character indeed.

And what if there had been no Harold Rothermere, hammering away, upsetting the Old Boys, conspiring with Winston and generally making a muddle of government policy? How then would the country have fared?

Maybe Harold made no impact whatsoever on public attitudes and government policy during the 1930s. Then again, maybe he did.

19

'Home'

Lilian was dying. Like other privileged persons before her, she had believed that, by refusing to admit to life's pain, she could escape it. Now she learned otherwise, and her bitterness was without end.

She had skated over the surface of life, empowered by her wealth, but, despite her seeming frivolity, she harboured a secret malevolence. At one moment her letters to her son were lively and cheering; at the next, patronizing and condescending.

'We are going daily to Herbert's Physical Culture classes,' she wrote to Esmond from Deauville in the mid-1920s,

> and skip about clad in a short skirt was bare head, back, arms and legs and feet! Jumping sunning climbing – playing ball – it's wonderfully healthy . . .
> Oh, you might persuade the Pater to sell me the Rolls for £1300.

When in this mode, she signed herself 'Bluebell', and chattered on about new clothes and gramophones, travel and motor cars.

But when the other side was upon her, more frequently as she grew older and life's pleasures began to pall, she more and more wrote to her son in the dark mode, often critically, and signing her letters with the faintly shadowy, 'Your Mother'. Typical of Lilian's advice was a letter dated only 'Saturday' but written some time well into the 1930s. It was addressed to 'Darling Mondy' and traced out in her careless, swirling hand, now barely legible.

> There is only one life to be lived and you are only half living and it makes my heart ache as your mother – regretfully it seems – in name only! I am grieved beyond words – I have tried to be your friend but that also seems to have failed. That is to say: you do not want me – My own life fortunately is so full and complete so perfectly happy that I can live without your love and 'attention' but it overflows to you and to all who are not so fortunate as I am and in spite of everything I am very grieved that you and I are not more united. I could have been of so much use to you in so many ways – and let me tell you now once and for all – from the beginning yours and Peggy's attitude towards me has been

entirely lacking in the most ordinary politeness and respectful 'attentions' usually accorded to the most ordinary mother-in-law and I have never interfered or proffered advice – well, there it is and so it is – friends real friends who are able to advise and tell one another the truth without fear are rare – and in your position they do not exist.

Good bye darling Boy – I am just leaving for Paris.

I beg of you to take advice from your doctor and others as I think you may be in a serious state of health, a state which if not taken in time – may be more serious still.

Your Mother.

Don't answer this letter – I hope we shall meet sometimes as usual – as to the rest – I am resigned.

By late February 1937, Lilian had been diagnosed as having cancer and had undergone painful surgery as a result. Harold and Esmond understood she wouldn't recover, but the blow was naturally softened for Esmond's children, who were thought to be too young to understand. With typical care, Harold gently explained to the eldest of his grandchildren, Lorna, what was happening to her grandmother, couching the cold fact of her approaching death amongst many reassuring terms of endearment.

He wrote in his own hand from La Dragonnière at Cap Martin:

My darling Grand-daughter,

I've not written before because I do not know exactly what your Father's plans are. He talks about going to see you at Easter time in which case I shall probably go with him.

I am glad you like your school in Florence. There's nothing like school for growing girls. They must be kept in order.

We have had wonderful weather here. I suppose you have had the same in Florence.

I think you are a very privileged girl to spend some part of your school life in such a wonderful city. Every well travelled person in the world goes to Florence and every artist or person who thinks he or she has artistic instincts also goes there. I expect you will emerge from Florence with quite a knowledge of what fine art should be.

Your Father plays a great deal of tennis here. He's been playing in the Monte Carlo Tournament. He looks better in health than I have seen him looking for some years.

Your Grandmother is, as you know, dangerously ill. She is showing no signs of recovery. The doctors do not understand how she has lived so long . . .

I hope you are a very good girl and doing everything to earn your Grandpapa's good opinion.

I am hoping you will come and stay with me at Stody in your holidays.

Your devoted Grandpapa

The second-eldest daughter of Esmond, Esme, noted that her grandfather was warm and demonstrative, and it seemed to her that her brother Vere was very much like him in that way. Like Harold, the boy also had a lively imagination, and he and Esme shared hours of pretend play:

Vere and I would start playing, and we understood one another. To us, a table could be a raft. Tables could be rocks. I can remember going up this river, with great crocodiles, and the great fun we had. He was imaginative like me...

Her grandmother, for all her smiles and chatter, was an undemonstrative woman, and Esmond, a lively character who loved practical jokes, took after his mother. Lilian also had a stoniness about her that Esmond seemed to share. But then Esmond took the brunt.

On her deathbed, Lilian wrote to her only living son her last testament – a disparagement of his father:

Dearest Esmond

Thank you for your chatty letter.

I am very sorry I cannot write in the same strain and that is why I have abstained from contacting you but I am still bruised and shaken by the cruelty of your father – who seized the occasion of my very serious illness to persecute me – last time at Marseilles – your father said to me complacently: 'I don't think Esmond has made the most of his life, do you?' Feeling very indiscreet I said: 'My dear, he has been terribly handicapped' (meaning to continue and tell him what I thought about his part in it!). Dorothy fearfully butted in and changed the conversation – quite unbelievable and I hope I shall never set eyes on him again.

He has been the evil genius of your life as well as mine and has imagined it well compensated for by money – Oh, how mistaken he is! – but you my dear boy also ever at his side – money is your 'God' also and neither you nor your father ever had or ever will have any real joy in life...

I am fed up with both of you – you have no 'guts' and no imagination so there it is – I pity you both.

Your Mother.

P.S I do not mention my health – as obviously it is a matter of very secondary consideration with you both and you have no doubt reports from all your 'spies' –

P.S You no doubt think I shall 'forget' all this don't delude yourself on that matter – the surgeon said too when I was screaming in agony: 'She will forget all this when she is better, it is nerves and she is hysterical'! Alas! I remember all that horror, every moment of agony and so it will be with this –

Lilian spoke in pain, no doubt under the influence of drugs, and her final reckoning was unquestionably shadowed by a death she feared. Her words were nevertheless soulless and cruel: Esmond was 'handicapped', he had no 'guts'. He had never had nor would he ever have 'any real joy in his life'. It was tantamount to a curse – a strange legacy for a mother to leave her son.

Gide's speculation that women like Lilian were cut from a cloth with no thickness perhaps had merit.

Fortune, intelligence, beauty – they seem to possess everything, except a soul . . . No past weighs upon them, no constraint . . . neither laws, nor masters, nor scruples . . .

Were the 'freedom and spontaneity' of Lilian's character, attractive as these features were, the very traits that cut her off from natural instincts of love? So the novelist had postulated. As she lay dying, Lilian Rothermere determined to leave everything except her villa in the South of France to the mystic Gurdjieff, whose cult exists to this day. It was her final gesture of despair.

It was baffling – this effect of money and privilege upon women. It appeared to do them no good.

Princess Stephanie Hohenlohe stalked Rothermere, complaining of her impoverished state. On 11 January 1935, Rothermere wrote her a cheque for duties discharged. Between then and the 14th – a matter of three days – she complained to him several times she needed more. Her son's future was in doubt, her style of living was under threat: he must do something.

Rothermere, harassed but sympathetic, wrote back immediately suggesting she 'move to a less expensive hotel . . .

After all, these are hard times for all of us. The ex-Queen of Wurtemberg travels second class on the railways and keeps no motor car.'

It was the closest to tough Harold was able to muster with a woman in distress. By the end of his letter he was promising to try to find her 'more remunerative work . . . in the cause of European peace'. In a postscript, he added: 'When your boy leaves Oxford send him to me. I can make him useful.'

Again, in February, Rothermere asked the Princess not to bring him any more 'letters regarding German or mid-European politics'. There was, he said, 'nothing more to be done'. Still again in November, he wrote a letter discouraging the Princess.

I do hope you are not coming to bring any messages from anyone. I do not want them...

Events will move towards their destined end.

At last, on 26 May 1936, he wrote his final word!

Dear Princess Hohenlohe,

I have felt it necessary to tell you that if I am to see you again you must cease your constant importunity for money and jewellery.

In my long life I have not hitherto met with a constant appeal from anyone for gifts of various kinds.

I have already handsomely acknowledged your services in endeavouring to establish a better relationship between Britain and Germany, but I do not think that unofficially this matter can be carried any further.

If at any time you wish to see me again I hope you will observe that I shall see you on the understanding you make no further appeals for financial or other assistance.

> With all good wishes,
> Yours very sincerely,
> Rothermere

By 15 July, Princess Stephanie Hohenlohe was back on salary.

The Hungarian princess was what is known in the parlance as a survivor. When at last she was severed from Rothermere's payroll, in January 1938, she quickly set about bringing a legal action against him, based upon claims that he had gained international fame resulting from her work for him, both in Hungary and in Germany; that her reputation had been impaired as a result of that work (she was now thought to be an international 'spy'); that Rothermere had undertaken to support her and her son indefinitely. This was the gist. The remedy she sought was a great deal of money.

Accordingly, in November 1939, Rothermere met her in court with no fewer than seventeen lawyers, including Sir Patrick Hastings and later Sir William Jowett. The result was that Princess Stephanie's claims were not upheld and Rothermere was awarded costs. In the aftermath of this public ordeal, Rothermere, knowing the distress of the Princess, sent word to her that he would meet all her expenses in the case, an offer that she accepted.

This was the final transaction between Rothermere and Princess Stephanie.

In the strange case of Princess Stephanie Hohenlohe the question must at last arise whether she was acting for Rothermere alone. So tempting is it to view Steph as a greedy, spoiled, self-indulgent amateur, dabbling in waters out of her depth, that it is easy to overlook the possibility she was in fact a Nazi sympathizer – or, to put it as the American newspapers did, 'Hitler's henchman'. Was Rothermere her dupe?

The evidence for the case was substantial. It was she who first approached the great English press lord, proposing to go to work for him; she who gave him the signal Hitler was ready to meet him in 1933. Later, when he tried to end the relationship, she stuck to him, leech-like, besieging him with missives from abroad and bleeding him for more and more money. His offer to put her son to work went unacknowledged – an opportunity most young men would have jumped at. The trial, too, seemed trumped up, the claims absurd. Was it an attempt to blackmail Rothermere into giving her yet more money by publicizing his correspondence with Hitler? If so, she had entirely misjudged her man.

Rothermere was not the sort to be blackmailed, nor did he shrink from defending his position in court. It would, of course, have been a matter of principle. By the same token, neither was he a man to take advantage of a destitute woman – as he believed Princess Stephanie to be – and he promptly paid her expenses in the suit after he had proven his innocence.

However the relationship began – whether through Hitler's machinations or Rothermere's – the press lord's every purpose in his relations with the German dictator was aimed at delaying a war he believed inevitable while attempting to publicize the urgent need for rearmament.

His open and ingenuous dealings with Hitler were part and parcel of the duality of his character: he could respect the dictator's achievements, admiring his strong leadership, while at the same time understanding the grievous danger he represented to Britain.

The offence of which Rothermere could justly be accused was only this: that he did not use a longer-handled spoon.

On 1 September 1939, General Walther von Brauchitsch, leading 1,250,000 men in sixty divisions, invaded Poland from north, west and south as Luftwaffe planes systematically bombarded all major cities and designated military targets. This close coordination of air and ground forces represented a new and irresistible plan of attack which came to be known as blitzkrieg.

At 9.00 a.m. on 3 September, the British delivered an ultimatum to the German Government to which Germany made no reply. It expired at

11.00 a.m., and the two countries were officially at war. Later in the day, France joined the British, and, with the inclusion of their colonies and those Dominions who quickly followed suit, the nomenclature 'Second World War' became apt.

A strange quietude followed. It was an intermission in the hostilities lasting some seven months – soon to be known as the 'Phoney War'. When at last it ended and the Germans resumed the *blitzkrieg*, the countries of Western Europe fell in a wave of surrender: in April, Denmark; some few weeks later, Norway. By the end of May, Holland and Belgium were securely in the hands of the Nazis and, on 21 June, France capitulated.

These first ten months of conflict gave dramatic notice of the new import of air power in the conduct of modern warfare. The sinking by German U-boats of the British passenger liner *Athenia* off the coast of the Hebrides and HMS *Courageous* off the south-western coast of England alerted the world to the changing nature of modern naval warfare. Meanwhile, the collapse of France destroyed the pre-war myth of that country's invincibility. Rothermere had repeatedly warned his countrymen against these very calamities, but being right carried little pleasure in these dark days.

Just prior to the outbreak of war, in the summer of 1939, Rothermere had had another of his intuitions. He wrote to Churchill, 'I can very well see a great responsibility may be placed upon you at an early date.' In light of this, Rothermere wrote, they would do well to renew their 'old bet'. He was referring to a running wager between the two whereby Winston would give up one form or another of alcohol for a specified period of time, thus winning a fabulous sum of money from Rothermere. This time, since Rothermere wished Churchill 'to be in the finest fettle when the day arrives',

> I bet you £600 that you will not be able to run from the given date to the same date next year without showing your predilection for cognac. Is it a deal?

Two days later, on 19 July 1939, Churchill wrote back:

> ... I accept the proposal which you make, in view of the many uncertainties of the future. The operative date will be to-morrow, July 20.
>
> Evidently a great 'crunch' is coming, and all preparations are moving forward ceaselessly to some date in August. Whether H. will call it off or not is a psychological problem which you can probably judge as well as any living man. I fear he despises Chamberlain, and is convinced that the reason he does not broaden his Government is because he means to give in once Parliament has risen ...

I am remaining entirely quiescent at the present time. Like you, I have given my warnings, and I am consoled for being condemned to inaction by being free from responsibility...

He proposed that he join Rothermere for a night or two at his villa on the Riviera at the end of summer, 'if you can find room'.

But once war was declared, Churchill was immediately returned to the Admiralty. By the following May, on the 10th, even as the countries on the Continent were folding one by one, he replaced Neville Chamberlain as Prime Minister. And on the 14th he appointed Max Beaverbrook to a newly created Cabinet post – Minister of Aircraft Production.

'The Ministry of Aircraft Production was torn from their very body,' Beaverbrook would later write of the Air Ministry. 'They saw the power and the authority passing elsewhere...' Summarily overruling all objections to Beaverbrook's appointment – as well as putting into the past his own chequered relations with the mercurial press lord – Churchill exonerated himself from all criticism by saying, 'I needed [Max's] vibrant and vital energy.'

The day after Beaverbrook was appointed, Rothermere wired him from France:

MY DEAR MAX OVERJOYED AT LAST SOME GOVERNMENTAL USE HAS BEEN FOUND AT THIS CRITICAL JUNCTURE FOR YOUR GLITTERING ABILITIES ... QUITE PREPARED TO HELP YOUR DEPARTMENT OTHER SIDE WITHOUT SALARY TRAVELLING EXPENSES OR CLERICAL EXPENSES FOR DURATION OF WAR IF NECESSARY STOP HAVE AS YOU KNOW CONSIDERABLE REPUTATION FOR MY SPECIFICATION BRITAIN FIRST STOP COULD I BELIEVE RENDER QUITE CONSIDERABLE SERVICE WITHOUT INTERFERING WITH PRESENT ARRANGEMENTS BUT COULD BE THERE FOR CONFERENCE AND DISCUSSION WHEN NECESSARY STOP NOT AN INTRIGUER OR PETTIFOGGER AS YOU KNOW.

On the same day he received the wire, Max sent back his reply: 'I WILL WANT YOUR SERVICES IN AMERICA AND HOPE YOU WILL GO THERE AT ONCE.' When Lord Halifax, now Foreign Secretary, objected to the enlistment of Rothermere, insisting Max rescind the order, Beaverbrook shunted him aside. 'I do not know where Rothermere is,' he said. 'I think he is already in the United States. In any case he is an old man.'

This was Max's way. Through the years, he might have flayed Rothermere in business, using the *Daily Mail* to finance the *Express*; he might crow when the circulation of the latter exceeded that of the former; he might have said a thousand things that diminished Rothermere in the eyes of others. But now, when the going got rough, he put aside the savagery of his own nature in surrender to the affection he felt for his good friend

Harold. Harold was old and failing and wanted to be of use. Very well, then, he would be put to use. Whatever characteristics Beaverbrook possessed, and some of these were most forbidding, loyalty was first and foremost.

He now turned his baleful eye to the production of aeroplanes. Harold had been right – the skies would be the decisive field of battle in the days that lay ahead.

Just after Dunkirk, in early June 1940, Esme Harmsworth, then seventeen, and her brother Vere, soon to be fifteen, were told they would be immediately evacuated to North America. Esme resisted, battling to stay in England; her grandfather, already in Canada buying aluminium for planes, took her side. He feared for the safety of Esme and her brother as they crossed the submarine-infested North Atlantic. They nevertheless made the crossing in a steamship, with six hundred other children, all of them bored and seasick and heartbroken to be leaving those they loved at home.

Vere was quickly enrolled in Kent School in Connecticut, and Esme went to Ridgewood, New Jersey, to stay in the house of one of her father's business associates, Frank Humphrey. There, she became desperately lonely, and to while away the time she accepted an unpaid job at a war relief organization in New York, taking the bus in from New Jersey and walking from the station to her work. When her grandfather discovered this, he became frantic with worry over her safety, irrationally demanding that she stay in Ridgewood – a demand, as a spirited teenager, she was bound to refuse. What Esme didn't know was that her grandfather had fallen ill, and for the last two weeks of June he had been in St Luke's hospital in New York, trying to find out what was the matter.

As he lay there, waiting for test results, fretting more and more about the direction the war was taking, a curious awakening was taking place in his country, a tangible buoyancy in the spirit of the populace. The growing optimism so confounded outsiders that one young reporter from the United States made note of it.* In the face of an adversity that did not exclude extinction, 'a wryly humorous defiance' had arisen amongst the people.

A ridiculous ditty, popularized by two well-known comedians, Flanagan and Allen, began to make the rounds. Soon, its lyrics could be heard in every pub in London and, sooner than anyone thought possible, in the Underground tunnels that served as air-raid shelters below London:

* The reporter was Drew Middleton, later military correspondent for the *New York Times*.

Run, Rabbit, run, Rabbit, run, run, run!
Don't give the farmer his gun, gun, gun!
He'll get by
Without his rabbit pie,
So run, Rabbit, run, Rabbit, run, run, run!

It must have had something to do with what was being called, all of a sudden, the 'spirit of Dunkirk' when 850 British vessels, many of them small fishing boats, slipped across the English Channel and evacuated more than 338,000 troops. They otherwise would have perished in the Battle of Flanders, thus obliterating Britain's fighting force.

It must have had something to do with the imperturbable determination of a country whose 'general strategy at present', as Winston Churchill put it, 'is to last out the next three months'.

The 'next three months' would turn out to be the Battle of Britain, and by the ingenuity, courage and wits of her young men, Britain would see them through.

In August 1939, amidst much secrecy, a number of trials began taking place at RAF Northolt involving a little-known device that permitted radio instruments to detect distant objects in the air. The device, known as 'radar' (Radio Direction and Ranging) had been in development ever since its invention in 1935 by Robert Watson-Watt.* By 1939, the area it covered included most of the eastern approaches to Britain, but now at Northolt the problem of successfully installing the device into aircraft was the prime object of a series of tests and trial runs. The plane selected for these first experiments with airborne interception radar was the latest model of Rothermere's Blenheim – the MkIV.

The Blenheim was not the fastest of the aircraft now lining up in defence of the nation, nor was it the most manoeuvrable. It was the large interior of the aeroplane that made it ideal for the installation of this rudimentary form of enemy aircraft detection.

After a number of trial runs over the Thames Estuary, the Blenheims moved to the North Sea, where by November the crews using airborne radar achieved a high level of confidence. Fewer than eight squadrons of Blenheims flew in the fifty-two mustered for Air Marshal Sir Hugh Dow-

* The following description of aircraft and radar comes from four principal sources: publications from the Museum at RAF Hendon, consultant Mungo Chapman; Drew Middleton's *The Sky Suspended*; A.J.P. Taylor's *English History, 1914–1945*; and Susan Joiner's compilation *Fighting Aircraft of World Wars I and II*, and a variety of encyclopedias, newspaper cuttings and other secondary sources.

ding's Fighter Command in the Battle of Britain, but because they were equipped with radar they were considered by the RAF to be 'the backbone of the nation's night fighter defences'.

Far more vital to the conduct of the battle now facing Britain's young pilots were the Hurricane and the Spitfire. Although the Hurricane was the principal weapon of the RAF during the Battle of Britain, the Spitfire, with its superior speed and grace when airborne, symbolized, more than any other aircraft, the crucial battle in the skies over Britain that raged for some three months between the young pilots of Britain and of Germany. The engine for these two aeroplanes – the Rolls-Royce Merlin – had been developed in 1931 for the Schneider Cup team, an effort financed by Lady Houston, the wealthy publisher of the *Saturday Review*, who agreed to sponsor the team when the Government refused.*

Right-wing and eccentric, Lady Houston's extreme political views had done much to engender the dislike of the British Establishment, who viewed her with suspicion and distaste. Although abjuring Hitler and his Nazi cohorts, she had publicly cheered Mussolini's early use of castor oil against Italian Socialists and thought it an idea worth emulating in Great Britain. Her origins as well – she was a former chorus-girl – hardly fitted into the ruling class's concept of a lady. She nevertheless threw her vital support into the campaign for the Spitfire, and without her the aircraft would never have come into production.

As to the Blenheim, whose original prototype had been produced five years before the battle, the slow progression of its obsolescence was considered something of a phenomenon amongst a small, well-informed group of air enthusiasts, and it was thought appropriate that the world's first combat victory using airborne radar, on the night of 22/23 July 1940, should have been carried out by a Blenheim fighter.

But Rothermere, shaky at first after his release from St Luke's Hospital and concentrating on what he believed to be an important mission in Canada, did not know that the aircraft he had donated to the nation was playing a vital part in its defence. Prone to worry at the best of times, his failing health increased his propensity for depression, and while he continued in his letters and telegrams home to express his unfailing belief that Britain would prevail, privately he despaired.

In late October, Rothermere told his granddaughter Esme he was having a cash-flow problem that made it necessary for him to go into a Sterling

---

* Four years before her death in 1936, Lady Houston also offered the Government a gift of £200,000 for the air defences of Great Britain, but this was refused on the grounds that Parliament alone had responsibility to determine appropriations for defence.

area, inviting her to come with him to Hamilton, Bermuda. To Esme, this was the chance she had been looking for – a possible stepping-stone back to England, and she accepted with delight.

> So we set sail on a Grace Line ship from New York to Bermuda, with my grandfather's secretary, Mr Morison, and his masseur, who also travelled with him ... So the four of us were on this ship.
>
> We arrived in Bermuda, and in those days on the island there were no motor cars, so we got into one of these little carriages – a kind of surrey with a fringe on top – and finally got to a small hotel – the big hotels had been taken over by the censors – and I had a bike to get around with, and my grandfather and I took all our meals together along with Mr Morison. Grandfather talked about politics and war and how sad the whole thing was, and at that time it looked as if we didn't have a chance of winning ... It looked pretty grim, so we had very sad conversations about the futility of war, and how we were going to lose it as well.
>
> Only a night or two after we arrived, they came to me in the evening and said, 'I'm very sorry, we've had to take your grandfather to the hospital.'

Rothermere had been suffering for some time from fatigue and, when carrying out his duties in Canada and New York, had several times faltered and fallen, on one occasion injuring himself seriously. Then, too, despite rigorous dieting, he had suffered continuous swellings, particularly at his joints and ankles. The night of his arrival in Bermuda, his secretary Morison sent for a doctor who examined his long-time employer and told him privately that Rothermere's 'heart was "leaking" badly and the swellings suggested dropsy'. The next morning, on the doctor's advice, he was checked into the King Edward VII Memorial Hospital. 'And every morning,' Esme later remembered,

> I would bicycle down to stay with him. And I used to sit there feeling very uncomfortable. I couldn't think of anything to say. I was embarrassed. 'I want to look at you because you look like my mother,' my grandfather would say to me.
>
> This went on for ten days or two weeks, and one morning, he had changed, his whole face had changed. His nose had changed. His cheeks were hollow. Of course, he was dying, but I didn't know it.
>
> The next day I was told he had died, and I was the only member of my family there and I had never even been to a funeral and I was sobbing my eyes out and at the funeral there were black horses with plumes – it was more than I could stand – and a young man came up in uniform and he came to pay his respects. My eyes were red and swollen, no make-up, it had all come off, and years and years and years later, I met him and by then he was the editor of the *Sunday*

Times, Frank Giles, and he said to me, 'You probably don't remember where I met you for the first time. It was at your grandfather's funeral. I was the Governor's ADC.'

After the burial of her grandfather, which took place one day after his death, on 28 November 1940, Esme was given the choice whether to return to America or to go back home. Esme chose England.

There followed a set of complicated arrangements that involved returning to Britain via Estoril, the only entry point back into Britain since Portugal remained neutral. It was necessary for her passport to be sent back to New York, where Frank Humphrey managed to procure the visa she needed, and then returned to Bermuda. 'Departure from the island', he wrote to Esmond, 'is very indefinite, very difficult.'

> The reason for this is that passenger accommodations are restricted by the weight of mails, petrol, stores and crew. It was put to me something like this: these [air] ships carry X pounds – the total weight of the mails petrol stores and crew is figured and then the difference between that and the total capacity of the ship are given over to passengers but, of course, there is a limit to the maximum number of passengers.

But Esme was unable to get a seat on the plane and only after much waiting managed to get aboard an American cargo boat. Once she reached Lisbon, she transferred to the Grand Hotel in Estoril, waiting to get in.

Estoril was much like Casablanca during the Second World War, the integration of refugees from both sides of the conflict making it a hot-bed for spies and intrigues. Esme spent her first solitary Christmas in the hotel; it was just another day of waiting. For six weeks she stayed by herself in Estoril, her only friend the former silent film actress, Virginia Cherrill, now Lady Jersey, who had played the blind flower girl in Charlie Chaplin's *City Lights*. Lady Jersey had taken Esme under her wing on the American cargo boat. Then one evening, Lady Jersey appeared in Esme's hotel room, saying she had managed to get two seats on an aeroplane returning to England. Could Esme be ready in fifteen minutes? 'Oh, yes, I can,' she answered.

By the time she and Lady Jersey arrived at the airport it was dark, and they walked out on to the runway. There, they saw 'this extraordinary sight – these two aeroplanes side by side all lit up, one with a swastika going to Berlin, the other with the English red, white and blue circles going to London'.

The two women climbed the steps to the British aeroplane and found seats.

Esme was going home.

Epilogue

A little over a year after Esme Harmsworth returned to Britain, her brother Vere flew home, one of the first to cross the Atlantic aboard the Boeing Flying Clipper, and resumed his studies at Eton.

Their father Esmond had become, in 1937, the Chairman of Daily Mail and General Trust Ltd, the name of the company having been changed in 1935. After his father's death, Esmond succeeded to the title and became the second Viscount Rothermere of Hemsted.

When his mother died, Esmond was not made an executor of her will, a fact which, he privately admitted, hurt him a great deal. Esmond nevertheless travelled to her house in France and paid off the man who had lived with her, giving him the yacht and a few household things, as was appropriate. Although none had been a more dutiful son than Esmond, it is likely he carried ambivalent feelings towards both his parents throughout his life.

Weakened by Harold's editorial policy, the *Daily Mail*, under Esmond, would become more and more a mouthpiece for the Establishment. Its moderate stance would carry it into a kind of stasis and, eventually, the flagship publication of the Harmsworth dynasty would be eclipsed by Beaverbrook's *Daily Express*. Thus would the *Daily Mail* fall upon hard times, until it seemed inevitable it would fold. The newspaper's revival would depend upon the untried leadership of Esmond's son Vere, who at the time of Harold's death was only a boy.

As for Rothermere's former courier, Princess Stephanie Hohenlohe, controversy continued to plague her career for many years to come. Accused of accepting the confiscated *schloss* of Jewish theatrical producer Max Reinhardt, Leopoldskron, as a gift from the Nazis, she also sustained attacks for taking money from prominent Jewish families, among them the Austrian Rothschilds, in exchange for their safe passage out of Europe.

At the outbreak of the Second World War, the Princess fled to the United States, where she was immediately interned for the duration of the conflict. Upon release, she managed to contract a romantic alliance with a well-connected Philadelphia millionaire and in 1947 was named as one of the Ten Best-Dressed Women in America.

She later became a business associate and close friend of Washington columnist Drew Pearson, and eventually went to work for Axel Springer. In this position, she personally arranged interviews with John F. Kennedy, the Shah of Iran, Princess Grace of Monaco and other luminaries of the age. A guest of honour at Lyndon B. Johnson's inaugural ball, she later became a personal friend of Richard Nixon. It is safe to conclude that any political convictions Princess Stephanie may have entertained over the years were strictly a matter of expediency.

In late November 1942, a vigorous gnome-like man in his middle sixties visited the churchyard of St Paul's, in Paget, Bermuda, which was situated in a little valley 'ablaze with hibiscus, bougainvillaea and poinsettia'. There, where some of the oldest Bermudian families and several Governors were buried, he stopped for some good time at the grave of the only peer of the realm.

Less than a week later, Beaverbrook wrote to Esmond,

In Bermuda last Sunday I visited your father's grave. He was great in vision, courage and loyalty. We do not make friends easily when old age overtakes us. And we do miss deeply the companionship we have relied upon in our journeys ... Nothing equalled his fun and fantasy in the days of his middle life before domestic disasters came to him.

The letter was handwritten and signed only 'Max'.

AUTHOR'S NOTE

I have taken the liberty of omitting ellipses from lengthy newspaper quotes, of which there are quite a few in this book. Please rest assured I have been careful to retain the original meaning of each dispatch.

As to documentation, each chapter is herewith sourced, with citations for major reference works consulted. A fully footnoted copy of this text is retained by the author in case of scholarly enquiries.

CHAPTER SOURCES

1: 'The Revenge of the Y.H.W.'

Reginald Pound and Geoffrey Harmsworth, *Northcliffe*, London: Cassell, 1959.

Hamilton Fyfe, *Northcliffe: An Intimate Biography*, London: George Allen & Unwin, 1930; another version of the education of Geraldine is found in Robert MacNair Wilson, *Lord Northcliffe: A Study*, London: Ernest Benn, 1927.

Cecil King, *Strictly Personal*, London: Weidenfeld & Nicolson, 1969.

Tom Clarke, *Northcliffe in History*, London: Hutchinson, 1950.

Paul Ferris, *The House of Northcliffe: The Harmsworths of Fleet Street*, London: Weidenfeld & Nicolson, 1971.

Bethnal Green Museum of Childhood, *Penny Dreadfuls and Comics*, London: Victoria and Albert Museum, 1983.

Kennedy Jones, *Fleet Street and Downing Street*, London: Hutchinson, 1920.

Tom Clarke, *My Northcliffe Diary*, London: Victor Gollancz, 1931.

Max Pemberton, *Lord Northcliffe: A Memoir*, London: Hodder & Stoughton, 1922.

John Montgomery, *1900: The End of an Era*, London: Allen & Unwin, 1968, quoting the musical, *Gentleman Joe*, pp. 134–5.

Interview with Daphne Macneile Dixon, South Godestone, 22 Mar. 1992.

Bernard Falk, *Five Years Dead: A Postscript to 'He Laughed in Fleet Street'*, London: Book Club reprint, 1938.

Sir Evelyn Wrench, *Uphill: The First Stage in a Strenuous Life*, London: Ivor Nicholson & Watson, 1934.

2: 'This Paper Will Go'

Frank Harris, *Frank Harris: His Life and Adventures, an Autobiography*, London: The Richards Press, 1947.

A. P. Ryan, *Lord Northcliffe*, Brief Lives, *London: Collins, 1943.*

Kennedy Jones, Fleet Street and Downing Street, London: Hutchinson, 1920.

Philippa Pullar, *Frank Harris*, London: Hamish Hamilton, 1975.

T.P. O'Connor, 'The New Journalism', *New Review*, Oct. 1889, pp. 423–34.

Hamilton Fyfe, *Northcliffe: An Intimate Biography*, London: Allen & Unwin, 1930.

Lincoln Springfield, *Some Piquant People*, London: T. Fisher Unwin, 1924.

Paul Ferris, *The House of Northcliffe: The Harmsworths of Fleet Street*, London: Weidenfeld & Nicolson, 1971.

Max Pemberton, *Lord Northcliffe: A Memoir*, London: Hodder & Stoughton, 1922.

9 Oct. 1994, *Evening News*.

Interview with Vere Rothermere, London, 10 Nov. 1992.

Reginald Pound and Geoffrey Harmsworth, *Northcliffe*, London: Cassell, 1959.

Bernard Falk, *Five Years Dead: A Postscript to 'He Laughed in Fleet Street'*, London: Book Club reprint, 1938.

Alfred Harmsworth, *The Romance of the Daily Mail*, London: Carmelite House, 1903.

Robert MacNair Wilson, *Lord Northcliffe: A Study*, London: Ernest Benn, 1927.

History of the Times, Vol. III: The Twentieth Century Test, 1884–1912, London: Printing House Square, 1947.

Northcliffe Papers, in the British Library, Add. MS 62292A, Vol. cxl.

Harry J. Greenwall, *Northcliffe: Napoleon of Fleet Street*, London: Allan Wingate, 1957.

3: 'Dead! and ... Never Called Me Mother!'

Alfred Harmsworth, *The Romance of the Daily Mail*, London: Carmelite House, 1903.

Reginald Pound and Geoffrey Harmsworth, *Northcliffe*, London: Cassell, 1959.

History of the Times, Vol. III: The Twentieth Century Test, 1884–1912, London: Printing House Square, 1947.

July 1898, *Saturday Review*.

8 June, 13, 17 Nov. 1896; 12 Feb., 11 Mar., 18, 21, 22, 23 June, 8 Oct. 1897; 7 May, 14, 17, 19, 20 July 1899, *Daily Mail*.

Lincoln Springfield, *Some Piquant People*, London: T. Fisher Unwin, 1924.

Hamilton Fyfe, *Northcliffe: An Intimate Biography*, London: Allen & Unwin, 1930.

Bernard Falk, *He Laughed in Fleet Street*, London: Hutchinson, 1933.

British Library, Add. MS 62292A, Vol. cxl.

Paul Ferris, *The House of Northcliffe: The Harmsworths of Fleet Street*, London: Weidenfeld & Nicolson, 1971.

Piers Brendon, *The Life and Death of the Press Barons*, London: Secker & Warburg, 1982.

Max Pemberton, *Lord Northcliffe: A Memoir*, London: Hodder & Stoughton, 1922.

John Montgomery, *1900: The End of an Era*, London: Allen & Unwin, 1968.

Interview with Daphne Macneile Dixon, South Godestone, 22 Mar. 1992.

Peter Mendelssohn, *The Age of Churchill*, London: Thames & Hudson, 1961.

Robert MacNair Wilson, *Lord Northcliffe: A Study*, London: Ernest Benn, 1927.

Kennedy Jones, *Fleet Street and Downing Street*, London: Hutchinson, 1920.

G. Ward Price, Unpublished MS, 1949.

A. P. Ryan, *Lord Northcliffe*, Brief Lives, London: Collins, 1943, p. 140.

4: 'Duke's Son, Cook's Son, Son of a Hundred Kings'

Robert MacNair Wilson, *Lord Northcliffe: A Study*, London: Ernest Benn, 1927.

James Dunn, *Paperchase: Adventures in and out of Fleet Street*, London: Selwyn & Blount, 1938.

Harry J. Greenwall, *Northcliffe: Napoleon of Fleet Street*, London: Allan Wingate, 1957.

17 Nov., 21 Dec. 1899; 2, 3, 5, 8, 11, 22, 29, 31 Jan., 27 Feb., 22, 23 May, 19 June, 1900, *Daily Mail*.

Lincoln Springfield, *Some Piquant People*, London: T. Fisher Unwin, 1924.

F. A. McKenzie, *The Mystery of the Daily Mail*, London: Associated Newspapers, 1921.

Lady Sarah Wilson, *South African Memories: Social, Warlike & Sporting*, London: Edward Arnold, 1909.

Lady Sarah Wilson, Dispatches on the Relief of Mafeking, 20 Mar., 11, 21, 22, 23, 25 Apr., 19, 22, 23, 28 May 1900, *Daily Mail*.

John Montgomery, *1900: The End of an Era*, London: Allen & Unwin, 1968.

Paul Ferris, *The House of Northcliffe: The Harmsworths of Fleet Street*, London: Weidenfeld & Nicolson, 1971.

Piers Brendon, *The Life and Death of the Press Barons*, London: Secker & Warburg, 1982.

Reginald Pound and Geoffrey Harmsworth, *Northcliffe*, London: Cassell, 1959.

5: 'Mr Alfred Worship'

Reginald Pound and Geoffrey Harmsworth, *Northcliffe*, London: Cassell, 1959.

Piers Brendon, *The Life and Death of the Press Barons*, London: Secker & Warburg, 1982.

Norman Angell, *After All*, London: Hamish Hamilton, 1951.

Hamilton Fyfe, *Northcliffe: An Intimate Biography*, London: Allen & Unwin, 1930.

Paul Ferris, *The House of Northcliffe: The Harmsworths of Fleet Street*, London: Weidenfeld & Nicolson, 1971.

J. A. Hammerton, *With Northcliffe in Fleet Street*, London: Hutchinson, 1939.

Sir Evelyn Wrench, *Uphill: The First Stage in a Strenuous Life*, London: Ivor Nicholson & Watson, 1934.

Tom Clarke, *My Northcliffe Diary*, London: Victor Gollancz, 1931.

Louise Owen, *The Real Lord Northcliffe: Some Personal Recollections of a Private Secretary 1902–1922*, London: Cassell, 1922.

July 1965, *Forme Magazine*.

British Library, Add. MS 62198, Vol. xlvi.

Bernard Falk, *He Laughed in Fleet Street*, London: Hutchinson, 1933.

Max Pemberton, *Lord Northcliffe: A Memoir*, London: Hodder & Stoughton, 1922.

Interview with Daphne Macneile Dixon, South Godestone, 22 Mar. 1992.

Alfred Harmsworth, *The Romance of the Daily Mail*, London: Carmelite House, 1903.

G. Ward Price, Unpublished MS, 1949.

Kennedy Jones, *Fleet Street and Downing Street*, London: Hutchinson, 1920.

F.A. McKenzie, *The Mystery of the Daily Mail*, London: Associated Newspapers, 1921.

Tom Clarke, *Northcliffe in History*, London: Hutchinson, 1950.

Hugh Cudlipp, *Publish and Be Damned*, London: Andrew Dakers, 1953.

29 Feb. 1952, *World's Press News*.

Alfred M. Gollin, *The Observer and J.L. Garvin*, Oxford: Oxford University Press, 1960.

History of the Times, Vol. III: The Twentieth Century Test, 1884–1912, London: Printing House Square, 1947.

6: 'Paper!'

Alfred Harmsworth, *The Romance of the Daily Mail*, London: Carmelite House, 1903.

Reginald Pound and Geoffrey Harmsworth, *Northcliffe*, London: Cassell, 1959.

David MacFarlane, *The Danger Tree*, Toronto: Macfarlane Walter & Ross, 1991.

Interview with Vere Rothermere, London, 21 Jan. 1993.

John Braddock, 'One Bold Venture', *The Atlantic Advocate*, Apr. 1968.

British Library, Add. MS 62230, Vol. lxxviii, 10 June 1908.

British Library, Add. MS 62230, Vol. lxxviii: half-monthly report, 15–31 Jan. 1908; Beeton to Northcliffe, 11 Aug. 1908, misc. letters written 10, 16 Aug.

9 Oct. 1909, p. 1, *Evening Chronicle*.

AND-Co. Company Archives, compiled 8 Sept., 1954.

Northcliffe to Kennedy Jones (letter), 30 Oct. 1909, British Library, Add. MS 62196, Vol. xliv.

Interview with Edward M. Martin, St John's, Newfoundland, 22 Sept. 1992.

G.N. Neary, 'Mining History of the Buchans Area', in *The Buchans Orebodies: Fifty Years of Geology and Mining*, ed. E.A. Swanson, D.F. Strong, J.G. Thurlow, Geological Association of Canada, Special Paper 22, 1981, quoting Aubrey Goodyear, Buchans' resident.

31 Dec. 1927, *St. John's News*.

Interview with Barbara Vincent-Jones, Eastbourne, 21 Mar. 1992.

Hamilton Fyfe, *Northcliffe: An Intimate Biography*, London: Allen & Unwin, 1930.

Interview with Robert Morrow, QC, Montreal, 10 Oct. 1992.

7: 'Those Magnificent Men in Their Flying Machines'

Ethel Violet Wallace, *Edgar Wallace*, London: Hutchinson, 1932.

Northcliffe to Winston Churchill (letter), 15 May 1908.

Ted Morgan, *Churchill: 1874–1915*, London: Jonathan Cape, 1982.

Randolph S. Churchill, *Winston S. Churchill, Vol. II, The Young Statesman, 1901–1914*, London: Heinemann, 1967.

Violet Bonham Carter, *Winston Churchill as I Knew Him*, London: Eyre & Spottiswoode and Collins, 1965.

All letters and copies between Northcliffe and Churchill come from the Harmsworth Archives:

Winston Churchill to Northcliffe (letter), 1 Sept. 1903.

Northcliffe to Churchill (letter), 11 May 1908.

Northcliffe to Churchill (letter), 13 May 1908.

Churchill to Northcliffe (letter), 14 May 1908.

Churchill to Northcliffe (letter), 24 June 1908.

Northcliffe to Churchill (letter), 24 June 1908.

Churchill to Northcliffe (letter), 30 Aug. 1908.

Northcliffe to Churchill (letter), 14 Mar. 1909.

Churchill to Northcliffe (letter), 13 May 1909.

Churchill to Northcliffe (letter), 23 Jan. 1911.

Northcliffe to Churchill (letter), 27 July 1909.

Northcliffe to Churchill (letter), 29 July 1909.

Churchill to Northcliffe (letter), 30 July 1909.

Northcliffe to Churchill (letter), 11 Aug. 1909.

Anne Chisholm and Michael Davie, *Beaverbrook: A Life*, London: Hutchinson, 1992.

F. A. McKenzie, *The Mystery of the Daily Mail*, London: Associated Newspapers, 1921.

19 Dec. 1903; 15 Nov., 10 Dec. 1906, *Daily Mail*.

News in Our Time, 1896–1946: Golden Jubilee Book of the Daily Mail, published on the Fiftieth Anniversary of the *Daily Mail*, London: Associated Newspapers, 1946.

Robert MacNair Wilson, *Lord Northcliffe: A Study*, London: Ernest Benn, 1927.

Sir Evelyn Wrench, *Uphill: The First Stage in a Strenuous Life*, London: Ivor Nicholson & Watson, 1934.

23, 25, 28, 29 June 1910; 7, 10 June, 8, 10, 23, 25, 26 July 1911, *Daily Mail*.

8: 'The Cult of Northcliffe'

Louise Owen, *The Real Lord Northcliffe: Some Personal Recollections of a Private Secretary 1902–1922*, London: Cassell, 1922.

Reginald Pound and Geoffrey Harmsworth, *Northcliffe*, London: Cassell, 1959.

British Library, Add. MS 62198, Vol. xlvi.

Hamilton Fyfe, *Northcliffe: An Intimate Biography*, London: Allen & Unwin, 1930.

Tom Clarke, *My Northcliffe Diary*, London: Victor Gollancz, 1931.

G. Ward Price, *Extra-special Correspondent*, London: Harrap, 1957.

J. A. Hammerton, *With Northcliffe in Fleet Street*, London: Hutchinson, 1939.

Tom Clarke, *Northcliffe in History*, London: Hutchinson, 1950.

July, 1965, *Forme Magazine*.

Harry J. Greenwall, *Northcliffe: Napoleon of Fleet Street*, London: Allan Wingate, 1957.

Interview with Henry Arnholz, 7 May 1952, Harmsworth Archives.

Northcliffe to Henry Arnholz, 10 May 1910, Harmsworth Archives.

Northcliffe to Henry Arnholz, 30 Apr. 1910, Harmsworth Archives.

Hannen Swaffer, *Northcliffe's Return*, London: Hutchinson, 1925.

Bernard Falk, *Five Years Dead: A Postscript to 'He Laughed in Fleet Street'*, London: Book Club reprint, 1938.

J.M.N. Jeffries, *Front Everywhere*, London: Hutchinson, 1935.

14 May 1910, *Daily Mail*.

24 Aug. 1951, *World's Press News*.

Paul Ferris, *The House of Northcliffe: The Harmsworths of Fleet Street*, London: Weidenfeld & Nicolson, 1971.

9, 12 Jan., 1 Feb., 26 Apr., 8, 15 May, 29 July, 5 Sept. 1911, *Daily Mail*.

Northcliffe to Marlowe, 27 Apr. 1912; British Library Add. MS 62198, Vol. xlvi. Vincent Jones to Northcliffe, 12 Feb. 1913, British Library, Add. MS 62231, Vol. lxxix.

Northcliffe to Vincent Jones (letter), 22 Apr. 1913, British Library, Add. MS 62230, Vol. lxxviii.

Northcliffe to Sutton (letter), 21 Sept. 1913 as quoted in Pound and Harmsworth, p. 447.

Interview with Barbara Vincent-Jones, Eastbourne, 21 Mar. 1992.

Robert MacNair Wilson, *Lord Northcliffe: A Study*, London: Ernest Benn, 1927.

F.A. McKenzie, *The Mystery of the Daily Mail*, London: Associated Newspapers, 1921.

Northcliffe to Churchill (letter), 18 Sept. 1911, Harmsworth Archives.

Northcliffe to Churchill (letter), n.d., Harmsworth Archives.

Northcliffe to Churchill (letter), 12 July 1912, Harmsworth Archives.

Northcliffe to Churchill (letter), 10 Mar. 1913, Harmsworth Archives.

9: 'The March of the Hun'

Paul Ferris, *The House of Northcliffe: The Harmsworths of Fleet Street*, London: Weidenfeld & Nicolson, 1971.

Tom Clarke, *My Northcliffe Diary*, London: Victor Gollancz, 1931.

Princess Evelyn Blucher, *An English Wife in Berlin*, London: Constable, 1920.

Reginald Pound and Geoffrey Harmsworth, *Northcliffe*, London: Cassell, 1959.

Hamilton Fyfe, *Northcliffe: An Intimate Biography*, London: Allen & Unwin, 1930.

Robert Blatchford, 25 Aug. 1914, *Daily Mail*; G. Ward Price, 'French within 18 Miles of Metz,' 21 Aug. 1914, Hamilton Fyfe, 21 Aug. 1914, *Daily Mail*.

18 Aug. 1913, *Daily Mail*.

Bernard Falk, *Five Years Dead: A Postscript to 'He Laughed in Fleet Street'*, London: Book Club reprint, 1938.

Harry J. Greenwall, *Northcliffe: Napoleon of Fleet Street*, London: Allan Wingate, 1957.

Alfred Harmsworth, *The Romance of the Daily Mail*, London: Carmelite House, 1903.

20 Oct. 1913; 17, 24, 25, 26, 28 Aug., 21, 22 Sept., 5, 6, 14, 16 Oct. 1914; 5 Mar., 22 May 1915, *Daily Mail*.

Punch, Vol. cxlviii, 17 Feb. 1915.

Max Pemberton, *Lord Northcliffe: A Memoir*, London: Hodder & Stoughton, 1922.

G. Ward Price, *Extra-special Correspondent*, London: Harrap, 1957.

Ferdinand Tuohy, *The Crater of Mars*, London: Heinemann, 1929.

James Dunn, *Paperchase: Adventures in and out of Fleet Street*, London: Selwyn & Blount, 1938.

Robert MacNair Wilson, *Lord Northcliffe: A Study*, London: Ernest Benn, 1927.

Leaders quoted: 27 Aug., 25 Nov. 1914; 21, 22 May, 15 June, 20 July, 24 July, 28 July, 23 Aug. 1915, *Daily Mail*.

Henry Wickham Steed, *Through Thirty Years, 1892–1922: A Personal Narrative, Vol. II*, London: Heinemann, 1924.

Northcliffe's Personal Notes for Leader in the *Daily Mail* of Monday, 24 May 1915, Harmsworth Archives.

Hannen Swaffer, *Northcliffe's Return*, London: Hutchinson, 1925.

10: 'The Remainder Were Not To Be Denied'

Reginald Pound and Geoffrey Harmsworth, *Northcliffe*, London: Cassell, 1959.

22 Feb., 7 May 1915, *Daily Mail*.

G. Ward Price, *Extra-special Correspondent*, London: Harrap, 1957.

9 Mar., 3, 17, 24 Sept., 18 Oct. 1915; 3 July 1916, *Daily Mail*.

William Shawcross, *Rupert Murdoch: Ringmaster of the Information Circus*, London: Chatto & Windus, 1992.

British Library, Add. MS 62179, Vol. xxvii.

British Library, Add. MS 62199, Vol. xlvii.

All correspondence from Vere to Esmond and Harold Harmsworth is held in the Harmsworth Archives:

Vere to Esmond Harmsworth (letter), 15 Oct. 1914.

Vere to Harold Harmsworth (letter), 7 June 1915.

Vere to Harold Harmsworth (letter), 23 June 1915.

Vere to Harold Harmsworth (letter), 27 Aug. 1915.

Vere to Harold Harmsworth (letter), 9 July 1915.

Vere to Harold Harmsworth (letter), 15 July 1915.

Vere to Harold Harmsworth (letter), 17 July 1915.

Vere to Harold Harmsworth (letter), 10 July 1915.

Vere to Harold Harmsworth (letter), 26 May 1915.

Vere to Harold Harmsworth (letter), 11 June 1915.

Vere to Harold Harmsworth (letter), 12 June 1915.

Vere to Esmond Harmsworth (letter), 7 June 1915.

Vere to Harold Harmsworth (letter), 26 July 1915.

Vere to Harold Harmsworth (letter), 10 Aug. 1915.

Vere to Harold Harmsworth (letter), 7 Nov. 1915.

Vere to Harold Harmsworth (letter), n.d. Sept. 1915.

Vere to Harold Harmsworth (letter), 27 Sept. 1916.

Henry Wickham Steed, *Through Thirty Years, 1892–1922: A Personal Narrative, Vol. II*, London: Heinemann, 1924.

Philip Magnus, *Kitchener: Portrait of an Imperialist*, London: John Murray, 1958.

Cecil King, *Strictly Personal*, London: Weidenfeld & Nicolson, 1969.

Paul Ferris, *The House of Northcliffe: The Harmsworths of Fleet Street*, London: Weidenfeld & Nicolson, 1971.

11: 'After the Somme'

Tom Clarke, *My Northcliffe Diary*, London: Victor Gollancz, 1931.

Tom Driberg, *Beaverbrook: A Study in Power and Frustration*, London: Weidenfeld & Nicolson, 1956.

2, 13 Dec. 1916, *Daily Mail*.

The headlines appeared on 6 Dec. 1916 in the *Daily Mail*.

Henry Pelling, *Winston Churchill*, London: Macmillan, 1974.

Reginald Pound and Geoffrey Harmsworth, *Northcliffe*, London: Cassell, 1959.

Paul Ferris, *The House of Northcliffe: The Harmsworths of Fleet Street*, London: Weidenfeld & Nicolson, 1971.

Anne Chisholm and Michael Davie, *Beaverbrook: A Life*, London: Hutchinson, 1992.

A.J.P. Taylor, *Beaverbrook: A Biography*, London: Hamish Hamilton, 1972.

David Lloyd George, *War Memoirs of David Lloyd George, Vols. I and II*, London: Odhams Press, 1938.

Louise Owen, *The Real Lord Northcliffe: Some Personal Recollections of a Private Secretary 1902–1922*, London: Cassell, 1922.

Northcliffe to Lady Northcliffe (letter), quoted in Pound and Harmsworth, p. 536.

Hamilton Fyfe, *Northcliffe: An Intimate Biography*, London: Allen & Unwin, 1930.

Northcliffe to Sutton (letter), 30 June 1917, Harmsworth Archives.

Northcliffe to Sutton (letter), 20 June 1917, Harmsworth Archives.

Northcliffe to Sutton (letter), 29 July 1917, Harmsworth Archives.

Northcliffe to Sutton (letter), 17 Aug. 1917, Harmsworth Archives.

Northcliffe to Sutton (letter), 17 June 1917, Harmsworth Archives.

Northcliffe to Major Davies (letter), 20 June 1917, Harmsworth Archives.

Dec. 1927, *National Review*.

Henry Wickham Steed, *Through Thirty Years, 1892–1922: A Personal Narrative, Vol. II*, London: Heinemann, 1924.

Northcliffe to Beaverbrook (letter), 23 Apr. 1918, Beaverbrook Papers, House of Lords Record Office.

Northcliffe to Beaverbrook (letter), 30 Apr. 1918, Beaverbrook Papers, House of Lords Record Office.

Sir Campbell Stuart, KBE, *Secrets of Crewe House*, London: Hodder & Stoughton, 1920.

Mrs C.S. Peel, *The Daily Mail Cookery Book*, London: Associated Newspapers, 1920.

Northcliffe to Marlowe (letter), 11 Dec. 1918, British Library, Add. MS 62199, Vol. xlvii.

The event took place at the end of November 1918. Pound and Harmsworth, p. 675.

14 Feb. 1918, *Eton College Chronicle*.

Richard Bourne, *Lords of Fleet Street: The Harmsworth Dynasty*, London: Unwin Hyman, 1990.

Vyvyan Harmsworth to Northcliffe (letter), 29 Jan. 1918, Harmsworth Archives.

Interview with Daphne Macneile Dixon, South Godestone, 22 Mar. 1992.

A.P. Herbert, *The Times Saturday Review*, 9 Nov. 1991, p. 12.

Harold Harmsworth to Esmond Harmsworth (letter), 23 May 1918, Harmsworth Archives.

12: 'Northcliffe Mad'

Northcliffe to F.W. Wile (letter), 24 July 1918, Harmsworth Archives.

Reginald Pound and Geoffrey Harmsworth, *Northcliffe*, London: Cassell, 1959.

Tom Clarke, *My Northcliffe Diary*, London: Victor Gollancz, 1931.

Carmelite Magazine, Harmsworth Archives.

A.J.P. Taylor, *Beaverbrook: A Biography*, London: Hamish Hamilton, 1972.

David Lloyd George, *War Memoirs of David Lloyd George, Vols. I and II*, London: Odhams Press, 1938.

A.J.P. Taylor, *The First World War: An Illustrated History*, Hamish Hamilton, 1963.

Northcliffe to Harold Harmsworth (letter), 10 Apr. 1919, quoted in Pound and Harmsworth, p. 712.

Paul Ferris, *The House of Northcliffe: The Harmsworths of Fleet Street*, London: Weidenfeld & Nicolson, 1971.

Bernard Falk, *Five Years Dead: A Postscript to 'He Laughed in Fleet Street'*, London: Book Club reprint, 1938.

Bernard Falk, *He Laughed in Fleet Street*, London: Hutchinson, 1933.

British Library, Add. MS 62199, Vol. xlvii.

Louise Owen, *The Real Lord Northcliffe: Some Personal Recollections of a Private Secretary 1902–1922*, London: Cassell, 1922.

Northcliffe to Marlowe (letter), 24 July 1919, British Library, Add. MS 61100, Vol. xlviii.

Northcliffe, *Leaves from a Peasant's Diary*, written by Alfred for his mother in 1919 in remembrance of his trip to Gorbio, Harmsworth Archives.

From 'Northcliffe's Throat Diary', kept in 1919 and held in the Harmsworth Archives.

Mike Carleton, 2 May 1993, p. 5, *Sunday Times*.

'Melba sings by wireless', 16 June 1920, p. 1, *Daily Mail*.

David MacFarlane, *The Danger Tree*, Toronto: Macfarlane Walter & Ross, 1991.

Henry Wickham Steed, *Through Thirty Years, 1892–1922: A Personal Narrative, Vol. II*, London: Heinemann, 1924.

Douglas Crawford to H.G. Price (letter), 19 May 1920, Harmsworth Archives.

Winston Churchill to Northcliffe (letter), 29 May 1920, Harmsworth Archives.

Northcliffe to Winston Churchill (letter), n.d. July 1920, Harmsworth Archives.

'State Aid for Civil Flying, Mr Churchill's Promise', 15 Oct. 1920, *Daily Mail*.

Piers Brendon, *The Life and Death of the Press Barons*, London: Secker & Warburg, 1982.

William Shawcross, *Rupert Murdoch: Ringmaster of the Information Circus*, London: Chatto & Windus, 1992.

Murdoch to Northcliffe (letter), 4 Mar. 1920, British Library, Add. MS 62179, Vol. xxvii.

Murdoch to Northcliffe (letter), 23 Apr. 1922, British Library, Add. MS 62179, Vol. xxvii.

Northcliffe to Murdoch (letter), 18 Apr. 1921, British Library, Add. MS 62179, Vol. xxvii.

Murdoch to Northcliffe (letter), 7 Dec. 1921, British Library, Add. MS 62179, Vol. xxvii.

Northcliffe to Murdoch (letter), n.d. Dec. 1921, British Library, Add. MS 62179, Vol. xxvii.

Murdoch to Northcliffe (letter), 30 Dec. 1921, British Library, Add. MS 62179, Vol. xxvii.

Northcliffe to Murdoch (letter), 25 Jan. 1922, British Library, Add. MS 62179, Vol. xxvii.

Murdoch to Northcliffe (letter), 12 Mar. 1922, British Library, Add. MS 62179, Vol. xxvii.

Murdoch to Northcliffe (letter), 24 Mar. 1922, British Library, Add. MS 62179, Vol. xxvii.

Punch, 27 July 1921, Vol. clxi.

Northcliffe to Marlowe (letter), 22 Nov. 1921, from SS *Nyanza*, off the China Coast, British Library, Add. MS 62200, Vol. xlviii.

Hamilton Fyfe, *Northcliffe: An Intimate Biography*, London: Allen & Unwin, 1930.

Kennedy Jones to Northcliffe (letter), 29 Apr. 1916, British Library, Add. MS 62196, Vol. xliv.

Northcliffe to Kennedy Jones (letter), 12 Dec. 1916, British Library, Add. MS 62196, Vol. xliv.

Hannen Swaffer, *Northcliffe's Return*, London: Hutchinson, 1925.

13: 'Rosebud'

Louise Owen to Northcliffe (letter), 19 Mar. [1922], Harmsworth Archives.

Steed to Northcliffe (letter), 31 Dec. 1919, British Library, Add. MS 62247, Vol. xcv.

Northcliffe to Marlowe (letter), 10 Feb. 1920, British Library, Add. MS 62200, Vol. xlviii.

History of the Times, Vol. III: The Twentieth Century Test, 1884–1912, London: Printing House Square, 1947.

Bernard Falk, *He Laughed in Fleet Street*, London: Hutchinson, 1933.

Bernard Falk, *Five Years Dead: A Postscript to 'He Laughed in Fleet Street'*, London: Book Club reprint, 1938.

Steed to Northcliffe (letter), 5 July 1920, British Library, Add. MS 62248, Vol. xcvi.

Northcliffe to Murdoch (letter), 12 May 1922, British Library, Add. MS 62179, Vol. xxvii.

Northcliffe to Murdoch (letter), 18 May 1922, British Library, Add. MS 62179, Vol. xxvii.

Murdoch to Northcliffe (letter), 22 May 1922, British Library, Add. MS 62179, Vol. xxvii.

Murdoch to Northcliffe (letter), 26 May 1922, British Library, Add. MS 62179, Vol. xxvii.

Northcliffe to Murdoch (letter), 29 May 1922, British Library, Add. MS 62179, Vol. xxvii.

Sir Robert Hudson to Sir George Sutton (letter), 16 June 1922, Harmsworth Archives.

Paul Ferris, *The House of Northcliffe: The Harmsworths of Fleet Street*, London: Weidenfeld & Nicolson, 1971.

Tom Clarke, *My Northcliffe Diary*, London: Victor Gollancz, 1931.

'Notes' by General Sir Alexander Godley, on the visit of Northcliffe to Cologne, May, June, 1922. An extract from *Life of an Irish Soldier* by General Sir Alexander Godley, GB, KCMG, written in 1939, expanded and refined from the original document.

Wickham Steed's 'Notes of My Intercourse with Lord Northcliffe, June 11 to 14' were dated and signed 22 June 1922, Harmsworth Archives.

Reginald Pound and Geoffrey Harmsworth, *Northcliffe*, London: Cassell, 1959.

Epilogue

Hannen Swaffer, *Northcliffe's Return*, London: Hutchinson, 1925.

Tom Clarke, *My Northcliffe Diary*, London: Victor Gollancz, 1931.

Louise Owen, *The Real Lord Northcliffe: Some Personal Recollections of a Private Secretary 1902–1922*, London: Cassell, 1922.

Paul Ferris, *The House of Northcliffe: The Harmsworths of Fleet Street*, London: Weidenfeld & Nicolson, 1971.

14: 'The River Fleet'

Interview with Graham McLean, London, 10 Apr. 1992.

Cecil King, *Strictly Personal*, London: Weidenfeld & Nicolson, 1969.

A.J.P. Taylor, *English History: 1914–1945*, Oxford: Oxford University Press, 1965.

Bernard Falk, *Bouquets for Fleet Street: Memories and Musings over Fifty Years*, London: Hutchinson, 1951.

Hugh Cudlipp, *Publish and Be Damned*, London: Andrew Dakers, 1953.

Richard Bourne, *Lords of Fleet Street: The Harmsworth Dynasty*, London: Unwin Hyman, 1990.

Cecil King, *Strictly Personal*, London: Weidenfeld & Nicolson, 1969.

Interview with Esme, Countess of Cromer, London, 14 Mar. 1992.

Martin Gilbert, *Winston S. Churchill, Vol. V, Companion Part I. Documents. The Exchequer Years, 1922–1929*, London: Heinemann, 1979.

Andrew Boyle, *Poor, Dear Brendan: The Quest for Brendan Bracken*, London: Hutchinson, 1974.

A.J.P. Taylor, *Beaverbrook: A Biography*, London: Hamish Hamilton, 1972.

Rothermere to Lloyd George (letter), 23 Apr. 1918, Harmsworth Archives.

Lloyd George to Rothermere (letter), 25 Apr. 1918, Harmsworth Archives.

Rothermere to Lloyd George (letter), 25 Apr. 1918, Harmsworth Archives.

Sir Evelyn Wrench, *Geoffrey Dawson and Our Times*, London: Hutchinson, 1955.

Anne Chisholm and Michael Davie, *Beaverbrook: A Life*, London: Hutchinson, 1992.

Rothermere to Bonar Law (letter), 3 May 1918, Harmsworth Archives.

Interview with Daphne Macneile Dixon, South Godestone, 22 Mar. 1992.

George D. Painter, *André Gide*, London: Arthur Barker, 1951.

Linette F. Brugmans, ed. and trans., *Correspondence of André Gide and Edmund Gosse, 1904–1928*, London: Peter Owen, 1960.

André Gide, *The Coiners*, London: Cassell, 1950, trans. from the French by Dorothy Bussy.

James Moore, *Gurdjieff: The Anatomy of Myth, a Biography*, Shaftesbury: Element Books, 1991.

Robert Sencourt, *T.S. Eliot: A Memoir*, edited by Donald Adamson, London: Garnstone Press, 1971.

Elizabeth Sprigge, *Gertrude Stein: Her Life and Work*, London: Hamish Hamilton, 1957.

Lady Rothermere to Esmond Harmsworth (letter), 12 Oct. 1931, Harmsworth Archives.

Tom Clarke, *My Northcliffe Diary*, London: Victor Gollancz, 1931.

Rothermere to Beaverbrook (letter), 10 Feb. 1921, Harmsworth Archives.

Beaverbrook to Rothermere (letter), 20 Apr. 1921, Harmsworth Archives.

Rothermere to Beaverbrook (letter), 3 May 1921, Harmsworth Archives.

Francis Williams, *Dangerous Estate: The Anatomy of Newspapers*, London: Longman, 1957.

Rothermere to Beaverbrook (letter), 18 Nov. 1922, Harmsworth Archives.

Beaverbrook to Rothermere (letter), 21 Nov. 1922, Harmsworth Archives.

Rothermere to Esmond Harmsworth (letter), 30 Dec. 1922, Harmsworth Archives.

Rothermere to Pomeroy Burton (letter), n.d., Harmsworth Archives.

Rothermere to Esmond Harmsworth (letter), Tues., n.d., 1923, Harmsworth Archives.

Rothermere to Harold (letter), n.d., May 1923, Harmsworth Archives.

15: 'Nomad'

Rothermere to Esmond Harmsworth (letter), n.d., Harmsworth Archives.

Rothermere to Esmond Harmsworth (letter), 10 Feb. 1921, Harmsworth Archives.

Rothermere to Esmond Harmsworth (letter), 30 Dec., n.y., Harmsworth Archives.

Rothermere to Esmond Harmsworth (letter), n.d., Harmsworth Archives.

Rothermere to Esmond Harmsworth (letter), n.d., Harmsworth Archives.

Rothermere to Esmond Harmsworth (letter), n.d., Harmsworth Archives.

Rothermere to Esmond Harmsworth (telegram), 23 Jan. 1924, Harmsworth Archives.

Interview with Aidan Crawley, Farthinghoe, Northants., 22 June 1992.

Interview with Esme, Countess of Cromer, London, 14 Mar. 1992.

Hugh Cudlipp, *Publish and Be Damned*, London: Andrew Dakers, 1953.

Robert Allen and John Frost, *Daily Mirror*, Cambridge: Patrick Stephens, 1981.

Rothermere to Esmond Harmsworth (letter), 22 Oct. 1921, Harmsworth Archives.

Rothermere to Beaverbrook (letter), n.d., from Venice, 1921, Harmsworth Archives.

Esmond to Rothermere (letter), 17 Jan. 1924, Harmsworth Archives.

Rothermere to Esmond (letter), 21 Jan. 1924, Harmsworth Archives.

Tom Driberg, *Beaverbrook: A Study in Power and Frustration*, London: Weidenfeld & Nicolson, 1956, quoting an interview with Stanley Baldwin in the *People*, 18 May 1924, pp. 179–80.

Rothermere to Esmond (letter), 8 Oct. 1924, Harmsworth Archives.

Lewis Chester, Stephen Fay and Hugo Young, *The Zinoviev Letter*, London: Heinemann, 1967.

Beaverbrook to Rothermere (telegram), 30 Oct. 1924, Harmsworth Archives.

Beaverbrook to Rothermere (letter), 3 July 1925, Harmsworth Archives.

G.M. Young, *Stanley Baldwin*, London: Rupert Hart-Davis, 1952.

Charles Edward Lysaght, *Brendan Bracken*, London: Allen Lane, 1979.

Keith Middlemas and John Barnes, *Baldwin: A Biography*, London: Weidenfeld & Nicolson, 1969.

Bernard Falk, *He Laughed in Fleet Street*, London: Hutchinson, 1933.

Cecil King, *Strictly Personal*, London: Weidenfeld & Nicolson, 1969.

Arnold Bennett, *The Journals of Arnold Bennett*, ed. Newman Flower, 3 vols, London: Cassell, 1932–3.

Richard Buckle, *Diaghilev*, London: Weidenfeld & Nicolson, 1979.

Northcliffe, *Leaves from a Peasant's Diary*, Unpublished MS, 1919, Harmsworth Archives.

Alice Nikitina, *Nikitina, By Herself*, trans. from the French by Baroness Budberg, London: Allan Wingate, 1959.

Viscount Rothermere, *My Campaign for Hungary*, London: Eyre & Spottiswoode, 1939.

Prince Franz Hohenlohe, *Steph – The Fabulous Princess*, London: New English Library, 1976.

Rothermere, 'Europe's Powder Magazine', 30 Aug. 1927, *Daily Mail*.

Martin Gilbert, *Winston S. Churchill, Vol. V, Companion Part I. Documents. The Exchequer Years, 1922–1929*, London: Heinemann, 1979.

Martin Gilbert, above, quoting Baldwin's letter to Churchill, dated 15 May 1928, p. 1287.

Cuttings made available by Major Vyvyan Harmsworth, Head of Corporate Affairs, Associated Newspapers.

16: 'The Glorious Twelfth'

Anne Chisholm and Michael Davie, *Beaverbrook: A Life*, London: Hutchinson, 1992.

Aidan Crawley, *Leap Before You Look: A Memoir*, London: Collins, 1988.

Interview with Esme, Countess of Cromer, London, 14 Mar. 1992.

Richard Bourne, *Lords of Fleet Street: The Harmsworth Dynasty*, London: Unwin Hyman, 1990.

Bernard Falk, *He Laughed in Fleet Street*, London: Hutchinson, 1933.

Interview with Aidan Crawley, Farthinghoe, Northants., 22 June 1992.

G. Ward Price, *Extra-special Correspondent*, London: Harrap, 1957.

Minutes, January 1928, Daily Mail & General Trust.

Interview with Eric Swansen, St John's, Newfoundland, 22 Sept. 1992.

Interview with Edward Martin, St John's, Newfoundland, 22 Sept. 1992.

G. N. Neary, 'Mining History of the Buchans Area,' in *The Buchans Orebodies: Fifty Years of Geology and Mining*, ed. E.A. Swanson, D.F. Strong, J.G. Thurlow, Geological Association of Canada, Special Paper 22, 1981.

From information dated 16 Oct. 1926 and summarized by R.C. Brooks on 14 Mar. 1960, Beaverbrook Papers, House of Lords Records Office.

Beaverbrook to Rothermere (letter), 21 Oct. 1926, Beaverbrook Papers, House of Lords Record Office.

5 Jan., 14 Feb. 1930, *Daily Mail*.

Keith Middlemas and John Barnes, *Baldwin: A Biography*, London: Weidenfeld & Nicolson, 1969.

Tom Driberg, *Beaverbrook: A Study in Power and Frustration*, London: Weidenfeld & Nicolson, 1956.

Henry Pelling, *Winston Churchill*, London: Macmillan, 1974.

Beaverbrook to Esmond Rothermere (letter), 18 Aug. 1961, Harmsworth Archives.

S.J. Taylor, *Stalin's Apologist: Walter Duranty: The New York Times's Man in Moscow*, Oxford: Oxford University Press, 1990, p. 72, quoting Duranty.

Denis Mack Smith, *Mussolini*, London: Weidenfeld & Nicolson, 1981.

William Shirer, *Midcentury Journey: The Western World through Its Years of Conflict*, New York: New American Library, 1961.

Richard M. Griffiths, *Fellow Travellers of the Right: British Enthusiasts for Nazi Germany, 1933–39*, London: Constable, 1980.

Rothermere to Lloyd George (letter), 10 June 1927, Harmsworth Archives.

17: 'The Blackshirts Are in the Wash'

Public Record Office, Kew, Home Office File 144/19069–70/486825.

Robert Skidelsky, *Oswald Mosley*, London: Macmillan, 1975.

Diana Mosley, *A Life of Contrasts*, London: Hamish Hamilton, 1977.

Harold Nicolson, *Diaries and Letters, 1930–1939* and *1939–1945*, ed. Nigel Nicolson, London: Collins, 1967.

Richard M. Griffiths, *Fellow Travellers of the Right: British Enthusiasts for Nazi Germany, 1933–39*, London: Constable, 1980.

G. Ward Price, '15,000 at Blackshirt Meeting', 8 Jan. 1934, *Daily Mail*.

Interview with Ralph Izzard, Tunbridge Wells, 1 Sept. 1992.

Oswald Mosley, *My Life*, London: Thomas Nelson & Sons, 1968.

Public Record Office, Kew, Home Office File 144/20142/674216/178.

Arthur Wareham, *Quiet Man of Fleet Street*, Unpublished MS.

Viscount Camrose, *British Newspapers and Their Controllers*, London: Cassell, 1947.

A.J.P. Taylor, *Beaverbrook: A Biography*, London: Hamish Hamilton, 1972.

Viscount Rothermere, *My Fight to Rearm Britain*, London: Eyre & Spottiswoode, 1939.

Collie Knox, *Collie Knox Calling! A Selection of the Famous Friday 'Week-end' Broadcasts Now Appearing in The Daily Mail*, London: Chapman & Hall, 1937.

Interview with Reginald Foster, by telephone, 27 Mar. 1992.

21 Nov. 1967, *Daily Mail*.

Interview with Selina Hastings, by telephone, 13 July 1993.

Interview with Rhona Churchill, London, 23 Nov. 1992.

Martin Gilbert, *Winston S. Churchill, Vol. V, 1922–1939*, London: Heinemann, 1976.

Winston Churchill, 5 Jan., 9 July, 17 Nov. 1932, *Daily Mail*.

Viscount Rothermere, 24 Sept. 1930; 10 July 1933, *Daily Mail*.

Prince Franz Hohenlohe, *Steph – The Fabulous Princess*, London: New English Library, 1976.

Rothermere to Princess Stephanie (letter), 1 Nov. 1933, Harmsworth Archives.

Franklin Reid Gannon, *The British Press and Germany, 1936–1939*, Oxford: Clarendon Press, 1971.

Ted Grant, *Menace of Fascism* [pamphlet], London: Militant, first published in 1948; revised 1978.

Bernard Falk, *Five Years Dead: A Postscript to 'He Laughed in Fleet Street'*, London: Book Club reprint, 1938.

G. Ward Price, *I Know These Dictators*, London: Harrap, 1937.

18: 'Butter'

Rothermere to N. Chamberlain (letter), 5 Oct. 1934, Harmsworth Archives.

Minute by Sir R. Vansittart, 19 Aug. 1934, Churchill College Cambridge, C.5957/28/18/1934.

Rothermere to Churchill (letter), 13 May 1935, Harmsworth Archives.

Rothermere to Tyrrell (letter), 1 Dec. 1933, Harmsworth Archives.

Rothermere to Lady Vansittart (letter), 19 Feb. 1934, Harmsworth Archives.

Rothermere to R. MacDonald (letter), 3 May 1935, Harmsworth Archives.

Rothermere to Churchill (letter), 13 May 1935, Harmsworth Archives.

G. Ward Price to Rothermere (letter), 13 Sept. 1936, Harmsworth Archives.

Rothermere to Churchill (letter), 17 July 1939; found in Martin Gilbert's *Winston S. Churchill, Vol. V., 1922–1939*, London: Heinemann, 1976, at pp. 1088–9; see also Viscount Rothermere, *My Fight to Rearm Britain*, London: Eyre & Spottiswoode, 1939.

Churchill to Rothermere (letter), 12 May 1935, Harmsworth Archives.

Rothermere to Churchill (letter), 31 Aug. 1934, Harmsworth Archives.

Rothermere to Oliver Stanley, MP (letter), 27 May 1935, Harmsworth Archives.

Rothermere to Princess Stephanie Hohenlohe (letter), 3 Apr. 1935, Harmsworth Archives.

Rothermere to Churchill (letter), 16 July 1936, Harmsworth Archives.

Rothermere to Churchill (letter), 22 Dec. 1937, Harmsworth Archives.

Gordon Beckles, *Birth of a Spitfire*, London: Collins, 1941.

Sir Kingsley Wood to Rothermere (letter), 6 July 1939, Harmsworth Archives.

Publication supplied by Royal Air Force Museum, Britain's National Museum of Aviation, Hendon, London, 'Bristol Blenheim', p. 33. Consultant, Mungo Chapman.

Susan Joiner, compiler, John Batchelor, illustrator, *Fighting Aircraft of World Wars I and II*, London: Phoebus, 1976.

Treasury announcement of Rothermere's gift of Blenheim Bomber to the R.A.F., n.d., Aug., 1935, Harmsworth Archives.

Viscount Rothermere, *Warnings and Predictions*, London: Eyre & Spottiswoode, 1939.

Rothermere to Churchill (letter), 26 Sept. 1938, Harmsworth Archives.

Rothermere to Churchill (letter), 30 Sept. 1938, Harmsworth Archives.

Rothermere to Churchill (letter), 6 Oct. 1938, Harmsworth Archives.

Rothermere to Churchill (letter), 6 Oct. 1938, Harmsworth Archives.

Rothermere to Ribbentrop (letter), 20 July 1939, Harmsworth Archives.

Rothermere to Ribbentrop (letter), 2 Aug. 1939, Harmsworth Archives.

Ribbentrop to Rothermere, 5 Aug. 1939, Harmsworth Archives.

Rothermere to the Minister of Agriculture (letter), 12 Apr. 1939, Harmsworth Archives.

Film clip [1938] of Rothermere with Esmond, held by Corporate Affairs in Northcliffe House.

F.E. Smith (Lord Birkenhead) to Rothermere, n.d. (1923?), Harmsworth Archives.

Bernard Falk, *Bouquets for Fleet Street: Memories and Musings over Fifty Years*, London: Hutchinson, 1951.

Unpublished interview with the 1st Viscount Rothermere, 14 Apr. 1934, conducted by George Popoff.

Interview with Vere Rothermere, London, 1 Nov. 1992.

Quentin Crewe, *Well, I Forget the Rest: The Autobiography of an Optimist*, London: Hutchinson, 1991.

Franklin Reid Gannon, *The British Press and Germany, 1936–1939*, Oxford: Clarendon Press, 1971.

Rothermere to Lady Vansittart (letter), 19 Feb. 1934, Harmsworth Archives.

Oswald Mosley, *My Life*, London: Thomas Nelson & Sons, 1968.

19: 'Home'

Lilian Rothermere to Esmond (letter), n.d. (c. 1921?), Harmsworth Archives.

Rothermere to Lorna Harmsworth, later Lady Cooper-Key (letter), 28 Feb. 1937, from her personal archive.

Interview with Esme, Countess of Cromer, London, 14 Mar. 1992.

André Gide, *The Coiners*, London: Cassell, 1950, trans. from the French by Dorothy Bussy.

Rothermere to Hohenlohe (letter), 14 Jan. 1935, Harmsworth Archives.

Rothermere to Hohenlohe (letter), 4 Feb. 1935, Harmsworth Archives.

Rothermere to Hohenlohe (letter), 5 Nov. 1935, Harmsworth Archives.

Prince Franz Hohenlohe, *Steph – The Fabulous Princess*, London: New English Library, 1976.

Drew Middleton, *The Sky Suspended: The Battle of Britain*, London: Secker & Warburg, 1960.

Rothermere to Churchill (letter), 17 July 1939, Harmsworth Archives.

Churchill to Rothermere (letter), 19 July 1939, Harmsworth Archives.

Anne Chisholm and Michael Davie, *Beaverbrook: A Life*, London: Hutchinson, 1992.

Rothermere to Beaverbrook (telegram), 15 May 1940, Harmsworth Archives.

Beaverbrook to Rothermere (telegram), 16 May 1940, Harmsworth Archives.

A.J.P. Taylor, *Beaverbrook: A Biography*, London: Hamish Hamilton, 1972.

Publication supplied by Britain's Royal Air Force Museum, Hendon, London: *The British Fighter Since 1912*, 'The Bristol Blenheim Bomber'.

Harry Morison to Arthur — (letter), 6 Dec. 1940, Harmsworth Archives.

Frank Humphries to Esmond Harmsworth (letter), 5 Dec. 1940, Harmsworth Archives.

Epilogue

Interview with Lady Cooper-Key, London, 1 June 1992.

Harry Morison to Arthur — (letter), describing the final resting place of Harold Rothermere, 6 Dec. 1940, Harmsworth Archives.

Beaverbrook to Esmond Rothermere (letter), 3 Dec. 1942, Harmsworth Archives.

SELECT BIBLIOGRAPHY

Allen, Robert and John Frost. *Daily Mirror*, Cambridge: Patrick Stephens, 1981.

Angell, Norman. *After All*, London: Hamish Hamilton, 1951.

Arming in the Air: The Daily Mail Campaign: Warnings of Three Wasted Years, London: Associated Newspapers, 1936.

Associated Newspapers Group Limited. Annual meeting minutes books, 1960–1974, access provided by Ian Jackson.

Baden-Powell, General. *Souvenir of the Siege of Mafeking*, introduction by Charles E. Hands, London: The Smith Premier Typewriter Co., 1901.

Balfour, Michael. *Propaganda in War 1939–1945: Organisations, Policies and Publics in Britain and Germany*, London: Routledge & Kegan Paul, 1979.

Baxter, Beverley. *Strange Street*, London: Hutchinson, 1935.

Beaverbrook, Lord. *Politicians and the Press*, London: Hutchinson, 1926.

Beaverbrook, Lord. *Men and Power*, London: Hutchinson, 1956.

Beckles, Gordon. *Birth of a Spitfire*, London: Collins, 1941.

Bennett, Arnold. *The Journals of Arnold Bennett*, ed. Newman Flower, 3 vols., London: Cassell, 1932–3.

Bennett, Arnold. *What the Public Wants: A play in four acts*, London: Chatto & Windus, 1921.

Bethnal Green Museum of Childhood. *Penny Dreadfuls and Comics*, London: Victoria and Albert Museum, 1983.

Bewsher, Captain Paul, DSC, RAF. *The Bombing of Bruges*, London: Hodder & Stoughton, 1918.

Bewsher, Paul. *The Dawn Patrol and other poems of an aviator*, London: Erskine Macdonald, 1917.

Bewsher, Paul. *'Green Balls': The Adventures of a Night-Bomber*, London: William Blackwood, 1919.

Blucher, Princess Evelyn. *An English Wife in Berlin*, London: Constable, 1920.

Bourne, Richard. *Lords of Fleet Street: The Harmsworth Dynasty*, London: Unwin Hyman, 1990.

Boyle, Andrew. *Poor, Dear Brendan: The Quest for Brendan Bracken*, London: Hutchinson, 1974.

Boyle, Andrew. *Trenchard*, London: Collins, 1962.

Brendon, Piers. *The Life and Death of the Press Barons*, London: Secker & Warburg, 1982.

Brex, Twells. *Adventures on the Home Front*, London: Methuen, 1918.

Brex, Twells. *Before Sunset*, reprinted from the *Daily Mail*, 8 Jan. 1920, London: Co-operative Printing Society.

Brugmans, Linette F., ed. and trans. *Correspondence of André Gide and Edmund Gosse, 1904–1928*, London: Peter Owen, 1960.

Buckle, Richard. *Diaghilev*, London: Weidenfeld & Nicolson, 1979.

Bundock, Clement J. *The National Union of Journalists: A Jubilee History 1907–1957*, Oxford: Oxford University Press, 1957.

Camrose, Viscount. *British Newspapers and Their Controllers*, London: Cassell, 1947.

Cardozo, Harold. *The March of a Nation: My Year of Spain's Civil War*, London: Eyre & Spottiswoode, 1937.

Carter, Violet Bonham. *Winston Churchill as I Knew Him*, London: Eyre & Spottiswoode and Collins, 1965.

Chester, Lewis and Jonathan Fenby. *The Fall of the House of Beaverbrook*, London: André Deutsch, 1979.

Chester, Lewis, Stephen Fay and Hugo Young. *The Zinoviev Letter*, London: Heinemann, 1967.

Chisholm, Anne and Michael Davie. *Beaverbrook: A Life*, London: Hutchinson, 1992.

Christiansen, Arthur. *Headlines All My Life*, London: Heinemann, 1961.

Churchill, Randolph and Helmut Gernsheim, eds. *Churchill: His Life in Photographs*, London: Weidenfeld & Nicolson, 1955.

Churchill, Randolph S. *Winston S. Churchill, Volume II, Young Statesman, 1901–1914*, London: Heinemann, 1967.

Churchill, Winston, S. *The World Crisis, 1911–1918*. Odhams Press, 1950.

Clarke, Mary and David Vaughan, eds. *The Encyclopedia of Dance & Ballet*, London: Pitman, 1977.

Clarke, Tom. *My Lloyd George Diary*, London: Methuen, 1939.

Clarke, Tom. *My Northcliffe Diary*, London: Victor Gollancz, 1931.

Clarke, Tom. *Northcliffe in History*, London: Hutchinson, 1950.

Clifford, Alexander. *Crusader*, London: Harrap, 1942.

Cobbett, W.W. and Sidney Dark. *Fleet Street: An Anthology of Modern Journalism*, London: Eyre & Spottiswoode, 1932.

Colvin, Ian. *The Life of Lord Carson*, Vol. III, London: Victor Gollancz, 1936.

Cowles, Virginia. *Winston Churchill: The Era and the Man*, London: Hamish Hamilton, 1953.

Crawley, Aidan. *Leap Before You Look: A Memoir*, London: Collins, 1988.

Crewe, Quentin. *Well, I Forget the Rest: The Autobiography of an Optimist*, London: Hutchinson, 1991.

The Criterion: A Quarterly Review. Published by R. Cobden-Sanderson, London, 1922.

Cromer, Esme. *From This Day Forward*, Stoke Abbott: Thomas Harmsworth Publishing Company, 1991.

Cudlipp, Hugh. *Published and Be Damned*, London: Andrew Dakers, 1953.

Daily Mail and General Trust Limited. Meeting minutes, yearly 1934–90.

Daily Mail and the Fight for London. A Handbook to the London County Council Election, Giving Both Sides, 1907.

Daily Mail Blue Book on the Indian Crisis, 1931.

The Daily Mail Bungalow Book: Reproductions of the Best Designs Entered in the Daily Mail Architects Competition for Labour-Saving Bungalows, London: Associated Newspapers, 1922.

The Daily Mail Ideal Houses Book: Reproductions of the Best Designs Entered in the Daily Mail Architects Competition, 1927, London: Associated Newspapers, 1927.

The Daily Mail Trade Union Mission to the United States: Full Story of the Tour and Members' Reports. London: Daily Mail, 1926.

Day, J. Wentworth. *Lady Houston: The Woman Who Saved Britain*, London: Allan Wingate, 1958.

Delgado, Alan. *Victorian Entertainment*, Newton Abbot: David & Charles, 1971.

Dilnot, George, compiler. *The Romance of the Amalgamated Press*, London: The Amalgamated Press, 1925.

Donald, Sir Robert. *The Tragedy of Trianon: Hungary's Appeal to Humanity*, London: Thornton Butterworth, 1928.

Driberg, Tom. *Beaverbrook: A Study in Power and Frustration*, London: Weidenfeld & Nicolson, 1956.

Driberg, Tom. *Ruling Passions*, London: Jonathan Cape, 1977.

Dunn, James. *Paperchase: Adventures In and Out of Fleet Street*, London: Selwyn & Blount, 1938.

Eade, Charles, ed. *Churchill: By His Contemporaries*, London: Hutchinson, 1953. [contains contributions by G. Ward Price, Sir Evelyn Wrench, and G.W. Steevens' original *DM* article].

Edelman, Maurice. *The Mirror: A Political History*, London: Hamish Hamilton, 1966.

Falk, Bernard. *Bouquets for Fleet Street: Memories and Musings over Fifty Years*, London: Hutchinson, 1951.

Falk, Bernard. *Five Years Dead: A Postscript to 'He Laughed in Fleet Street'*, London: Book Club reprint, 1938.

Falk, Bernard. *He Laughed in Fleet Street*, London: Hutchinson, 1933.

Ferris, Paul. *The House of Northcliffe: The Harmsworths of Fleet Street*, London: Weidenfeld & Nicolson, 1971.

Fyfe, Hamilton. *Behind the Scenes of the Great Strike*, London: The Labour Publishing Company, 1926.

Fyfe, Hamilton. *Northcliffe: An Intimate Biography*, London: Allen & Unwin, 1930.

Fyfe, Hamilton. *Press Parade*, London: Watts, 1936.

Fyfe, Hamilton. *Sixty Years of Fleet Street*, London: W.H. Allen, 1949.

Fyfe, Hamilton. *T.P. O'Connor*, London: Allen & Unwin, 1934.

Fyfe, Hamilton. *Twells Brex: A Conqueror of Death*, London: Cassell, 1920.

Gannon, Franklin Reid. *The British Press and Germany, 1936–1939*, Oxford: Clarendon Press, 1971.

Gardiner, Alfred G. *The Daily Mail and the Liberal Press: A Reply to Scaremongerings and An Open Letter to Lord Northcliffe*, London: The Daily News, 1914.

Gardner, Brian. *Churchill in His Time: A Study in a Reputation, 1939–1945*, London: Methuen, 1968.

George, David Lloyd. *The Truth about the Peace Treaties*, London: Victor Gollancz, 1938.

George, David Lloyd. *War Memoirs of David Lloyd George, Vols I and II*, London: Odhams Press, 1938.

George, W.L. *Caliban*. London: Methuen, 1920.

Gibbs, Sir Philip. *The Journalist's London*, London: Allan Wingate, 1952.

Gibbs, Sir Philip. *The Key of Life*, London: Hennel Lock, 1948.

Gibbs, Sir Philip. *The Pageant of the Years: An Autobiography*, London: Heinemann, 1946.

Gibbs, Sir Philip. *Street of Adventure*, London: Heinemann, 1909.

Gide, André. *The Coiners*, London: Cassell, 1950. Trans. from the French by Dorothy Bussy.

Gide, André. *Prometheus Unbound*, trans. by Lilian Rothermere, London: Chatto & Windus, 1919.

Gilbert, Martin. *Churchill: A Photographic Portrait*, London: Heinemann, 1974.

Gilbert, Martin. *Second World War*, London: Weidenfeld & Nicolson, 1989.

Gilbert, Martin. *Winston S. Churchill, Vol. V: 1922–1939*, London: Heinemann, 1976.

Gilbert, Martin. *Winston S. Churchill, Vol. V, Companion Part I. Documents, The Exchequer Years, 1922–1929*, London: Heinemann, 1979.

Gollin, Alfred M. *The Observer and J.L. Garvin*, Oxford: Oxford University Press, 1960.

Goodman, Jonathan. *The Crippen File*, London: Allison & Busby, 1985.

Grant, Ted. *Menace of Fascism* [pamphlet], London: Militant, first published in 1948; revised 1978.

The Great Adventure, 1896–1936. London: Associated Newspapers, Northcliffe House, 1936.

Greenwall, Harry J. *Northcliffe: Napoleon of Fleet Street*, London: Allan Wingate, 1957.

Griffiths, Richard M. *Fellow Travellers of the Right: British Enthusiasts for Nazi Germany, 1933–39*, London: Constable, 1980.

Hamilton, Everard, compiler. *Hamilton Memoirs: A Historical and Genealogical Notice of a Branch of that Family which Settled in Ireland in the Reign of King James I*. 1920, 2nd edition.

Hamilton, General Sir Ian. *Ian Hamilton's Despatches From the Dardanelles etc.* London: George Newnes, 1917. Introduction by Field Marshal Sir Evelyn Wood.

Hammerton, J.A. *With Northcliffe in Fleet Street*, London: Hutchinson, 1939.

Hansen, Ferdinand. *The Unrepentant Northcliffe*, Hamburg: Overseas Publishing Co., 1921.

Harmsworth, Alfred C. *The Romance of the Daily Mail*, London: Carmelite House, 1903.

Harmsworth, Cecil, Lord. *St John Harmsworth: A Brave Life (1876–1932)*, privately printed by the Tonbridge Printers, 1949.

Harris, Frank. *Frank Harris: His Life and Adventures, An Autobiography*, London: The Richards Press, 1947.

Harris, Frank. *My Life and Loves*, London: W.H. Allen, 1964.

Haskell, Arnold. *Balletomania*, Harmondsworth: Penguin Books, 1979.

Hastings, Max. *Bomber Command*, London: Michael Joseph, 1979.

The Herald and Weekly Times. *Keith Murdoch, Journalist.* Herald and Weekly Times: Melbourne, 1952.

History of The Times. Vol. III: The Twentieth Century Test, 1884–1912, London: Printing House Square, 1947.

History of The Times. Vol. IV: The 150th Anniversary and Beyond, Part I, 1912–1920, and Part II, 1921–1948, London: Printing House Square, 1952.

Hohenlohe, Prince Franz. *Steph – The Fabulous Princess*, London: New English Library, 1976.

Howells, Roy. *Simply Churchill*, London: Robert Hale, 1965.

James, Robert Rhodes. *Churchill: A Study in Failure, 1900–1939*, London: Weidenfeld & Nicolson, 1970.

Jeffries, J.M.N. *Front Everywhere*, London: Hutchinson, 1935.

Jenkins, Roy. *Asquith*, London: Collins, 1964.

Joiner, Susan, compiler. John Batchelor, illustrator. *Fighting Aircraft of World Wars I and II*, London: Phoebus, 1976.

Jones, Kennedy. *Fleet Street and Downing Street*, London: Hutchinson,1920.

King, Cecil. *Strictly Personal*, London: Weidenfeld & Nicolson, 1969.

Kipling, Rudyard. *The Muse among the Motors*, London: Daily Mail, 1904.

Kitchin, Harcourt. *Moberly Bell and His Times*, London: Philip Allan, 1925.

Knox, Collie. *Collie Knox Calling! A Selection of the Famous Friday 'Week-end' Broadcasts Now Appearing in The Daily Mail*, London: Chapman & Hall, 1937.

Koegler, Horst. *The Concise Oxford Dictionary of Ballet*, Oxford: Oxford University Press, 1977.

Koss, Stephen. *The Rise and Fall of the Political Press in Britain, Vols. I and II*, London: Hamish Hamilton, 1981.

Labour Research Department. *Who Backs Mosley? Fascist Promise and Fascist Performance*, London, 1938.

Lane, Margaret. *Edgar Wallace*, London: Heinemann, 1938.

Langguth, A.J. *Saki: A Life of Hector Hugo Munro*, Oxford: Oxford University Press, 1982.

Lewis, D.S. *Illusions of Grandeur: Mosley, Fascism, and British Society, 1931–81*, Manchester: Manchester University Press, 1987.

Lunn, Kenneth and Richard C. Thurlow. *British Fascism: Essays on the Radical Right in Inter-war Britain*, London: Croom Helm, 1980.

Lysaght, Charles Edward. *Brendan Bracken*, London: Allen Lane, 1979.

MacFarlane, David. *The Danger Tree*, Toronto: Macfarlane Walter & Ross, 1991.

McKenzie, F.A. *The Mystery of the Daily Mail*, London: Associated Newspapers, 1921.

Mack Smith, Denis. *Mussolini*, London: Weidenfeld & Nicolson, 1981.

Magnus, Philip. *Kitchener: Portrait of an Imperialist*, London: John Murray, 1958.

Mendelssohn, Peter. *The Age of Churchill*, London: Thames & Hudson, 1961.

Meral, Paul. *Paul Meral's Book of Recitatives*, trans. by Lilian Rothermere. London: Chatto & Windus, 1918.

Middlemas, Keith and John Barnes. *Baldwin: A Biography*, London: Weidenfeld & Nicolson, 1969.

Middleton, Drew. *The Sky Suspended: The Battle of Britain*, London: Secker & Warburg, 1960.

Montgomery, John. *1900: The End of an Era*, London: Allen & Unwin, 1968.

Moore, James. *Gurdjieff: The Anatomy of Myth, a Biography*, Shaftesbury: Element Books, 1991.

Morgan, Ted. *Churchill: 1874–1915*, London: Jonathan Cape, 1982.

Mosley, Diana. *A Life of Contrasts*, London: Hamish Hamilton, 1977.

Mosley, Oswald. *My Life*, London: Thomas Nelson and Sons, 1968.

Neary, G.N. 'Mining History of the Buchans Area', in *The Buchans Orebodies: Fifty Years of Geology and Mining*, eds E.A. Swanson, D.F. Strong, J.G. Thurlow, Geological Association of Canada, Special Paper 22, 1981.

New York Times. *Gaspesia*, New York: Corporate Records Library.

News in Our Time: Golden Jubilee Book of the Daily Mail 1896–1946, London: Associated Newspapers, 1946.

Nicolson, Harold. *Diaries and Letters, 1930–1939*, ed. Nigel Nicolson, London: Collins, 1967.

Nicolson, Harold. *Diaries and Letters, 1939–1945*, ed. Nigel Nicolson, London: Collins, 1967.

Nikitina, Alice. *Nikitina, By Herself*, trans. from the French by Baroness Budberg, London: Allan Wingate, 1959.

Northcliffe, Viscount. *At the War*, London: Hodder & Stoughton, 1916.

Northcliffe, Viscount. *My Journey Round the World*, ed. Cecil and St John Harmsworth, London: John Lane, The Bodley Head, 1923.

Northcliffe, Viscount. *Newspapers and Their Millionaires*, London: Associated Newspapers, 1922.

Owen, Frank. *Tempestuous Journey: Lloyd George His Life and Times*, New York: McGraw-Hill, 1955.

Owen, Louise. *Northcliffe: The Facts*, London: 21 Buckingham Gate, 1931.

Owen, Louise. *The Real Lord Northcliffe: Some Personal Recollections of a Private Secretary 1902–1922*, London: Cassell, 1922.

Painter, George D. *André Gide*, London: Arthur Barker, 1951.

Peel, Mrs C.S. *The Daily Mail Cookery Book*, London: Associated Newspapers, 1920.

Peel, Mrs C.S., ed., *The Daily Mail Fruit and Vegetable Preserving Book*, London: Associated Newspapers, 1920.

Peel, Mrs C.S. *Daily Mail War Recipes*, London: Constable, 1918.

Peel, Mrs C.S. *Life's Enchanted Cup: An Autobiography (1872–1933)*, London: John Lane, The Bodley Head, 1933.

Pelling, Henry. *Winston Churchill*, London: Macmillan, 1974.

Pemberton, Max. *Lord Northcliffe: A Memoir*, London: Hodder & Stoughton, 1922.

Phillips, Sir Percival. *Mesopotamia: The Daily Mail Inquiry at Baghdad*, London: Carmelite House, 1923.

Pound, Reginald and Geoffrey Harmsworth. *Northcliffe*, London: Cassell, 1959.

Price, G. Ward. *Extra-special Correspondent*, London: Harrap, 1957.

Price, G. Ward. *I Know These Dictators*, London: Harrap, 1937.

Price, G. Ward. Unpublished MS, 1949.

Pride, Emrys. *Why Lloyd George Met Hitler*, Risca, Great Britain: The Starling Press, 1981.

Pullar, Philippa. *Frank Harris*, London: Hamish Hamilton, 1975.

Ralph, Julian. *The Making of a Journalist*, London: Harper & Brothers, 1903.

Ralph, Julian. *War's Brighter Side*, London: C. Arthur Pearson, 1901.

Rees, Philip. *Fascism in Britain*, Brighton: The Harvester Press, 1979.

Reynolds, Rothay. *When Freedom Shrieked*, London: Victor Gollancz, 1939.

Rothermere, Viscount. *My Campaign for Hungary*, London: Eyre & Spottiswoode, 1939.

Rothermere, Viscount. *My Fight to Rearm Britain*, London: Eyre & Spottiswoode, 1939.

Rothermere, Viscount. *Solvency or Downfall? Squandermania and Its Story*. London: Longmans, Green, 1921.

Rothermere, Viscount. *Warnings and Predictions*, London: Eyre & Spottiswoode, 1939.

Ryan, A.P. *Lord Northcliffe*, Brief Lives, London: Collins, 1943.

Scaremongerings From the Daily Mail, 1896–1914, compiled by Twells Brex. London: Associated Newspapers, 1914.

Sedine, J. *Oeuvres Complètes*, introduction by Lilian Rothermere. Orléans: Imprimerie Orléanaise, 1917.

Sencourt, Robert. *T.S. Eliot: A Memoir*, ed. Donald Adamson, London: Garnstone Press, 1971.

Shawcross, William. *Rupert Murdoch: Ringmaster of the Information Circus*, London: Chatto & Windus, 1992.

Shirer, William. *The Western World through Its Years of Conflict*, New York: New American Library, 1961.

Simonis, H. *The Street of Ink: An Intimate History of Journalism*, London: Cassell, 1917.

Skidelsky, Robert. *Oswald Mosley*, London: Macmillan, 1975.

Sokolova, Lydia. *Dancing for Diaghilev*, ed. Richard Buckle, London: John Murray, 1960.

Sprigge, Elizabeth. *Gertrude Stein: Her Life and Work*, London: Hamish Hamilton, 1957.

Springfield, Lincoln. *Some Piquant People*, London: T. Fisher Unwin, 1924.

Steed, Henry Wickham. *The Fifth Arm*, London: Constable, 1940.

Steed, Henry Wickham. *The Press*, Harmondsworth: Penguin Books, 1938.

Steed, Henry Wickham. *Through Thirty Years, 1892–1922: A Personal Narrative, Vols. I and II*, London: Heinemann, 1924.

Steevens, G.W. *From Capetown to Ladysmith: An Unfinished Record of the South African War*, ed. Vernon Blackburn. London: William Blackwood & Sons, 1900.

Stein, Gertrude. *The Autobiography of Alice B. Toklas*, London: John Lane, The Bodley Head, 1933.

Stuart, Sir Campbell, KBE. *Secrets of Crewe House*, London: Hodder & Stoughton, 1920.

A Study in Malevolence. An Open Letter to Lord Northcliffe from a Member of Parliament, 1920.

Sullivan, Alvin, ed. *British Literary Magazines: The Modern Age, 1914–1984*, Westport, Connecticut: Greenwood Press, 1986.

Swaffer, Hannen. *Hannen Swaffer's Who's Who*, London: Hutchinson, 1929.

Swaffer, Hannen. *Northcliffe's Return*, London: Hutchinson, 1925.

Symons, Julian. *The General Strike: A Historical Portrait*, London: The Cresset Press, 1957.

Taylor, A.J.P. *Beaverbrook: A Biography*, London: Hamish Hamilton, 1972.

Taylor, A.J.P. *English History: 1914–1945*, Oxford: Oxford University Press, 1965.

Taylor, A.J.P. *The First World War: An Illustrated History*, Hamish Hamilton, 1963.

Taylor, S.J. *Stalin's Apologist: Walter Duranty: The New York Times's Man in Moscow*, Oxford: Oxford University Press, 1990.

Thomas, Bert, Wilton Williams and Lincoln Springfield. *One Hundred War Cartoons from London Opinion*, London: London Opinion, 1919.

Thurlow, Richard. *Fascism in Britain: A History, 1918–1985*, London: Basil Blackwell, 1987.

Tuohy, Ferdinand. *The Crater of Mars*, London: Heinemann, 1929.

Vansittart, Lord. *The Mist Procession*, London: Hutchinson, 1958.

Vine, Colin M. *A Little Nut-brown Man: My Three Years with Lord Beaverbrook*, London: Readers Union, 1968.

Viollis, André. *Lord Northcliffe*. Paris: Librairie Bernard Grasset, 1919.

Wallace, Ethel Violet. *Edgar Wallace*, London: Hutchinson, 1932.

The War Despatches, from the pages of the Daily Mail, London: Marshall Cavendish, 1977.

Wareham, Arthur. *Quiet Man of Fleet Street*. Unpublished MS.

Wells, H.G. *Experiment in Autobiography*, Vols I & II, London: Victor Gollancz and The Cresset Press, 1934.

What the Worker Wants, The Daily Mail Enquiry. London: Hodder & Stoughton, 1912.

Williams, Francis. *Dangerous Estate: The Anatomy of Newspapers*, London: Longmans, 1957.

Wilson, Robert Macnair. *Lord Northcliffe: A Study*, London: Ernest Benn, 1927.

Wilson, Lady Sarah. *South African Memories: Social, Warlike & Sporting*, London: Edward Arnold, 1909.

Wood, Alan. *The True History of Lord Beaverbrook*, London: Heinemann, 1965.

Wrench, Sir Evelyn. *Geoffrey Dawson and Our Times*, London: Hutchinson, 1955.

Wrench, Sir Evelyn. *Uphill: The First Stage in a Strenuous Life*, London: Ivor Nicholson & Watson, 1934.

Young, G.M. *Stanley Baldwin*, London: Rupert Hart-Davis, 1952.

Young, Kenneth. *Churchill and Beaverbrook: A Study in Friendship and Politics*, London: Eyre & Spottiswoode, 1966.

Zwar, Desmond. *In Search of Keith Murdoch*, Melbourne: Macmillan, 1980.

Periodicals

Braddock, John. 'One Bold Venture', *Atlantic Advocate*, April 1968.

Brooks, Sydney. 'Lord Northcliffe and the War', *North American Review*, 15 Aug. 1915, Vol. CCII, No. 717, pp. 185–96.

'England's Most Unpopular Editor', *Literary Digest*, 17 July 1915, Vol. 51, No. 3, pp. 125–6.

Forme Magazine. Associated Newspapers, July 1965.

Gardiner, Alfred G. 'The Times', *Atlantic Monthly*, Jan. 1917, Vol. CXIX, pp. 111–22.

'Grand Falls Festivities, Magnificent Banquet, 500 Guests', *Evening Chronicle*, St John's, Newfoundland, 9 Oct. 1909.

Harmsworth, Alfred. 'The Simultaneous Newspapers of the Twentieth Century', *North American Review*, Vol. CLXXII, Jan. 1901, pp. 72–90.

Harmsworth, Cecil. 'Toward International Amity', and Henry Wickham Steed, 'The Great Betrayal', in 'Munich: Two British Views' in *Forum*, Jan. 1939, Vol. CI, No. 1, pp. 21–3.

Hopkins, Frederick M. 'Harmsworth Collection Comes Home', *Publisher's Weekly*, 16 Apr. 1938, pp. 1629–31.

Literary Digest. 17 July 1915, pp. 125–6.

'Lord Northcliffe, The Man of War', *Nation*, 23 Aug. 1922, Vol. CXV, No. 2981, p. 180.

North American Review. July 1917, Vol. CCVI, No. 740, pp. 15–23.

National Review. Dec. 1917, p. 417.

National Review. Dec. 1927, p. 438.

Newton, W. Douglas. 'The Practical Vision', *Bookman*, Jan. 1917, Vol. LI, No. 304, pp. 124–6 [a review of 'At the War'].

Northcliffe, Viscount. 'If America Enters the War,' *North American Review*, Sept. 1915, Vol. CCII, No. 718, pp. 345–8.

Northcliffe, Viscount. 'Use and Misuse of the Press: How the Germans Bamboozled the Public. The English Press and the War', *Forum*, Oct. 1918, Vol. LX, pp. 395–7.

Northcliffe, Viscount. 'Win the War with Thrift: A personal message to America', *Forum*, Nov. 1917, Vol. LVIII, pp. 509–16.

O'Connor, T.P. 'The New Journalism', *New Review*, Vol. I, No. 5, Oct. 1889, pp. 423–34.

Punch, or the London Charivari. 17 Feb., 1915, Vol. CXLVIII, p. 130.

Punch, or the London Charivari. 27 July 1921, Vol. CLXI, p. 64.

Symons, Julian. 'The Cri', *London Magazine*, Nov. 1967, Vol. VII, No. 8, pp. 19–23.

Turnstile, Magnus. 'The Mail Affair', *New Statesman*, 23 Dec. 1966.

Vallance, Aylmer. 'Inquest on the British Press', *Nation*, Vol. CLXIV, No. 16, 19 Apr. 1947, pp. 451–2.

Wood, Eric Fisher. 'Northcliffe', *Century*, Oct. 1917, Vol. XCIV, No. 6, pp. 920–7.

World's Press News. 'Daily Mail Staff – A Battalion of the Best', 7 Jan. 1932, pp. 14–15.

Manuscripts, unpublished materials

Beaverbrook Papers, House of Lords Record Office. The following volumes, all Series BBK.C: BBK.C/254, Sir Oswald Mosley, 1928–63; BBK.C/261, Viscount Northcliffe, 1911–25; BBK.C/263, Frank Owen, 1936–51; BBK.C/264, Frank Owen, 1951–64; BBK.C/282, 1st Viscount Rothermere, 1912–14/20; BBK.C/283, 1st Viscount Rothermere, 1921–8; BBK.C/284, 1st Viscount Rothermere, 1926–30; BBK.C/285, 1st Viscount Rothermere, 1931–5; BBK.C/286, 1st Viscount Rothermere, 1936–40; BBK.C/287, 2nd Viscount Rothermere, 1929–64.

BBC 2 programme transcript. 'Napoleon of Fleet Street', in which Cecil King discusses his uncle, Lord Northcliffe.

Churchill (Chartwell) Archives, Churchill College, Cambridge.

Northcliffe Papers. British Library, Department of Manuscripts. Correspondence and papers of Alfred Charles William Harmsworth (1865–1922), Viscount Northcliffe 1917, journalist and newspaper proprietor; 1880–1922, n.d. Two hundred and forty-five volumes, Add. MSS 62153–62397. Presented by Sir Geoffrey Harmsworth, Bart, 1965 (the papers then acquired being reserved until 1972), 1973 and 1976; incorporated April 1982. Add. MS 62230, Vol. LXXVIII; Add. MS 62231, Vol. LXXIX; Add. MS 62232, Vol. LXXX; Add. MS Item 62277, Vol. CXXV; Add. MS 62179, Vol. XXVII, Keith Murdoch, 1915–22; Add. MS 62196, Vol. XLIV, Kennedy Jones, 1905–21, and Marine Dubbs, 1905–17; Add. MS 62198, Vol. XLVI, Thomas Marlowe; Add. MS 62199, Vol. XLVII, Thomas Marlowe, 1914–22, n.d.; Add. MS 62200, Vol. XLVIII, Thomas Marlowe, July 1919–22; Add. MS 62292A, Vol. CXL, General Correspondence 1891–Sept. 1905; Add. MS 62277, Vol. CXXV, Dr Seymour Price; Add. MS 62247, Vol. XCV parts A and B, H. Wickham Steed, July 1919–July 1920; Add. MS 62248, Vol. XCVI, H. Wickham Steed, August 1920–22, n.d.

Public Record Office, Kew. The following files: HO144/20142/674216/154–217; HO144/21041/674216/92–144; HO144/20144/674216/1–239; HO144/19069/486825/1–53; HO144/19070/486825/54–101; HO144/21061/692242/60–111; HO144/21060/692242/1–59; HO144/20140/674216/1–88; HO144/20145/674216/-350; HO144/20146/674216/-416.

Harmsworth Archives. Owned by the Daily Mail & General Trust, plc.

APPENDIX

There are two other sources. The first was Sir Evelyn Wrench, for a time his private secretary and later editor of the *Overseas Daily Mail*, who believed that Northcliffe had contracted the disease in 1909 on the basis that he had suffered a serious fever and seemed unreasonable and unkind afterwards. The second was J.L. Garvin, the editor of the *Observer*, who once commented that 'Northcliffe had paid greatly for his pleasures with women.' Stanley Morison, in the *History of the Times*, using Wickham Steed for his source, appeared for a time to accept the proposition that Northcliffe died of General Paralysis of the Insane, but later retreated from that position. Otherwise, many years later, Cecil King, the nephew of Northcliffe and Rothermere, who later became chairman of International Publishing Corporation, perpetuated the rumour by referring to it on a widely viewed television programme with Malcolm Muggeridge as the host.

On 25 October 1993, in an appointment with Professor M.W. Adler, head of the Department of Genito-Urinary Medicine at University College London Medical School, this author was informed of the unlikelihood that Northcliffe died of GPI on the basis of three criteria. The first included samples of Northcliffe's writing some three months before his death. Professor Adler concluded it would be 'highly improbable a man suffering from GPI could have written these documents'. The second was the fact that the Wassermann administered just before Northcliffe's death tested negative. It would have been 'highly unlikely a physician of Sir Thomas Horder's reputation would have falsified such a record, or indeed would have even administered the test at all if he had been trying to hide the fact the patient was dying of syphilis'. Finally, the symptoms Northcliffe displayed seemed more like those of endocarditis than of syphilis – although no conclusive diagnosis can be made now because of the passage of time.

On 11 December 1971, a lengthy and authoritative letter appeared in *The Times*, signed by Dr D.M. Lloyd-Jones, who had been working with Sir Thomas Horder on the Northcliffe case. He stated that Horder had been sure of his diagnosis, and in any case it had been substantiated by the other leading world authority on endo-carditis at the time, an American physician based in New York by the name of Dr Liebman, who also examined Northcliffe during his final illness. Finally, Dr Lloyd-Jones himself had been present at St Bartholomew's Hospital in London when Dr Joekes, a Dutch bacteriologist, called him to view the culture he had grown from a specimen collected from Northcliffe which proved conclusively he was infected with the streptococcus that, in conjunction with valvular damage of the heart, causes malignant endocarditis.

INDEX

Abbreviations: *DM* = *Daily Mail*; AN = Alfred, Viscount
Northcliffe; HR = Harold, 1st Viscount Rothermere